The GREATEST GIFT GUIDE EVER

2ND EDITION

REVISED & UPDATED

JUDITH KING

BETTERWAY BOOKS
CINCINNATI, OHIO

ACKNOWLEDGMENTS

I am grateful to the dozens of people who contributed ideas for this book. I particularly want to thank Susan Byrne, Janie Connelly, Christian Farmer, Russ Holder, Janet King, Marie Levine, Harold McManus, Robert Shelby, Jane Verm, Carol Victory, and Pam White for taking time out of their busy schedules to advise extensively in their areas of expertise. I am indebted to Emily Anne Croom for her invaluable help in research and data entry and to Amy Sneed for her capable assistance in data entry. I am grateful to Fred King for installing the data base that saved countless hours and to Fred, Tom, and Sarah King for their creative suggestions, constant encouragement, gracious help with data entry and research, and willingness to forgo home cooking while the book was completed. Support from friends and family is about the best gift one can receive. I am truly blessed.

Text illustrations by David Seal
Typography by Park Lane Publication Services

---

97 96 95 94 93   5 4 3 2 1

Library of Congress Cataloging-in-Publication Data

King, Judith.
  The greatest gift guide ever / Judith King. -- 2nd ed.
   p. cm.
  Includes index.
  ISBN 1-55870-314-4
   1. Shopping. 2. Gifts. I. Title
TX335.K434 1993
381'.4'5--dc20   93-24769
                    CIP

To Fletcher and P. B. Croom,
who gave me a rich heritage
and loving examples
of all that is good in this world

Contents

Introduction 7

1. Helpful Hints for Gracious Giving 9
Successful Gift Shopping Tips
Toy-Buying Tips
Wrapping It Up
Gift Shipping Tips
Creating a Gift Profile

2. Gift Ideas 19
Over 3900 gift ideas for 93 age and interest categories from Babies to Retirement Home Residents, Antique Collectors to Writers

3. Resources 115
Magazines: Gifts that will last all year
Catalogs: Convenient shopping at home

4. Gifts to Make 205
Simple directions for gifts for adults and children to make and share

Appendix 215
Small Electric Appliances
General Birthday Information
Anniversary Symbols & Gift Ideas
Perpetual Gift Occasion Calendar

Index 221

Introduction

Do you approach gift giving with apprehension, tension, or confusion because you have a hard time deciding what to give? Do you go blank when it's time for a high school graduation gift? Are you panicked because you just can't figure out what to give your new boss? Do you forget friends' birthdays? Do you miss out on bargains because you don't remember what size to buy for someone?

Then this book is for *you*. Whether you are giving to fulfill an obligation, to celebrate a special occasion, or just to make someone happy, you will find plenty of ideas here to set your imagination spinning. You can be confident that the gifts will be appreciated because they came from "wish lists" of persons with the various interests and hobbies included in the book and also from ideas gleaned from store clerks, specialty shops, and special interest catalogs and magazines. The lists include the newest hobby gadgets and the latest electronic products as well as ideas that never go out of favor.

Gift ideas in this book are not limited to a particular price range since different occasions and recipients may call for different levels of giving. Some of the gifts cost nothing more than a little time, and some can run hundreds of dollars. Your family may give each person one big gift on his birthday or you may like to have several smaller items. In either case, you will find many ideas here from which to choose. Prices for items are not given. Instead, the ideas are general enough to allow your imagination to interpret them as you (and your pocketbook) please. For instance, a gift of candy may mean homemade fudge or it may mean a bouquet of chocolate roses.

One suggestion made in several categories is the gift of coupons for services such as yard work, baby-sitting, etc. These can be made on index cards. Write your gift of time or effort on the card, decorate it if you like, and sign your name. These are wonderful gifts for children to make and give.

Even young children can be part of the gift selection process and learn valuable skills while doing so. Talk to them about the person who is to receive the gift. Ask them to tell you things that person likes to do or talk about and what they think that person would like. They'll surprise you with their observations. If at all possible, let them participate in making gifts for special friends or family members. A few easy crafts and recipes are mentioned in the *Gifts to Make* (page 115) section. Remember, too, that the purpose of their helping is not to produce a work of art, but to allow them to experience the joy of giving to other people and the appreciation that giving brings. Older children can learn about budgeting also if you take them shopping with you and let them help decide what can be bought for the specified amount.

❧ HOW TO USE THIS BOOK ❧

Start at the back of the book — at the *Perpetual Gift Occasion Calendar* (page 220). People love to have their birthday or anniversary remembered, but don't try to keep all that information in your head. Instead record it once on this calendar and impress your friends with your wonderful "memory"! If you write the year of the marriage or birth, then you can easily calculate when special anniversaries or birthdays come along.

Make 12 copies of the blank calendar. You may find it helpful to enlarge the calendar. A 129% enlargement is standard on the newer copy machines and will make the calendar the perfect size for a three-ring binder. Once you have twelve copies, fill in the provided spaces with each birthday, anniversary, or other occasion you will want to remember year after year in the space provided.

Then turn to *Creating a Gift Profile* (page 15). Think about each person to whom you will be giving and fill in as many blanks as you can. Don't wait for the next gift occasion to do this. Some time spent now will help you be prepared for early shopping and will prevent last-minute panic.

When it's time to select a gift, glance over your Gift Profile for the person's areas of interest. Skim the list of 93 gift categories in *The Greatest Gift Guide Ever* such as *Camper, Traveler, 3- to 5-Year-Old, Needleworker,* or *The Romantic* until you find one or several categories which apply to the person. Then read through the list and select some ideas for which to shop or which you can make. For even easier gift buying, order a few appropriate catalogs from more than 900 in the *Catalog* section. And for the easiest giving of all, order a subscription from the *Magazine* section, which contains more than 700 special interest magazines. If you are still at a loss, a copy of *The Greatest Gift Guide Ever* makes a great gift, too!

Gift giving does not have to be expensive or exhausting. Let it be fun with *The Greatest Gift Guide Ever*.

1.
Helpful Hints
for
Gracious Giving

℘ SUCCESSFUL GIFT SHOPPING TIPS ℘

Here is a strategy for cutting costs and reducing the number of returned gifts:

☐ Make 12 copies (or photocopies) of the *Perpetual Gift Occasion Calendar* at the back of this book; fill in each month with anniversaries, birthdays, and other annual events you want to acknowledge with a card or gift.

☐ As soon as you hear a "want" from someone on your list, jot it down in your Gift Profile notebook (see page 15, *Creating a Gift Profile*).

☐ Plan ahead! Before each shopping trip, check your *Perpetual Gift Occasion Calendar* for the next several months so you can look for sales or hard-to-find items for someone on your list.

☐ If possible, purchase a gift when you find it, even if the occasion is several weeks or months away.

☐ Select quality in a gift as if you were to be the receiver; select color and style to please the recipient.

☐ Remember that a gift does not have to be expensive to be appreciated or appropriate. Gifts that show you expended time and effort (in making the gift or in considering the person's preferences) are just as special as those with a high price tag.

☐ Keep a gift box or drawer of items you have made or bought on sale that can be used when you or your children need a last-minute gift.

☐ Save all receipts for about three months just in case a return or an exchange is necessary after a gift is worn or used a few times.

☐ Carry an up-to-date list of your family's sizes in your wallet so you can take advantage of unexpected sales or purchase that "just right" item when you find it.

☐ When purchasing accessories for equipment (such as a computer, sewing machine, camera, etc.), know the brand and size or model number of the main item to ensure compatibility.

☐ If possible, stick with the recipient's favorite brand (of cosmetics, sports equipment, tools, etc.).

☐ Record your gifts on each Gift Profile so you won't give the same gift next year!

❧ TOY-BUYING TIPS ❧

❏ Toys should be fun! Select a toy that the child can play with right now, not one he'll grow into. A toy that is too advanced can frustrate a child and make him feel inferior. Toys ideally will give the child experiences through which he learns more about himself and his abilities, gains self-confidence or social skills, or develops his creativity or physical skills.

❏ For younger children, choose something simple and durable. Simplicity encourages the use of imagination and creativity and allows for great variety in the kinds of play in which the toy is used.

❏ Generally avoid novelty or "trendy" toys (usually the most heavily advertised) that have little lasting value. Judge the toy on criteria other than name.

❏ A toy does not have to cost a lot to be loved and played with a lot.

❏ When possible, choose the toy for the particular child and her interests. Your niece may like to play in the sandbox with trucks while your nephew may like to bake or needlepoint. Put aside preconceived ideas of "appropriate" toys and encourage the child's individualism and special interests.

❏ Electric toys for children under six should be battery-powered. All electrical toys should carry the UL (Underwriters Laboratories) seal of approval. Include the proper number and size of batteries with a toy for immediate enjoyment!

❏ Above all, choose safe, sturdy toys that will last. Avoid the inexpensive, thin plastic trinkets that look so appealing but often don't last through one good playing session and, when broken, produce sharp, dangerous edges. For smaller children, look for non-toxic paint, smooth edges, and parts that cannot be pulled off and swallowed. Wood, thick plastic, cloth, and metal toys are the best values in the long run.

❏ Some sources of toys that are wholesome, educational, and lots of fun are teacher supply stores, arts and crafts fairs, and the catalogs under *For Children Only; Handcrafts;* and *Toys, Dolls, Games*.

❏ Remember that children enjoy many items other than toys.

⤷ WRAPPING IT UP ⤶

Sometimes the presentation of a gift is as appreciated as the gift itself. You are not limited to wrapping paper and bows. Be creative in the kind of container used to hold the gift and in the wrapping material. Here are a few ideas.

- ❒ Decorate boxes with colored macaroni, colored or pearlized beads, or sequins glued in a design.
- ❒ Include a loaf of bread and jar of preserves with a bread basket.
- ❒ Top a jar of homemade jelly or relish with a doily and tie with a ribbon or paint the lid and glue on a fabric heart, shamrock, Christmas tree, etc.
- ❒ For a Western theme, decorate the package with a little straw hat or wrap in a bandanna.
- ❒ Purchase wooden cutouts from a craft store or catalog. Paint or leave plain and attach to the gift box.
- ❒ Make a miniature wreath by stringing cranberries or beads on wire.
- ❒ Give a child a doll in a doll chair or doll bed with the doll holding the gift.
- ❒ Paint a clay flower pot and place the gift inside.
- ❒ Paint a tin pail or can with acrylic paint. Spray with matte clear acrylic spray to protect the paint.
- ❒ Place an awkwardly shaped gift in a new trash can and top with a Santa's or elf's hat (or other seasonal decorations).
- ❒ Make a Cherub Gift Bag (see *Gifts to Make*).
- ❒ Place the gift in a useful container (such as a toolbox, sewing basket, closet storage container, or cookie jar) and tie with ribbon.
- ❒ Place a gift certificate in a large box weighted down with a brick.
- ❒ Cross-stitch a jar lid for a special occasion.
- ❒ Fill a basket with Easter grass, a lace doily, a kitchen towel, baby's breath, napkins, an apron, curling ribbon, straw, or a cross-stitched bread cloth before placing the gift inside.
- ❒ Spray paint a six-pack bottle carrier and fill each slot. Possibilities include jars of honey or picante sauce, pencils, snacks, or toys.
- ❒ Cut a shape out of a sponge. Brush paint on the sponge and decorate a set of napkins or a tablecloth. Iron to set the paint after it is dry. Use this fabric to wrap a gift.
- ❒ Decorate six graham crackers or petit-beurre biscuits with icing, sprinkles, or candies. Glue together with icing for an edible box! Insert a toy.
- ❒ Tie packages with useful items such as measuring tape, shoelaces, a jump rope, or a scarf.
- ❒ Make a drawstring bag out of country prints or rich tapestry and use year after year for gifts.
- ❒ Insert a hobby tool, kitchen utensil, lollipop, or pencil in the bow or ribbon on the package.
- ❒ Play "hide and seek" with your packages. Hide the gift and give a clue as to where to find the next clue and so on until the package is discovered.
- ❒ Decorate packages with natural materials such as little pine cones, flowers, sweet gum balls, etc.
- ❒ Reuse the pictures on greeting cards for decorating a package.
- ❒ Make a face on a package with buttons or candies, or draw a scene and glue on appropriate miniatures (e.g., Matchbox car on a highway).
- ❒ Make a basket out of bread dough. Spray with clear acrylic spray. Line with a colorful towel or napkins.

❧ OFFICIAL USPS ABBREVIATIONS ❧

Streets		States, Etc.		States, cont.	
AVE	Avenue	AL	Alabama	NE	Nebraska
BLVD	Boulevard	AK	Alaska	NV	Nevada
CTR	Center	AZ	Arizona	NH	New Hampshire
CIR	Circle	AR	Arkansas		
CT	Court	CA	California	NJ	New Jersey
DR	Drive	CO	Colorado	NM	New Mexico
EXPY	Expressway	CT	Connecticut	NY	New York
HTS	Heights	DE	Delaware	NC	North Carolina
HWY	Highway	DC	District of Columbia		
IS	Island			ND	North Dakota
JCT	Junction	FL	Florida	OH	Ohio
LK	Lake	GA	Georgia	OK	Oklahoma
LN	Lane	HI	Hawaii	OR	Oregon
MTN	Mountain	ID	Idaho	PA	Pennsylvania
PKY	Parkway	IL	Illinois	PR	Puerto Rico
PL	Place	IN	Indiana	RI	Rhode Island
RD	Road	IA	Iowa	SC	South Carolina
STA	Station	KS	Kansas		
ST	Street	KY	Kentucky	SD	South Dakota
TPKE	Turnpike	LA	Louisiana	TN	Tennessee
VLY	Valley	ME	Maine	TX	Texas
		MD	Maryland	UT	Utah
Apartments, Etc.		MA	Massachusetts	VT	Vermont
APT	Apartment	MI	Michigan	VA	Virginia
PLZ	Plaza	MN	Minnesota	WA	Washington
RM	Room	MS	Mississippi	WV	West Virginia
STE	Suite	MO	Missouri	WI	Wisconsin
		MT	Montana	WY	Wyoming

↬ GIFT SHIPPING TIPS ↫

Compare delivery service rates (e.g., United Parcel Service or Federal Express) with the United States Postal Service rates. Sometimes the delivery service rates are better for longer distances or larger packages. Each company has its own weight and size limits. Call and get specifics before you wrap your package if it is very large or heavy or if it requires special handling.

Word of Warning

Most package carriers state that protection of the package contents is the responsibility of the mailer. Only certain types of containers and wrapping material are acceptable. These services have the right to refuse improperly packaged articles or items that do not meet their guidelines (including certain liquids, aerosols, or oversized or heavy loads).

Enclose both shipping and return addresses inside the package in case of accidental damage in transit.

Pay the small additional fee for package insurance and save your receipt until you hear that the package has been received and opened. (Some services automatically insure to $100, others do not; make sure you check.)

When to Send

If using the Postal Service, mail a week to ten days ahead of the occasion. At Christmas, mail by November 30 if possible. If later than December 13, you'll need to use priority mail or an alternative delivery service. Get to the post office early in the day for a shorter line. If using a delivery service, be sure to allow them their full estimate of time for delivery. For example, if your gift recipient is in UPS Zone 2, it will probably take the full two days for delivery.

Containers

❑ Choose a container that will be filled by the item you are mailing and adequate cushioning. This will prevent unnecessary shifting of the contents. If necessary, cut down a larger box to obtain a closer fit.

❑ The Postal Service and box stores sell various sizes of padded bags that are good for books, tapes, diskettes, and flat or soft goods such as clothing.

❑ The Postal Service has a chart based on the weight and measurements of the package showing the grade of box required for packages weighing over 20 pounds. Generally, you cannot mail a package over 70 pounds and more than 108" in length plus girth. The other services have their own specifications.

❑ Used boxes are fine to use, but first remove or mark through all previous labels and markings that might interfere with reading the new addresses.

Cushioning

❑ Possible cushioning materials include: foamed plastic, corrugated fiberboard, polystyrene, shredded newspapers, and popped corn.

❑ Protect all items from outside forces with at least 2" of cushioning on each side. Wrap each item separately and protect from each other inside the box.

❑ Cushion any fragile item. Stabilize any heavy item that might shift and harm other articles in the box. Do not place heavy items above lighter items within the same box.

❑ Liquids should be placed in double, leakproof containers, then marked "Fragile."

❏ Perishables should be packed in odor-absorbent materials and marked "Perishable."

❏ Cookies: Bar, drop, and fruit cookies transport best. Wrap four to six cookies in plastic wrap and seal with masking tape. Pack in an airtight container (such as a tin) with waxed paper or tissue paper to keep packages from shifting. Do not mix candies that absorb moisture (such as caramels, mints, or hard candies) with those that lose moisture (such as fudge). Do not mix soft and crisp cookies. Place the tin in a plastic bag from which as much air as possible has been removed. Put in a box with cushioning around the tin. Mark the box "Fragile" and "Perishable."

Wrapping

❏ If the box is adequate for shipping and the address is easy to spot, it is not necessary to wrap it in paper.

❏ If such wrapping is necessary, use a grocery sack (plain side showing) or a bag of equivalent (60-pound basis) weight.

Sealing

❏ Use pressure-sensitive, filament-reinforced tape or reinforced paper tape (at least 2" wide and 60-pound basis). Be sure to rub tape down well.

❏ *Do not use cellophane or masking tape.*

❏ Be sure tape extends at least 3" over the side of the box. Tape over the opening of the box; then apply several rows of tape across the opening for reinforcement.

❏ Twine and cord are not recommended for closure and reinforcement. They hang up on automatice box-moving equipment.

❏ Stapling is adequate for loads up to ten pounds if the staples are not more than 5" apart (or 2½" apart for heavier or more delicate loads). Be sure to tape over the staples on padded bags in order to protect your hands.

Addressing

❏ Address the package with waterproof, smudgeproof blue or black ink or marker. Other colors are hard to read. Cover ink with rows of transparent tape.

❏ Write the receiver's address as near the center of the package as possible. Write the complete return address in the upper lefthand corner.

❏ Print clearly in plain block letters. Use the official Postal Service abbreviations (page 12). Omit punctuation. Include the zip code on the same line with city and state. Use zip+4 code for faster delivery. Below is an example of the preferred style for addressing.

> MR TOM KING
> 121 W. BAYLOR AVE APT 1225
> HOUSTON TX 12345-6789

❏ If applicable, mark the package "Fragile," "Perishable," or "Do Not Bend," or ask the receiving clerk to stamp the appropriate label on the box. Place these markings *above* the mailing address and to the right of the return address. The Postal Service reads the address from the bottom up. Anything below the zip code might be mistaken for the zip code and cause misrouting.

❏ Mark the class of mail on all flaps of envelopes and all sides of packages.

ᰋ CREATING A GIFT PROFILE ᰋ

The best gift givers are those who can "get inside" another person's thoughts and see life from his or her perspective. The questions that follow are designed to help you do just that. You won't be able to answer every question about every person, but the more information you can gather, the easier it will be to select a gift for each person that will really please.

Either make copies of the blank Gift Profile that follows and file the copies in a three-ring binder or devote a bound notebook to your profiles. At the top of each page, write a person's name. As you learn more about the person (or as her interests change), jot down the information on the appropriate page. You'll be glad you did when a gift occasion arises.

Your information will come from listening and observing. Listen for the topics they initiate, the hobbies they mention, the dreams they share, a song they liked on the radio. Make mental notes about the style of clothing he wears, the books on her coffee table, the color of their dining room. Soon you will have a variety of notes from which you can select a gift or gift category.

1. Is the person married? Are there any children or grandchildren?
2. Will the gift be shared with a family or is it for the individual alone?
3. How old is the person? Are there any physical limitations that would influence the gift choice?
4. Where does the person live (in an apartment with others, in a retirement home, in a cold or sunny climate)?
5. How does she spend her weekends? What does she do in her spare time —garden, needlepoint, read, scuba dive, haunt antique shops, etc.?
6. What grade or profession is he in? Does she love her job or would she prefer not to be reminded of it at gift time? In what organizations is the individual active?
7. Does the person have a hobby or favorite craft? What does she collect— antique hymnals, miniature bears, Disney memorabilia?
8. What does she talk about—the environment, her kids, favorite restaurants, the home team?
9. What games does he play—bridge, crossword puzzles, softball?
10. Where is (or was) he in school? Where does he hope to attend? What is the mascot? What are the colors?
11. What does she like to eat or drink? Does he have a favorite restaurant or type of food? Does she like to eat out or cook for a group? Is she a chocoholic? Has he mentioned an allergy to a particular food?
12. What magazines or books does she read? What music does he like? Is she a sports fan? Does he go to the theater or to movies? What kind?
13. What equipment or tools does he borrow from you?
14. Where does he go on vacations — the mountains, the lake, the city? Where would he like to go? Does he stay in fancy hotels or does he prefer to camp?
15. Are her ears pierced? What style clothing and accessories does she wear —sophisticated, Western, conservative? Does she wear hair ornaments? What colors does he wear the most or look the best in? Does he wear jewelry?
16. Has she mentioned a favorite fragrance, flower, brand of cosmetics, candy, author, singer, or musician?
17. Does he care how his apartment or home is decorated? Does he have a

particular style in home furnishings—modern, Southwestern, European, antiques?
18. What colors are in the bath, kitchen, bedroom, living room, dining room?
19. Does he have pets?
20. Is she a casual or formal person? Practical or sentimental? A joker or strictly proper?

Got the idea? As you give your attention to the other person, you will gain insights into his likes and dislikes, interests and hobbies, and you will be able to make an appropriate gift choice for him.

❧ GIFT PROFILE ❧

Name _____

Birthday _____ Anniversary _____

Sizes

Belt _____ Blouse/top _____

Coat/jacket _____ Gloves _____

Hat _____ Lingerie _____

Pants (waist/length) _____ Ring _____

Shirt (neck/sleeve) _____ Shoes _____

Skirt/dress/suit _____ Underwear _____

Favorites

Author _____

Beverage _____

Candy _____

College _____

Color _____

Flower _____

Food _____

Fragrance _____

Kind of music _____

Singer/entertainer _____

Sport or team _____

Type of movie _____

Type of reading _____

Observations

Hobbies or special interests:

Topics of conversation:

Area of work/volunteerism:

Collections:

Home (colors, style, etc.):

Wishes expressed/dreams:

Specific gift ideas:

Other:

Gift Record

DATE: **GIFT:**

_____   _____

_____   _____

_____   _____

_____   _____

_____   _____

_____   _____

_____   _____

_____   _____

2.
Gift Ideas

❧ BABY ❧

While tiny newborn outfits are adorable, many babies outgrow them before they get to wear them because they have so many. Here is a wide variety of gifts to welcome a child (see *Gift Ideas: New Parents* for a different slant on baby presents). Choose toys and nursery accessories that encourage the infant to experiment with a variety of sounds, shapes, textures, and colors or to practice hand-to-eye coordination and eye focus. Be aware of small parts (such as plastic eyes on stuffed animals) that could be torn off and swallowed. Whenever possible, look for washable toys! Look under *Catalogs: Infant/Maternity Supplies; Clothing — Children thru Teens; Handcrafts;* and *Toys, Dolls, Games* for sources.

Proof set of coins or commemorative stamps issued in the year of birth
Newspaper from baby's birthplace on date of birth
Buy a savings bond or start a savings or mutual fund account in baby's name
Amagift   catalog of over forty gifts of equal value from which new parent
     chooses. You buy the Amagift album and present it much like a gift cer-
     tificate, only the recipient does not know the price of the gifts. The re-
     cipient chooses which item he wants and orders it directly from Amway
     via a postcard attached to the album. Shipping has already been paid.
     Available from Amway distributors (check your local telephone book
     under Amway).
Baby book; birth plaque — needlepoint, wooden, ceramic, cross-stitch, etc.;
     picture frame; paint a colorful wall mural in the nursery.
Pillow with music box (Buy a music box movement at a craft shop and insert
     into a handmade pillow or stuffed animal.)
Music box; stuffed animal or doll (simple design, washable, no buttons!)
Sturdy plastic toys that rattle or make noise (no sharp edges!)
Rubber squeeze toys or baby bath toys; rattle, pacifier, teething toys
Baby mirror (unbreakable)—as toy or to install on side of crib
Blocks—foam, plastic, cardboard, cloth
Books—nursery rhymes, children's songs, cloth, plastic with large pictures
     and ring binder, books in which main character shares baby's name
Cassettes of lullabies
Birthday candle (marked for each birthday up to 18)
Baby backpack, sling, bicycle seat; baby's travel mat and tote; padded lining
     for infant seat
Baby bracelet, ring, necklace; silver teething ring, cup, bank, rattle, spoon
Make Christmas stocking or tree ornament with baby's name.
Clothes—diaper shirts, easy-off outfits, bonnet (clothing up to one-year size is

appreciated) booties
Rompers, T-shirts, coveralls with parent's college logo; bunting
Baby sunglasses to protect eyes on outdoor strolls

Major Equipment
Crib, crib bumpers, folding portable crib, crib pad; bassinet
High chair (collapsible with removable tray); soft, wide "belt" to keep baby
    upright in high chair or shopping cart
Changing table, pad; diaper bag with waterproof lining and compartments
Bathtub, Bathinette, slanting bathtub that holds baby's head upright (fill with
    water toys, shampoo, washcloths, etc.)

Car seat, head support for car seat, protective rubber mat
    to go under car seat
Infant seat with several positions
Stroller, umbrella stroller, jogging stroller; walker, col-
    lapsible bounce chair
Baby swing for tree or doorway, or on stand with a crank;
    "jump-up" swing
Rocking chair; nursing stool with inclined top, nursing
    pillow

Nursery Supplies
Fitted crib sheet, waterproof pads; nap roll, chair seat; crib dust ruffle, canopy;
    toy box
Baby blanket—receiving size or longer for child to grow into; washable quilt
    (have friends or relatives embroider their names on the squares); crochet
    shell border around receiving blanket; sew two pieces of flannel together
    (with or without batting) and crochet shell border around them; bind 45"
    square of two-sided quilted material with wide bias tape.
Crib gym, crib activity box, mobile (maybe a musical one)
Hooded bath towels, baby washcloths
Diaper stacker, diaper pail; disposable diapers, baby wipes; cotton diaper lin-
    ers and diaper covers
Baby clothes hangers; sachets for drawers or potpourri for dresser to sweeten
    the room
"Goody box" full of diaper pins, pin lubricator, blunt nail scissors, baby
    powder, baby lotion, creams, baby washcloths, baby nail clippers, bibs,
    waterproof pads, pacifier, rattle, etc.; night light, nursery lamp; intercom
    baby monitor; personalized light switch plate
Cool-mist humidifier, vaporizer
Wall hanging, picture, growth chart to fit nursery theme (maybe one you
    painted or stitched)

Feeding Accessories
Bottle sterilizer, bottles, bottle brush, nipples, bottle warmer, bottle blanket
    (quilted sleeve to keep bottle warm)
Bibs, napkin clip to turn any napkin into a bib (great for traveling)
Shoulder burp pad
Portable baby seat that clamps to table (for restaurants)
Decorated dish set—plastic, stainless steel, or fine china; "Octopus" suction-
    cup plate holder (from dime store) to keep feeding dish firmly on table;
    weighted-base cup; food warming tray; baby-size eating utensils—silver

or stainless steel
Food mill or grinder; mini food processor with containers that freeze and store
Mini medicine bottle with nipple

✌ 1-YEAR-OLD ✌

Toddlers are attracted to bright colors, interesting noises, and movement. Look for toys that cater to these interests and that aid with large muscle development and hand-eye coordination. See *Catalogs: Infant/Maternity Supplies; Handcrafts; Toys, Dolls, Games;* and *For Children Only*.

Books — cloth, plastic, or cardboard pages; simple pictures or stories; nursery rhymes; one word and simple picture on each page
Big, soft ball
Toy telephone
Stacking toys, sorting toys
Hammering toys
Inflated, transparent tube or ball with items inside that jingle and roll as the tube is moved
Simple train set; small, sturdy cars, trucks, planes (big ones for outdoors); sandbox and plastic toys—pail, sifter, plastic bowls, shovel, etc.; small tricycle, riding toy, rocking horse; wagon full of plastic or wooden blocks; swing set, small slide, indoor gym house, indoor-outdoor see-saw
Soft rubber toys
Stuffed dolls, animals (washable! no buttons!)
Music box, musical toy, musical stuffed animal
Hard plastic people, animals, tools
Make a drawstring tub toy holder out of nylon net.
Bath toys, water play toys
Pull or push toys (especially *noisy* ones)
Blocks—cardboard, wood, plastic, cloth-covered foam, needlepoint
Toy box, shelves; non-tip stepstool; child's chair
Picture or stitchery for room; wall height chart; personalized light switch plate
Child's dishes, silverware, or cup with cartoon or storybook design
Clothes, overalls, mittens
Personalized Christmas tree ornament
Add to a savings account; buy a savings bond.
Waterbaby swimming classes
Enlarge baby's picture or give a coupon to have a portrait made.

✌ 2-YEAR-OLD ✌

Help channel a two-year-old's independence in a positive direction with toys that imitate adult activities (cooking, gardening, driving, etc.) and give experience in manipulating his own world (stacking or interlocking parts, role-play accessories). Anything that gives an outlet to all that energy is wonderful also (riding toys, balls, jungle gym). See *Catalogs: Handcrafts; For Children Only;* and *Toys, Dolls, Games* for some delightful choices.

Indoor gym house or toddler's gym

Full-size (for child) sturdy tug boat, tent, play house, or castle. *Fabulous Play House Plans*, by Kathy Smith Anthenat (Betterway Books, 1507 Dana Avenue, Cincinnati, OH 45207-1005, 800-289-0963) has many great ideas for building indoor or outdoor play houses (Fisher Price, Little Tikes, and Playskool, also have several pre-built types).

Wagon full of plastic or wooden blocks

Blocks—wooden, hollow cardboard, or plastic; preschool, interlocking plastic blocks (such as Duplo blocks made by Lego)

Small metal, wooden, or tough plastic cars, trucks, trains, or airplanes; tough plastic play sets—circus, village, farm, nursery school, house, etc.; hard plastic people (astronauts, cowboys, etc.) and animals (dinosaurs, domestic, horses); plastic tools (for gardening, cooking, house cleaning, and building); sorting toys (by size, color, shape, etc.)

Snap-together toys, stacking toys (large plastic or wooden pieces)

Toy telephone; cassette player for youngsters; rhythm instruments, musical toys, xylophone, drum; balls, balloons

Very simple puzzles (wooden with a few pieces, all big); large wooden beads to string

Outdoor equipment—slide, swing set, jungle gym, sandbox, tricycle, wagon, riding toy; large metal trucks, construction equipment, cars; sturdy shovel or spoon, bowls, sifter, funnel, empty plastic bottles, cups, pail; inner tube, arm float-supports for supervised swimming

Books—picture book, nursery rhymes, books with character of same name as child, counting book, alphabet book, labeling book

Large cloth blocks, books, or dolls with all kinds of fasteners; dolls—large, cuddly, soft, easy to handle and to love (for boys, too!); large-size doll furniture, buggy, bed

Small suitcase, tote bag

Costumes, big clothes, purse, etc., for make-believe or dress-up; play jewelry —rings, bracelet, necklace, beads, pins, barrettes; unbreakable polished steel mirror; mittens, caps, other clothes; smocked dresses; cross-stitch designs on overalls, sweatshirt (see *Catalogs: Clothing—Children thru Teens*)

Play dishes (unbreakable plastic or metal); junior silverware, dishes, cups in decorative pattern (Sesame Street, Muppet, and Disney characters are favorites.)

Small chair, table; toy box, shelves

Picture, monogram, stitchery for room

Light switch extender (helps child turn lights on)

Stepstool for bathroom; bath toys, terry-cloth hand mitt or puppet, shaped sponges; bubble bath, bath crayons; decorative toothbrush

Cartoon or personalized bath towel, sheets, pillowcases, beach towel; afghan, quilt

Personalized or unbreakable Christmas tree ornament

Add to a savings account; buy a savings bond.

Waterbaby swimming class

❧ 3- TO 5-YEAR-OLD ❧

Children of this age are ready to stretch their minds as well as their muscles. They are ready for puzzles, art supplies, building toys, role-play equipment, and beginning language, math, or science aids. For many first-class toys and gifts, see *Catalogs: Handcrafts; For Children Only;* and *Toys, Dolls, Games.*

For a party, hire a clown, storyteller, or magician.

Trip to circus, zoo, ice show, rodeo, amusement park, carnival, child's movie, child's favorite eating place, ball game, fire station, bakery, farm, or city (whichever is different from her everyday environment); ride on a train, airplane, boat, or horse.

Lessons in swimming, dancing, tumbling, sport, etc.

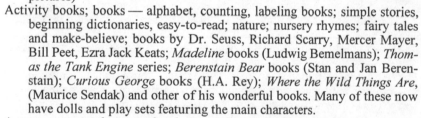

Art supplies—blunt scissors, crayons, chalk, felt-tip pens, paper (white and colored), finger paint, craft sticks, Play Doh (or see *Gifts to Make: Cooked Play Dough* for recipe), clay, paste, tablet, coloring books, pencils (personalized); old catalogs, wallpaper pattern books, sewing pattern books, magazines to cut up

Lite-Brite (child uses lighted, colored pegs to outline pictures)

Activity books; books — alphabet, counting, labeling books; simple stories, beginning dictionaries, easy-to-read; nature; nursery rhymes; fairy tales and make-believe; books by Dr. Seuss, Richard Scarry, Mercer Mayer, Bill Peet, Ezra Jack Keats; *Madeline* books (Ludwig Bemelmans); *Thomas the Tank Engine* series; *Berenstain Bear* books (Stan and Jan Berenstain); *Curious George* books (H.A. Rey); *Where the Wild Things Are*, (Maurice Sendak) and other of his wonderful books. Many of these now have dolls and play sets featuring the main characters.

A parent or grandparent who does not live near the child can buy a story book, read it on tape, and send the book and tape to the child

Bookmark, bookends, bookplates

Subscription (see *Magazines: Children*)

Blackboard, bulletin board; magnetic board with letters, numbers

Cassette player for little ones with tapes of a variety of music—for dancing, silly songs, children's classics, folk songs, lullabies, international sounds, etc.

Book/cassette (video or audio) combination; child's movie on video (see *Catalogs: Music & Movies; Religious;* and *For Children Only*)

View-Master and reels

Computer software for developing reading, counting, spelling skills

Board games (requiring no reading, but using identification and counting) such as Candyland, Chutes & Ladders, etc.

Matching games—playing cards, Old Maid, Lotto, dominoes

Sewing cards; craft sticks or popsicle sticks for craft projects

Play Doh and modeling (dough molding) sets

Outdoor Play Equipment

Swing set, jungle gym, slide, rope ladder, tire swing; stilts; tricycle, bicycle (with training wheels for beginner), bicycle license plate with child's name, wagon, scooter, sled, toboggan; skates (without ball bearing wheels for first roller skates); ice skates; snow skis

Construction vehicles, cranes, trucks, cars.

Wading pool, inflatable water toys, pail, water toys

Beginning sports equipment—balls of all kinds, $3/4$ or junior-size basketball, large plastic ball and bat, Frisbee, Velcro ball and catching disc, T-ball set of soft foam

Play house—It does not have to be a work of art. A child would love to get the wood, cardboard, or whatever and build it himself. Also child-size castle, fort, tent, store, or anything for fantasy play. A good source is *Fabulous Play House Plans*, by Kathy Smith Anthenat (Betterway Books, 1507 Dana Avenue, Cincinnati, OH 45207-1005, 800-289-0963)

Outdoor drinking faucet (attaches to outdoor faucet)

Role-Play Toys

Dolls—all sizes, kinds; baby dolls (don't overlook dolls for boys); flip-over dolls (Little Red Riding Hood on one end, the wolf on the other; Goldilocks and a bear; happy face and sad face); doll accessories—furniture, clothes, house, buggy, or stroller; paper dolls; doll or pillow with zipper, buttons, laces, snaps; hand puppets, finger puppets, puppet stage

Small-scale toy household items—kitchen appliances, apron, mop, broom, tea set, dishes, vacuum cleaner, mixer, etc.; small-scale toy lawn items—lawn mower, gardening tool sets, etc.; tools—Depending on child, you can introduce real hammer, nails, box of scrap wood, tool box, wrench, screwdriver, etc.; heavy plastic tools are still appropriate.

Costumes—old clothes, purse, costume jewelry, shoes; ready-made outfits for cowboy, Indian, astronaut, ballerina, princess, etc.

Hats—cowboy, Indian headdress, football helmet, crown (aluminium foil covered cardboard with sequins), fireman's, baseball, space helmet

Tepee (make it with three dowel sticks and circle of cloth); stick horse

Other Toys

Transportation toys—any size train set, cars, airplanes, spaceship, trucks, cranes, tractors

Construction set—blocks, interlocking block (such as Duplo by Lego) or log sets; giant or regular size

Small hard plastic or wooden people, animals

Space toys—dolls, sword, helmet, cape, spaceship, figures

Electronic items for ages three up (talking robot, clock radio with prerecorded melodies and night light, sing-along microphone, etc.); V-Tech Little Smart electronic, interactive toys

Plastic, colorful keyboards and monitors such as V-Tech Videopainter or Precomputer for ages five up

Foam toys—sports equipment, balls, blocks

Bath colors, bath toys, terry-cloth puppet

Bubblegum machine; trinket box

Music box; musical instrument—piano, xylophone, tambourine, drum, keyboard

Cookie cutter assortment; popsicle molds

Simple Science Equipment

Silly Putty; Slinky; flashlight; magnifying glass (mounted kind is nice); magnet; ant farm, bug house, seeds to grow, butterfly collection; kaleidoscope, octascope, dragon's eye; calculator, computer with preschool software; toy clock; telescope

For Child's Room
Small table, chairs, beanbag or rocking chair, bookshelf, wastebasket
For walls — long mirror, stitchery, picture, monogram, growth chart, personalized or decorative light switch plate, framed pictures of relatives (hang at child's eye level), calendar with pictures of interest to child, empty picture frame for child's art, blackboard
Linens—afghan, quilt; bedspread, sheets, pillowcases in cartoon, space, fairy tale, children's design
Throw pillow; slumber bag for overnight visits
Tooth-fairy pillow — pillow with small pocket attached to hold tooth and surprise from tooth fairy
Holiday decorations, small tree for child's room

Personal
Fancy comb, brush, hand mirror; barrettes, hair ribbons; little purse, suitcase, wallet; drawstring tote bag with child's name; lunch kit; real suitcase
Pretend make-up; children's jewelry—necklace, bracelet, rings (personalized items are nice); clothes—especially mittens, cap, T-shirt, belt, anything personalized; pajamas with cartoon or sport or movie theme; painted, cross-stitched, sequined sweatshirt or T-shirt, smocked dress
Personalized placemat, mug, dishes, bath towel, beach towel, Christmas tree ornament
Coin bank, coins, dollar bill
Wooden, felt, cloth nativity set for play and display
Foam booster seat for car after child outgrows car seat so he can see out window and still be in a seatbelt

❧ 6- TO 10-YEAR-OLD ❧

This is a marvelous age for introducing musical instruments, crafts, sports, and strategy games. Check under *Catalogs: For Children Only; Craft Supplies; Handcrafts; Models & Miniatures; Music & Movies; Science;* and *Toys, Dolls, Games* for some unique items or kits.

Hire a clown or magician for a party.
Trip to circus, movie, ball game, ballet, rodeo, carnival, historical monument, museum, favorite restaurant, theater, etc. Let child take one or two friends; ride on plane, train, or boat to some special place
Passes to movie theater, bowling alley, or skating rink, or coupons to an ice cream or pizza parlor or fast food restaurant
Lessons in swimming, gymnastics, ballet, karate, art, sport, musical instrument, etc.
Pet (with parental permission)
Add to a savings account; buy a savings bond.
One-of-a-kind handcraft (carving, doll, collectible, jewelry)
Shaped candies, e.g., chocolate baseball; cookie tin of favorite homemade cookies; gingerbread house (or make one with the child; flavored popcorn

Toys That Can Teach

Tape player or recorder, cassette tapes, compact disc (CD) player and compact discs (CDs)—variety of music such as folk songs, silly songs, children's classics, or soundtracks from family or children's movies

Video of child's favorite movie

Computer; educational software that teaches reading, math, spelling, thinking, writing, or problem-solving skills; or game software (see *Catalogs: Computing* and *For Children Only*)

Electronic keyboard, musical instrument, computer software for learning music skills

Subscription (see *Magazines: Children thru Teens*)

Books on sports, science, nature, fiction, fairy tales, animals, space; also child's dictionary or encyclopedia, simple biographies, comic books, or mysteries

Free Stuff for Kids (Meadowbrook Press, 1992)

The following series of books are well-liked—*Chronicles of Narnia* (C.S. Lewis), *Little House on the Prairie* (Laura Ingalls Wilder), *Boxcar Children* (Gertrude Chandler Warner), *Amelia Bedelia* (Peggy Parish), *Madeline* (Ludwig Bemelmans), *Curious George* (H.A. Rey), *Choose Your Own Adventure, Baby-Sitters Club, Baby-Sitters Little Sister*. Popular mysteries are *Nancy Drew, Hardy Boys, Bobbsey Twins, Tom Swift, Alfred Hitchcock,* and *Three Investigators*. Other popular authors are Beverly Cleary, Bill Peet, and Shel Silverstein.

A book from a recommended reading list for this age such as Partners in Excellence (selected by the American Library Association; call 800-621-8202 for a free list); bookends, bookmark, bookplates

Globe, wall map to mark where they have traveled

Pocket calculator, solar construction kit

Begin a collection of stamps, coins, rocks, shells, baseball cards, postcards, or dolls

Games — horseshoes, safe darts, ring toss, tether ball, badminton, racquet ball, croquet, volleyball, board games on reading level of child (or make your own on cardboard or plywood), simple card games, checkers, chess, dominoes, bingo, Ping-Pong

Some favorite games are Uno, Yahtzee, Monopoly, Chinese checkers, Parcheesi, Clue, Mastermind, Scattergories Junior, Topple, and Pictionary Junior.

Jigsaw puzzles (have one made from child's photograph)

Outdoor Toys

Roller skates, in-line skates, or ice skates, skating skirt; scooter; skateboard, helmet, protective gear; pogo stick, jumping shoes, stilts

Bicycle, carrier rack, chain lock, reflective pedals, basket, personalized license plate (see *Catalogs: Sports & Recreation* for motocross accessories)

Sports equipment — baseball, batting trainer, glove, bat; basketball (junior size for six- to seven-year-olds), hoop, backboard; soccer ball; tennis gear (see *Gift Ideas: Tennis*); football, helmet, pads (see also *Gift Ideas: Sports Fan,* and *Sports & Games*)

Baton; hula hoop; jacks, jump rope; sled, toboggan, inflatable snow tube; yo-

yo; Frisbee, Velcro ball and catcher's disc, ring toss; kites
Water toys—inflatables, rafts, beach ball, weighted diving rings; beach towel
Clubhouse or material to make one
Bug house, butterfly net, insect mounting kit, ant farm

Creative Toys

Activity books—dot-to-dot, mazes, word puzzles
Art supplies — pencils (personalized), eraser, tape, stapler, paper clips, crayons, felt-tip markers, craft sticks, construction paper, blank jigsaw puzzles to color, coloring books (check teachers' and art supply stores for historical, science, etc., themes), rubber bands, scissors, glue, string, label maker, etc.
Come Look with Me: Enjoying Art with Children, by Gladys S. Lizzard (Thomasson-Grant, 1991)
Pencil sharpener in cute shape; rubber stamps with designs, stickers (see ***Catalogs: Craft Supplies—Rubber Stamping***); paint-by-number kits
Sewing machine (play size), book of easy sewing projects
Crafts kits—potter's wheel, candle making, string art, leather craft, glass cutting, needlework, shrink-art, birdhouse kit, weaving, wood burning, printing, etc. (select kit by age printed on kit and maturity of child)
Tools—nails, screws, hammer, screwdriver, handsaw, toolbox, brace and bit, ruler
Science kits, microscope, telescope, crystal radio, etc.; magic set
Books of simple science experiments such as *How Science Works*, by Judith Hann (Reader's Digest, Dorling Kindersley, 1991)—One hundred ways parents and kids can share the secrets of science; *Eyewitness Juniors* (Alfred A. Knopf, publisher) series with books on topics from butterflies to bikes; *Eyewitness Visual Dictionaries* (Dorling Kindersley, publisher) series with detailed illustrations of animals, ships, music, physics, etc.
Models of cars, planes, spaceships, sailing ships, trains, skeleton, miniature furniture to build; construction sets—interlocking blocks; erector sets
Children's cookbook, apron, miniature pans

For Child's Room

Desk, desk light; clock, radio; blackboard, bulletin board; posters, wall mirror, needlework picture, framed photographs from a trip or of a friend or family; beanbag chair
Throw pillow with initial, fancy bed linens, quilt, slumber bag for slumber parties; tooth fairy pillow—pillow with small outside pocket to hold tooth and surprise from the tooth fairy
Type case or shadowbox for miniatures, treasures
Picture calendar (many photo stores will make a calendar from your pictures)
Holiday or seasonal decorations

Other Toys, Gifts

Stickers—Special varieties are "puffies", "googlie eyes" (moving eyes), and "smellies" (scented).
Personalized address labels, stationery
Racing car set, small cars, trucks, vehicles, airplanes, trains, spaceships
Small people, animals; dolls, doll house and accessories, doll clothes, collector dolls, paper dolls; matching outfits for girl and her doll or for girl and her mother; stuffed animals

Kaleidoscope or octascope (reshapes the world outside); walkie-talkie; flash-
light
Video cassettes—blank or of a favorite movie or subject
Scrapbook, photograph album; camera, film
Coin bank, cash; raise child's allowance (or start one!)
Suitcase or tote bag for overnights, ballet, or gymnastics lessons; sports bag;
satchel,; backpack for school; umbrella; insulated, reusable lunch kit
Fancy comb, brush set, hand mirror, hair ribbons, barrettes
Watch; jewelry (especially personalized)—ring, necklace, bracelet, pin, ear-
rings; jewelry box
Decorative tin, wooden, crystal, or ceramic boxes for trinkets; music box
Clothing—jeans belt, funny T-shirt, anything personalized, sweater, paja-
mas, nightgown, fancy socks, tights, sweatshirt, etc. (see *Catalogs:
Clothing—Children thru Teens*)
Personalized or funny placemat, mug, glass; items with emblem of Scouts,
Campfire Girls, or other organization to which child belongs
Model train set—track, cars, engines, power pack, side buildings (kits to
make), landscaping items

∽ 11- TO 14-YEAR-OLD ∾

Youths' favorite areas of interest are music and clothes, but many are open to
experimenting with musical instruments; crafts such as models or cross-
stitch; scientific kits including crystal radios or radio-controlled cars; and
new leisure activities including aerobics or art lessons. Listen carefully to the
young person you are giving to and see what he talks about that might be ex-
plored through a specialty magazine or classes or supplies. You'll find plenty
of sources for just the right gift under *Catalogs: Books & More; Collectibles; Craft Supplies; Electronics; Handcrafts; Jewelry; Models &
Miniatures; Music & Movies; Outdoors; Science;* and *Toys, Dolls, Games*.

Gift certificates for bowling, miniature golf, roller or ice skating, movie theater, video rental store, ice cream, yogurt, or pizza parlor or favorite fast
food restaurant; tickets for sporting event, performing arts group, amuse-
ment park, sports card or doll show, etc.; season's pass to a local museum,
entertainment facility, or theme park
Membership in swimming or tennis club or recreational facility like YMCA
Take a few friends to movie, pizza parlor, skating rink, museum, etc.
Lessons in dance, art, musical instrument, sport, gymnastics, sewing, swim-
ming, karate, woodworking, drama, craft, etc.
Tuition for a baby-sitting, first-aid, or modeling course
Tuition to church or Scout camp or retreat
Begin a collection of ceramic figurines, stuffed animals, miniatures of a fa-
vorite animal, mascots, cars, regional crafts, patches, etc.
Pet (with parent's permission)
Subscription (see *Magazines: Children thru Teens)*
Books—biographies, science, fiction, mystery (*Hardy Boys* or *Nancy Drew*),
encyclopedia, comic books, adventure, sports, etiquette, baby-sitting,
dictionary, hobby how-to, history; *Anne of Green Gables* or other books
by L.M. Montgomery; *Eyewitness Books* (Alfred A. Knopf), detailed
illustrations and explanations of such diverse subjects as money, art, fos-

sils, and flying machines; books by Klutz Press such as *Kids Shenanigans—Great Things to Do That Mom and Dad Will Just Barely Approve Of*, *The Official Icky Poo Book*, or Klutz books on clowning, the art of bubble blowing (foot-long ones!), juggling, etc. (each book contains an item to use in the activity)

A book from a recommended reading list for this age such as Partners in Excellence (selected by the American Library Association; call 800-621-8202 for a free list)

Comic collections such as *Calvin & Hobbes*; bookends, bookplates, bookmark, bookshelf; child's own public library card

Stereo, tape player, tapes, tape holder, CD player, CD holder or rack, CDs; carrying or storage case for tapes or CDs

Computer; computer game software, educational software; software for making banners, certificates, or greeting cards (see also *Gift Ideas: Computer Enthusiast*); pocket calculator

Especially for Teens

Own telephone extension or line, decorator telephone; answering machine-phone combination, long cord for telephone, cordless telephone

Special telephone services such as speed calling, call waiting, or call cue (redials last local number called)

Radio, clock-radio, clock, alarm clock; Walkman (portable cassette player), Discman (portable CD player), and good earphones; Karaoke sing-along system

Bulletin board; block of note paper

Autograph book, diary, decorative pillow, stuffed animal; address book, stationery, telephone book, personalized stickers or address labels

Scrapbook, photograph album, sports album

Notebooks with movie star's or cartoon character's picture

Wall posters of singers, movie personalities, slogans, nature scenes

Backpack for school

Shaped candies (e.g., a chocolate telephone); tin of favorite cookies; bucket of flavored popcorn

Cosmetic organizer and carrying case, zippered cosmetic bag, mood lipstick, cosmetics (scented bath powder, eye shadow collection, etc.)

Creative Gifts

Camera, film

Construction sets—interlocking blocks or metal parts

Models of airplanes, cars, ships, trains, rockets

Model train set—track, cars, side buildings (kits to make them), engines, power pack, bridges, landscaping accessories

Doll house and miniatures (or kits to make them)

Art kits, calligraphy kit, rubber stamping supplies, blank jigsaw puzzles

Space pen that writes at any angle

Craft kits—rock tumbling, stitchery, wood burning, macramé, sand painting, printing, ceramics, fabric painting, weaving, shrink-art, etc.

Science kits—crystal radio, microscope, telescope, chemistry lab, radio-controlled cars or planes, solar experiments, etc.

Sewing machine, sewing basket, supplies (see *Gift Ideas: Seamstress*)

Kit to make Christmas ornaments or other seasonal decoration

Just for Fun
(see also *Gift Ideas: Sports & Games*)

Skateboard, protective gear, in-line skates; bicycle, carrier rack, basket, reflector pedals, motocross equipment (see *Gift Ideas: Cyclist*)

Sports equipment — baseball batter training set, throwback net, glove, bat; football, helmet; soccer ball; or basketball, backboard, or hoop; T-shirt, cap, or notebook with favorite team's logo

Frisbee, yo-yo, kite, darts, table tennis

Beach towel, beach ball, inflatable raft or floats, sun hat, weighted diving rings, beach chair or umbrella

Camping gear (see *Gift Ideas: Camper* and *Outdoors Lover*) or equipment for other outdoor activity (see *Gift Ideas: Tennis; Water Skier; Snow Skier; Runner/Jogger/Walker;* and *Backpacker,* etc.)

Small ice chest or folding insulated carrier

Small cars, miniatures (soldiers or doll house miniatures or other collectibles); space toys, spaceships, Star Trek memorabilia; stuffed animals

Yahtzee, Scrabble, Risk, Pictionary, other board games, strategy games, checkers, chess, card games, dominoes, table games

Battery-operated games, computer games

Outdoor games—croquet, volleyball, archery, horseshoes, badminton

Jigsaw puzzles, brain teasers, games of skill, solitaire games; book of group games, crossword puzzles, mazes

For Room
Throw pillow—initials, shapes like seashell or butterfly, lace-trimmed, personalized; sleeping bag for slumber parties; afghan

Beanbag chair, pillow with arms; trinket box, coin bank; pictures, picture frame, wall hangings, wall mirror, hand mirror, vanity tray or dresser set; teen bed or bath linens, satin pillowcases; matching sheets, comforter; small potted plant; type case, shadow box, or shelves for miniatures and treasures; music box; desk lamp

Storage or space-making supplies for organizing the desk or closet; matched set of tape dispenser and stapler; stacking storage containers

"Do not disturb" sign for door knob

Christmas tree ornament—personalized or handcraft

Slightly Personal
Funny T-shirt, one with slogan or design that matches youth's interests

Almost anything personalized—purse, pencils, jewelry, plaque, memo pads

Jewelry — ID bracelet, locket, earrings, neck chain, anklet, chain bracelet, watch; wallet, purse, key ring

Soft luggage, tote bag, insulated carrying case for curling iron

Clothes—especially sweat suits, no-slip sock slippers, holiday socks, gowns, pajamas, jeans, fancy or cute lingerie, matching robe and slippers, boxers

❧ 15- TO 18-YEAR-OLD ❧

Gifts for this age group can come from the previous age category or from any of the other gift categories. Many youths have already determined a special interest that you can foster through a gift. If you don't know what that is, try a gift certificate or one of the many ideas below.

Cash (never inappropriate!)

Open a savings account, purchase penny stocks, or make initial investment in a mutual fund.

Behind-the-wheel driving course

Course, book, or video instruction on baby-sitting, auto repair, relationships, craft or hobby (photography, fabric painting, cake decorating, wood-working, etc.)

Lessons in dance, aerobics, music, sports, crafts, sewing, art, karate, etc.

Gift certificates to movie theater, miniature golf, amusement park, bowling alley, ice cream parlor, fast food restaurant, video rental store; season's pass to a local museum, entertainment facility, theme park; two tickets to sports event, ballet, theater, entertainment event (and money for snacks)

Gift certificate to favorite clothing or craft store, restaurant dinner for two

Pet (with parent's permission)

Especially for Teens

Amagift—catalog of over forty gifts of equal value for teens. You buy the Amagift and present it much like a gift certificate, only the teen does not know the price you paid. The teen chooses which item he wants and or-ders it directly from Amway via a postcard in the back of the album. Shipping has already been paid. Available from Amway distributors (check your local telephone book under Amway).

Key chain for new privilege of car keys

Sun shade or license plate holder with favorite sports team or college logo

Membership in American Automobile Association (1000 AAA Dr., Heath-row, FL 32746-5080) or other organization that furnishes emergency road service

Cosmetic organizer and carrying case; stacking storage organizers

Stuffed animal

Spiral notebooks with sports figure, entertainer, or popular slogan on cover

Diary, address book; autograph book; scrapbook, photograph album; picture frames

Gift certificate to favorite hairdresser, manicurist, makeup consultant, photo-grapher

Own telephone line or extension, decorator telephone, long cord for tele-phone, retracting telephone cord, answering machine, answering ma-chine-phone combination, cordless telephone

Special telephone services (see *Gift Ideas: Adult—Basic*)

Alarm clock, clock, clock-radio, clock/tape/radio combination; CD player, CD of favorite music; CD holder, carrier, or rack

Stereo, tape player, cassette tapes, tape holder or carrier; portable tape or CD player and radio; earphones or headphones for tape player, stereo, or radio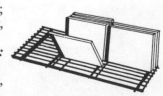

Videos—music or area of interest (see *Catalogs: Music & Movies*), video rewinder

Computer; software for learning to type, calendar, resumé writer, spelling checker, type styles, banners, certificates, greeting cards, publish-ing, training for the SAT or ACT, other areas of interest

Posters of entertainers, singers, slogans, nature, cartoon character, Scripture verse

Karaoke sing-along system

Tank of gas, gas credit card, auto safety device or alarm

Own credit card with a monthly limit for clothing or other purchases

Bucket of flavored popcorn, case of favorite snacks, shaped candies (e.g., chocolate rose or dollar bill)

Just for Fun

Subscription (see *Magazines: Children thru Teens* or other topic of interest)

Books on famous people, sports or sports figures, young love, mystery, growing up, etiquette, adult development, science, adventure stories, career possibilities, relationships, science fiction, cartoons

Begin or add to a collection—stamps, thimbles, coins, bears, miniatures, etc.

Star Trek or favorite show memorabilia

Jigsaw puzzles, crossword puzzle books, brain teasers (see *Catalogs: Toys, Dolls, Games*)

Table games such as games of skill and strategy, chess, checkers, playing cards, Michigan Rummy, Yahtzee, Scrabble, Pictionary, Taboo, Skipbo, Uno (see also *Gift Ideas: Sports & Games*)

Outdoor games like volleyball, badminton, Frisbee, Ping-Pong

Battery-operated game, computer game, video game

Hobby equipment, tools

Sports equipment for football, tennis, baseball, etc.; bicycle, skateboard, safety helmet, accessories (see *Gift Ideas: Cyclist*); in-line skates, safety helmet, knee or elbow pads

Exercise equipment, clothing (see *Gift Ideas: Fitness Buff*)

Membership in fitness or health club

Baseball cap, T-shirt, sweat suit, etc., with favorite team's logo

Beach towel, beach ball, inflatable raft, beach umbrella or chair; small ice chest, thermos

Other Gifts

Type case or shelves for treasures

Stationery, personalized stickers or note pads, address labels; desk, drawer, or closet organizers (see *Gift Ideas: The Organizer*); pen and pencil set, pen or pencil holder; personalized clipboard; bulletin board, message board

Typewriter, calculator, computer, TV, VCR

Wall or hand mirror, lighted or standing makeup mirror

Teen bed or bath linens—sports, romantic, nature themes; matching sheets, comforter; personalized or handmade throw pillows, quilt, afghan, wall hanging or picture (or kit to make any of these); beanbag chair

Craft or science kits such as needlework, wood burning, macramé, models, pompom craft, transistor radio kit, digital computer kit (see *Catalogs: Craft Supplies* or *Science*)

Sewing machine, sewing basket and supplies (see *Gift Ideas: Seamstress*)

Clothes — especially T-shirts, nightclothes, accessories (hair bows, purses, scarves), fancy lingerie, matching robe and slippers

Sachet, scented drawer liners, satin padded clothes hangers

Scarf (wool or ski), leather gloves or driving gloves

Jewelry—personalized, locket, earrings, neck chain, bracelet, pin, pendant, watch, ring

Jewelry box; decorative tin, wooden, or ceramic box for trinkets

Cosmetics (eye shadow collection, scented bath products, new type of product, fancier brand than she buys for herself), cologne, cosmetic bags for travel

Shower tote or caddy; hair dryer, electric razor, or other personal care appliance (see *Appendix: Small Electric Appliances*)

Wallet (how about a surprise inside?), purse, compact

Luggage, soft luggage, garment bag, sports tote bag

Camera, film, camcorder, video camera

Potted or silk plant for room

❧ ADULT — BASIC ☙

If you aren't sure of the special interests of your gift recipient, try an idea from this list. See also *Gift Ideas: Man—Basic; Woman—Basic; Bachelor; Single Woman; Family; Electronic Marvels,* and other interest categories. Order a few catalogs from the *Art & Special Treasures; Books & More; Smorgasbord; Food; Handcrafts,* or *International/Regional Specialties* sections to find these and other sure-to-please gifts.

Tuition for a defensive driving course; tuition for a leisure course—quilting, rock climbing, photography, round dancing, gourmet cooking, etc.

Anything you make well—ceramic bowl, wooden trivet, homemade bread or jelly, cross-stitched picture, etc.

Installation and several months of special telephone service (not available from all telephone companies)—call waiting, call forwarding, selective call forwarding (allows you to forward calls from up to three local numbers; all others go to your home), call trace (initiates a trace of the last local call you received; this information is sent only to the telephone company), three-way calling, speed calling (lets you dial frequently called numbers with one or two digits), touch tone, call return (redials your last local caller even if you don't know who just called you), call cue (calls back the last local number you dialed whether or not your call was answered), call blocker (blocks calls from at least three local numbers and prevents the last number that called from reaching you again), priority call (identifies up to three local numbers that will signal you with a special ring), personalized ring

Decorator telephone, gift certificate from telephone company for long distance calls, cellular telephone

Personalized bumper sticker, car license plates, or license plate holder

Erasable memo board that attaches to car visor for jotting notes or reminders

Offer to inventory household goods for insurance (and take snapshots or video of valuable items and furniture).

Membership in local educational television station (find out what amount entitles recipient to receive monthly program listing)

Installation and several months of special cable television service

For 80th and subsequent birthdays, request a card from the mayor or governor. For greetings from the president of the United States, write four weeks in advance to Greetings Office, OEOB, Room 94, Washington, DC 20500. Include the recipient's full name, address, zip code and complete date of birth.

Take him/her out to dinner, a show or special entertainment event.

Tickets to a sports event, the opera, the theater, a concert, etc.

Two-for-one or discount coupon book for services, meals, or merchandise

Coupons for car wash, movies, ice cream, yogurt, pizza, maid service, etc.

Locking gas cap for car (see also *Gift Ideas: Security & Safety Conscious*)

Coupons for you to do chores — lawn mowing, mending, weeding flower beds, baby-sitting, etc.

Amagift—catalogs of several dozen gifts of equal value from which recipient chooses. You buy the Amagift in the price range you want and give the recipient the colorful album. The recipient (unaware of the price) chooses which item he wants and orders it directly from Amway. Shipping has already been paid. Available from Amway distributors (check your local telephone book under Amway).

Items relating to profession or hobby—magazine, book, miniature, needlework plaque, mug, T-shirt, note pad, tools, etc.

Call long distance; send a cassette or video of you or his family.

Singing telegram (see *Gift Ideas: Extra Special*)

Book on adult development, money management, hobby, how-to, time management, biography of person he admires, special interest area, favorite cartoon (*Calvin & Hobbes* or *Far Side*)

Family genealogy chart or book such as *Unpuzzling Your Past*, by Emily Anne Croom (Betterway Books, 1507 Dana Avenue, Cincinnati, OH 45207-1005, 800-289-0963)

Stress relievers such as pinhead sculpture (leaves a 3-D impression of anything pressed into it), small squeezable ball, kaleidoscope or octascope, lava lamp, CRDL (diamond-shaped chips on a magnetic base that can be shaped any way you like), safe darts and dart board

Always Appropriate

Wallet, key case, or key ring; automatic or purse-size umbrella; magazine rack; cassette, video, or CD holder or carrying case; subscription (see *Magazines*); bookends, bookmark (make one), bookplates; desk calendar, pencil or pen holder, paperweight, memo board, desk accessories, letter holder; briefcase, attaché case

Directory of toll-free telephone numbers (call Worldwide Directory at 800-SWB-BOOK for current price and ordering information)—consumer directory lists more than 60,000 published AT&T 800 numbers alphabetically and in yellow pages format

Exercise bicycle or other exercise equipment (see *Gift Ideas: Fitness Buff*)

Membership in local spa or health club

Organizers for desk, belts, shoes, ties, or closets (see *Gift Ideas: The Organizer*); stationery, notecards, personalized postcards or address labels

Gift certificate to favorite store, specialty shop, or catalog

Terrarium, flowers, potted plant, hanging basket, topiary, silk flower arrangement (see *Catalogs: Floral Gifts*)

Large-number outdoor thermometer

Radio, CB, cassette player, CD player, alarm clock, clock-radio

TV, computer, VCR, VCR Plus (automatically programs up to 14 different shows at a time); remote control, remote control holder; copy of a favorite movie, documentary on a favorite subject, or travel video (see *Catalogs: Music & Movies*)

Cassette tape, video, or CD of favorite singer, group, or type of music

Computer program for personal finances, calendar, mailing labels or lists, banners, greeting cards, forms or legal documents, health and diet, genealogy, other area of interest (see *Gift Ideas: Computer Enthusiast*)

Nutcracker, package of nuts; homemade edibles (see *Gifts to Make*) — cookies, cake, bread, jelly, candy, venison sausage, instant mixes; gift pack of ham, fruit, cheese, or regional specialties (see *Catalogs: Food*); selection of dessert sauces, preserves, honey, candies; coffee grinder, varieties of coffee or tea, spiced tea mix (see *Gifts to Make*), teapot or tea cozy; popcorn popper, ice cream maker (see *Appendix: Small Electric Appliances*)

Playing cards, brain-teaser puzzle, jigsaw puzzles (put pieces in a jar and keep the box!) (see *Catalogs: Toys, Dolls, Games*)

Watch; luggage, tote bag, sports bag

Pocket calculator; folding opera glasses, binoculars

Garment bags for shoes, dresses, suits

Enlarge a favorite picture; have old pictures copied or restored; convert slides or home movies to video.

Your choice of photograph on mug, calendar, plate, six-sided puzzle, or Christmas ornament (see local photo dealer); photograph album, camera, film

Board or table game — checkers, chess, backgammon, Michigan Rummy, Scrabble, Pictionary, Trivial Pursuit, Taboo

Outdoor game—croquet, Frisbee, horseshoes, badminton

Decorative candle or handcraft; throw pillow (stitchery, needlepoint, letter-shaped, lacy); linens for table, bath, or bed (flannel sheets are great)

Personal Items

Bath sheet; large wrap-around towel; driving gloves; scarves, neck scarf, scarf hanger; clothing—shirt, blouse, nightclothes, robe, belt, sweater, T-shirt, lingerie; cosmetics—bath powder, bath oil, cologne, perfume, nail polish, after-shave lotion, any product in person's favorite fragrance; jewelry — ring, earrings, bracelet, neck chain, pendant, stick pin, pin; jewelry box; ultrasonic jewelry cleaning system; manicure set; cosmetic bag; shower massage (see also *Catalogs: Environmentally Friendly*); memory box—shadow box filled with meaningful miniatures or treasures; picture of family for office, desk, or wallet; personal care appliances (see *Appendix: Small Electric Appliances*); write a poem or song; T-shirt or mug with special slogan, person's name, college logo or crest; flowers

ᕽ ANNIVERSARIES ᕽ

Anniversaries usually mean a gift for the couple. If both enjoy a particular interest, check that category. See also *Gift Ideas: Extra Special; Family;* and and *Wedding,* and *Appendix: Anniversary Symbols & Gift Ideas*. Please avoid those gifts inscribed "25th Anniversary."

Make a scrapbook of family photos, letters, or remembrances.

Write friends and ask them to send a card or letter mentioning a special memory involving the couple.

Make a family quilt with each family member making a square. Children can draw with permanent ink markers; composite picture frame filled with

family photos; enlarge and frame a favorite photograph.; picture frame
or photo album; take a portrait of the couple or give a gift certificate to a
photography studio.; frame the wedding invitation or announcement.;
restore the wedding picture.; painting or photograph of their house,
church where they married, or other sentimental spot

Family history—genealogy charts, written or taped experiences

Candy; their favorite wine; basket of fruit, jellies, or cheeses

Cassette tape or CD of favorite kind of music

Give an open house.; guest book, if they have a party

Bake a wedding cake. Just a white cake with white icing, topped with flowers
or a plastic bride and groom from the variety store, will suffice if you
aren't a cake decorator.; cake knife—silver or porcelain handle; two silver, crystal, marble, or pewter goblets

Arrange a conference call with all the children.

Restage the honeymoon as nearly as possible (same place, same menu, etc.).

Write local mayor or governor (no more than four weeks in advance) request-
ing that an anniversary greeting be sent to the couple. For a greeting from
the president, write four weeks in advance to Greetings Office, OEOB,
Room 94, Washington, DC 20500. Usually they will send greetings for
50th or subsequent wedding anniversaries. Include recipients' full names,
address, zip code, and complete date of marriage (month, day, and year).

Memory box or shadow box filled with memorabilia

Silver or handmade bookmarks

Matching reclining chairs; double bed lamp with separate dimmer switches

Dinner at a nice restaurant; tickets to special program or event they enjoy

Bulbs, shrub, tree, or rose bush for their yard or give to local park or church
in their names.; flowers or a potted plant

Give altar flowers for their church in their names.

Original artwork or handcraft — stained glass, painting, sculpture, needlepoint, woodcarving, etc.

✎ ANTIQUE COLLECTOR ✎

Find out which period, style, and kind of antiques are preferred if possible.
Does she or he like 18th-century European or Oriental or colonial American
items? Or does she collect a particular item such as bells, spoons, toys, or
books? You will find some quality reproductions in *Catalogs: Art & Special
Treasures*.

Take pictures for insurance or pay for an appraisal;
shelves or display rack, shadow box for display;
decorative items of the period to complement
furniture pieces (such as vase, napkin rings,
candlesticks, or bookends); make a craft from
her favorite period of history such as a sunbon-
net or a Renaissance design needlepoint.

Tickets to an antique show

Registry book

Book on restoration, identification, or pricing of antiques, e.g., *Kovel's Antiques and Collectibles Price List,* by Ralph Kovel and Terry Kovel
(Crown). This is updated with a new edition each year.; books on silver

marks or particular items collected such as bottles, art pottery, Depression glass, American dinnerware, dolls, buttons, etc.

Pass down a family heirloom with a written history of the item and maybe some personal anecdotes or data about some of the owners.

Restore a picture of the family, old homestead, or hometown long ago.

If your recipient has another hobby, find an antique used in that hobby (such as an old book for an avid reader, an antique thimble for a seamstress, old tools for a handyman, old kitchen utensils for a cook, etc.)

Jewelry from the period

Subscription (see *Magazines: Arts & Antiques*)

ꙮ AMATEUR ARCHAEOLOGIST ꙮ

For those who love to dig for buried bones and bits of history, give something from this list. Other ideas might come from *Gift Ideas: Camper* and *Backpacker* if they go on digs lasting more than a day.

Subscription (see *Magazines: Science*)

5-inch mason's pointing trowel (Marshaltown — preferred brand); tool box; line level; measuring tape (automatic, spring-loaded) — both metric and inches; assortment of dental picks; brushes — small, camel-hair; dust pans; quilted vest with lots of pockets; sun hat, rain gear; picnic supplies; folding camp stool or chair; compass; reproductions of artifacts as decorative items; arrowhead sets; dues in a local or state archaeology society; book or video on regional archaeological studies or others in area of special interest or on the people group being studied; topographic maps of area; camera, film

ꙮ ARTIST ꙮ

Know your recipient's favorite medium (watercolor, oil, pen and ink, etc.). See also *Gift Ideas: Crafts Enthusiast*. You'll find suggestions under *Catalogs: Craft Supplies* and finished works under *Catalogs: Art & Special Treasures* and *Handcrafts*.

Tickets to a gallery show

Gift certificate to an art supply house, a craft catalog, or a picture framing shop

Membership in an art gallery or a museum (allowing entry to all shows for the year or season)

Art lessons in person's field; tuition to workshop

Books on technique, design, favorite medium, favorite artist

Drawing computer software

Calendar, T-shirt, mug, notecards, or other item with famous art print on it

Studio apron

Staple gun

100% rag tracing paper, rub-on letters; sketch pad or board for person's medium, e.g., pen and ink, charcoal, watercolor, etc.

Portfolio, tote bag, canvas
Easel, easel binder, or carrying case
Mat cutter (used in mounting pictures)
Top quality brushes, brush holder
Desk top organizer
Art bin box for carrying supplies
Collection of paints
Drawing pencils, pastel kit, charcoal pencils, eraser
Adjustable mannequin
Swivel-head lamp
Stool for studio or folding stool for outdoors
Collection of frames, stretcher strips
Palette, palette pad, palette knife (for oil, acrylic, or china painting), paint tray
China painting—pieces of white china or jewelry to paint, sable brushes, liners, pointers, oil or china paints, airtight flat storage containers to put mixed paints in to freeze and reuse, decals, adjustable magnifier on stand
Pen and ink—refillable drawing pen, Bristol board or paper, India ink, pen points
Sculpting—wooden mallets, chisels, X-Acto knife, modeling stand to hold pieces while working; armatures, mannequin; carving tools, knives, rasps; modeling wheel

❧ BACHELOR ❧

We often think of bachelors as being a bit on the wild side, but underneath a carefree exterior, there often hides someone who would enjoy some help with the holiday decorating or a taste of home cooking (see also *Gift Ideas: Adult —Basic; Man—Basic; Cook; Fireplace Gifts; Host/Hostess; Housewarming;* and hobby categories).

Barbecue grill, hibachi
Picnic basket, ice chest, thermos
Gift pack of cheese, jellies, relishes, fruit, sweets (see *Catalogs: Food*)
Membership in a health club, dinner club, YMCA
Two tickets to a sporting event, symphony, play, ballet, art or home show, etc.
Passes to movie theater, bowling alley, miniature golf range, driving range, etc.
Gift certificate to nice restaurant
Gift certificate to clothing, hobby, hardware, or auto parts store
Have him over for a home-cooked meal.
Flavored popcorn
Frozen, home-cooked meals in one-serving size (see Extended Family Home-Cooked Mail-Order Meals under *Catalogs: Food—Assorted*); home-made bread, cake, cookies, casserole, etc. Let him keep the dish.; coupons for mending, cooking
Gift certificate to a house-cleaning service or car wash
Subscription (see special interest area under *Magazines*)
Book on money or time management, adult development, relationships, hobby, cooking terms; money

You're one in a million!

Anything with college or favorite team emblem on it—mug, T-shirt, glasses, cap, etc.

Lessons in country and western, ballroom, or square dancing

Tuition for course in woodworking, painting, photography, scuba diving, bridge, gourmet cooking, etc.

Frame a picture.

More Personal Items

Soap on a rope, cologne, after-shave lotion; anything handmade—afghan or throw, throw pillow, T-shirt, cross-stitch, painted picture, bookends, stained glass ornament, or whatever you do best; jewelry—neck chain, bracelet, medallion, cross; key ring; cigarette lighter or stop smoking kit or course; write him a poem or song.; bath sheet, giant size towel, or towel that fastens around waist; humorous T-shirt; personalized license plates, bumper sticker

Things for the House

Extra loud alarm clock; smoke detector (see also *Gift Ideas: Security & Safety Conscious*)

One-cup drip coffeemaker, popcorn popper, ice cream freezer, burger cooker (see *Appendix: Small Electric Appliances*); nice set of glasses, dishes, or flatware; coasters; serving dishes; cookbook — especially for quick meals or microwave ovens; microwave oven

Bar supplies (see *Gift Ideas: Bar Gifts*); wine rack, wine, liquor, wine glasses, ice bucket

Bed, bath, kitchen, or table linens; variety pack of decorative paper napkins, coasters, plates for entertaining; no-iron cloth napkins; laundry basket with detergent, stain-removal spray, roll of quarters

Book of household hints (stain removal, food substitutes, etc.)

Address book, daily or weekly planner

Calendar with notations of family or other birthdays, anniversaries, etc.; calendar from your choice of photographs (see local photo developing store)

Portable TV, radio, CD, VCR, CD player; cassettes, videos, CDs; answering machine, telephone/answering machine combination, decorator telephone, portable telephone, telephone services (see *Adult—Basic*); Comedy answering machine messages

Computer, software (see *Gift Ideas: Computer Enthusiast*)

TV trays, card table, folding chairs

Iron, ironing board; sewing kit

Plants, hanging basket, terrarium, silk flower arrangement

Plaque, painting, poster, needlework, cross-stitched picture

Holiday ornaments or decorations (handmade is especially nice)

❧ BACKPACKER ❧

For a backpacker, less is more. He or she needs essential survival gear, but in compact form. Some new materials are available for clothing to keep him or her warm and dry and that rolls into amazingly small bundles. See more ideas in *Gift Ideas: Camper* and *Outdoors Lover*. Check also *Catalogs: Outdoors* and *Sports & Recreation* for sources.

Clothing

Identification necklace or bracelet, with medical alert information if applicable; nylon or GORE-TEX jacket, poncho, parka, vest; wool shirt, chamois shirt; turtleneck sweater; sock liners, wool or thermal socks; wool pants; stocking cap, sock cap, down hood; insoles for shoes; rain gear; hiking boots; boot wax, sealer, conditioner; snowshoes, snow goggles; bandannas; gloves; thermal, insulated, or silk underwear

Cooking Gear

Metal match, waterproof matches, plastic match box; backpacker's grill; pack stove, fuel bottle or pump; nesting camp cook set; pot gripper, long oven mitt; collapsible water jug; G.I. can opener; water purifier, water purification tablets; fold-up camp bucket; dried food; quick-energy or non-perishable foods—beef jerky, peanut butter, nuts; spice wheel or small containers of spices

Emergency Equipment

Small first-aid kit, first-aid book; compass; whistle—especially for children; aerial flare, signal mirror; instant ice cold compress; walkie-talkie; space, emergency, or reflector blanket

Other Ideas

Gift certificate to outdoor catalog or store

Walking stick

Pack, pack frame, shoulder bag, drawstring stuff bag, rucksack

Sleeping bag (get lightweight backpacker's kind that rolls up very small)

Backpacker's tent

Air pillow, thin air mattress or foam pad

Hammock (lightweight)

Light plastic sheet, ground cloth

Camera, camera strap, camera harness, close-up lens, filters, film, waterproof camera bag

Binoculars; pocket knife, sheath knife, Swiss Army knife; small mill file, sharpening stone, honing oil; folding saw, hatchet; ice ax; folding scissors; repair tape for all fabrics, small sewing kit

Compact waterproof flashlight, extra batteries and bulb; crush-proof eyeglass caddy

Plastic tube (map keeper); break-down fishing rod; travel alarm clock; pocket calendar

Outdoor, or backpacking magazine (see *Magazines: Outdoors*)

Book or video on birds, snakes, wildflowers, trees, stars, wild animals, geology, and packing tours in a particular part of country (see *Catalogs: Outdoors; Music & Movies;* and *Books & More*); topographic maps of area of interest (see *Catalogs: Science*); small journal; harmonica or kazoo

❧ BAR GIFTS ❧

See *Catalogs: Housewares* for some sources of stylish glasses and other serving aids.

Glasses — cocktail, champagne, cordials, martini, wine, highball, old fashioned, whiskey sour, brandy snifter, mint julep; decanter; wine or liquor bottle labels; wine, liquor; wine rack; wine cooler; cocktail napkins, picks, stir and dip straws, paper party napkins; bottle and can opener, corkscrew, waiter's corkscrew with wire cutter; cocktail strainer; lime squeezer; pourer, siphon; jigger — silver, crystal, with college logo; muddler spoon, jigger spoon, bar spoon; ice bucket, ice tongs; ice crusher; bar towel; bar light

❧ BAR OR BAT MITZVAH ❧

Jewish 13-year-olds celebrate reaching the age of religious responsibility with a special service and usually a party. A gift from this list or *Gift Ideas: 11- to 14-Year-Old* would be a nice way of helping them mark this important time. See *Catalogs: Religious* and *Art & Other Treasures*.

Watch with Hebrew numerals; collector's crystal dreidel
Religious jewelry, Star of David; mezuzah, menorah, chai
Star of David quilt, pillow, or handmade stitchery
Prayer book, Torah, Holy Scriptures (Chumash)
Biography of Jewish hero, heroine, famous Jews in sports or arts
Stories, poems, or music by a Jewish author or composer
Savings bond; add to savings or mutual fund account.
Clock radio, CD player, camera, watch
Picture frame, photo album
Kiddush cup
Shabbet candlestick (girl)
Subscription to Jewish magazine (see *Magazines: Religious*); Israeli art object, double candlestick, handcraft, or coin made into medallion; Israeli stamps or jewelry; Passover seder plate from Israel; donation to a charity in the child's name; plant a tree in Israel in the youth's name. Contact the Jewish National Fund, 42 E. 69th St., New York, NY 10021 (212-879-9300) or the local office.

❧ BILLIARDS PLAYER ❧

Pool cue and/or carrying case, gift certificate to billiard center, chalk for cue, set of balls, certificate for cue repair (re-tipping), cue-repair kit

❧ BOATER ❧

See also *Gift Ideas: Fisherman; Water Skier;* and *Outdoors Lover*. Catalog sources are listed under *Catalogs: Outdoors*.

Book or video on boating, fishing, marine life, maritime history, sea tales, boat repair or design, skills, or places to go
Course or video on water safety, racing, or technique (call the BOAT/U.S. Foundation Course Line at 800-336-BOAT for free courses on boat safety, regulations, equipment)

Model of type of boat with name of boat on it
Gift certificate to restaurant at the marina
Tickets to a boat show
Certificate for free month's slip rental at marina
Desk or household items or clothing (tie, sweatshirt, T-shirt, cap, jewelry) with nautical motif
Subscription (see *Magazines: Boating & Sailing*)
Life vests (for pets, too!); inflatable air mattress, boat, or life raft
Flares, strobe light, air horn, emergency whistle, distress flag, paddle; First-aid kit (waterproof)
Fake rattlesnake to scare away seagulls and keep the deck cleaner
Inflatable underwater viewer for a clear look under the surface from deck or dock
Boat bumpers; anchor (every boat needs two!); boat flag (even for small boats); fishing rod holder; weather radio; Hydroslide or kneeboard
Picnic basket, ice chest with flotation in sides, thermos; collapsible water jug; insulated drink holders (the kind that freeze with a blue ice component to keep drinks cold for hours after removal)
Floating knife, key chain, flashlight; binoculars, floating marine binoculars; sports or waterproof watch; disposable waterproof camera; compass; chart book of maps for favorite river or bay
Nylon (or new material such as GORE-TEX) poncho, windbreaker, pants; swimsuit or cover-up, sun hat, thongs; beach towels; beach chair; nylon tote bags, pouches, cushion with zippered pockets, ditty bag; rigger's bag (canvas tool bag with pockets)
Trailer lock; boat cover; outboard motor lock, case of motor oil, motor cover, motor weed guard; dry land test flush (to clean motor); battery charger; boat light; marine engine tune-up kit; ski rope, ski gloves

Big Boats

T-shirt with name of boat or reading "Captain" or "Crew"
Nautical charts from National Oceanographic Service, 6501 Lafayette Ave., Roverdale, MD 20737-1199 (or call 301-436-6990)
Deck shoes, sandals, rubber boots; foul weather gear
Sailing gloves, all-weather gloves; sailing cap
Nautical napkins with name of boat; non-slip unbreakable dishware, nautical dishware and mugs
Small refrigerator; boat barbecue grill; seafood or galley cookbook
Portable, folding fan; cabin dehumidifier to prevent mildew
Yacht bell
Log book
Cabin magazine rack, lights; folding table, chairs; deck chair; portable toilet
Boarding ladder; novelty pennants or flags; flag staff; ship's clock, chronometer, barometer
Piloting aids—sextant, speed/time/distance computer, range finder
Gauges—thermometer, wind chill, rain gauge, wind indicator
Chart case, chart holder, chart weight
Illuminated magnifier; spotting scope; sailing timer; nautical almanac
Tools for boat—adjustable end wrench, slip joint pliers, pipe wrench, vise grip, several sizes of screwdrivers, box end wrench set, hammer, plug wrench, etc.; toolbox

Waterproof box of spare parts—distributor points, condenser, coil, spark plugs, fuel pump, fuel filter (for diesel engine)

Rigging knife; boat burglar alarm; fog horn; floating rescue light; fire extinguisher, smoke detector; safety netting to protect area between railing and deck; dock edging; sail repair kit, yachtsman's sewing kit; magnetic playing cards; insulated boat blanket; spillproof, windproof ashtray; screw-in metal cup holders that swivel

ഏ BOWLER ல

Bowling ball without holes (must be drilled to fit fingers); bowling bag (with wheels is great); bowling shoes; bowling towel; bowling ball polisher, buffer; bowling glove, wrist support; passes to bowling alley; tickets to or entry fee in bowling tournament; book or video on technique or tournaments; subscription (see *Magazines: Sports*); anything with bowling motif—T-shirt, mug, plaque, miniature figure, key chain, pillow; comedy bowling ball (brick with two or three holes)

ഏ BRIDESMAID ல

For a special thank you, give something that will last. See also *Gift Ideas: Silver Gifts; The Romantic;* and *Woman—Basic*.

Jewelry—pin, necklace, bracelet, earrings, neck chain, pendant, locket

Jewelry box, ring box, crystal ring holder

Vanity tray or set, inlaid hand mirror

Perfume

Satin or lace sachets

Bud vase, china or silk flower arrangement

Stained glass window or table ornament, home decorating item

Picture frame, photo collage frame, monogrammed or leather photograph album; photograph of wedding party; personalized notecards or stationery with elegant writing pen; silver or crystal candy, relish, or compote dish; silver or crystal jigger; serving tray, serving bowl, Revere bowl; silverplate, pewter, wood, or brass trivet; crystal or silver-plate coasters; wood or crystal and silver salt and pepper shakers; monogrammed linen roll cover, table linens; any item made by bride—pottery bowl, needlepoint bookmark, embroidered pillowcases, calligraphy, painted or cross-stitched picture; handcraft—jewelry, decorative art piece, regional folkart

ഏ CAMPER ல

See *Gift Ideas: Backpacker* and *Outdoors Lover* for more suggestions. Catalogs with camping equipment are listed under *Outdoors*.

Golden Eagle Passport to national parks (see *Gift Ideas: Traveler* for details)

Books or videos on camping with children, equipment, campsites, first aid, birds, wildflowers, trees, wild animals of the area, star gazing

Subscription (see *Magazines: Outdoors* and *Animals, Birds, Fish & Wildlife*)

Humorous laundry bag (drawstring); elastic or nylon clothesline; portable toilet; portable or catalytic heater; small fan (battery-operated or electric); heavy-duty extension cord; steel mirror; baby-carrying devices—sling, cradleboard, backpack carrier

Thermal, insulated, or silk underwear; cold-weather clothes, parka, outdoor clothing (hiking boots, poncho, chamois shirt, etc.); personalized name tags to sew or iron onto youngsters' clothing; matching flannel shirts, nightshirts

Film; weather radio; automobile roof rack with cover

Spray for ants, ticks, or flying insects; fly swatter; insect repellent; mosquito coils

Canteen, bota, folding cup, water bottle

Basic Gear

Sleeping bag, ground cloth, inflatable pillow or air mattress, foam pad, cot, free-standing mosquito net dome for placing over the upper body while in a sleeping bag

Foot pump or 12-volt air compressor for blowing up air mattresses

Tent, screened room, tent bag, tent frame bag

Waterproof flashlight, extra batteries and bulb

Lantern (lightweight and reliable)

Ax, hatchet, folding saw, shovel, folding hand shovel

Folding chairs, stool, or table

Folding canvas water bucket, collapsible water jug; portable solar shower; canvas or nylon duffel bag, stuff sacks, soft luggage, backpack, fanny pack, or day pack

Binoculars; good sunglasses; pocket knife, Swiss Army knife; plastic bottles for liquid toiletries, soap holder, toothbrush holder

Safety Equipment

Small first-aid kit and book, sting stopper; compass; whistle for everyone; fire extinguisher; signal mirror; emergency or reflective blanket

Cooking Gear

Camp toaster

Portable stove, reflector stove (and appropriate fuel)

Outback oven and baking mixes

Collapsible oven

Charcoal, waterproof matches

Dried food; grocery staples—instant hot drinks, soup, cereals, peanut butter, non-perishables

Nesting cookware; unbreakable plastic or metal dishes or mugs; dutch oven

(cast iron or thick aluminum); oversized frying pan or griddle (cast iron or aluminum); insulated ice chest, thermos; long oven mitt; long-handled fork, tongs, spatula, spoon; outdoor cookbook; picnic basket; picnic tablecloth or blanket (washable, please!), tablecloth clamps; folding net "umbrella" to cover food

Trailer Camper

Wooden stove cover to double as cutting board or counter; catalytic heater; heavy duty extension cord; vent pillow; folding portable step; *Trailer Life Campground & RV Services Directory* (P.O. Box 7500, Agoura, CA 91301-7500)—guide to more than 3,000 campgrounds, RV (recreational vehicle) service centers, tourist attractions, LP (propane) gas locations

❧ CANOEIST/KAYAKER ❧

See also *Gift Ideas: Backpacker; Camper;* and *Outdoors Lover.*

Classes on water safety, Red Cross lifesaving; swimming lessons

Video or book on technique, equipment, river tours, rescue procedures

Waterproof watch, camera, camera bag, drawstring stuff bags, insulated coolers, dry bags

Floating compass, flashlight

Exercise equipment for cross-training (see *Gift Ideas: Fitness Buff*)

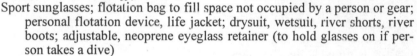

Sport sunglasses; flotation bag to fill space not occupied by a person or gear; personal flotation device, life jacket; drysuit, wetsuit, river shorts, river boots; adjustable, neoprene eyeglass retainer (to hold glasses on if person takes a dive)

Roof rack for car for carrying canoe or kayak; boat carrier on wheels; paddle rack for storage

Canoeist

Knee pads; small ice chest, insulated canned drink holder that fastens to a frame member or thwart; rain suit; GORE-TEX or similar jacket or suit that is lightweight but very warm and waterproof; hat; foam oar grips, blade protectors, quick-release spare oar holder; paddling jacket, pants, overalls; folding camp chair, canoe seat backrest, canoe chair; bags made to attach under seat or into end of canoe

Kayaker

Kayak stroke simulator; rescue rope bag (with rope that unwinds when you throw it); helmet, helmet liner

❧ CAR ENTHUSIAST ❧

Subscription (see *Magazines: Automobiles* or magazine about his favorite make or model)

Book or video on car restoration or repairing, classic cars, history of the auto industry

Personalized license plates, license plate frame; meaningful bumper sticker

Car wash supplies—polish, wax, chamois cloth, sponges, chemically-treated duster, brush, wheel brush; anti-fog mitt for cleaning inside of windows

Gift certificate to auto parts store or car wash

Portable air ionizer for neutralizing pet, tobacco, or other odors or pollens

Steering wheel cover

Heavy-duty liner for vehicle cargo area; compartmentalized trunk storage bag
Decorative floor mats
Electric vacuum that plugs into cigarette lighter
Drink holders, trash bag, car caddy for holding tissues and drinks
Locking gas cap, screw-on gas cap that prevents gas spills
Sun shade for inside, magnetic windshield cover for outside

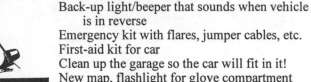

Alarm system; steering wheel or column lock
Back-up light/beeper that sounds when vehicle
is in reverse
Emergency kit with flares, jumper cables, etc.
First-aid kit for car
Clean up the garage so the car will fit in it!
New map, flashlight for glove compartment
Cellular telephone, inside antenna
Retractable antenna
Upgrade radio, cassette, CD player, or speakers
Parking sensor (mount it in garage and it
changes colors to tell driver how close he
is to desired parking spot)

Heater that plugs into cigarette lighter for instant warming of car interior and
defrosting of windows
Rear window defogger
Car cover with storage bag
Certificate for oil change or tune-up

✸ CHRISTMAS SPECIALS ✜

It takes several years to build up a supply of Christmas decorations. You can
give a child an early start by giving him an ornament each year. By the time
he has his first dorm room or apartment, he will have decorations with a
touch of home.

Give "The 12 Days of Christmas." Give one item on the first day (December
13), two on the second day, etc. Gift can be as simple or as elaborate as
you like (a six-pack of a favorite beverage on day six; a 10-oz. box of
candy on day 10; a calendar (12 months) or a dishware set for 12 on day
12. Or give something with the appropriate number in the title.
Tickets to "The Nutcracker" or other special holiday entertainment
Holiday bell pull, hand towel, apron, vest, tie, pillow, cross-stitched picture
or jar lid; door or doorknob decorations
Holiday clothing—button covers, earrings, tuxedo shirt with holly or bells,
sweatshirt or sweater with Santa or a Christmas tree, decorated socks,
tights with candy canes, hair barrettes with jingle bells
Giant, inflatable ornament balls for outside trees
Lawn decorations
Wreath—greenery, pine cones, nuts, candy, sweet gum balls, braided fabric,
straw, bread dough, grape vines, painted wooden cutouts
Artificial Christmas tree, tree stand
Tree skirt—quilted fabric, stitchery, patchwork, felt, sequined
Centerpiece—with candles, greenery, mini-tree, basket of small pine cones
with red bows, shiny Christmas balls; holiday tablecloth and napkins

Fancy plate, dish, or tin filled with homemade goodies; plate of shaped cookies (include the cookie cutter!); Christmas-decorated dinnerware, serving pieces; mints, cookies in holiday shapes; fruitcake, bread, jellies, pickles, relishes; brandy snifter full of candy and decorated like face of Santa Claus

Advent calendar (wall or door hanging with 25 spaces for the first 25 days of December)—Make in shape of calendar, plaque, or Christmas tree (use felt or fabric or paint on posterboard). Add small toy, ornament, candy cane, or decoration to one space each day.

Stockings for adults

Make your own Christmas cards—an original block print, poem, drawing, puzzle, carol; card with family photograph.

Christmas music—CDs, cassette tapes, concert tickets, song books, sheet music; video of Christmas or Christian movie or songs; book on Christmas—decorations, customs, stories, art, carols

The Best Christmas Pageant Ever, by Barbara Robinson (several editions)

The Christmas Lover's Handbook, by Lasley F. Gober (Betterway Books, 1507 Dana Ave., Cincinnati, OH 45207-1005 (800-289-0963)

Christmas figure, bell, nativity set, angel, nutcracker of collectible quality

Prepare a family or neighborhood Christmas pageant.

Nativity scenes—fabric, ceramic, wood, one for the children to play with

Go caroling at a nursing home or home of a shut-in or special friend.

Contribute to a charity in honor or memory of someone.

Small tree for child to decorate for her own room

Card holder—basket lined with bright fabric

Ornaments

Kits to make—wooden, felt, sequined, stuffed, or needlework; stained glass, crocheted, knitted, needlepoint, cross-stitched, or painted; dough ornaments (see *Gifts to Make*); cookie cutters tied with gingham or red ribbon; wooden (natural finish or painted)—Trace cookie cutters onto $1/8''$ plywood and cut out shapes with a jigsaw.; heirloom—crystal, etched glass, gold-plated, silver, Gorham, Hallmark

❧ CLERGY ☙

Of course, clergy enjoy golf, tennis, camping, and other interests just as lay people do, but sometimes you may want a gift that relates more directly to his work. Here are some ideas. For others, see *Catalogs: Religious*.

Business cards (with church's name on them, too); notecards

Medallion or other religious jewelry

Stole, hand-embroidered or in liturgical color

Personalized copy of denominational hymn book or antique hymn books, book on history of hymns

Antique Bibles or denominational books; religious reference book

Literal translations of the Bible from Greek and Hebrew texts

Video by a favorite theologian, on the Holy Land, on church history or topic of special interest in her ministry

Mementos from the Holy Land, Vatican, or other place of special religious significance for the person

Christmas decoration or tree ornament; nativity sets from around the world

Door plaque with scripture verse or religious symbol

Gift certificate to book store, other favorite store, religious book catalog

Subscription to special interest or religious magazine

Cassette tape or CD of a favorite choir, singer, or instrumentalist

Tickets for family to the theater, symphony, ball game, etc.

Homemade goodies; gift pack of cheese, sausage, jellies, fruit (see *Catalogs: Food*); any handcraft by you (or see *Catalogs: Handcrafts*)

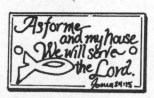

Door plaque with scripture verse or religious symbol

Give book, tree, shrub, hymnals, equipment, or furnishings to the church in his name; make a contribution to the American or International Bible Society or other religious organization in her name.

Include his family in your family activities.

For Office
(see also *Gift Ideas: Desk Dweller*)

Plaque, picture, figurine, or stitchery meaningful to him (serious or humorous); picture frame for desk; desk organizers; have diploma or certificates matted or framed.; personalized memo pads, pencils; computer, computer software (especially Bible reference)

❧ COLLECTOR ❧

Adding to a collection is a fun way to give a gift. My mother collected roadrunners and we delighted in finding roadrunner notecards, stitcheries, mugs, pins, pewter figurines, placemats, and who knows what else. See *Catalogs: Collectibles*. Look also under *Art & Special Treasures; Handcrafts; International/Regional Specialties; Models & Miniatures; Toys, Dolls, Games,* or other special interest category for unique additions to collections of certain animal or sport paraphernalia, dolls, miniatures, teapots, etc. The ideas here go beyond the collection itself to useful equipment and accessories that might apply to different kinds of collections. Specific suggestions are listed for two common collectibles: stamps and coins.

Subscription (see *Magazines: Collectors*)

Gift certificate to shop or catalog that carries what he/she collects

An item of collectible quality such as Hummel, Precious Moments, David Winters, etc.

Tickets to a show featuring his collectible such as gun show, sports card show, or doll show

Book on identifying silver hallmarks, cut-glass signatures, or other special markings; book on the appropriate collectible—its history, how-to (if a craft), antique or rare items, museum collections, price lists

Doll house furniture, accessories—be sure item is same scale as house (most are scaled 1" to 1') and in correct era (Victorian, Early American, etc.)

A piece for the collection; antique or foreign item

Display shelves, plate holder, stand, glass display dome; line a shadow box with velvet for displaying small items; lighting for display shelves

Album for postcards, stamps, matchbooks, etc.

Registry or inventory book or database software for listing the items in the collection with a place for purchase, insurance, and appraisal information

Current pricing guides

Take pictures of collection for insurance.

Jewelry or art work related to the collection, e.g., coin pendant, framed enlarged print of a stamp

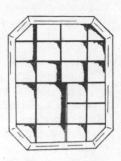

Stamp Collector

Stamp album, stock books, first day cover album; stamp tongs, hinges, acetate or glassine envelopes, magnifying glass, perforation gauge, color gauge; watermark detector fluid, tray; stamp map, atlas, globe; save commemorative stamps off your mail and include undamaged ones with a card.; from post office, "theme" packets of stamps, mint stamps, first day covers, plate blocks, albums with stamps included (or call 800-STAMP-24 to order); stamp press; stamp lift (for removing old hinges); new stamps from any foreign country you visit; special commemorative cachet, envelope, or plate block for a topic of interest (profession, favorite sport, hero or heroine, historical place, etc.); *Collecting Stamps for Pleasure & Profit* and *Advanced Stamp Collecting*, both by Barry Krause (Betterway Books, 1507 Dana Ave., Cincinnati, OH 45207-1005. 800-289-0963)

Coin Collector

Coin mounts, holders, tubes; stock book, album; acetate envelopes, plastic coin holders; magnifying glass, loupe; silver dollars, mint coins; proof set of new year coins (write Bureau of the Mint, 633 3rd St. NW, Washington, DC 20220 or call 202-874-6450 for ordering information); proof set of his birth year; *Guide Book of United States Coins*, R.S. Yeoman (Western Publishing Co.). New edition every year.; *Collecting Coins for Pleasure & Profit* by Barry Krause (Betterway Books, 1507 Dana Ave., Cincinnati, OH 45207-1005. 800-289-0963)

❧ COLLEGE GRADUATION ❧

See also *Gift Ideas: Man — Basic; Woman — Basic; Adult — Basic; Bachelor; Single Woman;* and other special interest categories.

Frame the diploma.

Class ring

Car or special trip

Luggage, soft luggage, sports bag, garment bag

Mug, plaque, T-shirt, anything with school's logo

Membership in alumni or professional association

Gift certificate to medical, architectural, dental, or other professional supply house

Reference book or tools in graduate's field

Subscription to professional or hobby magazine

Tickets to entertainment event

Gift certificate to nice restaurant, résumé writing or typing service

Framed portrait of the graduate

Watch, jewelry; clothes for work, attaché case; pocket calculator, radio, answering machine, telephone; camera, camcorder; photograph album; typewriter, computer, software for personal finances, résumé writing, or in his field; sewing machine; items for setting up housekeeping (see *Gift Ideas: Cook; Host/Hostess;* or *Housewarming*); quilt, handmade stitchery or sculpture; cash; wallet (with cash inside!); book on job hunting, money management, investments (probably in that order!); book on time management, adult development, degree field; bookends; pen and pencil set; supplies for hobby or sport

❧ COLLEGE STUDENT ❧

Here are some things that will be appreciated by a college student and a few extras that are unique to those living away from home whether across town or out of the city, in a dorm or an apartment. Other gift ideas are listed under *Bachelor; Single Woman; Adult—Basic; Woman—Basic; Man—Basic;* and special interest categories. For students living in apartments, see *Gift Ideas: Host/Hostess; Cook;* or *Housewarming*.

Money

Telephone credit card, pay for private telephone, gift certificate for long distance telephone calls or special services from telephone company

Decorator telephone, cordless telephone, answering machine

Magazine subscription (maybe in the field of study or a weekly news magazine or something frivolous for a change of pace from studying)

Take student out to eat.

Passes to movie theater, bowling alley, fast food restaurant, ice cream or pizza parlor (in college town)

Gift certificate to a nice restaurant (in college town)

Gift certificate to college's book store

"Care package" of non-perishable food—beef jerky, sunflower seeds, fruit rolls, dried fruit, canned fruit, crackers, peanut butter, honey, nuts, raisins, coffee, tea, candy, cookies

Any gift in a decorative reusable container

Special pastry or candy (see *Catalogs: Food—Sweets*)

Personalized coffee mug, flavored coffee

Small insulated ice chest (for picnics)

Typewriter, computer, software (especially word processing, training for LSAT or GRE, résumé writer, grammar/spelling checker, calendar, games, banners, greeting cards)

Pocket-size electronic dictionary/thesaurus; Desk lamp

Folding backjack chair (for backrest while sitting on the floor), bean bag chair, director's chair

Calendar with pictures on a subject student is interested in (nature, Scripture, cartoons, etc.) or one made with your own pictures at a photo specialty store; perpetual calendar or dated calendar with sayings, cartoons, photographs (maybe from her area of the country if she is attending a school out of state); daily planner notebook

Portable bookcase, small chest of drawers

Wastebasket with school or sports team colors or logo

Space-savers for closet (shoe racks, belt holders, stacking pants/skirt hangers); storage bins for under the bed; padded hangers, scented drawer liners, sachets

Bookends, book plates, bookmark; address book; Block of note paper

Desk supplies — electric pencil sharpener, pencil holder, transparent tape, scissors, stapler, removable self-stick notes; bulletin board and thumbtacks; blank book and fountain pen; bag of ball-point pens, pencils (personalized)

Photo album, scrapbook, camera, film

Cassette tape or CD player; cassette tapes, videos, CDs

Alarm clock (loud!); clock radio, portable radio, small TV, VCR

Luggage, tote bag, garment bag, luggage tags

For traveling — jewelry roll, shoe protectors, lingerie roll, insulated bag for hot curling iron, travel-size plastic containers in a waterproof bag

Travel-size hair dryer or other personal care appliance (see *Appendix: Small Electric Appliances*)

Clothes with school's name or mascot on it

Fleece-lined slippers, non-slip socks

Bed and bath linens, blanket, afghan, throw pillows, quilt, comforter

Wall posters, pictures, cross-stitched plaque

Manicure kit

Potted plant

Smoke detector

Car anti-theft devices (such as The Club)

Board games, playing cards, outdoor games and sports equipment

Workout/aerobics clothing, equipment

Lots of mail; tickets for transportation home; telephone calls from home, visits from hometown folks; subscription to hometown or church newspaper

Stationery (addressed and stamped!), roll of stamps, stamped postcards

Cookie jar (full of homemade cookies); homemade goodies (cake, candy, cookies) or fresh fruit

Heating element for coffee, soup; microwave oven (if allowed); small coffee pot, set of flatware and dishes; popcorn popper, small refrigerator, combination refrigerator/microwave oven (if allowed in dorm); fan

Basic tool set — small hammer, screwdrivers, sticky fastener for hanging items on walls when nails are not allowed

Shower shoes, shower tote

Drip-dry, no-care clothing; cute laundry bag or clothes basket with roll of quarters; personalized labels for clothes, linens; clothes drying rack, elastic clothesline, mesh sweater drier

Iron, ironing board; basic sewing kit

Something from home state for out-of-state students, e.g., a flag, T-shirt, poster, bumper sticker

❧ COMPUTER ENTHUSIAST ❧

In picking a gift for a computer user, it will be helpful to know something about the system used. Is it IBM or Macintosh compatible? Are the disks 5¼" or 3½"? If you don't know, there are plenty of ideas that don't involve software and would be welcomed by a user. If in doubt, save the receipt or give a gift certificate! See *Catalogs: Computing* for sources.

Subscription (see *Magazines: Computing*)

Tuition for a course or workshop

Book or video on a particular software program; subscription to national bulletin board service such as Compuserve (800-848-8199) or Prodigy (800-776-0836, ext. 917)

Modem; fax modem

Upgrade the computer, monitor, printer, or operating system.

Hard disk compression software

Sound board (sound-making capability)

CD-ROM drive, CD-ROM disc

Scanner

Reliable power surge protector (some guarantee the device plugged into it)— get a remote control one for someone who has difficulty bending to the floor to turn one on.; system stand (keyboard slides into a slot under the monitor)—space saver for a small desk; under-desk keyboard holder or keyboard carrel; printer stand, computer table or desk

Blank diskettes (pre-formatted is a nice extra), diskette file (box or notebook)

All kinds of software—screen-saver (what shows when screen has been idle for a few minutes), grammar/spelling checker, design, banners, certificates, greeting cards, calendar, games, type styles, publishing, finances, update a program he has (newer release), Windows (visual presentation used as background for many programs); program to do something in another area of interest such as designing quilts, astronomy, genealogy, Bible reference, etc.

Mini-vac to clean keyboard or mini-attachments for full-size vacuum cleaner

Book/diskette combinations for learning popular software programs

Decorated computer paper (for holiday, celebrations, stationery, etc.); mouse, mouse pad, mouse cover; track ball; copy holder—an arm that attaches to computer or a standing type to hold documents

Good desk lamp; anti-glare filter for screen; keyboard wrist rest; carrying case for laptop or notebook computer

❧ COOK ❧

Whether the cook you have in mind grills, braises or microwaves, you can make preparation easier with suggestions from this section. For more ideas, see *Appendix: Small Electric Appliances — Food Preparation & Serving Aids* and *Gift Ideas: Host/Hostess*. Various equipment and other appropriate gift items are found under *Catalogs: Cookware; Food;* and *Housewares*.

Gift certificate to nice restaurant, cooking class

Subscription (see *Magazines: Food & Entertaining*)

Microwave oven, convection oven, portable convection oven fan (turns ordinary oven into convection oven)

Kitchen clock, kitchen timer

Food processing machine, accessories

Herb garden in pretty pots or planter; sprouting kit

Absorbent kitchen towels; oven mitts and pot holders

Apron—canvas with pockets, or patchwork, holiday, or pinafore style

Baking dish, skillet, or cake pan full of casserole, cookies, etc. Let cook keep the dish.

Indoor stovetop grill

Cookbooks of all kinds—quick meals, freeze-ahead meals, foreign fare, microwave or slow cooker recipes, low fat, no salt, gourmet, or favorite organization's cookbook

Collection of family recipes in handwriting of relative(s) if possible

Computer software for organizing recipes, keeping track of food intake and ingredients

Better Homes & Gardens Complete Guide to Food and Cooking (Meredith Corp., 1991)—alphabetical explanation (with illustrations) of all kinds of cooking terms; great for a new cook

Once-A-Month Cooking, by Mimi Wilson and Mary Beth Lagerborg (Focus on the Family, 1992)—call 800-932-9123, how to organize, shop for, and prepare healthy, home-cooked meals for a month in one day

Amagift—Gourmet Gifts catalog of several dozen items of equal value from which recipient chooses one. You purchase the album (the cost includes shipping) and present it as a gift. The recipient orders the item he wants directly from Amway. Available from Amway distributors (check your local telephone book under Amway).

Cookbook holder (Lucite); recipe holder, recipe box, decorative recipe cards, plastic sleeves for recipe cards

Measuring cups (two- to four-cup size is nice, too), spoons; spatula, sifter (electric kind is available), wire whisk, tongs, pastry brush, baster, fat-skimmer cup or ladle

Bottle pourer (cork with pouring spout attached, for controlling flow of liquid); mixing bowls (covered ones are useful), colander; spoon rest; cutting board (wood, ceramic, or Lucite)

Thermometers—meat and poultry, candy, oven, refrigerator

Freezer-to-oven cookware, non-stick cookware, dishwasher- and microwave-safe cookware

Cookware—double boiler, roasting pan, baking pan (with cover), bread pan, muffin tin, cake or pie pan, skillet, soup pot

Airtight plastic storage containers or canister set

Stainless steel oil cans—airtight with non-drip spout that allows you to keep cooking oils near the stove for convenience

Cooling racks; food scale; jar opener

Knives — French chef, bread, butcher, roast slicer, boner, utility, paring, frozen food, steak set; knife holder, knife block; sharpening steel or ceramic hone

Pastry cloth, rolling pin cover, pastry board, bread baking or pizza stone

Spice rack

Microwave cookware — browning tray, muffin pan, cake pan, bacon rack, casserole or baking pans, popcorn popper, steamer

Pizza pan, pizza paddle, pizza brick, pizza cutter; omelet pan; fondue pot, fondue forks; wok set

Butter warmer, butter molds

Pressure cooker; Food dehydrator

Slow cooker, bread and cake bake pan for slow cooker; sausage maker kit; salad spinner; meat grinder, coffee grinder; vegetable steamer; roaster

Food chopper; cheese grater (hand held at table), cheese slicer

Shrimp cleaner and sheller, crab shears

Meat tenderizer

Garlic press, radish cutter, melon baller, meatball press, tomato corer, pineapple cutter, peeling machine; apple parer, corer, slicer; lemon zester

Pot racks—wrought iron, copper, brass

Three-tier hanging basket for fresh vegetables, fruit

Sieves, spatter top, pot drainer, double-boiler maker

Kitchen shears, poultry shears; shish kabob skewers

Canning equipment—jars, lids, labels

Cookie sheets (air-cushion kind prevents over-browning), bread pans

Cake pans (with cover; different sizes), pie plates, pie crust shields, cake carrier, pie carrier; springform pan

Cake decorating kit; shaped cake pans; book, video, class, or home-study course from Wilton (call 800-323-1717, operator 440 or write to 2240 W. 75th St., Woodridge, IL 60517-9985 for details); accessories — decorating tips and nozzles, pastry bags, turntable, decorating comb, coupler, flower nails, tapered and angled spatulas, icing colors

Cookie cutters or cookie press; candy molds, dipping sets; fillings, coatings

Salad molds (copper or ceramic ones can double as kitchen decorations)

Wheeled chopping block; bread box

Pretty serving dishes (see *Gift Ideas: Host/Hostess*)

Door or wall rack to expand pantry space

Folding stepstool, rolling cart

Cheese or wine tasting course; tuition for gourmet cooking class

Dinner at gourmet restaurant

Hard-to-find seasonings, foreign food items (see *Catalogs: Food*) or gourmet foods such as pheasant, caviar, pâté, lobster tails, shad roe, sun-dried tomatoes

Wine label album

Asparagus or artichoke steam rack; canapé maker, lobster scissors, steak hammer; garlic storage jar; ginger grater

Marble rolling pin and pastry board; soufflé dish, pâté en croûte dish; quiche pans—ceramic, glass, stainless steel; au gratin dishes; wooden utensils, chopsticks (disposable or decorative), whisk, whip; clay bread pans, roasting pot

Bakers' black steel baking pans, bread pans, jelly roll pan; cast iron or copper cookware; carbon steel or stainless cutlery, food slicer

Pasta maker, pasta cooker, tortilla press, tortilla steamer

Pepper grinder; rolling mincer

Tart tamper, tart pan

Outdoor Cook

Napkins out of colorful terry-cloth or no-iron fabric; barbecue grill, hibachi, portable grill; charcoal, fire starter, long matches, electric charcoal lighter; grill cleaning brush, gas grill cover; grill attachments—second layer, rib rack, broiler basket, corn and potato grill, tray; long handled tools — tongs, fork, spatula, baster, knife, spoon; oven mitt; outdoor cookbook; electric rotisserie; shish kabob skewers; box of decorative paper plates, napkins, cups; wicker paper plate holders; plastic dishware; insulated glasses, mugs, serving dishes; steak serving plates; picnic table, tablecloth, tablecloth clamps; lawn furniture, folding chairs; chef's apron; mesh or net food cover

❧ CRAFTS ENTHUSIAST ☙

Often a person who loves to make things enjoys trying new kinds of crafts. If you can't find what you want in her particular area, try a kit (complete with necessary supplies) in a different medium. See also *Gift Ideas: Artist; Handyman; Needleworker; Seamstress;* or *Wood Hobbyist* for more suggestions. You will find additional sources under *Catalogs: Craft Supplies*.

Gift certificate to craft store or catalog

Tickets to a show featuring person's specialty such as a gem and mineral show, doll show, quilting show, etc.

Glue gun, battery-powered scissors; paint storage and carrying case (airtight)

Shelves, display rack, or box for displaying finished work

Craft worktable (durable, easy-clean top), swing-arm lamp

Lessons in a new or favorite craft area

Subscription (see *Magazines: Crafts*)

Book or video on the craft — techniques, variations, famous collections, instructions, new patterns or designs

Crafts Supply Sourcebook by Margaret Boyd (Betterway Books, 1507 Dana Ave., Cincinnati OH 45207-1005. 800-289-0963)

Kits for the crafts listed below or for papier-mâché, decoupage, tole painting, plastic molding, string art, weaving, wire art, pompom craft, plaster casting, shrink art, woodcarving, sequin or felt crafts, paint-by-number, mosaics, model building, metal enameling, clear casting

A finished piece in her favorite craft area such as a pompom refrigerator note holder, pottery pitcher, hand-painted wooden Christmas ornament, cornhusk doll, hand-woven shawl, etc.

Basketry—Reeds, dyes, raffia, Spanish moss, coiling; tapestry needle, jute, yarn, string, wire, woodburner for signing

Batik—Bamboo brushes (or any other natural brush), alcohol lamp, stretcher frame; white silk, cotton, linen, or other natural fiber material; dyes, tjanting tools for outlining, paraffin and beeswax, melting pot, materials for making stamps (pipe cleaners and other textured items), iron

Calligraphy—Pen and nibs, ink or cartridges, parchment or special papers, style books

Candle Making—Coloring wax (or a box of old crayon stubs), candle thermometer, molds, candle holders, candle scents, wicks

Ceramics/Pottery—Greenware, glazes, molds, slip, cleaning tools, pattern cutting tools, decals for decoration, brushes, basket or carrying case for supplies; potter's wheel; rolling pin, knives, scrapers, sponges, plastic dishpan and waste cans for storage or cleanup; good brushes; tools for trimming, decorating, and carving; glazes and stains (lead-free, if possible); 25 to 100 pounds of clay (many types and colors); rolling boards; kiln; balance scales to weigh glaze chemicals; any handmade pottery piece; pottery lifter

Doll Making—New mold, fabrics, patterns, accessories (furniture, toys, hat box, etc.)

Enameling—Metal kiln; enameling rack, fork, and spatula; swirling tool, tweezers; copper shapes, copper light switch plates; powdered enamel, hard enamel flux; fine paint brushes and thick leather gloves

Fabric Painting—Fabric paint pens, brushes, paints, ColorPoint applicators for paint stitching (leave a bead of color; make designs similar to cross-stitch)

Jewelry Making—Book on identifying stones and minerals, field guide to gem and mineral localities; anvil, bench pin, jeweler's saw, pin or bench vise, tin snips, metal shears, cutting broach, dapping punches, cutters, blocks to shape and cut metal and wax, pivot and twist drills, hand drill, hammer mallet, wire cutter, mandrel, pliers, metal stamp; buffing kit; buffing cloth; burnisher; emery paper, files; magnifying glass or loupe; ring stick or measuring gauge; metal scales, metal test kit; soldering gun, accessories; electric engraver; jeweler's work bench; jeweler's casting machine; miniature power tool kit; accessories for polishing, cutting, sanding; rock tumbler, polisher; polished gemstones; mountings for gems (stick pin, pendant, brooch, earring, ring, belt buckle); wooden shapes for earrings (coyote, butterfly, candy cane, etc.); velvet-lined boxes for finished work; clasps

Leathercraft—Package of scrap leather; anvil, mallet, tooling kit, stamping kit; leather stripper, leather shears, sewing awl, lacing needle, snap button fastener, edge bevelers, hole punch set, leather point machine needles, X-Acto knife; belt buckle

Macramé—Macramé board, cord or jute, rings, beads

Miniaturist—Kits for doll houses, accessories, furniture, or dolls in proper scale (usually ½" to 1' or 1" to 1'); books on patterns, techniques, collections; small vise, woodworking tools, Dremel tools; jigsaw; mold and paint for figures; glue gun, glue sticks

Paper Making—Mold (frame and deckle), blender, plastic basin, fabric dyes, materials to add to pulp (feathers, glitter, dried flowers, potpourri, threads, etc.)

Rubber Stamping—Rubber stamps of all kinds—Victorian, animals, sayings, seasonal, etc. (see *Catalogs: Craft Supplies*); wooden storage tray for stamps; colored or rainbow stamp pads; selection of colors of embossing powder, flossing powder, glitter, brush markers; glue pen; stamp roller (designs on rollers for continuous decoration); shaped papers (for cards, notes, invitations, etc.); self-healing cutting mat; heat gun for embossing

Silk Painting—Resists, dyes (resin or silk), brushes, stretcher, natural silk fabric

Stained Glass—Pattern books, copper tape, lead, soldering iron, glass or circle cutter, glass pliers, glass handler's gloves, soldering tool stand, belt sander, "L" square or glass cutter's square, carborundum stone for smoothing rough spots

ও CYCLIST ঙ

Know whether your cyclist rides around the neighborhood for exercise, participates in races or takes cycling vacations. Each activity calls for slightly different accessories. For equipment sources, see *Catalogs: Sports & Recreation*.

Safety helmet
Clothing — biking shorts, cleated cycling shoes, gloves, neoprene socks; lightweight, breathable, waterproof rain gear; sports bra
Face mask, ear band, cycling glasses or overshields for wearers of prescription glasses, arm and leg warmers
Sleeveless training top
Tire pump
Personalized license tag
Child seat with foot guard for parent's bike
Rear-view mirror that snaps on helmet, glasses, or handlebar

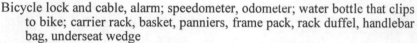

Bicycle lock and cable, alarm; speedometer, odometer; water bottle that clips to bike; carrier rack, basket, panniers, frame pack, rack duffel, handlebar bag, underseat wedge
Reflectors; reflective clothing, ankle bands, and pedals
Padded seat or seat cover; waist pack
Horn, bike radio
New bicycle; bicycle rack for car, storage rack for garage or hall; certificate for "tune-up"
Books on cycling vacations, racing, physical fitness, consumer guide to bicycles, biking atlas, *Spinning: A Guide to the World of Cycling*, Paul McCallum (Betterway Books, 1507 Dana Ave., Cincinnati, OH 45207-1005, 800-289-0963)
Membership in
   ❏ *International Bicycle Touring Society*, P.O. Box 6979, San Diego, CA 92166-0979 (619-226-TOUR) (must be 21 or older). Sponsors tours in U.S. and Europe.
   ❏ *League of American Wheelmen*, 190 W. Ostend St., Ste. 120, Baltimore, MD 21230-3731 (800-288-BIKE). Monthly magazine, information on getting involved in local cycling events and clubs, bulletins on tours in U.S. and abroad.
   ❏ *United States Cycling Federation*, 1750 E. Boulder St., Colorado Springs, CO 80909 (719-578-4581). Controlling organization for racing in U.S.
Motocross—Pads for frame, cross bar, stem; grips for handlebars; number plates
Racer—Tights, zip T-neck, jerseys, gloves, underwear, socks out of warm but lightweight materials; clipless pedals; toe clips and straps; cycling cap, protective helmet; cycle computers (mount on handlebar; show distance traveled, trip distance, 24-hour clock, stop watch, average and maximum speed, current speed, heart rate, cadence, etc.); training rollers, resistance fan, trainer rack; in-line skates (as training alternative); Racers don't want accessories because of the excess weight.
Tourist—Guide book on bike paths; book or video on area to be toured; lighting set; wool leg, arm, foot warmers; lightweight, waterproof, warm zippered jacket with hood; jerseys, tights out of microfiber fleece or neoprene; rain poncho made for cyclists so loose ends won't catch in

spokes; clips for pants to keep them from catching in spokes; fingerless gloves with padded palm and mesh back; cyclist's tent, mattress, pad; travel case for bicycle (hard or soft cover); bicycle radio, AM/CB bicycle base transceiver; panniers, other touring bags, belt pack, over-the-shoulder bag; plastic saddle cover (for rainy weather); fanny pads; bicycle repair tools; compass; rearview mirror to clip to glasses, helmet, or handlebar; waterless hand cleaner; swiss Army knife (screwdriver, slicing knife, bottle opener are necessities)

❧ DANCER ☙

Dancing can mean do-si-do or cha-cha or arabesque. Here are some general ideas and then some more specific suggestions for a few of the different styles of dance.

Lessons in her favorite or a new kind of dance
Music for his type of dance; book or video of demonstrations, famous dancers
Item such as tote bag or cross-stitched picture with her particular kind of
  dancer on it
Ballet — Bodywear, legwear, leg warmers; bag to carry clothes to studio; portable barre; gift certificate to dance accessory and clothing store; tuition to a special workshop; tickets to ballet; subscription to *Dance Magazine* (see *Magazines: Arts & Antiques*)
Ballroom—Videos of Fred Astaire, Ginger Rogers, and Gene Kelly movies; gift certificate to store with ballroom clothing or shoes; memorabilia; tickets to competitions

Country Western — Western style clothing—beaver (for her and him) or straw hats, bolo tie, yoked poplin shirts, vests, clothing decorated with rhinestones or sequins, tuxedo shirt with Southwest design, split skirt, broomstick and prairie skirts, denim clothing; gaucho silver belts, suede and leather jeans; western button covers; bandannas; ropers (boots); country music cassettes (see also *Gift Ideas: Western & Equestrian*)
Square Dance—For the woman—dresses, bloomers, pettipants, silk or net petticoats, belt, apron, pinafore, T-strap or rhinestone-studded dance footwear
For the man — neckerchief, shirt to match her skirt, bolo tie, stick pins for hat, money clip or tie tack with square dancer motif, beaver or straw hat, horsehair hat band, fancy boots, yoked shirt
Hook that attaches to belt with hand towel; collar tips; cassettes of calls; tickets to an exhibition; entry fee to a competition

❧ DESK DWELLER ☙

Do you need an idea for your boss or secretary or a co-worker? Here are some suggestions. See other gift idea categories such as *A Little Remembrance; Adult—Basic; Man—Basic; Woman—Basic; Bachelor; Single Woman; Computer Enthusiast;* or a hobby area he has mentioned.

A raise, cash bonus

Magazine subscription (a professional periodical or one for a leisure interest)

Book or computer software about her business

Subscription to a business book summary service such as Executive Book Summaries (see *Catalogs: Books & More*) which sends two or three eight-page summaries a month of books that advance careers, save time, and increase profits and productivity

Gift certificate to major department store or small specialty shop

Amagift—catalogs of several dozen gifts of equal value from which recipient chooses one. Albums are offered in various price ranges or with a theme (Men's Super, Women's Super, Gourmet Gifts, Sweets & Treats, Jewelry). You purchase the album and present it as a gift. The recipient (unaware of the price) orders the item he wants directly from Amway. Shipping is included in the price you pay. Available from Amway distributors (check your local telephone book under Amway).

Coffee mug with person's name or significant slogan or theme on it (with a package of tea or flavored coffee); vacuum carafe that keeps beverages hot or cold for eight hours; assortment of flavored coffees, teas, jellies

Gift pack of cheeses, sausages, regional treats, snacks, candies, etc. (see *Catalogs: Food*); flavored popcorn in decorative canister

Soundless, vibrating alarm for a punctual end to presentations without the distraction of checking a watch

Attaché case, portfolio, organizer brief, clipboard, pad holder, business card holder; luggage if the work requires travel (see *Gift Ideas: Traveler*)

Business cards, personalized notes, stationery, or memo pads; name plate for desk; supply holders—pen or pencil holder, tape holder, tissue holder, letter holder, magnetic paper clip holder

Drawer or desk organizers; paperweight; unusual pens, pen and pencil set, mechanical pencil; electric pencil sharpener or stapler

Desk calendar or desk diary; perpetual calendar (spiral-bound calendar that you turn each day to show a page with an inspirational or humorous saying for the day); electronic calendar (shows full calendar for any month far into the future, also shows time and current date and has an alarm)

Desk or wall clock or picture frame, desk clock with slot for business cards

Laminated wall calendar; daily planning notebook

Chair cushion or new chair for office

Pager (local, regional, national, or all-in-one)

Holiday ornament or decoration; add to a collection.

Wallet-size calculator, calculator stand, pocket calculator

Potted plant for desk, fresh or silk flower arrangement, vase

New dictionary, spell checker, *Roget's International Thesaurus*

Covered sectioned dishes for microwave; insulated lunch bag

Mug that can be frozen and then filled to keep a drink cold for hours without diluting drink

Letter opener; telephone shoulder rest, retracting telephone cord; bulletin board for office

Personal yellow pages—journal for recording suppliers, associates, consultants, etc.; list finder or roto-phone file with removable pages

Book—cartoons, biography of person in line of work, success tips; cassette of favorite music or singer; video (travel, hobby, how-to, favorite film); computer software for a hobby or special interest

❧ ELDERLY AT OWN HOME ❧

In addition to ideas from hobby and interest categories, here are some gifts that are particularly appropriate for someone who isn't as active as he used to be and who is more interested in giving away mementos than in collecting more. For other suggestions, see *Gift Ideas: Nursing Home Resident; Special Health Needs; Security & Safety Conscious; Adult—Basic; Man—Basic;* and *Woman—Basic.*

Do a home project—paint a room, clean the garage, do yard work, etc.
Coupon book for shopping, yard work, rides, etc.
Go Christmas caroling at his/her home; take refreshments.
Holiday or seasonal decoration, Christmas tree or ornament
Ask mayor, governor, or president to send birthday greetings. Contact mayor's or governor's office or see *Gift Ideas: Anniversaries* for White House address.
Large-print telegram (call Western Union at 800-325-6000)
Tuition for leisure class—bridge, photography, ceramics, etc.
Tuition for Elderhostel, 75 Federal St., Boston, MA 02110-1941 (617-426-8056—catalogs are sent to all public libraries). Educational adventure for persons 60 and over and their spouses. Over 1,800 colleges and universities around the U.S. and overseas offer low-cost residential, academic study in diverse areas from glacial history to musical theater. Standard fee for six-night, state-side stay is $285 (plus transportation to the city).
Membership in American Association of Retired Persons, 601 E. St. NW, Washington, DC 20049 (202-434-2277). Special rates on insurance, drugs, travel, etc.; bimonthly magazine (*Modern Maturity*)
Arrange conference call with scattered family members.
Tape (video or audio) a family gathering and send them the tape.

Radio, TV, VCR; multiple item remote control; small electric heater or fan
Cassette recorder or player, tapes
Photo of family, wallet photos, photo wheel or album
Have old photographs copied or restored.
Visit on a special day; visit on any day and it will be special.
Dinner at your home or a restaurant
Books, bookmarks; magazine subscription
Assorted greeting cards, stationery, stamps
Lots of mail; anything made by grandchildren or children
Have grandchildren draw a picture, call, or send a note.
Tickets and transportation to entertainment or sports event, movie, etc.
Golden Age Passport to national parks (see *Gift Ideas: Traveler*)
Bible, other books or magazines in large print (see *Magazines: Special Needs*)
Calendar—inspirational, nature scenes, area of interest, one made with your photographs at a photo finishing store
Gift certificate to beauty parlor to have hair fixed (once a month for a year)
Afghan, electric blanket, quilt; new linens
Gift certificate from telephone company; special telephone services such as call return (reconnects with the last local number that called), call waiting, three-way calling, speed calling (dials often called numbers with just one or two digits), call cue (calls back the last local number dialed whether or not the party answered)

Telephone amplifier; telephone/answering machine combination

Energy-saving improvements — sun screen, weather stripping, storm door, storm windows, etc.; automatic garage door opener, heat-activated porch or driveway light; smoke detector, alarm system; deadbolts (install them, too!); door viewer; touch-sensitive lamp control, remote light control

Railing for outdoor steps; bathtub railing

Large-print or waist-level display bathroom scale

Electric pill box with timer and clock

Hand-held vacuum cleaner, non-electric carpet sweeper, or lightweight vacuum cleaner; air-purifying system

Meals for freezer

Box of fruit, candy, cheese, teas, coffees (see *Catalogs: Food*)

Small appliance like burger cooker, coffee pot (see *Appendix: Small Electric Appliances*)

Jar opener; zipper pull; lighted magnifying glass; assortment of light bulbs

Bird feeder or birdbath; wind chimes; sun-catcher for window

Seeds, potted plant, flower bulbs, terrarium

✎ ELECTRONIC MARVELS ✐

This list is a tribute to the imagination. You'll say, "Well, I never!" over some of these ideas. See also *Appendix: Small Electric Appliances*.

Digital travel compass

Heat and massage car seat

Environmental sound machine; wireless stereo speakers; antenna that connects to AC wall receptacle to substitute for outside antenna or rabbit ears

AM/FM/TV band radio (fits into shirt pocket or clips on belt; picks up audio portion of TV shows); backseat TV (attaches to front car seat headrest)

Karaoke/sing-along system; radio concealed in a baseball cap

Video transfer system (use any camcorder to transfer slides, still prints, or old movie film onto video cassette tapes); video title maker

VCR Plus — keyed to many local TV listings, for one-step programming of up to 14 programs

Wireless intercom for home (to monitor nursery, sick room, etc.)

Laser pointer pen

Hand-held address computer or organizer

Labeling system

Desktop paper shredder

Digital car compass

Pill dispenser and timer

Computerized chess, bridge, blackjack, crossword puzzle solver, etc.

Wireless wall switch that controls lamps, TVs, stereos, other appliances plugged into wall outlet up to fifty feet away

Remote control for several devices; remote control retriever (attaches to bottom of remote control; find it by whistling!)

Alarm clock that projects time onto ceiling or one with two alarm settings

Answer telephone (answering machine/telephone combination)

Headphone for hands-free telephone/radio

Cordless headset for TV, video, or stereo

Telephone conversation recorders
Microcassette recorder (records up to two hours; portable, size of a candy bar)
CD cleaner
Portable wireless telephone jack that turns any standard outlet into a tele-
  phone jack
Heated towel stand; slippers with lighted toes for walking in a dark house
Regulated pet food dispenser
Digital bathroom scale; water-resistant radio for shower or hot tub
Blood-pressure recording watch
Prenatal sound amplifier (allows you to hear baby's hiccups, kicks, heartbeat
  by third trimester)
Air-filtering system
Jar opener; automatic mug warmer
Checkbook calculator (stores balance for three accounts)
Cordless bug sucker (traps bugs in wand for easy disposal); electronic
  mosquito repellent that mimics the sound of the dreaded mosquito hawk
Digital distance measurer (ultrasound)

᧔ ENVIRONMENTALIST ᧖

See *Catalogs: Environmentally Friendly* for gifts that give to future genera-
tions as well as to a person in the present one.

Art out of Cyclestone, made out of recycled glass and plastic
  (looks like marble), or Rainforest tagua (looks like ivory);
  garden sculpture from recycled items
Anything made from recycled paper (stationery, home paper
  products)
Paper-making kit; any handcraft (ready made or kit to make);
  solar energy experiment kits
Book or video on alternative energy, recycling, rainforests, en-
  dangered species
Recycling organizer bins or bags
Aluminum can crusher or Recyclor (by Sjoberg Industries), a fully-automatic
  beverage can recycling appliance
Cloth shopping bags; natural fiber clothing and linens
Make reusable gift bags from colorful cotton; tie with grosgrain ribbon.
Slogan on bumper sticker, T-shirt
Subscription (see *Magazines: Politics & Opinions*)
Donation to National Arbor Day Foundation, 100 Arbor Ave., Nebraska
  City, NE 68410 (402-474-5655). For $10, a gift membership will be
  entered which includes six bimonthly issues of *Arbor Day.* Also ten 6"
  to 12" tree seedlings will be sent to your friend during a suitable planting time for her area. Another gift option (also $10) is membership in
  the Rainforest Rescue Program. A gift card will be sent to you to give. It
  includes an honorary deed guaranteeing the preservation of 2,500 sq. ft.
  of endangered rain forest.
Donation to Trees for the Future (11306 Estona Dr., P.O. Box 1786, Silver
  Spring, MD 20915-1786), which plants fast-growing seedlings in areas
  where forests are being destroyed and the native people depend upon
  trees for their way of life

Membership in a conservation organization such as
- ☐ Sierra Club (see *Gift Ideas: Outdoors Lover* for address)
- ☐ Nature Conservancy, Membership Dept., P.O. Box 79181, Baltimore, MD 21279-0181
- ☐ World Wildlife Fund, P.O. Box 224, Peru, IN 46970

Leaf vacuum/mulcher; composting system, composting pail for kitchen, rotating composting drum; reusable coffee filters

Juicer, food dehydrator; any kitchen supplies for canning or freezing fresh food

Nylon, insulated, reusable lunch bag or cooler

Nature sound machine or recordings of running water, birds, rain, waterfall, surf, jungle, etc.

Clothes line, clothes pins, drying rack

Solar powered watch, radio, outdoor lights, flashlight

Portable, solar-powered generator; candles (to save on electricity) or halogen or compact fluorescent light fixtures or lamps

Any gift picturing an endangered species (jewelry, T-shirt, art, game, etc.)

Air purifier, kit to test home for toxins

Bottled water dispenser and service; water filter, low-flow showerhead, faucet aerator; rain barrel with rain spout that runs into the barrel

Water timer or computer to set lawn sprinkler for a certain amount of time or for certain hours; thermostat timer

Fire starters, fireplace equipment (see *Gift Ideas: Fireplace Gifts*)

Rechargeable batteries, button battery charger (for solar charging of mercury hearing aid batteries, cameras, watches, hand-held electronic games, etc.)

Storm glass—glass flask that serves as a weathercasting barometer

Nuclear-free smoke alarm

Rag rug

Non-electric floor sweeper; organic cleaning products

❧ EXTRA SPECIAL ❧

A gift from this list will be long remembered. Don't wait for an official occasion to give these to someone. Use them to say, "You are special to me."

Membership in professional, historical, scientific, or alumni association

Membership in Young Men's (or Women's) Christian Association, community center, swim club,, or local museum, zoo, or cultural arts society (entitles person to discounts and special events)

Cookie bouquet (see *Delectable Edibles* or *Cookie Bouquet* under *Catalogs: Food—Sweets*)

Tuition for a leisure or academic class

Children can make coupon books for parents or special friends for free yard mowing, weeding, dishwashing, housework, baby-sitting, etc.

Select a pet from the local animal shelter.

Keep someone's children overnight or for a weekend.

Donate a book in her name to the local, church, or school library.

Dedicate a book to him or her.

Write a song, poem, or story for the person.

Create an original painting, stitchery, sculpture, etc.

Matching outfits for mother/child or for the whole family

Create a software program for an unusual hobby or interest.

Use photographs of the person for huge poster, calendar, mug, plate, Christmas tree ornament, puzzle, or T-shirt; convert slides, photographs, or movies to video.

One-of-a-kind handcraft (see *Catalogs: Handcrafts;* or *International/Regional Specialties*)

A collectible quality gift (see *Catalogs: Collectibles*)

Make a quilt, banner, or pillow using significant photographs or illustrations (see Gramma's Graphics under *Catalogs: Craft Supplies—Assorted*)

Antique or family heirloom with a written history of the item

Have older member of family tell on tape (video or audio) about his childhood, special trip, or other interesting part of his life. Copy tapes for other family members.

Record on paper or tape or as a scrapbook or illustrated book special events from that person's life — stories about him from his childhood, nice comments from significant people, funny sayings and happenings.

Research the family genealogy and present in charts or book form.

Subscribe to the Galaxy Project (4600 Park Rd. #107, Charlotte, NC 28209; 800-438-1242), an experiment in which subscriber's letters, photographs, and documents are recorded on CDs, which are sent to major world libraries and time capsule planners and are also transmitted by high-powered radio transmitters throughout the galaxy in the hope that advanced worlds may intercept and read the information.

Call or write if you haven't in a long time.

Give a gift in your friend's name to a charity, church, or school.

Plant a tree at a local park, church, or school in the person's name.

Plant a tree or perennials (roses, lilies, azaleas, etc.) in his or her yard.

Quarter of beef for freezer

Once-a-month flowers, fruit, candy service (see *Catalogs: Food;* or *Floral Gifts*)

Loan a gasoline credit card for a trip; pay for the whole trip; pay for the car; pay for the car insurance.

Say "I love you."; send flowers or a happy telegram to the office.

Bottle of champagne or liquor delivered with red roses, crystal glasses, or other specialty item (call 800 Spirits at 800-BE-THERE)

Hot tub

Unusual message services:

❑ *Balloon Bouquets* — balloon arrangements and various gift items (call 800-424-2323 for office nearest you)

❑ *Eastern Onion*—songs or comedy acts to be delivered by telephone or in person with choice of crazy costumes (consult local telephone directory for nearby office)

❑ *Western Union*—singing telegrams by telephone, also Braillegrams and large-print telegrams (call 800-325-6000)

৬ FAMILY ৵

Sometimes you want a gift for the entire family instead of for an individual. Here are suggestions that will appeal to families with varied interests.

Subscription to a magazine like *National Geographic, Smithsonian*, a regional travel magazine, or one in area of family interest

Subscription to magazine about their state (check with state highway department)

Book — encyclopedia; stargazing, bird, or wildflower guide; games, art, travel guide, road atlas, regional history; holiday theme, cartoons (*Family Circus* or *Calvin & Hobbes*), medical guide

Bookends; song book; cassette tape, CD, holder or carrier for these

Video player, videos (blank or favorite movies — see *Catalogs: Music & Movies*), video rewinder; video — movie, nature, family aerobics, one you made, place they have visited, how-to in activity they are interested in

VCR instant programmer; radio, clock, TV, VCR

Universal remote control for up to 12 preprogrammed devices

Subscribe to a special cable channel: sports, movie, Disney, Discovery (science and adventure), Nickelodeon (kids' movies, games, music), CNN, A&E (entertainment, drama, documentaries, performing arts), or TNT (classic movies, children's programming, specials)

Computer, computer game or software in their area of interest; Prodigy or Compuserve — computer bulletin boards that allow access to various services such as weather information, sports scores, shopping services, etc. (see *Gift Ideas: Computer Enthusiast* for telephone numbers)

Playing cards, board games, dominoes, chess, checkers, Chinese checkers, Parcheesi, Taboo, Trivial Pursuit (or extra questions for), Pictionary, Scattergories, Split Second, Family Feud, Jeopardy, Play It By Ear (a CD game for ages sixteen up), Yahtzee, Scrabble

Jigsaw puzzle (for more challenge, hide box until they work the puzzle), brain teasers, mazes, games of skill

Outdoor games — croquet, badminton, baseball, bocce, shuttle or paddle games, tetherball, etc.

Ping-Pong, pool table

Exercise equipment (see *Gift Ideas: Fitness Buff*)

Biorhythm charts or kit

Address book

Wireless intercom

Tickets to special sports or entertainment event; passes to movie theater, ice cream or pizza parlor, bowling alley, miniature golf, etc.

Membership in dinner club (one free meal for one bought); membership in Young Men's (or Women's) Christian Association, community or recreation center, swim club, local museum, or cultural arts society (allows for discounts on classes and special events); membership in local educational television station (so they can receive monthly program listings)

Membership in discount warehouse club

Gift certificate to a restaurant or portrait studio

Telephone amplifier; telephone extension or decorator telephone, cordless telephone, cellular telephone; gift certificate from telephone company, an 800 number, special telephone services (see *Gift Ideas: Adult—Basic*)

Directory of 60,000 toll-free 800 numbers (call Worldwide Directory at 800-SWB-BOOK for current price and ordering information)

Bulletin board, memo board

Tape dispenser, desk organizers, pencil sharpener, pencil holder

Big school bell (to call the kids home)

Bird feeder, bird house, bird bath; wind chimes

Topiary in cute shape—hanging monkey, duck, bear, giraffe, etc.

Porch swing, hammock; beach umbrella; lawn furniture, folding table or chairs; barbecue grill (see *Gift Ideas: Cook—Outdoor Cook* for other ideas); picnic equipment—thermos jug, ice chest, picnic basket, ground cloth; *Picnic! Recipes and Menus for Outdoor Enjoyment*, by Edith Stovel (Garden Way Publishing, 1990). Workday picnics, sandy picnics, elegant picnics, romantic picnics, etc.

Hanging basket, pot plant, terrarium

Tree, shrubs, bulbs, perennials, or rose bush for yard

Pet door, a pet (with their permission), pet food or toys

Aquarium set-up kit and gift certificate for fish; water purifier or replacement filters for it

Safety devices—smoke detector, fire extinguisher, alarm system, automatic timer for lights, door peephole, deadbolts (see *Gift Ideas: Security & Safety Conscious*)

Fireproof lock box

Energy-saving devices—sun screen, weather stripping, storm windows or doors, etc.

Small appliance—ice cream freezer, yogurt maker, popcorn popper (see *Appendix: Small Electric Appliances*)

Fireplace equipment (see *Gift Ideas: Fireplace Gifts*)

Linens for bed, bath, kitchen, table

Camera, camcorder

Photo album, photo wheel, film; composite picture frame

Family photos made into calendar, poster, puzzle, Christmas ornament

Family tree—picture composite, narrative, outline, genealogy charts (filled in), genealogy computer software; *Unpuzzling Your Past*, by Emily Anne Croom (Betterway Books, 1507 Dana Ave., Cincinnati, OH 45207-1005, 800-289-0963) to assist them with tracing their ancestors

Assemble a family cookbook with all the relatives' favorite recipes.

Make a home movie or video of family members for those who live far away.

Holiday ornament or seasonal decoration

Make a throw pillow; cross-stitch, needlepoint, or paint a picture; embroider hand towels; make something with your hobby—ceramic bowl, woven placemats, wooden bookends, etc.

Coupons for baby-sitting, car wash, yard work, etc.

Homebaked goods; preserves, pickles, jelly, etc.; gift pack of fruit, candy, cheese, meats, nuts, dessert sauces, jellies (see *Catalogs: Food*); basket with samples of everyone's favorite foods or case of their favorite soft drink or prepared food; gingerbread house, specially decorated cake; gingerbread house mold, shaped candy or candy molds, cookie cutters

Matching T-shirts, nightshirts

ᔥ FAREWELL GIFTS ᔥ

Saying good-bye is seldom easy, but sending along something to be remembered by helps ease the pain. You may want to give a gift from a special interest category or one aimed at the new residence and memories of the old.

Something local to remember the area by—photograph or painting of a local scene, area craft, T-shirt with local slogan, book of landmarks, cookbook of regional dishes, picture calendar of the area, playing cards or note paper with local scene

Subscription to local paper; subscription to old or new area magazine

Bird feeder for new location

Address book (put your name in!); change-of-address postcards

Give an open house for them.

Bulbs for new yard; flower pot (empty)

Box of tissues

Potted plant delivered by florist after they arrive in new residence

Stained glass window ornament, refrigerator magnet (how about one with a picture frame and your picture in it?); wind chimes

Stationery—with new address if you know it

Return address labels with new address

Write a note and mail it so it will be waiting at new house for them.

Muslin or autograph pillow; napkins or tablecloth signed in permanent ink by their friends

Friendship quilt or patchwork pillow—each square by a different friend

Collection of photos of good times together; photograph album

Have them for a meal on moving day or a few days before; baby-sit on moving day; help on moving day

❧ FIREPLACE GIFTS ❧

Fire screen or glass door fire screen; stainless steel reflecting screen that stands behind the fire to reflect it into the room; pay for a visit from a chimney sweep.; andirons, indoor wood rack or log holder; outdoor log rack, canvas cover for it; wood splitter, cord of wood, gas logs, artificial logs; firewood carrier, utility cart; tools—tongs, poker, brush, turner, broom; bellows; long-handled popcorn popper, special fireplace grill; fireplace matches, colored flame makers, fire starters; fireplace potpourri; fireproof hearth mat; fireplace vacuum for collecting cold ashes

❧ FISHERMAN ❧

When buying gifts for a fisherman, keep in mind the kind of fishing he does —fly fishing, deep sea fishing, surf fishing, or lake fishing. More ideas are listed in *Gift Ideas: Outdoors Lover* and *Boater*. See *Catalogs: Outdoors* for some sources.

Gift certificate to local fish market

Gift certificate to sporting goods store or catalog

Subscription (see *Magazines: Outdoors*); book or video on fishing

Tickets to boat show, recreational vehicle show, camping show

Pay fee for fishing guide for a day at favorite lake.

Pay entry fee for fishing tournament.

Fish cookbook; smoker (for cooking his catch)

Fish mounting kit; ice chest; insulated spillproof mug, thermos, canteen

Pocket camera, weather radio; fishing chair, stool; rod, reel, electric fishing
   reel; rod or reel carrying case; rod rack, tackle cabinet; fishing rod
   holder, belt caddy
Line counter (measures how deep she is fishing or how much line she is
   trolling); live bait tank, bait bucket; fisherman's vest, sportsman's belt;
   tackle box, fly or lure box, soft folding tackle box, tackle pack that fits
   over back of chair; fishing pliers, fish hook remover, hook sharpener,
   hone, folding scissors
Pocket scales (digital is nice), stringer
Lures, baits, spinners, or flies, or kits to make them
Box of assorted hooks, weights
Knives—scaling, filet, floating, pocket
Floating key case
Floating or waterproof flashlight
Small first-aid kit, air horn
Plastic tube for holding maps, leaders
Fighting belt (for bringing in the "biggies")
Fisherman's float; landing net, creel
Wading staff, wading boots, hip boots
Spikes that clamp to shoe soles, strike sensor alarm, ice shuttle or
   tent (for ice fishing)
Stream thermometer
Head-net hat, sunglasses
Fingerless gloves
Rain gear, emergency blanket

✎ FITNESS BUFF ❧

Choose a gift from this list whether the person frequents the gym or just
watches his diet. Also see *Gift Ideas: Runner/Jogger/Walker* or other sports
categories. Catalogs offering some of these items are listed under *Health &
Beauty*.

Subscription (see *Magazines: Health & Fitness*)
Book on biofeedback, stress reduction, family medical guide, exercise, aero-
   bics, healthy eating, stop-smoking cure
Journal for keeping records of exercise, calories, etc.
Membership in health club, swim club, YMCA or YWCA, tennis club, golf
   club
Warmup suit, terry bathrobe, sports bra, leotard, workout clothes or gloves

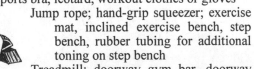

Jump rope; hand-grip squeezer; exercise
   mat, inclined exercise bench, step
   bench, rubber tubing for additional
   toning on step bench
Treadmill; doorway gym bar, doorway
   punching bag, chin-up bars, push-up
   bars; gymnastics ball; pool-exercise
   buoyancy belt
Rebound jogger, wheel for strengthening abdominal muscles
Stationary bicycle or stand for converting regular bicycle into one
Videocycle — videos of scenic areas with music and cycling tips to be

watched while using an exercycle; filmed as if cyclist were actually on the road; book stand or wide seat for exercise bicycle

Barbells, ankle weights, wrist weights, weighted sit-up strap; resistance bands (for stretching); weight belt

Digital watch, pedometer, stop watch, ring-style lap counter; bathroom scale

Blood pressure monitor, pulse monitor, first-aid kit, electronic thermometer

Tape or video of aerobic dance or exercise music (see *Catalogs: Music & Movies*) or video of the exercises themselves with favorite kind of music (from rock to Christian to Big Band)

Computer software program for tracking food intake, exercise sessions, ingredients in recipes, medical information

Digital pedometer that attaches to waistband and displays distance covered, calories burned, time spent

Padded innersoles for shoes

Tote bag for taking clothes to gym

Shower massage, heat massage, hour's massage at a spa, massaging sandals

Dietary food scale; water filter for faucet; dust masks

Air purifier or "smokeless ashtray" for home or office; "Thank You for Not Smoking" sign or desk plaque, perhaps hand-painted or needlepoint; stop-smoking class or kit

Basket of bath and beauty products (for skin care, healthy hair and nails, etc.)

Hot or cold therapy wraps, infrared heat therapy instrument

✤ GARDENER ✤

Here are gift ideas for those who keep you supplied in fresh produce through the summer and for those who always win the "Best Yard" award from the civic club. Gift sources can be found under *Catalogs: Gardening*.

Subscription (see *Magazines: Gardening*)

Gift certificate to local nursery or gardening catalog

Software for designing a garden or for landscaping

Stationery, jewelry, pictures, hand towels, etc., with flower or vegetable designs

Farmer's or garden almanac for the coming year

Book or video on plant care, gardening, organic gardening, local area gardening, flower arranging; *Rodale's All-New Encyclopedia of Organic Gardening* (Rodale Press, 1991)

12-24-12 fertilizer, garden gypsum, super phosphate, organic fertilizers

Bench on wheels with space for garden tools under the seat

Compost bin; kitchen compost bucket

Tool bucket or carry-all, tool apron

Garden clogs or boots

Cordless grass trimmer

Rake—expanding or regular

Weed pruner, pruner on rod

Harvest basket, one on a long pole to eliminate need for ladder

Wheelbarrow, drop spreader, hand spreader

Garden gloves, sun hat, knee pads, rubber boots, kneeling pad

Tools — trowel, gardening fork, clippers, pruning shears or saw, ratchet shears, dibble (punches holes for planting), seeder

Several seed packets or bulbs in a flower pot tied with gingham ribbon; fruit or other kind of tree; bulbs, bedding plants, seeds of all kinds; potting trays, potting soil, potting bench; soil test kit

Portable, roll-up path made of boards

Garden hose, canvas soaker hose, hose hanger, hose nozzles, garden hose reel; sprayer; sprinkler (some have automatic timer and cut-off); watering can—rustproof, large capacity

Underground irrigation system; water timer or computer to set lawn sprinkler for a certain amount of time or for certain hours

Moisture meter, rain gauge, or pH meter

Plastic markers for plant identification, waterproof marking pen; twist-ties

Humorous markers for garden

Tomato supports, frames

Garden tower, multi-tiered garden, trellis, English-style trellis in shape of various trees

Cold frame (to cover plants in cool weather); heating cable (for cold frame); greenhouse, portable solar greenhouse

Wall of water plant protectors (water-filled tepees); hot kaps

Canning jars, lids, labels, equipment

Tube of liniment or hand cream; Bag Balm

Decorative Items — wind chimes; bird bath, bird feeder, bird seed, bird house; bronze decorative faucets; garden sculpture; topiary; hanging basket, plant hangers (indoor and outdoor); bench, swing, or hammock for relaxing and enjoying what is growing

Flower Arranging — Book or video on technique, preserving flowers; tuition for course on flower arranging; gift certificate to floral shop; vases; silver or other centerpiece bowl with frog (to hold stems); flower cutters, clippers; assorted flower holders, needlepointer (for fixing needlepoint holder); flower press; spray that cleans silk or dried arrangements; wire cutter

Indoor Gardening — Mister, indoor watering hose, humidifier, small watering can, mini-tool set; humidity tray; plant light or seed starting lamp; electric mat (for providing bottom heat); timer for plant light; ceiling track for hanging baskets; plant dolly (dish on casters), plant display stand; vase, decorative pot or planter—copper, brass, ceramic, clay, etc.; terrarium (or small aquarium); automatic plant waterer; moisture meter

✦ GENEALOGIST/FAMILY HISTORIAN ✦

Tracing one's roots is a popular pastime. People pursue their ancestors with varying degrees of intensity, but these ideas should facilitate the process. See also *Gift Ideas: History Buff* and *Traveler*.

Subscription to or membership in family or ethnic association; regional, state, or county genealogical society in the area of residence or research

Membership in National Genealogical Society (4527 17th St. N, Arlington, VA 22207-2399)

Subscription to Everton's *Genealogical Helper* (The Everton Publishers, Inc., P.O. Box 368, Logan, UT 84321)—has ads and lists of other genealogical associations and organizations in six yearly issues

Archival material such as acid-free paper, storage boxes, sheet protectors, or ink, available from such sources as The Preservation Emporium, P.O. Box 226309, Dallas, TX 75222-6309 (214-331-8902)

Books on genealogical how-to such as *Unpuzzling Your Past,* by Emily Anne Croom (Betterway Books, 1507 Dana Ave., Cincinnati, OH 45207-1005, 800-289-0963), reference books such as *The Handy Book for Genealogists* (Everton Publishers, address above), research guide to the research area available from National Genealogical Society (address above) or genealogy booksellers, or social history of research area or ethnic group such as *The Scotch-Irish,* by James G. Leyburn (University of NC Press, 1962).

Gift certificate to bookstore (new or used books)

Antique map of state or city where family lived, especially if date of map is close to the time the family lived there

Good atlas of United States or world; road maps, county maps or topographical maps of research areas

Research supplies: three-hole punch, large three-ring binders, magnifying glass, pencils (many libraries require use of pencils, not pens), mechanical eraser, stamps, legal-size envelopes

Computer software for word processing, form-making, data base, genealogical data; laptop computer, page scanner

Camera, film for research travel

"Copicard" for use at favorite library

Roll of coins for copy machines and parking meters during research

Donation to library or society in honor of the genealogist

Personalized stationery and envelopes, especially of the size or quality for use in a computer printer or copy machine

Originals or copies of old family photographs; mementos that belonged to an ancestor, including jewelry, documents, photographs, personal belongings, books, diaries, letters, etc. (with any information on that relative)

Material for tombstone rubbing (blank newsprint paper, crayons, charcoal, chalk)

Insulated lunch bag or carrier for all-day research trips

Coupons for baby-sitting services while researching

✎ GOLFER ✎

For sources, see *Catalogs: Sports & Recreation*.

Tickets to professional golf tournament

Golf lessons; book or video on technique, tournaments, world-wide courses

Subscription (see *Magazines: Sports*)

Take a video of his golf swing for him to analyze.

Electronic golf tutor with hanging ball (as ball is hit, computer analyzes the spin and calculates ball travel and distance)

Computer software that analyzes her hits, greens, putting stats, etc., so she'll know what to practice

Golf clubs, golf club covers (knit, crocheted, drawstring)

Sports bag; shoe bag

Golf club care kit, golf club cleaner

Golf Links (personalized with name and telephone number
 in case golfer leaves a club somewhere; snaps into
 hole at end of club grip)

Identification tag for golf bag (needlepoint, maybe)

Golf umbrella, seat, or cane

Golf shirts, shoes, gloves

Mesh bag for carrying golf spikes in a suitcase

Golf bag, bag strap pad, bag on wheels, bag cart, bag rain
 gear; solar-powered, ventilated golf cap

Dozen golf balls, tees (biodegradable, personalized), wiffle or foam practice
 balls; ball and tee pouch to attach to belt; golf ball monogrammer; golf
 ball retriever, shag bag

Scorecard holder or album; golf towel (personalized)

Electric putting cup, home putting green and cup, chipping mat, driving mat

Golf practice net

∾ GRANDPARENTS ∾

These items especially recognize a person's role as grandparent and are great
for grandchildren to give. Of course, consider gifts from other appropriate
categories also.

Keep a photograph album all year and give it to them at the end of the year.

Picture frame, photograph album, photo wheel; "brag book"—purse-sized
 photo album; pictures—wallet-size, school, family, portrait; refrigerator
 magnet child has made to hold her artwork or one with grandchild's
 picture on it; make a collage of pictures, notes, or drawings.; draw a picture or write a poem or story for them.

Write a "book." Have children write about some things they enjoy doing and
 illustrate their own stories.

Rocking chair

Coupons for yard work, housecleaning, or other chores
 by the grandchildren

Send a taped letter or video.; VCR so they can watch
 videos of the family; copy old slides or home
 movies onto video.

Toy box or basket filled with toys for the grandchildren

An antique toy or book or one from his/her childhood

Tablecloth or napkins of muslin decorated by the
 grandchildren with fabric paints

Cookie jar

Call, visit, or write them often.

Ornament for Christmas tree with grandchild's picture
 and date or one the child has made

Stitchery pictures, e.g. "If mother says no, ask grandmother."

Bumper sticker or plaque—e.g., "Ask me about my grandchild(ren)."

Grandmother's Precious Moments, by Gwendolyn and Steve Hines (Thomas
 Nelson, 1990)—book for her to record her favorite family stories, girl-
 hood fashions, hobbies, romances, etc., and give to the grandchildren.

❦ GROOMSMAN ❧

See also *Gift Ideas: Man—Basic*.

Silver or crystal jigger; bottle of wine; pewter tankard; pocket knife; bookends; wallet, money clip; belt buckle, cuff links, tie tack; key ring; neck chain, bracelet, ring (only if he wears jewelry); man's jewelry box or dresser top organizer; fountain pen and pencil set, letter opener; picture frame; soft luggage, travel kit

❦ HANDYMAN ❧

To list every kind of tool for electricians, carpenters, auto mechanics, plumbers, and other do-it-yourselfers would take another book. For more exhaustive ideas, try some catalogs under *Handyman; Electronics;* and *Craft Supplies*.

Subscription to do-it-yourself magazine (see *Magazines: Handyman & Hobbyist; Metalworking;* and *Woodworking*)
Gift certificate to hardware store or catalog or lumber yard
Book or video on repairs or special interest area
Tuition for course in automotive repair, cabinetwork, etc.
List of plumbers or electricians who make emergency calls
Toolbox, multi-drawer cabinet
Magnetic tool tray (so nails, screws, etc., don't get lost)
Pegboard for hanging tools; shelves in workshop
Tool pouch, nail bag, carpenter's apron; heavy-duty work gloves
Heavy-duty extension cord; ladder, ladder with extended handle and wide top step for holding supplies; saw horses
For shop—workbench, broom, paper towel holder, waterless hand cleaner, fan, heater; level; drill, attachments; sander, assorted grades of sandpaper; saws—handsaw, jigsaw, sabre saw, etc.; miter box
Assorted sizes of nails, screws, washers, nuts, picture hangers, bolts, wire
Good paint brushes, rollers, paint pans; brush storage bucket with airtight cover for interrupted paint sessions; roller washer that spins roller clean in minutes
Tools — screwdrivers, hammers, wire-cutter pliers, tin snips, jeweler's screwdriver, utility knife, pipe wrench, channel lock, contour gauge, C-clamps, etc.
First-aid kit for shop
Caulking gun, soldering gun, staple gun
Power tape measure, flexible ruler
Box of household adhesives—Super Glue, masking tape, electrician's tape, duct tape, silicone sealer, epoxy, Elmer's glue, wood glue, weather-strip adhesive, etc.
Antique or unusual tools
Chain saw

❦ HIGH SCHOOL GRADUATION ❧

Help the student celebrate this special achievement or give her a head start on her future plans—college, first job, first apartment, marriage, etc. Many ideas will come from *Gift Ideas: Adult—Basic; Man—Basic; Woman—Basic;*

Bachelor; Single Woman; Wedding; College Student; Housewarming; Cook; or an area of special interest.

A job offer
Frame for diploma; portrait of graduate or frame for one
Give a party.
Gift certificate for two to a nice restaurant; passes to a movie theater, a bowling alley, or a miniature golf, or a driving range; tickets to special entertainment or sports event; special trip
Membership in fitness club

Luggage, travel kit, garment bag, suit bag, tote bag, soft luggage, jewelry roll, lingerie bag, shoe covers, insulated bag for hot curling iron, cosmetic bags (waterproof, with mirror)
Sun shade for the car (maybe with college logo)
Backpack, book bag
Camera, film, camcorder
Photograph album, scrapbook, collection of favorite tales of his growing up (adventures, embarrassing or funny moments, special things he did for people, inside family jokes, etc.)
Address book (with important addresses already entered), stationery, personalized memo pads or notes, stamps; autograph book
Favorite photographs made into calendar, ornament, plate, mug, T-shirt, or puzzle
Posters

Calendar for wall or desk with family's and friend's anniversaries and birthdays filled in; perpetual calendar (each day has a Scripture, cartoon, or saying; calendar can be used again and again)
Typewriter, computer, or computer software (see *Gift Ideas: Computer Enthusiast*)
Dictionary, *Roget's International Thesaurus*, book of famous quotations, other reference book
Book of etiquette (a modern version if you want it used!); books on adult development, money management, self-improvement, time management, choosing a career, college life, or job hunting; devotional book or calendar; book of poetry, "wise sayings," or cartoons
Bookends; handmade, personalized, or silver bookmarks; book plates
Magazine subscription (in a leisure area of interest or possible career field)
Desk accessories and organizers, pencil sharpener, pencil holder, pen and pencil set, desk lamp; bulletin board and thumbtacks; memo board
Box of office supplies for the dorm—stapler, paper clips, pens (red, blue, and black), ruler, scissors, transparent tape, rubber bands, self-stick removable notes, computer diskettes, etc.
Cash, savings bond; add to a savings account; begin a mutual fund account.
Order designer checks or checkbook; open a personal checking account.
Wallet (with money inside!)
Clothing—sweat suit, lingerie, sweaters, sweatshirt or T-shirt with personal slogan or college logo, robe, pajamas, nightgown, workout clothes, clothes for work; gift certificate to favorite clothing store or book store

Umbrella (size to fit in purse, backpack, or attaché case or automatic kind)

Anything with emblem of chosen college—mug, bumper sticker, tote bag, key chain, notebook, etc.

Watch, jewelry, jewelry box, dresser top organizer; vanity tray, dresser set

Scented toiletries

Start a silver flatware set for her.

Coffeemaker or teapot (with special flavors of coffee or tea)

Radio, clock radio, non-electric alarm clock, Walkman, Diskman, or head-phones

Pocket calculator (one with graphing capabilities if student plans to study engineering, economics, etc.)

Cassette player, stereo, VCR, TV, CD player, videodisc player

Cassette tape, video (music, favorite movie, aerobics, sports, lessons in area of interest), or CD; tape holder or carrier

Answering machine, answer telephone, telephone, cellular telephone or air time; gift certificate for long-distance telephone service

Small hair dryer, other personal care appliance (see *Appendix: Small Electric Appliances*)

Iron, travel iron, ironing board; fan; sewing kit, sewing machine

Basic tool set or hammer with screwdrivers hidden in handle

Closet organizers, space-savers for closet or under bed; stacking storage containers; Carry-all for cosmetics, etc.

Linens for bed, kitchen, or bath; afghan, quilt

Quilt depicting special childhood memories

Humorous laundry bag (e.g., "Hi, mom! I'm home!"), clothes hamper, laundry detergent, rolls of quarters; folding drying rack

Beach towel, beach chair, clip-on umbrella

Small ice chest, thermos, picnic supplies

In-line skates (see also *Gift Ideas: Sports & Games*)

State flag, T-shirt, poster or other memorabilia of home state if going to an out of state college or job

Holiday or seasonal decorations—personalized Christmas ornaments, nativity set, door wreath, shaped candles or figures

Bouquet of flowers, vase; decorative container with potpourri

Chocolate in different shapes—heart, flower, car, computer, telephone, etc.

৬ HISTORY BUFF ৵

Learn whether there is one particular period of history that your friend favors —American Civil War, Renaissance, European, Roman Empire, etc. Then try to find something from this list that applies to that time and place. Used bookstores are great places for rare finds. See also *Gift Ideas: Genealogist /Family Historian*.

Tickets to place of interest (national monument or historical site) or local traveling exhibit

Book or periodical published during the period; book about a favorite period, historical event, or person, history of his town or area

Subscription (see *Magazines: History & Military*) or single issues of magazines that deal with the period

Biographies of people who lived during the period

An item from the period such as documents, coins or currency, stamps, buttons, clothing, glassware, art objects

Copies of crafts or decorator items of the period such as dolls, toys, clock, needlework, quilt, dishes, furniture, candlesticks, or jewelry

Famous autographs or maps from the period

Art that depicts the period

Family history or family tree (filled in as much as possible)

Copy of newspaper or magazine from her day of birth; coins or stamps from year of birth

Tape of radio program, speech, music, or video documentary from the period

Commemorative stamps depicting a historical event; copy of old newsreels

Video or cassette tape or notes from elderly family members on family anecdotes, events, members, memories

An American flag for flying outside, flag mount

✎ HOST/HOSTESS ✎

Some people have a gift of hospitality and others entertain to fulfill social or business obligations. In either case, these gifts will enhance their ability to please their guests. Other ideas are listed under *Gift Ideas: Bar Gifts; Cook;* and *Silver Gifts.* Hostess gifts are under *Catalogs: Cookware; Food; Home Furnishings; Housewares;* and *Smorgasbord.* Also see *Appendix: Small Electric Appliances.*

Book of party games; bridge tallies or score pads; personalized or assorted invitations, notecards, or postcards; dinner bell; guest book; guest soap, soap dish; assorted cheeses, mints, coffees, jellies, relishes (see *Catalogs: Food*); favorite wine, liquor; "Thank You for Not Smoking" sign —needlepoint, painted, wooden; smoke eliminator, ashtrays, air purifier; plant or flower arrangement; pacific cloth or flannel bags for silver items

Linens—Cocktail or dinner napkins; make coasters out of quilted material.; placemats, tablecloth, table runner, matching napkins, napkin rings; linens in a style to match the kind of food he likes to serve (e.g., for Southwestern dishes, handwoven placemats from South or Central America); guest towels, pretty towel holder; pillows, pillowcases, bed linens, decorative pillows; roll cover (for bread basket)

Decorations—Vase; flower arrangement—china, fabric, wood, dried; fresh flowers; candlesticks, candelabra, candles (beeswax, scented, or shaped); ice sculpture art molds

Beverage Aids—Glassware, mugs; coasters; coffee beans and electric coffee mill; coffee urn, espresso, or cappuccino maker; pitcher; decanter set, liquor labels; insulated vacuum server; punch bowl, cups, ladle; wine rack, wine cooler; ice bucket, tongs; wooden stemware holder; demitasse cup set; ice crusher—manual or electric

Serving Accessories—Snack set (small trays with cups); dessert set; decorated paper plates, matching paper napkins and cups; paper party napkins (initialed or printed with name); serving dishes (e.g., chip and dip set for casual entertainers, fine china bowl for a formal table); serving trays (all

sizes)—silver, wood, enamel, plastic, painted, crystal; warming tray, one- or two-burner buffet range; buffet caddies; electric plate warmer; hors d'oeuvre knives or forks, cocktail forks; steak knives, carving set; cake or pie serving knife; grapefruit or melon spoons; trivets; lazy Susan; salt shaker, peppermill; salad molds; TV trays, card table, folding chairs, serving cart

Special Function Dishes—Cruet; small dishes for relishes, mints; condiment server; cheese board, knife; cheese saver with cover; chip and dip set; bread basket; cookie jar; cake plate; salad bowl, salad servers, individual bowls, salad stand; soup tureen; chafing dish; casserole dish (oven-to-freezer is useful); microwave dishes; gravy separator; parfait glasses, sherbets, banana split dishes

❧ HOUSEWARMING ❧

If you like to take a gift the first time you visit someone's new home, here are some ideas. Other gifts are included in *Catalogs: Food; Handcrafts; Handyman; Home Furnishings; Housewares; Gardening;* and *Smorgasbord.*

List of reliable repairmen, doctors, 24-hour groceries, or drugstores nearby
Take pictures of house during construction and present to new owners.
Offer to help paint.
Take prepared meal or have them for a meal before or after moving.
Gift certificate to hardware store
Change-of-address cards; return address labels or stationery with new address
Book on home energy conservation, home repair, do-it-yourself projects, local gardening information, *Complete Guide to Four-Season Home Maintenance,* by Dave Heberle and Richard M. Scutella (Betterway Books, 1507 Dana Ave., Cincinnati, OH 45207-1005, 800-289-0963)
Subscription to home decoration, home improvement, or gardening magazine (see *Magazines: Gardening; Homes & Decorating;* or *Handyman & Hobbyist*)
Computer program for home inventory or landscaping
On Moving Day—Keep the children. Take them a picnic lunch; have them over for a quick meal. Take a cooler of drinks, cookies, sandwiches, or fruit. Lend a strong back. Take an emergency kit of Band-Aids, paper towels, paper cups, soap, toilet paper, scissors, dust rags, all-purpose cleaner, pen and note pad, anything they might need and can't locate.
Outside Ideas—Front door plaque with family's name; front door knocker; mailbox—decorated or with family's name; door mat (personalized); house numbers for door or lawn; new garbage can (decorated if you want), garbage can caddy; outdoor bell to call kids home; lawn furniture; wind chimes; potted plant or hanging basket, topiary; tree, shrubbery, flowers, bulbs, grass seed, rose bush, perennials; lawn mower, blower/vac, grass trimmer; snow scoop with wheels

Safety Devices—Door peephole, dead bolts, door chain, window locks, door alarm; automatic light timer, heat-activated light for driveway or porch; motion-detecting flood lights; smoke detector, fire extinguisher, fire escape ladder, alarm system; fireproof lock box. (see also *Gift Ideas: Security & Safety Conscious*)

Indoor Ideas—Bath set, towels, guest towels, bed or table linens; fancy soap — scented, initialed, shaped; candles; "Thank You for Not Smoking" sign — hand painted, needlepoint; ashtrays; vase; silk flower arrangement or tree; wine rack, bottle of wine; personalized cocktail napkins; collection of light bulbs; guest book; closet organizers; fireplace equipment (see *Gift Ideas: Fireplace Gifts*); wall decoration—plaque, picture, stitchery, photograph; toolbox, assorted tools (see *Gift Ideas: Handyman*); broom, mop, bucket, vacuum cleaner; assorted nails, screws, picture hangers, wire; household adhesives—masking tape, Super Glue, epoxy, electrician's tape, etc.

❧ HUNTER ❧

A hunter's needs depend upon the time of year he hunts, what he hunts, and whether he shoots guns or bows. Other ideas are in *Gift Ideas: Outdoors Lover* and *Camper*. For many sources of gifts, see *Catalogs: Outdoors*.

Gift certificate to sporting goods store or catalog

Tickets to gun or hunting show, recreational vehicle show, camping show

Smoker; meat processing equipment—grinder, sausage stuffer, jerky cure

Glasses, mugs, picture, print, dishes, T-shirt with hunting motif or the animal he hunts

Mounting plaque for horns, head, birds

Subscription (see *Magazines: Outdoors* or *Animals, Birds, Fish & Wildlife*)

Book or video on weapons, hunting, wildlife, conservation, game processing

Detailed map or aerial photo of hunting area—Check with highway department or Agriculture Stabilization and Conservation Service (ASCS) office in county where land is located.

Camp stool with pockets; hot seat (stadium seat) cushion that stores and reflects body heat

Weather radio, AM-FM radio with earphones

Binoculars; flashlight that doesn't rattle or shine

Folding table

Small first-aid kit

Hunting knife, knife sharpening set

Game scissors, meat saw, rope

Stainless steel, wide-mouth thermos, canteen, ice chest

Food bars

Game bag (orange or camouflage)

Scents (depends on prey); calls (moose, etc.)

Winch, utility vehicle storage boxes or liner, hitch-haul carrier for back of vehicle

Snake guards; snake-proof chaps, pants, gaiters; hunting boots

Face paint, face mask, balaclava, or toque—camouflage

Clothing—(Many new fabrics are more effective against cold and water than the old ones. Check for the latest improvement.); rain suit or poncho;

hooded sweatshirt; fur-lined cap or gloves; water-resistant hat; socks (heated, wool, or GORE-TEX); thermal or silk underwear; chamois or flannel shirt; camouflage or blaze orange suit, caps, shirts, pants, vest, bib overalls, sweatshirt, gloves, sportsman's collar; insulated or wool parka, overalls, coveralls; shooting jacket; pack vest (with roomy backpack pouch and front pockets); shooting gloves, shooting mitt with flap for trigger finger, hand warmer, heater gloves; shooting glasses

Gun Equipment—Gun lock (prevents its firing); gun cleaning supplies; gun case, gun sling, wide shoulder strap; reloading equipment (correct caliber or gauge is vital); ammunition case; ear protectors (different kinds for shooting range and field); scope, scope covers; gun safe for home; gun rack for truck, home; membership in National Rifle Association, 1600 Rhode Island Ave. NW, Washington, DC 20036 (202-828-6000)

Bird Hunter — Bird bag; decoys; bird dog, gun dog training kit, dog grooming aids; book or video on training dog to point, hold, retrieve, hunt dead; calls (duck, goose, quail, turkey, dove, etc.)

Archer—Bow, bow strings, bow case; quiver, arrows; gloves, finger tips, finger tabs, arm guard; arrow straightener, fletching tools, kit for making arrows; broadheads, small game points, shafts (correct size and weight are vital); target, matte, easel, 3-D target; bow and arrow rack

❧ LEFTIES ❧

When someone comments that a lot of things are not right in this world, he may be a pessimist—or he may be left-handed! If you are right-handed and have ever tried using scissors with your left hand, you will understand the problems of lefties in accomplishing many simple, everyday tasks. The following items can be found with handles or openings reversed or otherwise altered for left-handed use.

Kitchen knives, corkscrew, utensils, ladle, can opener, vegetable peeler, ice cream scoop, measuring cup, cake server

Scissors, pinking shears; pocket knife, screwdriver

Fishing reel; catcher's mitt; fielder's glove; golf, bowling, or tennis glove; archery bows; golf clubs

Playing cards with numbers in all four corners

Pitcher, mug with handle on right

Camera with shutter button on left

Watch that winds on left

Spiral notebooks or checkbook bound on right

Left-handed ruler numbered right to left

Lefty T-shirt, mug, note paper, tote bag, bumper sticker

Manuals on left-handed craft work, golf, calligraphy, guitar; teaching left-handed children; etc.

Membership in Lefthanders International, P.O. Box 8249, Topeka, KS 66608 (913-234-2177). Magazine, product information, etc.

❧ A LITTLE REMEMBRANCE ❧

Sometimes it's fun to give a gift for no special reason except to encourage, thank, or express your appreciation for that person. You may also find an idea in the category for a special interest that person has. For unique gifts, check a catalog under *Handcrafts; International/Regional Specialties; Art & Special Treasures;* or *Smorgasbord*.

Small handcraft—teacozy. scented trivet, etc.

Box of notecards, pretty postcards or stationery, funny or personalized memo pads

Holder (hand-decorated) for pencils, rings, tissues, letters, etc.

Bridge tallies or score pads

Perpetual calendar

Scented, shaped, or initialed soaps

Hand towel, apron

Candle, beeswax, scented, or meaningful shape; candleholder

Homemade goodies—cookies, molded salad, cake, pie, bread, pickles, casserole

Plate of shaped cookies plus the cookie cutter

Favorite wine or liquor

Gift basket of fruit, cheese, teas, candy (see *Catalogs: Food*)

Mix a recipe of spiced tea (see *Gifts to Make*) and put in a decorated tin, good storage container, or pretty jar.

Gift from your garden

Potted plant, fresh flowers, hanging basket, flower pot, topiary

Fabric, silk, or china flowers

Favorite music or type of reading; video of favorite movie or special interest area

Long-distance telephone call

Seasonal decoration

Jewelry—initialed, pin, earrings, necklace, bracelet, pendant, ring

Personalized key ring

Refrigerator magnet

Decorated trinket box—tin, crystal, silver

Figurine, small print, or stitchery reminding you of the person

Handcraft

Write a note telling what her friendship means to you.

✎ MAN—BASIC ✐

These ideas are just a beginning; so be sure to check *Gift Ideas: Bachelor; Adult—Basic;* and appropriate interest categories.

Pocket knife, multipurpose folding tool

Belt buckle, belt caddy

Tie, neck scarf, tie rack (maybe one that rotates)

Shirt—sport, dress, knit, rugby, flannel

Workout suit, sweatshirt

Handkerchiefs (monograms are nice, but no-iron fabric is nicer!)

Travel kit, soft luggage, garment bag

Calendar filled in with family's or friends' birthdays, anniversaries, and special occasions

Cosmetics, cologne, after-shave lotion; valet

Electric shoe polisher
Jewelry—neck chain, bracelet, cuff links, watch, ring, tie tack
Book on being a man today, fatherhood, male "mid-life crisis," relationships
Coupons for yard work, car wash, etc.
Reclining chair
Magazine subscription
Amagift—catalog of several dozen gifts for men from which he chooses one. You purchase the album and present it to him. He then (unaware of the price) orders the item he wants directly from Amway by returning a card in the back of the album. Shipping has already been paid. (Gourmet Gifts, Sweets & Treats, and albums of mixed gifts in various price ranges are also offered.) Available from Amway distributors (check your local telephone book under Amway).

❧ MOTORCYCLIST ❧

Leather anything—clothes, riding pants (different grades of safety and durability); helmets with intercoms, cassette player, CB, radar detector, visor, full-face; riding gloves, steel-toe boots (for safety); saddlebags, hard bags; sheepskin seat cover; drink holders; safety locks, alarm system; rain gear

❧ MUSICIAN ❧

Adapt these ideas to the particular instrument or talent of your musician. *Catalogs: Music & Movies* includes audio and video cassettes of music and concerts, LP albums, CDs, instruments, accessories, and musical gifts. Handmade instruments are listed under *Catalogs: Handcrafts*.

Lessons (also available on video and cassette)
Metronome, pitch pipe
Music stand, carrying case for music stand, beverage holder, or light tray that attaches to stand; clip to hold music on stand
Antique instrument
Tickets to concert or musical program
Opera glasses
Tape a recital or program in which he performs.
Gift certificate to music store or catalog
Caricature of musician using art prints or magazine picture and inserting face of your friend.
Carrying case for instrument, identification label, new strap for case; instrument polish
Briefcase for music
Self-inking stamp or address labels for labeling music
Music storage cabinet, files
Book on famous artist in friend's favorite medium; book or video on technique; history of favorite hymns, songs, or symphonies
New Illustrated Family Hymn Book (Hal Leonard Publishing, 1992) including designs from the Hallmark collection; arranged for piano, voice, and guitar

Subscription (see *Magazines: Music*)
Cassette tape in particular field of interest—organ, jazz, flute, guitar, etc.
Blank cassette tapes, tape holder or carrier; same for CDs
Music computer software for composing
Holiday sheet music, record, CD, or tape
Headphone that plugs into electric guitar, organ, keyboard
Music dictionary
Collections of music; book-record combinations
Sheet music (old copies are interesting gifts)
Pencils, staff paper
Framed program from concert he has participated in
Custom design a program for a special recital.
Scrapbook of programs and recitals over a period of time
Laminate or frame your friend's favorite piece of music or personal composition
Items with musical symbols—jewelry, note paper, picture, tote bag, posters, mugs, etc.; T-shirt or sweatshirt with a musical logo or slogan
Miniatures of instrument, musician, director
Old or antique hymnal for a church musician
Choral musician—membership in Chorister's Guild, 2834 W. Kingsley Rd., Garland, TX 75041
Drummer—percussion instruments, sticks, practice pad
Guitarist—extra set of strings, variety of picks, guitar strap, cords, capo
Pianist—Piano tuning, piano lamp, needlepoint piano bench cover

ஒ NEEDLEWORKER ஒ

You can adapt these general ideas for your needleworker's specialty — needlepoint, stitchery, knitting, crewel, latch-hook, crochet, quilting, etc. She might enjoy a kit in a new type of needlework also (please be sure kit includes necessary supplies). Additional ideas are found under *Gift Ideas: Seamstress*. Good sources are listed under *Catalogs: Craft Supplies*.

Kits to make
Subscription (see *Magazines: Crafts*)
Gift certificate to needlework store or catalog or frame shop
Tote bag or storage basket for current project
Tracing wheel, tracing paper, design transfer equipment, hot iron transfers
Caddy for armchair or sewing table with detachable litter bag, pin cushion, magnetic strip

Stand that holds pattern and needlework, knitting or crocheting project — for one-handed crafter or those with weak hands
Yarn or thread palette or box (for separating by color)
Magnifying glass (one that hangs around the neck is especially nice), high-intensity magnifying lamp
Portable light (runs on batteries)
Scissors holder or pocket (fabric pouch for storing scissors in sewing bag to protect searching fingers)
Tatting shuttle, thread; thimble, needle threader, crewel needles; blocking board

Lap desk with cushioned bottom, clip for charts, and magnetic strips for scissors and threaded needles

Lessons, pattern books in her area of interest

Frame or make a pillow from a picture she worked.

Embroidery hoop, needles, thread assortment; complete set of DMC embroidery floss with storage box

Book easel with attached frame for current project, utility tray for supplies, magazine rack for other project books or magazines

Table clamp and frame to allow working alongside a table

Light box to backlight one's work (great for dark fabrics), attaching frame

Good shears, folding scissors, scissors with slanted blade for cut-work and appliqué

Crochet—set of hooks, big cone of crochet cotton

Cross-stitch—Graphing software for computer (such as PC Stitch, 800-800-8517), magnetic board for holding patterns, frame for working pieces; items ready to be decorated such as baby bibs, hand towels, bookmarks out of cross-stitch fabric; counted or stamped cross-stitch kit

Knitting—needles, circular needle, stitch and row counter, bobbins, stitch holder, point protectors, ring markers, yarn-end weaver, cable stitch needle, gauge ruler and knitting needle measure

Needlepoint—frame for working pieces; non-bleeding markers, canvas

Quilting—quilting frame or hoop, quilting scissors, quilting needle, long quilting pins, water-erasable marking pen, leather thimble with metal tip or finger guard, templates for patterns, quilting spoon (basting tool), computer software for designing patterns (PC Quilt, Electric Quilt, and Quilter's Design Studio are a few available), extra long tape measure (100 feet), T-square ruler, fabric grips, cushioned quilter's pressing and squaring board, quilt soap for heirloom quilts

❧ NEW PARENTS ❧

Sometimes you might want to honor the parents in addition to the new baby by giving one of these gifts. These are especially appropriate for the parents when number three, four, etc. come along. See also *Gift Ideas: Baby.*

Sterling silver diaper pin for mother to wear

Mother's basket—filled with her favorite scents, perfume, soaps, bath crystals, candles, teas, candies, etc.

Coupons for baby-sitting

Family genealogy with baby's name included

"Cents off" coupons for disposable diapers

Donation to charity in child's name

Gift certificate to nice restaurant or entertainment event (offer to baby-sit!)

Offer to keep other children when father needs to go to hospital

Maid service once a week; diaper service

Clothing suitable for nursing

Frozen meals for when they are too tired to cook; take dinner to them.

Cabinet door latches, caps for electrical outlets, door gate

Child carrier for parent's bicycle

Portable telephone, monitor with intercom for baby's room

Loan parents baby equipment.
Rocking chair
Subscription to parenting magazine (see *Magazines: Family Life*)
Book on parenting, first aid, child development, bedtime stories, devotionals for parents; family medical guide
Potted plant, tree, or rose bush
Camera, film, photograph album, picture frame
Camcorder, VCR, blank videos
Gift certificate for massage or personal pampering (hair dresser, etc.)

❧ NURSING HOME RESIDENT ❧

The needs and wants of nursing home residents are often so simple that we feel apologetic and end up frustrated trying to select a "larger" gift. In general, they enjoy something to cheer up the room and anything that brings a visitor with it. Be aware that fire regulations may prevent plastic items from being kept in the rooms and that space for displaying items is often limited. Depending upon the health of the resident, check *Gift Ideas: Retirement Home Resident; Special Health Needs;* or other categories for more ideas. Helpful sources are listed under *Catalogs: Special Needs*.

Fresh flowers in vase, small potted plant, hanging basket
Note paper, pretty postcards with stamps
Wall calendar with large numbers, pretty pictures, moon signs
Pretty decoration for wall
Subscription to hometown or church newspaper
Individual magazines rather than subscription
Large-print books or magazine (see *Magazines: Special Needs*)
Large-print telegram (call Western Union at 800-325-6000)
Greetings for birthday or anniversaries from mayor, governor, or president (see *Gift Ideas: Anniversaries* for details)
Go Christmas caroling at the home (children's voices are especially welcome) and take simple refreshments (if allowed) or take a group to sing or perform any time of the year.
Visit often even if the patient doesn't respond to your visit. Sometimes the patient receives more consistent care if the nursing home staff knows someone checks in frequently.
Install a private telephone. Telephone often.
Send a taped letter.
Plan a trip out of home (if allowed) for dinner, movie, visit at a home.
Decorate the room for a holiday. (check home's fire regulations; plastic and paper decorations are sometimes banned)
Give a small party in the nursing home. Take a picnic lunch to eat on the patio.
Do his shopping for him.
Anything made by children or grandchildren or made especially for resident
Photo wheel with lots of family pictures
Collage photo frame with pictures of family, old friends
Small bulletin board (change items on it frequently)
Wheelchair caddy or carrying bag

Folding TV or bedside table on wheels

Lap desk, pens, pencils

Lighted magnifying glass

Assorted greeting or holiday cards with stamped envelopes

Cassette recorder, radio, TV with earphones (put permanent identification on it or check it with desk)

Pretty pillowcases

Lap robe, synthetic sheepskin throw, afghan; soft, washable blankets

Washable foam rubber cushion and side pillows for bed, chair, or wheelchair

Washable bedroom slippers

Personalized clothing labels; handkerchiefs, tissue box cover; toilet articles, bath powder, room fresheners, body lotion, cologne, after-shave lotion

Crossword puzzle books, dominoes, playing cards, bean bag toss

Box of hard candies in sealed container

Homemade food (with permission) in metal tin to keep it fresh

Fresh fruit (with permission)—bananas, grapes, any easy-to-eat fruit

Coin purse with coins (take a few each time rather than leaving a lot since coins "disappear" easily)

Box of flexible straws

For Women—Lacy, back-closing hospital gown; front-opening wash-and-wear dress, brunch coat, robe, nightgown; hose—knee or ankle length; socks, slippers; jewelry; shawl, cardigan sweater; zipper pull

For Men—Pajamas, robe, socks, house slippers; sports shirt; wash-and-wear cardigan sweater; tie, tie tack, belt; wallet with plenty of photo space (include photos)

❦ THE ORGANIZER ❦

If a person is organized in one area of his life, he often likes to be in all areas. Humor him with organizers for a "pet peeve" area or one he hasn't tackled yet.

Removable self-stick notes; cube of memo paper

Personalized memo pads, pencils, stationery, telephone message pads

Shower dispenser that pumps shampoo, liquid soap, conditioner

Filing cabinet; card file, coupon organizer, car document organizer for glove compartment (labeled for insurance papers, owner's manual, service record); desk drawer or desk top organizers (pencil holders, memo paper holder, stacking trays); storage boxes for computer disks, videos, audio cassettes

Bicycle storage racks, sports equipment storage racks (special ones for baseball, tennis, golf, etc.)

Computer software for personal accounting, income tax preparation, recipes, home inventory, activity scheduling, investments and family finances, mailing lists and labels, spreadsheet, database, road atlas, diet planner

Rolodex organizer (electronic file for business cards, reminder notes, call sheet, monthly calendar, currency exchange, etc.)

One-day-at-a-time calendar, perpetual calendar for birthdays and anniversaries, daily planner notebook

Calendar personalized with important anniversaries, birthdays, events (call Uniquely Yours calendar at 800-551-1224)

Photo album, scrapbook; photo marker (to mark on photographs or in albums)

Storage units or space savers for closet, kitchen, bathroom
cabinets; shoe racks, turntables; belt, tie, or scarf
hangers; stacking skirt or pants hangers; hanging or
stackable clothes bags, sweater bags or storage boxes,
shoe bags or boxes
Shelves for the garage, attic, closet, pantry
Shelves that attach to inside of doors
Label maker
Clear plastic storage boxes with airtight (bug-proof) covers for attic and
basement storage; special containers for slides, negatives
Computer program for producing slide labels such as CRADOC Caption-
Writer (602-945-2001) or for inventorying slides or photos
New city or state map
Notebook for keeping track of expenses, mileage
Telephone conversation recorder, microcassette recorder to carry in pocket or
purse for recording reminders to yourself
Portable desktop laminator; time/date stamper
Attaché case

❧ OUTDOORS LOVER ❧

Whether your outdoors lover belongs to a birding group or hikes mountain
trails, you will find a gift for him or her here. For other, more specific ideas,
see *Gift Ideas: Backpacker; Boater; Camper; Cyclist; Fisherman;* or
Hunter. Gift sources are listed under *Catalogs: Outdoors.*

Membership in a conservation organization such as
☐ *Sierra Club*, Box 7959, San Francisco, CA 94120-9943.
☐ *National Wildlife Federation*, 1400 16th St. NW, Washington, DC
20077-9964 (800-432-6564).
☐ *Ducks Unlimited*, One Waterfowl Way, Memphis, TN 38120.
☐ *Cousteau Society*, 870 Greenbrier Circle, Ste. 402, Chesapeake, VA
23320
Subscription (see *Magazines: Outdoors* or *Animals, Birds, Fish & Wildlife;*
most state wildlife agencies have magazines)
Rainforest Preservation Kit—$20 from National Wildlife Federation (address
above), represents purchase of 100 square feet bordering on existing
rainforest parks in Costa Rica, poster, map, information on rainforests.
Book on birds, wildlife, first aid, snakes, trees, wildflowers, stars, trails,
campsites, adventurers, solar cooking, minerals, shells, geology
Peterson's or Audubon Society's field guides to animal tracks, birds, shells,
butterflies, mammals, reptiles, rocks, trees, insects, wildflowers, stars
Audio recordings of nature sounds
Topographic quadrangle maps from U.S. Geological Survey, Map Sales, Box
25286, Denver, CO 80225 (303-236-7477)
Glasses, mugs, picture, print, jewelry, notecards, hat, T-shirt with outdoor
motif
Make first-aid kit in small plastic box with disinfectant, adhesive tape, sterile
cotton or gauze, aspirin, burn and chap ointment, insect repellent, folding scissors, first-aid book, Band-Aids, pre-moistened tissues, instant
cold compress.

Survival kit in light backpack—waterproof matches, candle, map, compass, 100 feet of strong fishing line or copper wire, dehydrated food and beverages, signal mirror, whistle, antiseptic bandages, reflective blanket, cup, parka or poncho, extra socks, knife

Compass, range finder

Binoculars (auto-focus is a new feature for continuous sharp focus)

Solar-powered or waterproof watch (for rain storms); combination altimeter, barometer, thermometer, stopwatch, watch

Pocket camera, camera harness, watertight camera bag, telephoto lens for camera

Small cassette recorder for recording nature sounds

Pocket barometer-altimeter, wind chill meter, wind speed meter

UV sensometer (measures intensity of ultra violet rays and tells what strength sunscreen to use)

Camp stool with pockets, folding chair or seat

Mosquito net, mosquito coils, insect repellent

Cot, hammock, sleeping bag, tent

Ensolite pads (light, water resistant), air cushion, or mattress; drawstring stuff bag, equipment bag, or tote bag (nylon or waterproof)

Fanny pack that holds water bottles

Backpack, child carrier backpack, or day pack

Waterproof tarp

Beach umbrella, chair

Rope hoist

Air horn, signal mirror

Waterless hand cleaner

Picnic blanket (washable), space blanket, all-weather blanket

Waterproof flashlight, pocket-size flashlight with powerful beam, swivel light on headband for night hiking

Fluorescent or propane lantern and extra bulbs or fuel canisters

Repair kit—sturdy needles with large eyes, a few yards of strong nylon or Dacron thread, thin fishing line, small roll of copper wire, nylon repair tape, polyethylene tape for mending any surface

Clothing—Fanny pack, ankle wallet; embroidered or hand-painted denim shirt; parka (hooded is nice), poncho, windbreaker; warm socks (top quality virgin wool, synthetic/wool blend), electric socks; hiking boots, tennis shoes, snowshoes; boot jack; electric footwear drier; light cotton work gloves, leather gloves, removable wool glove liner; hand warmer; bandanna, wool scarf; warm hat (wool), sun hat, head net (to keep bugs away); good quality sunglasses; insulated, or silk underwear; rainsuit (GORE-TEX and nylon covered with neoprene are first rate); down-insulated vest, jacket; wool shirt or jacket, chamois shirt; wool or heavy-duty pants, jeans; beachwear — bathing suit, cover-up, beach towel, beach bag, beach shoes; for children — bright red or yellow (easy to spot) jacket, shirt, stocking cap or hat; whistle

Eating Equipment — Flat G.I. can opener; thermos, ice chest, collapsible water jug; box of large trash bags; swiss Army knife or pocket knife—carbon steel or stainless steel blades; folding drinking cup; waterproof matches; wild game or outdoor cookbook; portable grill; nesting cookware, dishes; picnic basket, unbreakable plates and silverware; insulated canteen or vacuum server, bota; solar oven, solar tea jug

✎ PERSON LIVING ABROAD ✎

Sometimes it's the little things a person misses most—like her favorite brand of hot sauce or jeans. A gift for a person overseas takes special consideration, i.e., following postal and customs regulations into the country of residence and weighing the cost of shipment against the cost of the gift itself. American military personnel and families often have a wide selection of American goods available in the PX, but missionaries and other employees may long for the latest album of a favorite singer or a magazine from the states. See also *Gift Ideas: Traveler*.

Hometown T-shirt
Latest American-style clothing
English language books
Subscription to a hometown newspaper or American magazine
Familiar brands of cosmetics, toothpaste, soap, cigarettes
Food or other items not easily found there (soft toilet paper is one commonly mentioned)
Packages of dried food — spaghetti sauce, chili seasoning mix, etc.
Small cassette or CD player; tape (video or audio) from family and friends (be sure they have access to a compatible American brand tape player)
Tape of favorite sports team playing (or series of games)
Pictures from home
Art history book on country of residence, book of favorite cartoons
Guidebooks for the area (more are usually available in the states than in the particular country)
Electric current converter
Air mail stationery
Dictionary or phrase book of the language of the country (cross-referenced with English); foreign language lessons on cassette or video
Homemade cookies (bar kind that won't crumble) or candy (kinds that last a long time) packed in airtight coffee cans
Money to buy souvenirs of the area or to purchase necessary household or clothing items that would be prohibitive to ship

✎ PETS & PET LOVERS ✎

I sometimes think pet toys bring more pleasure to the pet owner than to the pet. Below are ideas for either.

Pet car seat, pet carrier
Fancy collar, tags
Leash, harness leash, trolley (attaches to tree to keep dog in yard), self-retracting leash
Bicycle dog exerciser
Toys, catnip toys for cats
Dog sweater
Pet furniture — something to climb, scratching post, fancy cage, bed, pillow, cushion; pet door
Personalized feeding dishes, placemats, automatic feeders on timers, wall-

mounted food dispenser, food bowls on a stand for tall dogs
Reflective clothing for walking dog after dark
Cookie cutters, cake pans in animal shape
Brush, comb, claw clipper; motorized brush or hand vacuum for cleaning pet hair off furniture
T-shirt, cross-stitch, mug, keychain, bumper sticker, household accessories (clock, dishes, pillows, linens, etc.) with appropriate pet on it
Pet magazine; book or video of training, care, different breeds; subscription (see *Magazines: Animals, Birds, Fish & Wildlife*)
Grooming accessories, training gear, tickets to pet store
Electronic training mat (for sofa or other forbidden place) that teaches pet to stay off; invisible fence and collar
Donation to the local Society for the Prevention of Cruelty to Animals (SPCA) or animal care shelter
Aquarium decorations, color bar over fluorescent lights, hanging thermometer
Gift certificate to fish shop or pet store
Bird or gerbil cage accessories such as ladders, bells
Pet treats, treat storage jar

✎ PHOTOGRAPHER ✎

Whether a person mainly takes snapshots at family occasions or tries to rival *National Geographic*, you'll find a gift idea here. For those who develop their own film, check out the darkroom equipment ideas. For most gift ideas, you will want to know the brand of camera, and the size and type (slides or prints) of film used. Look under *Catalogs: Photography* for sources.

Subscription (see *Magazines: Photography*)
Book or manual on technique, special effects, developing, exposure, film, famous photographs, photographers, etc.
Tuition for photography course
Tickets to special photography exhibit
Gift certificate to picture frame shop, photography store, or film developing store
Have slides, photographs, or movies converted to video.
Have some of her photographs enlarged or printed on T-shirt, plate, Christmas ornament, puzzle, poster, or calendar
Computer program for producing slide labels such as CRADOC Caption-Writer (602-945-2001) or for inventorying slides or photos (or the income from each print or slide)
Tripod, around-the-neck tripod for camcorder or video camera
Panoramic camera
Photograph album, picture frame
Negative and slide files, sleeves, pages
Film; prepaid mailers for film developing
Camera bag, case—large enough for extra lenses, film accessories; over shoulder or fanny pack for photo gear
Camera bracket
Video film editor, splicing tape
X-ray-safe film bag for travel
Disposable underwater camera

Camera strap, harness

Projection screen, slide projector, slide trays, sorter, editor, or lighted viewer

Camcorder, video camera, blank video cassettes

Slide or video cassette title lettering set

Filters—all kinds (need to know lens size); light meter

Lens (know camera size, brand, and model); lens hood, lens case, lens cleaner

Small strobe unit, slave trigger for strobe, nicer strobe with head that can be angled, flash extension cable, reflector pads; cable release cord

Cropping guide

Darkroom Equipment—Developing chemicals (find out preferred brand); chemical storage containers; developing trays, tanks, reels; film-changing bag; film washer; photo paper dispenser, photo paper; photo texturizing kit, texture screens; paper trimmer; dry mounting materials; darkroom lamp, safelight; enlarger, enlarger lens enlarging easel; focusing cloth; automatic enlarger timer, digital darkroom timer; contact printer; print drier; slide ready mounts; color processing or slide processing equipment, chemicals, thermometer; kit or chemicals for making prints from slides; cotton gloves, sponge tip tongs; water filter; automatic tray siphon, automatic print washer; darkroom graduate (for measuring); loupe, magnifier; print squeegee, film clips; dodging kit, burn-in kit, vignetter; re-usable film cartridges, bulk film loader; accessory drying rack; retouching colors and equipment

❧ RETIREMENT HOME RESIDENT ❧

Retirement homes are basically apartment complexes with a minimum age requirement. Most residents live there for convenience rather than because of a physical reason. Therefore, many of your gift ideas will come from *Adult —Basic; Man—Basic; Woman—Basic;* or special interest categories. Some ideas from *Nursing Home Resident* or *Elderly at Own Home* categories are appropriate also. Some units have kitchens and so open up other gift possibilities. Most apartments are already crammed with mementos and keepsakes; so unless you know an item would make living more enjoyable or comfortable, lean toward the consumable choices.

Home-cooked meals for the freezer (or see Extended Family Home-Cooked Mail-Order Meals in *Catalogs: Food—Assorted*), simple pre-mixed foods

Take person out for dinner (especially a home-cooked one), movie, entertainment.

Terrarium, potted plant; fresh flowers

Restore or copy old photos; photo wheel

Cassette player-recorder or stationery (with stamps) to keep in touch with family or friends; TV, VCR, radio, clock radio

Stained glass window ornament; holiday door, table, or wall decoration

Tickets to sports event, cultural or entertainment event

Tuition for Elderhostel (see *Gift Ideas: Elderly at Own Home*)

Magazine subscription

Greetings for birthday or anniversary from mayor, governor, or president (see *Gift Ideas: Anniversaries*)

Large print books, Bible, magazine (see *Magazines: Special Needs*); books, religious music, or Bible study on tape (see *Catalogs: Books & More* and *Religious*); bookmark (make one!)

Playing cards, checkers, board game, scoring pads and accessories

Small refrigerator, hot plate if apartment does not have a kitchen; toaster-broiler, microwave oven; small coffee pot

Linens, afghan; quilt with children's and grandchildren's names on squares

Decorator telephone, telephone services (see *Adult —Basic*)

Video of favorite movie, area he has visited or would like to visit, historical event, sports competition, etc.

Rent in a mini-storage facility

✎ THE ROMANTIC ✎

If she likes lace and roses, you are safe with a gift from this group.

Classical music

Book of poetry, about the Victorian period or Victorian decorating

Tapestry or satin anything—pillow, jewelry box, travel accessories, check book, cosmetic bag, book cover

Beaded evening purse

Victorian style button covers or jewelry (locket, hand-painted jewelry, cherubs, cloisonné, colored glass, ornate hearts, bow pins, brooch)

Jewelry box or armoire

Feminine lingerie (lots of lace, satin, and silk)

Sweet-smelling body gel, soap, after-bath splash, bubble bath, perfume, cologne, lavender water, rosewater, handmade glycerin soap, French vanilla or lavender potpourri or candles

Perfume atomizer

Pillows with lace or fringe

Linen or lace apron, dresser scarf, roll cover, doily, shawl

Hat or trinket boxes or baskets (any size) covered in fabric

Stationery, notecards, or return address labels with flowers, hearts, hats, lace, ribbon, cherubs; sealing wax and brass seal for letters

Real silk stockings, blouse, dress, slip; camisole, chemise; blouse with lace, high collar, puffy long sleeves; poet's shirt (oversized with puffy sleeves)

Scented or padded satin clothes hangers; sachets, scented drawer liners

Satin or silk pillowcases, sheets

Lace parasol

Candles, Victorian table linens and dishes

Holiday decoration in Victorian style

Ruffled, lace-trimmed, or satin photograph album

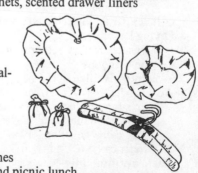

Dried swag with roses and ribbon

Ornate, silverplated desk accessories

Doll or paper dolls in Victorian styles

Wire bird cage (with or without bird!)

Antique rosebushes or a trellis for roses or vines

Wicker basket filled with tablecloth, wine, and picnic lunch

◆ RUNNER/JOGGER/WALKER ◆

You should not "run" out of ideas with this list. Whether your friend is a serious athlete or a playful occasional walker, consider this list. See also *Gift Ideas: Fitness Enthusiast*.

Identification tag (with any medical information)
Subscription (see *Magazines: Sports*)
Book or video on running or race-walking technique, philosophy of running,
    aerobics, other topics of interest
Massage oil, liniment
Certificate for professional massage; hour's paid massage at spa
Sports bag; fanny pack, wrist pack
Jogging suit or shorts, sports bra, athletic socks; reflective clothing; knitted
    cap, gloves for winter jogging; visor

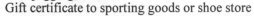

    Gift certificate to sporting goods or shoe store
    Shoe laces, key holder that attaches to shoe laces, jog-
        ging shoes, heel repair kit
    Ring-style lap counter
    Slogan T-shirt; sweatbands (wrist and head)
    Leg weights, hand weights
    Pedometer
    Digital stop watch
    Wrist radio or earphones
    Non-spill water pitcher or thermos, small ice chest
Entry fee to race-walking or running competition; go along to competition to
    cheer them on.

◆ SCUBA DIVER ◆

If your scuba diver rents his equipment, you can build up his inventory from the Basic Equipment list. If he owns his gear, the Accessories list would be a better place to look. Find catalogs under *Sports* or *Outdoors*.

Subscription to diving magazine or one on the world underwater (see *Magazines: Water Sports* or *Science*)
Book or video on diving, underwater world, reefs, *Scuba Diving Handbook*
    or *Underwater Adventures,* both by Paul McCallum (Betterway Books,
    1507 Dana Ave., Cincinnati, OH 45207-1005, 800-289-0963)
Gift certificate to diving equipment store or catalog
Diving lessons
Underwater camera equipment, watch; spear-fishing equipment; scoops,
    sieve scoops
Waterproof wallet, duffel bag, gear bag
Accessories—Diving watch; wetsuit shampoo, defog solution; mask strap,
    fin strap, knife strap; snorkel lock; rubber marking paint, rubber preser-
    vative; international "Divers Below" flag for boat; dive markers; catch
    bag, carry bags; underwater writing slate, emergency cue cards; under-
    water camera, film
Basic Equipment—Neoprene wetsuit, drysuit, jacket, pants, T-shirt, gloves,
    hood; grabber gloves or boots; thinsulate undergarments, socks; depth or
    pressure gauge, compass, thermometer, console for gauges; hose pro-

tector; CO_2 cartridge for air device; cylinder, backpack, regulator, spare air canister; face mask, fins, snorkel; buoyancy compensator; diving vest; repetitive dive charts; underwater lights; safety whistle; diver's knife; hooks, buckles for belt; weight belts, weights

✎ SEAMSTRESS ✎

The right equipment can turn some tasks into hobbies. More ideas for crafts such as quilting or cross-stitch are found under *Gift Ideas: Needlework*. The magazines listed under *Magazines: Crafts* often have the directions for various projects each month to give an ongoing supply of ideas. See *Catalogs: Craft Supplies* for sources.

Sewing machine, serger, pleater for smocking; sewing machine cover
Cabinet for sewing machine (pay for installing machine in cabinet, too!)
Sewing bench with storage; chair on wheels
Freestanding lamp or lamp to clamp on cabinet
Attachments for sewing machine — buttonhole maker, decorative stitches, creative feet (ribbon foot, sequin foot, satinedge, topstitching, elastic, etc.), Jean-A-Ma-Jig (for sewing on heavy fabric like denim), etc. (know model number and make of machine)
Subscription to craft or sewing magazine (see *Magazines: Crafts*)
Book or video on sewing, tailoring, appliqué, alterations, etc.
Sewing lessons (available at many fabric stores in all ability levels from beginning to tailoring)
Video on sewing techniques such as *Suddenly You're Sewing* by Daphne Maxwell Reid and McCall's Patterns (four videos and patterns to teach sewing basics)
Personalized fabric labels ("Made for you by...")
Gift certificate to fabric store
Gift certificate for sewing machine cleaning or scissors sharpening
Length of material (up to two yards for child, three yards for adult)
Button covers in various styles, assortment of buttons
Sewing kit, thread box
Magnetic tray for keeping pins, scissors, snaps, etc., from spilling
Good quality scissors, pinking shears (maybe the rolling kind), shears for cutting knits or nylon, rotary cutter for straight edges, left-handed scissors for a lefty, bent trimmer (blades at an angle)
Pattern weights; cutting board or table, self-healing gridded cutting mat
Long wall mirror; body form
Pin cushion (wrist type, magnetic, or make one); silver or decorative thimble
Steam iron, fabric steamer, ironing press

Useful Gadgets

Tape measure, metal yardstick, curved measuring gauge, curve ruler, pressure-sensitive tape measure, transparent ruler; tailor's chalk, marking pencils, tracing paper, tracing wheel; hem marking clips, hem marker on stand; top-stitch or zipper guide; box of new pins, ball-point pins for knits; hem-bonding tape; bias tape maker; press mitt, press ham, sleeve board, needleboard for pressing piled fabrics, press cloth to prevent scorching or shine; point turner; seam ripper; appliqué scissors, nippers;

knit fabric mender; baste-and-sew glue; body ruler pattern fitter, pants pattern fitter; pattern storage box (decorate it yourself); fabric eraser; travel sewing kit; extra bobbins, bobbin box; needle threader, assortment of needles; assorted colors of good quality thread; little boxes to hold pins, snaps, buttons, etc.

ᕔ SECURITY & SAFETY CONSCIOUS ᕗ

The reality of today's world is that more of us need to take precautions for personal safety. Here are some items for the home and for carrying when alone or in areas of questionable security. Security measures should be selected so as to interfere the least with a person's lifestyle (or the item may go unused). For instance, a smoke detector that can have its battery tested by shining a flashlight up onto it is more likely to be regularly tested than one that requires standing on a chair to reach a button.

Dues in a community patrol association or civic club
Mail slot to inside of house
Deadbolts for doors, door peephole or Doorscope, door alarm, door chain, locking screen door
Automatic timer for lights in home, sensor that turns lights on at dusk and off at dawn, heat-, motion-, or noise-activated light for porch, driveway, or yard area
Battery-powered emergency light in major traffic area of house
Porch lights
Plug-in, rechargeable flashlight
Electric garage door opener
Barking dog alarm that is triggered by noise
Smoke detector, fire extinguisher
Fire escape ladder
Fire-safe security file or box
Large, clearly visible house numbers
Small whistle on necklace, hand-held siren or spray deterrent (mace) for purse
Alarm system for the home, motion-breaking glass detector that plugs into AC outlet
Solid core wood or metal outside doors; locks for sliding doors; storm windows or storm doors
Secret storage containers that look like books, cleaning products, etc.
Course in self-defense, karate, rape prevention, firearms use and safety, swimming, CPR, first aid (Red Cross has good courses in many of these)
Membership in American Automobile Association (check local telephone book or see *Gift Ideas: Traveler* for address) or other travel club that has emergency road service
Cellular telephone, CB for car; automobile alarm, anti-theft devices such as steering column lock, locking gas cap; remote controlled car security light —turns on car's interior lights from 50 feet away (see Company of Women under *Catalogs: Smorgasbord*); key ring with flashlight attached
Back-up light/beeper for car (beeps when vehicle is in reverse)
Telephone answering machine; home telephone tap detector, voice-changing telephone to discourage unwanted calls

Kit for testing one's home for toxic substances such as radon, carbon monoxide, lead, etc.

Non-slip ice mat for steps in winter

Electric engraving pen for engraving ID number (from police department) on valuables

❧ SILVER GIFTS ❧

Silver can make any occasion one to be remembered. You can choose between sterling, silver-plate, and non-tarnish silver-plate or mix with crystal for an elegant gift.

Jewelry—spoon ring, charm, pendant, bracelet, earrings, chain, pin, stickpin, cuff links, tie tack, medallion, ring

Belt buckle

Comb and brush set, vanity tray

Baby items—teething ring, cup, eating utensils, jewelry, diaper pins, comb and brush set

Pendant or cross made from woman's silverware pattern

Tooth fairy box

Picture frame

Cigarette box, lighter, silent butler

Flower pot, bud vase, centerpiece with frog

Trivet, napkin rings, coasters, salt and pepper shakers

Antique silver items

Revere bowl, compote, candy dish, relish dish, or jelly dish with spoon

Candelabra, candlesticks

Casserole with removable glass liner

Covered vegetable dish, serving dishes

Trays, bread tray

Water goblets, wine glasses, jigger

Cream and sugar set, gravy boat, butter dish

Flatware holders for a party (hold up to 12 forks, spoons, knives), flatware, steak knives, carving set; complete a set of flatware—for hard-to-find or discontinued silver or silver-plate flatware patterns, contact Walter Drake Silver & China Exchange (Drake Bldg., Colorado Springs, CO 80940) or Replacements, Ltd. (see *Catalogs: Housewares*)

Have damaged silver piece repaired or antique piece resilvered.

Demitasse spoons, pastry set

Coffee service, tea service

Christmas tree ornaments; bell; trinket box

Pacific cloth or flannel bags for silver items, silver polish

❧ SINGLE WOMAN ❧

More gift ideas are given in *Adult—Basic; Woman—Basic; Security & Safety Conscious;* and special interest categories.

Membership in American Automobile Association (check local telephone book or see *Gift Ideas: Traveler* for address) or other travel club that has emergency road service

Big flashlight, extra batteries
Course in karate, self-defense, rape prevention
Small whistle on necklace, hand-held siren or spray deterrent (mace) for purse
CB radio, cellular telephone for car
Course in basic auto or home repairs
Names of trusted auto mechanic, repairmen
Jumper cable, emergency kit, or locking gas cap for car
Coupons for car wash, yard work, maid service, etc.
Tickets to movie theater, bowling alley, ice cream parlor, miniature golf, etc.
Two tickets to sporting or entertainment event
Take her out for dinner or have her over for dinner.
Single serving meals for freezer (see Extended Family Home-Cooked Mail-Order Meals under *Catalogs: Food—Assorted*)
Book or video on hobby, money management, adult development
Jar opener; stepstool
Anything made just for her—throw pillow, cross-stitched picture, custom earrings, knit sweater, etc.
Enlarge a photograph from a memorable event.
Anything personalized—T-shirt, mug, jewelry, key ring, beach towel, tote bag, etc.
Linens—bed, bath, table, kitchen
Popcorn popper, small coffee pot, etc. (see *Appendix: Small Electric Appliances*)
Tuition for leisure course—photography, scuba diving, ceramics, gourmet cooking, etc.; lessons in ballroom or country western dancing
Money
Cosmetics (collections, scented bath products)
Potted plant, terrarium, aquarium
Take her photograph; paint her portrait; write her a song or poem.
Personalized car license plates; bumper sticker or license plate holder with college logo
Magazine subscription
Daily planner, calendar with important dates already filled in
TV, radio, alarm clock, VCR
Telephone answering machine; comedy answering machine messages
Wine, candy, flowers, video, cassette tape, or CD
Holiday or seasonal ornaments or decorations
Card table, folding chairs, TV trays
Dishes, glasses for entertaining
Barbecue grill, ice chest, picnic basket
A pet (with permission)

❧ SNOW SKIER ☙

Find gift sources under *Catalogs: Outdoors* and *Sports & Recreation*.

Subscription (see *Magazines: Winter Sports*)
Book or video on skiing technique, competitions, *Downhill Skiing Handbook*, by Paul McCallum and Christine Lariviere McCallum (Betterway Books, 1507 Dana Ave., Cincinnati, OH 45207-1005, 800-289-0963)

Ski machine for strengthening necessary muscles before getting on the slopes
Book of ski lift tickets, season pass for ski area
Transportation to and from favorite resort
Clothing — Knit cap, ski mask, wool scarf, head band, ear muffs, earflap
wool hat; ski helmet for children; ski gloves, leather mittens, waterproof
gloves, glove liners, hand warmer; goggles (fog-free), sunglasses with
wind visor and green or yellow lenses, goggles glove (storage pouch to
prevent scratches; hooks to jacket); ski boots, boot bag,
boot tree, hiking boots, after-ski boots, snow gaiters;
boot drier; boot-carry strap; heavy socks, sock liners,
knee socks, leg gaiters, sock warmers (battery-powered); silk underwear or glove liners (very warm);
long underwear, thermal underwear; sweater — front-
zip turtleneck, turtleneck, or other kind; stretch pants,
insulated ski pants, warm-up suit, ski bib; flannel
slacks, blazer, sport jacket, shirt; parka, nylon wind
shirt; headlight, face shield; fanny pack, belt pouch

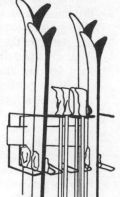

Equipment — Wine bota (flask), drink belts; new poles,
skis; pole grips with watch and stopwatch built in; ski
bag, ski lock, ski ties or carrier; car rack or home storage rack for skis; ski wax kit; lip and sun cream; thermometer

❧ SPECIAL HEALTH NEEDS ❧

Hearing Impaired
Besides ideas from other categories, these gifts may be especially appreci-
ated. See *Catalogs: Special Needs* for sources.
Course in lip-reading, sign language
Subscription to *Deaf American* (see *Magazines: Special Needs*)
Items such as books, T-shirts, stationery, mugs, poster, jewelry, etc., with
sign language on them
Books about famous deaf persons, latest research
Aid-o-phone (to carry to use on a telephone), clarity enhancing telephone
Vibrator wake-up device or alarm clock
Clock with flashing lights
Sentry or sound lamp—device hooked up to react to the sound of the door-
bell, TV, baby crying, etc.
Telecommunication machine — teletypewriter attached to telephone that
transmits to similar machine on another telephone
Telephone amplifier
Personal television amplifier (enables television sound to remain at normal
level for others in room); closed captioned system that hooks to TV,
VCR, cable TV, or satellite receiver to supply captions and/or sound
Sign language dictionary

Mentally Ill
The needs of each person will vary depending upon the degree of illness and
where he lives. Persons with mental impairment will often enjoy the
same gifts as others in their age group. Lean toward the simpler items

and avoid the overly abstract and complicated ones. Children will enjoy the same clothing fads as other children, but select toys that are not too advanced so that they do not frustrate the child.

If the recipient lives in an institution or home, check with the staff for any regulations or restrictions on items you could bring (see also *Gift Ideas: Nursing Home Resident*). For those with severe disabilities, clothing and personal care items are always appropriate. Look at catalogs in the *Special Needs* section for equipment to assist with unique disabilities.

Fresh fruit; homemade cookies, candy, or cake

Non-perishable food—peanut butter, crackers, nuts, candy, gum, packages of punch or tea

Paper cups and dispenser; party napkins, favors

Any clothing item which is easily laundered—robe, pajamas, dress, socks, bathing suit, shorts, slacks, slippers, sweater, raincoat, underwear, shawl, head scarf, etc.

Make-up or cosmetics of all kinds; comb, brush, mirror

Fancy soap, soap dish; toothbrush, toothpaste

Wheelchair robe, wheelchair caddy

Jewelry, jewelry box

Purse, wallet, coin purse, tote bag

Hair curlers, hair dryer, hair nets, curler bag, ribbons, barrettes

Hanging basket, gardening tools, gloves, seeds, potting soil

Books, magazines, newspaper subscription

Posters, pictures, bulletin board, fresh or silk flowers, anything to brighten the room

Wall clock, clock, clock radio, radio, TV

Lamp, throw pillows, afghan

Art supplies — paper, paints, felt markers, scissors, pencils, glue, rubber stamps, etc.

By-number painting kits, needlecraft kits, bird feeder kit, other craft kit

Sewing notions, fabric, patterns

Tools—hammer, nails, screwdriver, wood chisel, saw, pliers, etc.

Outdoor games — horseshoes, jump rope, basketball, volleyball, baseball, croquet, etc.

Indoor games—bingo, checkers, puzzles, playing cards, etc.

Musical instruments—guitar, harmonica, etc. with instruction books

Song books, tapes, tape player, video cassettes, VCR

Assorted greeting cards, stationery, stamps, pencils, pencil sharpener

Holiday decorations

Physically Disabled

Many physically disabled persons will enjoy gifts from other special interest categories. Here are some ideas that address their unique needs. Of course, the type and extent of a person's disability will influence your choice of gift. Also see *Gift Ideas: Nursing Home Resident* or *Elderly at Own Home*. Catalogs that offer aids for persons with disabilities are found under *Special Needs*.

Take the person out shopping, to entertainment event, to restaurant.

Prepared meals

Non-slip mat to go under cookware for stirring

Shopping bag on wheels, folding shopping cart

Shirt buttoner
Portable cane seat
Wheelchair carry-all, wheelchair beverage carrier
Walker with detachable tray or tote bag
Bedside pouch
Folding cane, decorative cane
Lap desk with pencil tray
Telescoping magnet, reaching tongs
Extending mirror

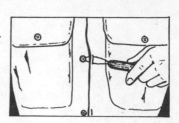

Coaster or ashtray that snaps onto wheelchair or bed railing
Bed ladder for pulling up to a sitting position while in bed
Foot mop
Card shuffler, card holder
Arm for holding telephone receiver
Remote switch for TV, lamp, etc.
Automatic page turner
Doorknob opener
Elastic shoelaces, stocking or sock pull-on, extra-long shoe horn, zipper pull, dressing stick
Front closure lingerie, clothing
Harness for one-handed fishing
Weighted ballpoint pen for writing without exerting pressure
Safety Aids — Portable raised toilet seat, safety arm rest for toilet; power failure security light, smoke detector with emergency light; bathtub safety rail or mat; bath chair, bath lift; railing for outside steps; telephone dialer stick; telephone holder hand clip; (see also *Gift Ideas: Security & Safety Conscious*)
Kitchen Helpers — Pan handle holder; curved butcher knife; swivel eating utensils, thick-handled utensils, gripper-handled utensils; suction-base food chopper, grinder, plate; serving cart with casters; mounted jar opener; one-handed jar, can, or bottle opener; box-top opener; vacuum cup for drinking in semi-reclined position; two-handled mug with spout

Physically Ill

To cheer up someone at home in bed or in the hospital, consider something from this list as well as items from other special interest categories.
Book satchel to hang on side of bed; bed caddy, fabric bag to tie to hospital bed railing
Fill bag with little gifts for each day — lipstick, cologne, playing cards, dry shampoo, baby powder, hand lotion, toothbrush, pencil and note pad, small book, card, small toys
Small bell to ring for assistance
Pajamas, gown, robe, tennis socks (to wear in bed), washable slippers; shawl
Nice bed sheets, pillowcases (flannel ones are great for winter)
Soft pillows in cheerful fabric (14" square or 9" x 18", stuffed with thin layer of polyester filling)
Light reading, audio or video, magazine or newspaper
Cards, cards, cards (include cartoon or funny clipping or make a card with words appropriate to the situation cut from magazines)
Shallow basket for card holder
Roll of masking tape so hospital patient can tape cards on wall

Crossword puzzle or maze book; game for one or two; bingo, playing cards, checkers, etc.; book of solitaire card games and quality playing cards

Handle for pulling up to a sitting position while in bed

Lap desk (with pencil tray); bed tray; prop-up pillow

Personalized cup, mug, glass, plate

Colorful or seasonal paper napkins for bed tray

Visit for no special reason; just take time to be there.

Bring patient's favorite ice cream, gelatin, custard, etc., or basket of fresh fruit (with doctor's permission), or fresh flowers in a vase

Take a party to hospital — colorful napkins, silver flatware, special food (depending on patient's diet).

Portable cassette or CD player with cassettes or CDs

Especially for Children—Activity book; Comic book or other book, pop-up book, light reading, picture book, or storybook; Art box—coloring books, tablet, crayons, scissors, glue, tape, colored pencils and pens, pipe cleaners, etc.; Origami book and special colored paper; Puzzle, brain teaser, game of skill; Paper dolls, doll, stuffed animal; Autograph pillow or animal for visitors to sign, little guest book; Catalog or old sewing or wallpaper pattern book to cut up; Paint-by-number kit, art kit, tracing supplies; Hand puppet; Kaleidoscope, octascope, or dragon's eye; Xylophone; Small cars, toys; View-Master, reels; Children's movie on video; Game software for the computer; A pet (with parental permission) — perhaps a fish tank or gerbil that can stay in the room

Visually Impaired

A person who is visually impaired has not necessarily lost all sight. For some, large-print and Braille or raised dot items are useful aids. Children will benefit from a wide range of sounds, textures, and shapes. For items with these characteristics, look under *Catalogs: Special Needs*.

Talking books, Braille books or magazines, books on tape (see *Catalogs: Special Needs* and *Books & More*)

Children's Braille books, scratch and sniff books, touch and feel books

Subscription to Braille magazine (see *Magazines: Special Needs*)

Enrollment in Choice Magazine Listening, P.O. Box 10, Port Washington, NY 11050 (free service providing selected magazine articles, stories, and poetry on cassettes for the blind)

Braille Book Review, National Library Service for the Blind and Physically Handicapped, Library of Congress, 10 1st St. SE, Washington, DC 20540. Write for free list of Braille books and magazines available through libraries or call 202-707-5104.

Instructional aids, tools, supplies, and books and magazines (Braille, large type, recorded, and computer disk form) are also available from the American Printing House for the Blind, 1839 Frankfort Ave., P.O. Box 6085, Louisville, KY 40206-0085 (502-895-2405).

Book stand

Greeting cards in Braille (see Prophecy Design in *Catalogs: Special Needs*)

Braillegram or large-print telegram (call Western Union at 800-325-6000)

Braille or large-print playing cards or table games such as Monopoly, Scrabble, Chinese checkers, magnetic games

Braille and tactile T-shirts and jewelry
Beep ball (electronic beeping system inside), audible ball (with bell inside)
Special sports equipment for visually impaired
Toys—musical, smooth wooden, stuffed, foam
Cassette recorder, audio tapes
Variable speech control recorder-player
CDs, records, Braille or large-print sheet music, or music lessons
Magnifier—tweezer, over-the-head, foldable, swivel arm,
     lighted, on floor stand, for the thermostat
Light sensor, audicator, print locator, light detector
Modified automotive gauges, equipment
Talking calculator or electronic calculator with Braille
     print-out
Braille counter, Braille or large-print labeling equipment
Braille slate, paper, stylus
Braille typewriter or computer printer
Braille compass, ruler, tape measure (with tactile indicators)
Large-print telephone dial or touch-tone telephone attachment, device that
     speaks the numbers as you dial
Signature guide, writing guide, envelope-addressing guide
Braille or talking watch, clock, alarm clock
Television magnifier
Educational or enlarging computer software (magnifies text and graphics)
Alternative computer keyboards
Speech synthesizer
Talking or large-print thermometer
Magnetic padlock
Smoke detector, motion-activated alarm system for the home
Kitchen timer, pots, blender, mixer, etc., with raised dots on controls; large-
     print digital timer
Slicing guides for cake, pie, bread, meat
Cake caddy (cuts and lifts triangular piece of cake)
Electronic liquid level indicator
Braille cookbook
Automatic needle threader
Sock sorter; aluminum clothing tags (to indicate colors)
Bathtub safety bars or scale with raised dots (or talking or large print)

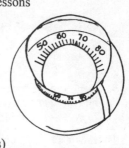

❧ SPORTS FAN ☙

These are ideas for those who prefer to be spectators rather than participants,
but whose loyalty to their team can't be questioned. See *Catalogs: Sports &
Recreation* for some unique gifts.

Tickets to sporting event
Book on major sports figure, sports records
Video of favorite sport or particular event
Subscription (see *Magazines: Sports*)
Baseball cap, cap holder that cleans cap in dishwasher
Varsity-letter-style jacket
Stadium seat or cushion, stadium blanket

Thermos, small ice chest
Binoculars
TV, TV antenna, transistor radio with earphones
Sports equipment
Anything with team's logo on it—T-shirt, jacket, mug, notebook, cap, waste-
    basket, memo pad, pennant, license plate frame, bumper sticker
Key ring, jewelry, figurine, or small print or picture relating to favorite sport
Autographed ball, picture, uniform, etc., from a special player
Electronic baseball encyclopedia

✋ SPORTS & GAMES ✌

Some people just like to be active and test their agility; others love to participate in team activities. Here are some gift ideas for the serious or casual
player. See also individual sports and *Gift Ideas: Fitness Buff*.

Subscription to magazine (see *Magazines: Sports*)
Video or book on technique, famous participants, competitions, or games
Tickets to an exhibition or game
Anything autographed by a professional or famous player of the sport or with
    professional team's logo
Equipment bags
Basic uniform and equipment items, training aids (such as basketball back-
    board, baseball pitching machine)
Fees for participating on a team or for joining a club
Lessons, fee for workshop or sports camp
Novelties with the particular sport motif — T-shirts, bumper stickers,
    watches, puzzles, mugs, etc.

Darts, dart board case with board inside
Burp gun (shoots Ping-Pong balls)
Sports radar gun (for tracking speed of baseball pitch,
    football pass, tennis serve, ski run, etc.)
Velcro ball with catcher's disk
Nerf slingshot (ages six up), Bow 'n Arrow (ages eight
    up), Master Blaster (ages six up), T-Ball set (ages
    five up)
Skateboard, roller skates, skating gloves, knee pads,
    elbow pads, helmet
Air-pressure water gun (for responsible 11-year-olds or older; misuse can be
    dangerous)
Nintendo entertainment system, Game Boy, games, game caddy or carrying
    case, game preserver (plastic case), game light, controller handles, joy-
    stick controller, power glove (controller that fits on top of hand)
Group games such as Taboo, Trivial Pursuit (or extra questions for), Tripoly,
    Pictionary, Scattergories, Split Second, battlefield strategy games (e.g.,
    Axis and Allies), Family Feud, Jeopardy, Life, Play It By Ear (a CD
    game for ages 16 up), Yahtzee
Archery (see also *Gift Ideas: Hunter*)—arrow holder that clamps onto bow
Electronic radio-controlled cars, boats, planes — rechargeable Ni-Cad
    batteries and charger, battery tester, miniature tools, magnifier lamp,
    kits, gift certificate to model store or catalog

Fencing (sabre, foil, epée)—equipment bag, shoes, vest and pants, mask, weapon, old Three Musketeers movie!

In-line skates (such as Rollerblade), crash helmet, knee pads, shin guards, wrist supports, elbow pads; in-line hockey stick, shin guards, pucks, balls; roller poles

Paintball—boots, holsters, camping or survival gear, camouflage clothing, fee for a game, paintball gun, mask or goggles, sport gloves, backpack with supertube pouches

Racquetball—glove, racquet, gym bag, racquet cover, membership in racquetball club

Rock climbing—crampons, high energy food bars, climber's backpack, belay/rappel devices, good sunglasses, workout equipment (for hands, fingers, forearm), rock boots, double boots, winter clothing, ice tools, probe pack, beacon, fanny pack, harness

Soccer—balls, goalkeeper glove, shin guard, padded shorts, socks or hose, goalkeeper jersey, training goal

Target shooting—see *Gift Ideas: Hunter*

Volleyball—knee pads, wrist supports, ball and net set

❧ STOCKING STUFFERS & HANUKKAH GIFTS ❧

Here are some small surprises that will fit nicely inside a Christmas stocking or help round out the Hanukkah shopping. Look for many more under the appropriate age category for children or an interest category for adults.

Children

Anything they have to have, but in a fancy style—underwear, socks, barrettes, hair ribbons, belt, shoe laces, comb, brush, mirror

Decorative or personalized pens or pencils, erasers, crayons, chalk, notepads, coloring book, pencil sharpener, ruler, scissors, decorative rubber stamps

Dreidel; Hanukkah gelt (chocolate coins)

Candy, gum, fruit, favorite snack

Any small toy or game; model or craft kit

Decorated toothbrush; soap sculpture

Bubble bath, shampoo in cute containers

Balloons, jacks, jump rope, marbles, playing cards

Jewelry

Bookmark, small book, book plates

Book of cartoons, holiday story, other favorite subject

CD or cassette tape, movie on video; video cassette on Christmas or Hanukkah or their religious traditions — Brentwood Music (*Mother Goose Gospel*), Maranatha Music (*Kids' Praise* series), Integrity Music, Tyndale (*Superbook* and *Kingdom Adventure* series), Focus on the Family (*McGee and Me*), and Oxford Vision (*Children's Video Bible*) are just a few publishers of wonderful videos for Christian children. *Shalom Sesame* from Children's Television Workshop is a fun-filled series for Jewish children ages two to twelve (800-428-9920).

Packet of coins, currency, or collectibles (stamps, baseball cards, stickers, patches, etc.)

Card announcing a magazine subscription (see *Magazines: Children thru Teens*)

Gift certificate to bowling alley, fast food restaurant, movie theater, video rental store, favorite clothing store, etc.

Christmas ornament (personalized or handmade), small individual menorah

Adult

Notecards, pretty postcards, stationery, stamps, address labels

Pens, pencils, notepads

Wallet-sized photos

Gift certificate for restaurant, car wash, hobby store, long-distance telephone calls, etc.; card announcing a magazine subscription

Bookmark, small book, book plates

Film

Decorative candle or handcraft for office or home

Key chain or key ring

Seatbelt adjuster

Jewelry; comb, compact, lipstick, nail polish

Scented or initialed soap, bath powder, body lotion; small bottles of shampoo, hand lotion, cologne, perfume, or after-shave lotion

Hose, gloves, socks, scarves, belt, small umbrella

Handkerchiefs, purse-size tissue holder

Washable lint remover

Candy, gum, fruit, nuts, favorite canned food (e.g., oysters, bean dip), homemade jelly or relish

Bottle of wine or favorite soft drink

Kitchen utensils, cookie cutters, magnetic memo holders

Small tools for hobby

Golf tees or balls, tennis balls

Gun shells (can't mail these legally with Postal Service; check other services such as UPS); fishing tackle, flies, worms

Flower bulbs, seed packets

Fireplace matches, decorative book matches, cigarette lighter

Thermometers—cooking, indoor-outdoor

Rechargeable batteries; pocket-sized flashlight; pocket calculator

Christmas ornament

Any small gift from other gift categories

❧ SWIMMER ❧

Lessons on swimming or diving

Video or book on technique, famous meets, or famous swimmer

Swimsuit, sweat suit, thongs, cover-up, cap

Underwater watch, stopwatch

Special waterproof pouch that holds a radio for swimming to music

Buoyancy belt for water exercise, underwater lap counter

Goggles (a kind is made that accepts prescription lenses), fins

Kickboard, hand paddles

Tote bag

Small insulated cooler

Snorkeling equipment

Membership in club or YMCA with an Olympic-size pool
Beach towels; towel of viscose that absorbs water, then wrings out to dry again and again
Moisturizing body oil to counteract effects of sun and chlorine

❧ SWIMMING POOL OWNER ☙

Inflatable or foam floats; water games such as water volleyball set; gift certificate for a cleaning or to a store for chemicals and supplies; poolside furniture, plants; storage box for weather-sensitive pool or patio accessories like chair cushions or vinyl pool toys; floating beverage holder; life preserver, long pole; outdoor, waterproof clock or thermometer; candles that float in pool for party; solar insulating cover or cover for winter; solar pool purifier

❧ TEACHER ☙

A gift from this list is sure to rate with your teacher. Check *Gift Ideas: Desk Dweller* and *A Little Remembrance* categories for other suggestions.

An appreciative note
Gift of money to school, designating that it be used for teaching aids chosen by your teacher for her room
Donate a tree, shrubbery, perennials, outside bench, playground equipment, audio-visual equipment, anything needed at the school in his honor.
Give book to school library in her name.
Book (new or very old) or video on his favorite subject
Computer software on her subject, banners, certificates, calendar, publishing (for class newsletters), puzzles (that might be adapted to the classroom)
Supplies for his subject — maps, models, clip art, demonstration materials, posters
Laser pointer pen for attention-grabbing presentations
Magazine subscription in her subject area (or see *Magazines: Teaching*)
Small potted plant, fresh flowers in vase
Pretty cookie tin or tray full of cookies
Candy or condiment dish
Pretty basket filled with fresh fruit, homemade cookies, bread
Assortment of flavored coffees, teas; spiced tea mix (see *Gifts to Make*)
Stickers, balloons, stamps, certificates to give out to students
Big box of #2 pencils, ball-point pens, felt-tip pens, red pens or pencils
Airtight storage containers, filing cabinet
Fountain pen to hang around neck; personalized pencils
Desk picture frame
Cute note pads, self-stick removable notes
Memo board
Stationery, notecards, pretty postcards
Any craft you do well, handcraft or decorative item
Decorate a tissue box or letter holder.
Anything from your garden or kitchen

Desk top or drawer organizer, tape holder, pencil holder, stapler, staple remover, box of staples

Bookends, book plates, bookmark

Coffee mug, set of coffee mugs

Decorative candle

Scented or initialed soap

Hand towel

Pin, bracelet, pendant, neck chain, earrings

Personalized tote bag

Holiday or seasonal decoration or ornament you made

❧ TENNIS PLAYER ❧

Your tennis fan will "love" one of these gifts. You can find additional items in *Catalogs: Sports & Recreation*.

Tickets to a tennis tournament; take a video of his playing for him to study.;

 lessons or fee for a workshop; subscription to tennis magazine (see *Magazines: Sports*); book or video on tennis technique or tournament play; racket, racket cover (needlepoint or handmade); can of tennis balls, tennis ball belt, basket for balls; hanger for racket and balls (fits on clothes rod); locker bag, tennis bag; tennis trainer (base with ball on string), practice rebound net; tennis socks, shoes, hat, cap with visor, tennis glove; tennis shorts, skirt, dress, panties; warm-up suit; sweatband (head or wrist); small ice chest, thermos; kit for stringing or re-gripping a racket

❧ TRAVELER ❧

Choose a gift from this list for those who travel for business or for pleasure. *Catalogs: Smorgasbord* and *Travel* have lots of specialty items.

Give a bon voyage party or host a picture show after traveler's return.

Subscription (see *Magazines: Travel*)

Book or video on part of world he likes (or hopes) to visit, historic spots, bed and breakfast accommodations in area, travel health, packing tips

Rand McNally's Business Traveler's Road Atlas (1992)—city and state maps, airports and accommodations in major cities, coupons

Whistler Interstate Tripmate—a database for services along every major interstate highway in continental U.S.

AT&T 800 Travel Directory — lists more than 6,000 travel organizations around the world with toll-free numbers (call 800-426-8686)

Road atlas, current highway map, road atlas computer program, distance-measuring map pen

Passes to nearby museums, national parks, etc.

Golden Eagle Passport: $25 per permit holder, good January 1 through December 31 for admission to any national park, monument, recreation area, historic site, wildlife refuge (Golden Age Passport free with proof of age over 62)—can be purchased from Department of Interior, National Park Service, P.O. Box 37127, Washington, DC 20013-7127 (202-208-4747) or at any federal area where fees are charged

Annual park pass (for a particular national park)

Membership in Hosteling International, 733 15th St. NW, Ste. 840, Washington, DC 20005 (202-783-6161) or check local telephone book for local chapter—allows use of hostels in U.S. and Europe

Literature on national parks from National Park Service (address above)

Coupons for house sitting—watering plants, feeding pets, checking mail, mowing lawn, etc.

Membership in travel club or American Automobile Association, 1000 AAA Dr., Heathrow, FL 32746-5080 (check local telephone book for local office)—benefits include emergency road service, touring information, road maps, insurance, etc.

Travel diary, small address book

Photograph album; slide trays, slide sorter, slide viewer; camera, camcorder, film, prepaid film mailers; holders for videos; camera bag, X-ray-safe film bag, camera fanny pack

Pocket-size binoculars; compass

Children's travel games, cassette tapes, CDs (for tape deck or portable CD or cassette player)

Book on crossword puzzles or word games for next trip, travel games

Towel of viscose that absorbs water, then wrings out to dry again and again

Anti-bacterial wipes, spot removers

Waterproof (also leakproof) cosmetic kit; drawstring laundry bag.

Package of travel detergent, inflatable clothes hangers, elastic clothesline

Portable iron, fabric steamer, Wrinkle Free (spray that removes wrinkles without ironing), Static Guard (spray that removes static cling)

Nylon inflatable sweater dryer (inflate with hair dryer)

Travel sewing kit; clothes brush

Shoeshine kit, shoe mittens (cloth bags for shoes)

Luggage, carry-on luggage, garment bag, men's shaving kit, tote bag, clothes bag, luggage with wheels and pulling handle

Luggage identification tags, personalized luggage straps, luggage wheels, collapsible luggage cart

Luggage handler—enables carrying two suitcases easily in one hand

Purse-size umbrella, folding cane

Jewelry roll or bag, insulated cover for hot curling iron

Travel-size hair dryer, curling iron

Unbreakable mirror

Hanging baby seat (for restaurants)

Travel coffee set—cup, spoon, immersion heater, and assorted coffees (or teas) in zippered bag

Compact sound machine (natural sounds of rainfall, surf, etc., to lull traveler to sleep in noisy hotel room)

Weather radio

Rain gear that rolls up very small

Portable combination lock or burglar alarm for hotel door

Automatic light timers to leave at home (get one for radio, too); automatic pet feeder (measures fresh food at regulated intervals for pet left at home)

Money belt, security wallet, personal safety devices (portable smoke or door alarms)

Travel alarm clock (a talking one perhaps)
Inflatable pillow
Make a carry-all, cosmetics case, jewelry case, jewelry roll, or shoe socks
(drawstring bags for shoes to fit in)

Car Traveler
Pre-trip car tune-up
Automobile burglar alarm, anti-theft devices (e.g., steering column lock)
Car first-aid kit
Driving gloves
Commuter mug (insulated, spillproof), insulated beverage holder, thermos,
or small ice chest
Coffee console (plugs into car lighter); car snack tray, wastebasket, or caddy
Cellular telephone, air time; CB radio; phone number index that fits on visor

Car visor organizer, sun shade
Vacuum, or clothes bar
Luggage rack with cover
Folding snow shovel, ice scraper
Emergency reflector blanket
Personalized hood ornament
Air compressor; car thermometer
Fire extinguisher; flashlight (small enough for glove compartment)
Mileage counter and timer; auto compass
Trunk or hood light; flare, signaling wheel cover

Foreign Traveler
The Safe Travel Book: A Guide for the International Traveler, by Peter Sav-
age (Free Press, 1988)—lots of tips from a former foreign service officer
on packing, planning a trip, safety en route and on arrival, security mea-
sures at your destination and on returning home, etc.
Foreign language course, records, cassettes, or software
Hand-held language translator; English-foreign language dictionary (should
translate from both languages) phrase book in various languages
Foreign currency converter and/or calculator, foreign telephone line adapter
Sight-seeing guide, travel guide (Arthur Frommer's or Fodor's are good)
Envelope of coins in the foreign currency so he will have change for tips
when he arrives; money belt or small cloth pouch (hangs around neck) to
hold passport, traveler's checks
Voltage converter, dual-voltage appliances, adapter plugs
Acoustic coupler that allows traveler to transmit data from a laptop computer
anywhere in the world on any telephone
Dual time-zone watch
Sleeping bag liner (for staying at hostels)
Painting or art print of place she's been
Water purifiers, filters

❦ VEGETARIAN ❧

Also check *Gift Ideas: Cook; Environmentalist;* and *Gardener*.

Juicer; yogurt maker; food dehydrator; flour, grain, seed mill; mortar and pes-
tle for grinding; canning and food processing equipment; slow cooker;

soup bowls, soup tureen; vegetable steamer; food slicer, grater; food processor; herb garden, sprout kit, patio tomato plant; dried fruit, honey; vegetarian jerky; nut bowl, nutcracker, nuts; basket of fruit, fruit bread; corn or pea sheller; salad spinner; cookbooks, books on vegetarian nutrition; gift certificate to vegetarian restaurant or health food store; subscription to vegetarian magazine (see *Magazines: Food & Entertaining*)

✎ WATER SKIER ✎

See also *Gift Ideas: Boater*.

Subscription (see *Magazines: Water Sports*); lessons; beach towel, swimsuit, suit coverup; water ski wetsuit; ski rope, ski gloves; skis, slalom ski; ski carrying case; athletic eyeglass holder; ice chest, thermos, insulated beverage holder

✎ WEDDING ✎

The ideas below supplement those found in *Gift Ideas: Host/Hostess; Cook; Housewarming; Family;* and *Silver Gifts*.

If you know soon enough, give computer software on planning weddings or subscription to a bridal magazine (see *Magazines: Women*).

Offer to take wedding pictures, snapshots, or video at reception.

Tape the ceremony.

Make the rice bags.

Address wedding invitations.

Give a dinner or party.

Make bridal gown.

Make traditional garter, ring bearer's pillow, satin purse.

Make hors d'oeuvres or wedding cake or cater the wedding.

For outdoor summer wedding, party, or reception, make heart-shaped fans (white posterboard edged in wedding color and glued to tongue depressor).

Frame wedding picture or invitation.

Bride's book

Family Bible

Wedding plaque with wedding date and couple's names in needlepoint, stitchery, or paint

Make wedding bells—Cut 18" high out of white satin, burlap, or felt. Trim in satin ribbon, lace, and pearl beads. On one, bead or embroider names of bride and groom. On other, put the wedding date. Display with satin rope.

Send champagne or flowers to honeymoon spot.

Anything in couple's chosen patterns—stainless flatware, sterling flatware, everyday or china dishes, crystal stemware

Anything in sterling, silver-plate, crystal, or pewter

Silver knife for cutting wedding cake
Bed pillows
Handmade quilt, afghan
Holiday decorations
Recipe collection from family and friends
Recipe box with your favorite recipes inside
Matching bath sarongs, robes, pajamas
Silver chest; pacific cloth bags with Velcro closures for silver pieces
Zippered storage bags for china
Stationery with new name (and address if couple will be there at least a year)
Jewelry — necklace, pendant cross in bride's silver pattern, pin, bracelet, locket
Home decorations you make — photograph, needlework pillow or picture, painting, stained glass, wooden trivets, etc.
Pillowcases—satin, monogrammed, embroidered with couple's name
Bed and bath linens (monogrammed), table linens
Blanket (find out bed size); electric blanket (dual control)
Candlesticks, candelabra—wood, silver, pewter, brass, crystal
Two silver, crystal, or pewter goblets or champagne glasses
Set of glasses (see also *Gift Ideas: Bar Gifts*)
Small electric appliance (see *Appendix*)
Picture frame, photograph album; camera, film
Vase, flower pot, potted plant
Spice rack (already stocked)
Laundry basket full of kitchen utensils, staples, paper and cleaning products
Clock radio, wall clock, alarm clock
TV, VCR, radio, stereo, CD or tape player
Vacuum cleaner; sewing machine; ironing board, iron
Framed photographs of bride and groom as children
Family genealogy
Anniversary candle
Book on etiquette, household hints, money management, adult development, marriage
Amagift — catalog of dozens of wedding gifts of equal value from which couple chooses one. You present the album to the couple and they order the item they want by returning a card to Amway. Shipping has already been paid. (Other albums are also available in several price ranges between $10.99 and $750.) Available from Amway distributors (check your local telephone book under Amway).
List of birthdays, anniversaries, names of relatives on both sides of family
"His and her" tool sets
Card table, folding chairs, TV trays
Lingerie for her, silk boxers or pajamas for him
Stock the medicine cabinet—thermometer, heating pad, Band-Aids, ice pack, disinfectant, etc.
Card file and index cards for recipes, addresses, wedding gift record, etc. (decorate the box)
Address book

❧ WEDDING SHOWERS ☙

Regardless of the theme of the shower, you'll find some ideas for gifts in this list. Refer also to *Gift Ideas: Cook; Housewarming; Host/Hostess; Adult— Basic;* and *Handyman* for more ideas.

Appliance shower—see *Appendix: Small Electric Appliances*

Bathroom shower—linens, towel holder, hand mirror, scented soap, soap dish; medicine chest items, thermometer, heating pad; cleaning items; plumber's friend

Couple shower—two of anything (pillowcases, matching T-shirts, robes, pajamas, "his and her" mugs, towels, bath sheets, place settings of pottery or flatware, etc.)

Embroidery shower—at the party, guests embroider their names or design on dish towels, quilt squares, cocktail napkins, etc.

Freebie shower—Things a couple collects only with time (rags, empty jars or plastic storage containers, free cookbooks, good recipes)

Groom's shower (couples or men only)—tools, handyman books, pajamas, robe, heavy-duty extension cord, yard equipment (see *Gift Ideas: Gardener; Handyman;* and *Man—Basic*)

Kitchen shower—small electric appliance (see list in *Appendix*), utensils, dish towels, cookbooks, cookware, aprons, food staples, storage containers (see *Gift Ideas: Cook*)

Linen shower—towels (hand, bath, kitchen, guest), washcloths, blanket, bed linens (check bed size), pillows, mattress pad, placemats, tablecloth, napkins, hot roll cover, bath set, quilt, afghan

Lingerie shower—slip, panties, gown, robe, slippers, lounging gown, hose, bra, silk pajamas, chemise, camisole, teddy

On-the-go shower—gift certificates to movie theater, restaurant, bowling alley, theater, miniature golf, sporting event, frozen yogurt or pizza parlor

Pantry shower—canned goods (with or without labels!), food staples, cupboard organizers, paper goods, spices

Paper shower—paper towels, napkins, toilet tissue, shelf paper, placemats, plates, cups; cookbooks, handyman books, household hints book; wedding book; stationery, magazine subscription, photo album, blank journals

Potluck shower—guests bring food to eat and leave the bride and groom the recipe and serving dish

Recipe shower—guests bring a favorite recipe and at least one ingredient (non-perishable) used to prepare it

Spice shower—guests bring a bottle of spice and a recipe using it

Trousseau shower—linens, clothing, or jewelry for bride

❧ WESTERN & EQUESTRIAN ☙

There are as many styles of gifts for horse lovers as there are styles of riding. Look under *Catalogs: Western & Equestrian* for riding equipment, Western clothes, and gifts with horse motifs. See also *Gift Ideas: Dancer—Country Western* and *Square Dancer*.

Western shirt, jeans, riding pants, vest, chambray shirt, jeans jacket, duster coat; western hat, hat band (horsehair), stick pin (rhinestone or rodeo theme); boots, boot socks, boot shaper, boot jack; belt buckle, silver or fancy belt tips or belt keeper; personalized belt

Women—leather Indian princess dresses, moccasins, clothing decorated with rhinestones or sequins, decorated tuxedo shirts, split skirts, broomstick and prairie skirts, vests

Men—poplin shirts (yoke front and back)

Western art; lariat wreath

Gaucho silver belt; Western, turquoise, rhinestone jewelry; Western watch

Bola tie, oblong neck scarf, silver collar tips, bandanna

Engraved boot tips or heel scallops

Snuff box cover

Suit bag with pocket for boots

Country music tape

Sun shade or decorated mud-flaps for pick-up truck

Anything out of denim—skirt, purse, book cover, tote bag, vest, etc.

Items with horse or ranch motif—picture, lamp base, desk accessories, calendar, needlepoint pillows, etc.

Subscription (see *Magazines: Animals, Birds, Fish & Wildlife* and *Country Living*)

Book or video on the West, horses, ranching, horsemanship, competition, jumping, racing, etc.

Wrap gift in a bandanna.

Riding jacket, jodhpurs, saddle suit vest, English riding accessories; pads, saddle, bridle

Rodeo Riders—Belt holder; bull riding glove; resin bag; rope pad, rope can; stirrups, spurs; rigging bag

Working Cowboy or Cowgirl—Rain slicker; deerskin gloves; chaps; roping can, new ropes; practice steer head; bridle, halter, head stall, or breast collar for horse; favorite kind of bit or tie-down; skid boots for horse; saddle bags; saddle pad or blanket; pocket knife; portable spittoon (non-spill) for pick-up truck

✍ WOMAN—BASIC ✍

Many women's gift ideas are covered in other categories (see *Gift Ideas: Single Woman; Adult — Basic; The Romantic;* and other interest categories). Here are a few extras.

Book on being a woman, mother, working woman, widow, grandmother, wife

Coupons for baby-sitting, cooking, housework, car wash, lawn mowing, typing, etc.

Course in self-defense, rape prevention

Police whistle, tear-gas device for purse (see also *Gift Ideas: Security & Safety Conscious*)

Cellular telephone

Gift certificate to her favorite hairdresser or manicurist or really pamper her with a combination hair styling, manicure, pedicure, facial, massage, and elegant brunch ("trendy" hair salons often offer these)

Amagift—catalog of several dozen gifts for women from which she chooses one. You purchase the album and present it as a gift. The recipient (unaware of the price) chooses which item she wants and orders it directly from Amway. Shipping has already been paid. (Other albums that are appropriate are Gourmet Gifts, Jewelry, Sweets & Treats, and albums in various price ranges up to $750.) Available from Amway distributors (check your local telephone book under Amway).

Needlepoint purse or eyeglass case

Embroider, appliqué, cross-stitch, or paint a design on a skirt or shirt.

Crochet an airy shawl; knit a sweater.

Jewelry — ring, necklace, neck chain, religious pendant, bracelet, earrings, watch, ring watch; ring box or holder, earring tree, jewelry box; vanity tray, dressing table set, hand mirror

Potpourri, sachets, padded clothes hangers

Cologne, perfume

Cosmetics—body powder, bubble bath, bath oil, nail polish, scented soap

Comb, compact

Blouse, skirt, dress, shoes, handbag, gown, robe, slip, sweater, scarf, belt, gloves

Gift certificate to favorite clothing store or catalog

Subscription (see *Magazines: Women* or interest categories)

❧ WOOD HOBBYIST ❧

These ideas are general enough to please those with many specializations in woodworking. See *Catalogs: Craft Supplies; Handcrafts; Handyman;* or *Models & Miniatures*.

Book of patterns, ideas, techniques, tools in his specialty area; video on how-to

Subscription (see *Magazines: Handyman & Hobbyist*)

Tuition for woodworking class at hobby store, community college

Gift certificate to hardware store, lumber yard, tool catalog

Small stickers reading, "Handcrafted for you by ..."

First-aid kit

Assortment of sandpaper, wood screws, nails, bolts, nuts, brads

Files, rasps, rifflers, clamps, gauges, ruler, hammers, screwdrivers, pliers, vise-grip pliers, set of wrenches

Power tools — lathe, jigsaw, table saw, disc sander, grinder; router bits in various shapes; foot switch for power tools

Workbench or table, thick vinyl pad to place beside table to stand on and reduce fatigue

Goggles, nose mask, ear protector, industrial respirator

Combination square, mitre square, dovetail square

Molding cutter, scroll saw, inlay cutter; blade caddy for storing saw blades

Vinyl-covered magnetic clamp pads

Canvas tool rolls to protect carving tools

Miter box and saw, Japanese saws

Turning tools

Twist-lock marking tool

Hand plane

Good paintbrushes

Tool sharpening stone

Miniature tool set

Level, plumb bob

Precision ruler, caliper, folding extension rule, profile gauge that conforms to
any shape
Heavy-duty vacuum cleaner; heavy-duty extension cord
Soft, wide broom for sweeping up sawdust; dust pan
Storage cabinet with small, transparent drawers
Workshop apron (leather lasts the longest), tool belt
Pocket microscope for seeing detail work
Industrial task lamp that attaches to work bench, bandsaw, or anything else
Woodcarving tools—chisels, whittling knives, turning tools, carving knife,
blades, punches, gouges, mallets, scoops, study birds, book or video on
wildlife he carves, clamping jig
For workshop—good lock, paper towel holder, lint-free shop cloths, inter-
com or telephone extension, peg board and hooks

✎ WRITER ✐

Give an autograph party for a new book.
T-shirt reading, "Ask me about my book."
Subscription to writer's magazine or magazine in specialty area (see *Maga-
zines: Writing* and other areas)
Tuition for a writing workshop or class or dues in a local writing group
Book on style (punctuation, usage, grammar, etc.)
Book by or about an admired author, about the area of specialty, or a refer-
ence book in author's field
Book on writing markets—*Writer's Market* is a good one, published yearly
(Writer's Digest Books, 1507 Dana Ave., Cincinnati, OH 45207-1005,
800-289-0963).
New dictionary every five or so years for new terminology; on-line computer
dictionary
Roget's International Thesaurus, Bartlett's Familiar Quotations
Bound book with blank pages (unlined also allows for sketching)
Filing cabinet or boxes, file folders
Typewriter, typewriter ribbons (know brand and model of typewriter)
Coupons for manuscript typing
Computer; word processing, desktop publishing, spell checker, small busi-
ness finances software; letter-quality printer; blank diskettes; diskette
mailers (see *Gift Ideas: Computer Enthusiast*)
Letterhead stationery on 25% rag bond paper or good quality computer prin-
ter paper. Select business-like type. It could read, "Nancy Bell, writer."
Give address (with zip code) and telephone number (with area code).
Legal pads, typing or computer paper: watermark, 25% rag bond paper (white)
Personalized clipboard; bookends, book plates, bookmark
Personalized address labels or #10 envelopes
Box of #10 envelopes or manila envelopes (9" x 12" or 9½" x 12½")

Rubber stamps — "Do Not Bend," "First Class,"
"Photos"
Postal scale; roll of stamps
Index card file, index cards
#2 pencils, paper clips, pencil holder, pencil sharpener
Briefcase
Desk or drawer organizer; desk lamp

3.
Resources

ᦔ MAGAZINES

Magazines are wonderful gifts that keep giving all year. The topics available are endless—from gourmet cooking to herpetology (the study of reptiles and amphibians) to aviation. The ones listed here represent only a fraction of those available. Few gifts are as easy to give since many publishers have toll-free numbers that you can call and charge the cost to your credit card. If you are not sure whether a particular magazine will be appropriate, ask the publisher about ordering a sample copy. If you are really unsure (for instance, there must be over 100 magazines about cars), buy a sample of two or three and let the recipient choose which he likes best.

The only drawback to giving magazines is the length of time it usually takes to receive the first issue. Plan at least two months in advance if you want the first copy to arrive close to the date of the gift occasion.

Unless otherwise noted in this listing, publication is monthly. Prices are subject to change. Overseas rates are usually more; so call or write if you'll be sending to an overseas address. Throughout these listings, the descriptions in quotations are what the publishers say about their own publications.

Animals, Birds, Fish & Wildlife

American Cage-bird Magazine, One Glamore Ct., Smithtown, NY 11787. 800-359-BIRD. $21.95.

Animals, Massachusetts SPCA, Circulation Dept., 350 S. Huntington Ave., Boston, MA 02130. $19.94/6 issues.

Aquarium Fish Magazine, Subscription Dept., P.O. Box 6040, Mission Viejo, CA 92690-9953. $23.97/14 issues.

Audubon, National Audubon Society Membership Data Center, P.O. Box 52529, Boulder, CO 80322. 800-274-4201. $20/6 issues.

Cat Fancy, Subscription Dept., P.O. Box 52864, Boulder, CO 80323-2864. $23.97.

Cats Magazine, P.O. Box 420240, Palm Coast, FL 32142-0240. $18.97.

Dog Fancy, Subscription Dept., P.O. Box 53264, Boulder, CO 80322-3264. $23.97.

Dog World, P.O. Box 6500, Chicago, IL 60680. $28. "World's largest all breed dog magazine."

Equus, P.O. Box 57919, Boulder, CO 80322-7919. $24.

Freshwater & Marine Aquarium, P.O. Box 487, Sierra Madre, CA 91025. 800-523-1736. $22. "Dedicated to the tropical fish enthusiast."

Good Dog!, Attn: Subscription Dept., P.O. Box 31292, Charleston, SC 29417-1292. $14.95/6 issues. "Consumer magazine for dog owners."

Horse & Rider, Subscription Service Dept., P.O. Box 529, Mt. Morris, IL 61054. $19.95.

Horse Illustrated, Subscription Dept., P.O. Box 6040, Mission Viejo, CA 92690-9953. $22.97/14 issues. Guide to responsible horse care.

International Wildlife, 1400 16th St. NW, Washington, DC 20077-9964. 800-432-6564. $16/6 issues. Includes associate membership in National Wildlife Federation (or combine with *National Wildlife* for $22 and world membership).

National Wildlife, 1400 16th St. NW, Washington, DC 20077-9964. 800-432-6564. $16/6 issues. Includes associate membership in National Wildife Federation (or combine with *International Wildlife* for $22 and world membership).

Parrot Society, The, 1086 Fenlake Rd., Bedford, England MK4 0EU. $17.

Practical Fishkeeping Magazine, c/o Motorsport, RR1, Box 200D, Jonesburg, MO 63351. $42.

Practical Horseman, P.O. Box 367, Mt. Morris, IL 61054-7740. $24.95.

Reptile and Amphibian Magazine, RD 3, Box 3709-A, Pottsville, PA 17901. $12/6 issues.

Tiger Tribe, 1407 E. College St., Iowa City, IA 52245-4410. 800-862-6759. $18/6 issues. "Holistic health and more for cats."

Tropical Fish Hobbyist, TFH Publishing Co., Inc., P.O. Box 427, Neptune, NJ 07754-9989. $30.

Vivarium, American Federation of Herpetoculturists, P.O. Box 1131, Lakeside, CA 92040-0905. $26/6 issues. For those who maintain and breed reptiles and amphibians in captivity.

Zoolife, P.O. Box 363, Mt. Morris, IL 61054-0363. $14.95/4 issues. "Exploring the world of wildlife and nature."

Arts & Antiques

(see also *Magazines: Crafts; Metalworking;* and *Woodworking*)

Air Brush Action, Subscription Service, Box 3000, Denville, NJ 07834. $27/6 issues.

American Artist, 1 Color Ct., Marion, OH 43305. 800-347-6969. $24.95. "Leading magazine for fine artists."

American Craft, American Craft Council, P.O. Box 3000, Denville, NJ 07834. 800-562-1973. $40/6 issues.

American Indian Art Magazine, Circulation Dept., 7314 E. Osborn Dr., Scottsdale, AZ 85251. $20/4 issues.

American Theatre, 355 Lexington Ave., New York, NY 10017-0217. $27.

Applied Art, 885 Don Mills Rd., Ste. 324, Don Mills, Ontario, Canada M3C 1V9. $49/5 issues. Industrial and graphic arts.

Art & Antiques, P.O. Box 1638, Des Moines, IA 50340-1697. $27/10 issues.

Art in America, P.O. Box 1947, Marion, OH 43306-2047. 800-247-2160. $39.95. Galleries, museums, artists, trends.

Art of the West, P.O. Box 1702, Minnetonka, MN 55345-9900. $21/6 issues.

Artist's Magazine, The, P.O. Box 2121, Harlan, IA 51593. $24. How-to magazine for artists—watercolor, pastels, acrylics, etc.

ARTnews, P.O. Box 2083, Knoxville, IA 50197-2083. 800-284-4625. $32.95.

Dance Magazine, P.O. Box 57401, Boulder, CO 80321-7401. $29.95.

Design Times, 714 Boylston St., Boston, MA 02116. $30/6 issues. Interiors, fashion, architecture, furniture.

Equine Images, P.O. Box 916, Ft. Dodge, IA 50501-9991. $49/6 issues. Equine art.

Fiberarts, 50 College St., Asheville, NC 28801. $21/5 issues. Textiles.

Folk Art, 61 W. 62nd St., New York, NY 10023-7015. $35 individual/$25 student, or senior citizen/4 issues. Includes membership in Museum of American Folk Art in New York City.

Glass Magazine, 647 Fulton St., Brooklyn, NY 11217. $28/4 issues. Exhibitions, international artists, book reviews.

Handwoven, Interweave Press, 201 E. 4th St., Loveland, CO 80537. $21/5 issues. For handweavers.

I.D., P.O. Box 11247, Des Moines, IA 50340-1247. 800-284-3728. $55/6 issues. International design.

Latin American Art Magazine, P.O. Box 9888, Scottsdale, AZ 85252-3888. $24/4 issues.

Minerva, Subscriptions, 7 Davies St., London, United Kingdom W1Y 1LL. $28/6 issues. "International review of ancient art and archaeology."

Sculpture, P.O. Box 91110, Washington, DC 20077-7320. $55/6 issues. Includes membership in International Sculpture Center.

Southwest Art, P.O. Box 53185, Boulder, CO 80322-3185. $32.

Step-by-Step Graphics, P.O. Box 8641, Boulder, CO 80328-8641. $42/6 issues. "How-to magazine for traditional and electronic graphics."

Theater Week, 28 W. 25th St., 9th Fl., New York, NY 10010. $49/52 issues.

Wildlife Art News, P.O. Box 16246, Minneapolis, MN 55415-9912. $29.95/6 issues.

Automobiles

Automobile Magazine, P.O. Box 55752, Boulder, CO 80322-5752. $18.

AutoWeek, 965 E. Jefferson, Detroit, MI 48207-3185. 800-678-9595. $28/52 issues.

Car & Driver, P.O. Box 52906, Boulder, CO 80322-2906. $19.94.

Car Collector & Car Classics Magazine, Circulation Dept., P.O. Box 171, Mt. Morris, IL 61054. 815-734-6309. $32.

Cavallino, P.O. Box 810819, Boca Raton, FL 33481-0819. $24/6 issues. "The enthusiast's magazine of Ferrari."

Collectible Automobile, 7373 N. Cicero Ave., Lincolnwood, IL 60646-1613. 708-676-3470. $24/6 issues.

Four Wheels, P.O. Box 2046, Harlan, IA 51593. $17.87.

Motor Trend, Petersen Publishing Co., 8490 Sunset Blvd., Los Angeles, CA 90069. 800-800-MT4U. $19.94.

Petersen's 4 Wheel & Off-Road Magazine, P.O. Box 58753, Boulder, CO 80322. 800-800-4294. $19.94.

Road & Track, P.O. Box 55279, Boulder, CO 80321-5279. 800-877-8316. $19.94.

Special Interest Autos, P.O. Box 196, Bennington, VT 05201-9940. $12.95/6 issues.

Sports Car International, Subscription Service, P.O. Box 366, Itasca, IL 60143. $17.95. American and other sports cars.

Thoroughbred & Classic Cars, IPC Magazines, P.O. Box 272, Haywards Heath, W. Sussex RH 16 3FS United Kingdom. $60.

Vintage Motor Sport, P.O. Box 2895, Lakeland, FL 33806-2891. 813-686-3104. $35/6 issues.

Aviation

Aeroplane Monthly, Reed Business Publishing, 205 E. 42nd St., New York, NY 10017. $53.

Air & Space/Smithsonian, P.O. Box 53261, Boulder, CO 80322-3261. $18/6 issues. Includes membership in National Air & Space Museum, discounts.

Air Classics, 7950 Deering Ave., Canoga Park, CA 91304. $31.50. "World's leading publication on vintage and veteran aircraft."

Air International, P.O. Box 353, Whitestone, NY 11357. $49.

Air Progress, 7950 Deering Ave., Canoga Park, CA 91304-9980. 800-562-9182. $19.95.

Aviation, P.O. Box 368, Mt. Morris, IL 61054-7739. $16.95/6 issues.

Aviation Heritage, P.O. Box 368, Mt. Morris, IL 61054-7738. $16.95/6 issues.

Aviation Week & Space Technology, P.O. Box 503, Hightstown, NJ 08520-9899. 800-525-5003. $82/weekly. News, people, legislation.

Flight Training, P.O. Box 14236, Parkville, MO 64152-9972. $25. "Aviation training and careers magazine."

Plane & Pilot, Box 52411, Boulder, CO 80321-2411. $16.95.

Private Pilot, Subscription Dept., P.O. Box 55064, Boulder, CO 80323-5064. $23.97.

SAGA International Aviator, Sport & General Aviation, Inc., Evergreen Professional & Technological Center, 6851 Hwy. 73, Evergreen, CO 80439-9969. 800-446-SAGA. $40/4 issues. Photos, aviators, what you need to go places in light aircraft, future of aviation.

Sport Pilot, 7950 Deering Ave., Canoga Park, CA 91304-9980. $31.50.

U.S. Aviator, 3000 21st St. NW, Winter Haven, FL 33881. 800-356-PROP. $25. "Featuring the entire world of aviation."

World Air Power Journal, Airtime Publishing, Inc., Subscription Dept., 10 Bay St., Westport, CT 06880. $17.95 each/quarterly (really a book!).

Boating & Sailing

Boating, P.O. Box 51055, Boulder, CO 80323-1055. $17.97.

Boating World, P.O. Box 564, Mt. Morris, IL 61054-7996. $23/8 issues.

Classic Boating, Dept. D, 280 Lac La Belle, Oconomowoc, WI 53066. $20/6 issues. Restoration tips, features.

Cruising World, P.O. Box 3029, Harlan, IA 51593-4090. 800-727-8473. $24. Cruises, maintenance, techniques.

Hot Boat, P.O. Box 16927, N. Hollywood, CA 91615-9966. $19.95. "Family performance boating's leader."

Houseboat, 520 Park Ave., Idaho Falls, ID 83402. 800-638-0135. $8.95/6 issues. "Family magazine for American houseboaters."

Living Aboard, 54 Dalraida Rd., Ste. 119-XC, Montgomery, AL 36109. $20/4 issues.

Motor Boating & Sailing, P.O. Box 7156, Red Oak, IA 51591-2156. $15.97.

Ocean Navigator, P.O. Box 569, Portland, ME 04112-9947. $21/7 issues. "Marine navigation and ocean voyaging."

Power and Motoryacht, P.O. Box 57546, Boulder, CO 80322-7546. $19.95.

Powerboat, P.O. Box 556, Mt. Morris, IL 61054-7810. 800-827-0385. $27/11 issues. "World's leading performance boating magazine."

Sail, P.O. Box 56397, Boulder, CO 80321-6397. 800-745-7245. $19.95.

Sailing, Box 249, Port Washington, WI 53074-9975. $24.75.

Showboats International, P.O. Box 56319, Boulder, CO 80323-6319. $24/6 issues. Luxury boats.

Wooden Boat, Subscription Dept., P.O. Box 492, Mt. Morris, IL 61054-9852. $22.95/6 issues. "For wooden boat owners, builders, and designers."

Yachting, P.O. Box 52277, Boulder, CO 80321-2277. $16.97.

Yachting World, 205 E. 42nd St., Ste. 1705, New York, NY 10017. $65.

Buying Guides

Consumer Reports, Subscription Dept., P.O. Box 53009, Boulder, CO 80321-3009. $22/11 issues. Independent ratings of all kinds of products.

Consumer's Digest, P.O. Box 3074, Harlan, IA 51593-4138. $15.97/6 issues. Ratings of appliances, cars, services, products of all kinds.

Children Thru Teens

American Girl, P.O. Box 420210, Palm Coast, FL 32142-9896. $19.95/6 issues. Ages 7 up. Games, crafts, paperdolls, stories, trends.

Barbie Bazaar, Murat Caviale, Inc., 5617 6th Ave., Kenosha, WI 53140-4101. $25.95/6 issues. "Barbie collector's magazine."

Boys' Life, Boy Scouts of America, 1325 Walnut Hill Ln., P.O. Box 152079, Irving, TX 75015-2079. $15.60. Adventure, outdoor tips for all boys.

Child Life, Children's Better Health Institute, 1100 Waterway Blvd., Indianapolis, IN 46202. $13.95/8 issues. Health, exercise, safety, nutrition for ages 8-10.

Children's Digest, Children's Better Health Institute, 1100 Waterway Blvd., Indianapolis, IN 46202. $13.95/8 issues. Health, exercise, safety, nutrition for ages 10-12.

Children's Playmate, Children's Better Health Institute, 1100 Waterway Blvd., Indianapolis, IN 46202. $13.95/8 issues. Health, exercise, safety, nutrition for ages 6-8.

Cobblestone, 7 School St., Peterborough, NH 03458. $22.95/10 issues. "The history magazine for young people." Ages 8-12.

Cricket, Box 387, Mt. Morris, IL 61054-7823. $29.97.

Disney Adventures, P.O. Box 380, Mt. Morris, IL 61054-7728. $14.95. Ages 10-14.

Game Player's Guide to Nintendo Games, Signal Research, P.O. Box 29364, Greensboro, NC 27429. $26.50. Availability and upcoming releases.

High Adventure, Gospel Publishing House, 1445 Boonville Ave., Springfield, MO 65802. $1.75/4 issues. *Royal Rangers* magazine for boys. Religious and inspirational articles.

Highlights for Children, 2300 W. 5th Ave., P.O. Box 182346, Columbus, OH 43272-2706. $19.95. "Fun with a purpose" for ages 2-12.

Hopscotch, P.O. Box 164, Bluffton, OH 45817-0164. $15/6 issues. "To challenge young girls to enjoy and make the utmost of those few and precious years of childhood". For girls age 6-12.

Humpty Dumpty's Magazine, Children's Better Health Institute, 1100 Waterway Blvd., Indianapolis, IN 46202. $13.95/8 issues. Health, exercise, safety, nutrition for ages 4-6.

Jack & Jill, Children's Better Health Institute, 1100 Waterway Blvd., Indianapolis, IN 46202. $13.95/8 issues. Stories, activities, etc.

Kid City Magazine, P.O. Box 51277, Boulder, CO 80322-1277. $15.97/10 issues. Early elementary—ages 6-10.

Kid Sports, P.O. Box 55497, Boulder, CO 80322-5497. $15.94/6 issues.

Sports magazine for children 7-14.

Kids Discover, P.O. Box 54206, Boulder, CO 80323-4206. $17.95/10 issues. Elementary ages; each issue on a different scientific, historical, or cultural theme.

Ladybug, Box 592, Mt. Morris, IL 61054-7665. 800-827-0227. $29.97. Stories, songs, poems, games for ages 2-6.

Merlyn's Pen, P.O. Box 1058, E. Greenwich, RI 02818-1058. 800-247-2027. $18.95/4 issues. "National magazine of student writing" — award-winning, grades 7-10, new senior edition, grades 9-12.

My First Magazine, Scholastic, Inc., P.O. Box 3735, Dept. 6004, Jefferson City, MO 65102-9962. 800-631-1586. $10/6 issues. Ages 3-4.

National Geographic World, National Geographic Society, 17 & M Sts. NW, Washington, DC 20036. $12.95. Factual stories on outdoor adventure, natural history, sports, science, and history for children 8-13.

Noah's Arc, 8323 SW Frwy, Ste. 250, Houston, TX 77074. $8. Tabloid for Jewish children 6-12.

Ranger Rick, National Wildlife Federation, 1400 16th St. NW, Washington, DC 20078-6420. 800-432-6564. $15. Ages 6-12.

Right On!, Lexington Library, 355 Lexington Ave., New York, NY 10017. $17.99. Black young adult entertainment.

Sesame Street Magazine, P.O. Box 52000, Boulder, CO 80322-2000. $16.97 /10 issues. Ages 2-6.

16 Magazine, Subscription Dept., c/o Macfadden Publishing, Inc., 233 Park Ave. S, New York, NY 10003. $16.95. "Pin-ups, interviews and scoops on your 'faves.'"

Spark, P.O. Box 5028, Harlan, IA 51593-4528. $21.95/9 issues. "Creative fun for kids."

Sports Illustrated for Kids, P.O. Box 830606, Birmingham, AL 35282-9487. 800-334-2229. $18.95. Stories, games, photographs for ages 8 up.

Stone Soup, P.O. Box 83, Santa Cruz, CA 95063-0083. 800-447-4569. $23/6 issues. "Magazine by children."

Surprises, P.O. Box 20471, Bloomington, MN 55420-9802. $14.95/6 issues. "Fun activities for kids and parents."

Teen, P.O. Box 51683, Boulder, CO 80323-1683. $15.95.

3-2-1 Contact Magazine, E=MC Sq., P.O. Box 51177, Boulder, CO 80322-1177. $16.97/10 issues. Science, nature, technology for ages 8-12.

Turtle, P.O. Box 7133, Red Oak, IA 51591-0133. $13.95/8 issues. For preschool children.

U.S. Kids, P.O. Box 8957, Boulder, CO 80322. $20.95/8 issues. "A weekly reader magazine."

Where's Waldo? Magazine, P.O. Box 7560, Red Oak, IA 51591. $7.80/4 issues. Elementary grades.

YM, P.O. Box 3060, Harlan, IA 51593-2124. $18/10 issues. Older teen girls.

Young Judean, Hadassah Zionist Youth Commission, 50 W. 58th St., New York, NY 10019. $5/6 issues.

Young Voices, P.O. Box 2321, Olympia, WA 98507. $15/6 issues. "Magazine of young people's creative work."

Your Big Backyard, National Wildlife Federation, 1400 16th St. NW, Washington, DC 20078-6420. 800-432-6564. $12. Ages 3-5.

Zillions, Consumer's Union of U.S., Inc., 101 Thurman Ave., Yonkers, NY 10703. $15.95/6 issues. Consumer testing, purchasing education, etc.

Collectors

Autograph Collector, 541 N. Main St., Ste. 104-352, Corona, CA 91720. 714-734-9636. $38.

Baseball Cards, Circulation Dept., 700 E. State St., Iola, WI 54990. $18.95.

Cartwright's Journal of Baseball Collectibles, 10340 Camino Santa Fe, Ste. A, San Diego, CA 92121. $32/4 issues.

Coins, 700 E. State St., Iola, WI 54990-0001. $19.95.

Collect!, P.O. Box 1637, Glen Allen, VA 23060-0637. 800-394-9445. $12.95/4 issues. "For non-sports collectors."

Collectible Toys and Values, Attic Books, Ltd., 15 Danbury Rd., Ridgefield, CT 06877. $48. From superheroes to trading cards to trains.

Collecting Toys, P.O. Box 1612, Waukesha, WI 53187-9950. $19.95/6 issues.

Collector Editions, P.O. Box 1941, Marion, OH 43305. $22.95/6 issues. "Figurines, cottages, prints, plates, glass, antiques."

Collector's Mart Magazine, P.O. Box 12830, Wichita, KS 67277-9924. $23.95/6 issues.

Collector's Showcase, Customer Service, P.O. Box 59022, Boulder, CO 80322-9022. 800-766-3058. $49.90.

Collectors News Box, 156 Grundy, Center, IA 50638. 800-352-8039. $18/24 issues.

Contemporary Doll Magazine, Scott Publishing Co., 30595 Eight Mile, Livonia, MI 48152-9868. $29.70.

Doll Life, P.O. Box 514, Mt. Morris, IL 61054-7950. $15.95/6 issues.

Dolls, P.O. Box 1972, Marion, OH 43306-2072. $34.95/9 issues.

Inside Collector, The, 225 Main St., Ste. 300, Northpoint, NY 11768-9874. $36/9 issues. "Indispensable guide to popular antiques and collectibles."

Miniature Collector, P.O. Box 631, Boiling Springs, PA 17007-9985. $14.95/4 issues.

Non-Sport Update, 409 Green St., P.O. Box 5858, Harrisburg, PA 17110. 717-238-1936. $16/4 issues.

Numismatic News, 700 E. State St., Iola, WI 54945. $27.95/53 issues. "Coin market newspaper."

Scott Stamp Monthly, Subscription Dept., P.O. Box 828, Sidney, OH 45365. $16.95.

Teddy Bear and Friends, P.O. Box 466, Mt. Morris, IL 61054-7898. $17.95/6 issues.

Teddy Bear Review, P.O. Box 1948, Marion, OH 43306-2041. $22.95/6 issues.

Toy Box, 8393 E. Holly Rd., Holly, MI 48442. 800-437-1218. $12.95/4 issues. "For collectors of childhood treasures."

Trading Cards, Subscription Dept., P.O. Box 16928, N. Hollywood, CA 91615-9960. $17.95.

Tuff Stuff, P.O. Box 1637, Glen Allen, VA 23060-0637. 800-394-9445. $24.95. "Nation's favorite trading card magazine."

Computing

(The *S* after a listing suggests a magazine appropriate for a serious user. Be sure the magazine and the type of computer match.)

Atari Explorer, P.O. Box 6488, Duluth, MN 55806. $14.95/6 issues.

Boardwatch Magazine, 7586 W. Jewell Ave., Ste. 200, Lakewood, CO 80232. $36. Electronic bulletin boards.

Byte, Subscription Dept., P.O. Box 558, Hightstown, NJ 08520-9409. $29.95. New products, book reviews, news, features. *S*

Compute, P.O. Box 3244, Harlan, IA 51593-2424. $19.94. For beginners to intermediate users.

Computer Gaming World, P.O. Box 730, Yorba Linda, CA 92686-9963. 800-827-4450. $28.

Computer Shopper, P.O. Box 51020, Boulder, CO 80321-1020. $19.97. Good for keeping up with the market. *S*

Database Programming & Design, P.O. Box 51247, Boulder, CO 80321-1247. $37. *S*

Electronic Gaming Monthly, P.O. Box 7524, Red Oak, IA 51591-2524. 800-444-2884. $27.95.

Game Pro, P.O. Box 55527, Boulder, CO 80322-5527. $24.95. Video games.

Home Office Computing, P.O. Box 51344, Boulder, CO 80321-1344. $10.99. Great for small business owners.

Kids and Computers, P.O. Box 730, Yorba Linda, CA 92686-9963. $12/6 issues. "Magazine for parents."

Mac World, Subscription Dept., P.O. Box 51666, Boulder, CO 80321-1666. $18.95. *S*

MacUser, P.O. Box 52461, Boulder, CO 80321-2461. $27. *S*

Microsoft Systems Journal, P.O. Box 56622, Boulder, CO 80322-6622. $50. *S*

Midnight Engineering, Resources, & Insight for the Entrepreneurial Engineer, 1700 Washington Ave., Rocky Ford, CO 81067-9900. $19.95/6 issues. *S*

Mobil Office, Subscription Dept., P.O. Box 57268, Boulder, CO 80323-7268. 800-627-5234. $23.90.

NewMedia, Customer Service Dept., P.O. Box 1771, Riverton, NJ 08077-9771. $48. Multi-media technologies for desktop computer users. *S*

PC Computing, P.O. Box 50253, Boulder, CO 80321-0253. $14.97. Highly recommended for novices.

PC Games, P.O. Box 802, Peterborough, NH 03458-9971. $19.95/8 issues.

PC Home Journal, P.O. Box 469, Mt. Morris, IL 61054. 800-827-0364. $17.95. "Magazine for work, play, education" (non-technical).

PC Magazine, P.O. Box 57068, Boulder, CO 80321-7068. $29.97/22 issues. Testing results. For intermediate to advanced users. *S*

PC Novice, P.O. Box 85380, Lincoln, NE 68501-9815. 800-545-5200. $24. "Personal computing in plain English." Very good for beginners.

PC Sources, P.O. Box 50237, Boulder, CO 80321-0237. $12.97. Products and markets. *S*

PC Techniques, 7721 E. Gray Rd., Ste. 204, Scottsdale, AZ 85260-9747. $21.95/6 issues. *S*

PC Today, P.O. Box 85380, Lincoln, NE 80321-1833. 800-545-5200. $24. Computing for small businesses.

PC World, Subscription Dept., P.O. Box 51833, Boulder, CO 80321-1833. $29.90. For novices.

Portable Computing, Subscription Dept., 21800 Oxnard St., Ste. 250, Woodland Hills, CA 91367-9731. $28.80. For users of portable computers.

Windows User, P.O. Box 56630, Boulder, CO 80323-6630. $19.97. For users of Windows software.

Country Living
Adirondack Life, P.O. Box 97, Jay, NY 12941-9988. $17.95/7 issues.

Back Home, P.O. Box 70-H2, Hendersonville, NC 28793. 800-992-2546. $16/4 issues. "Hands-on and down-to-earth."

Backwoods Home Magazine, 1257 Siskiyou Blvd. #213, Ashland, OR 97520. $17.95/6 issues. "Practical journal of self-reliance."

Country, 5925 Country Ln., P.O. Box 994, Greendale, WI 53129-0994. $16.98/6 issues. "For those who live in or long for the country."

Country America, 1716 Locust St., P.O. Box 10678, Des Moines, IA 50380-0678. $16.97/10 issues. Country life and entertainment.

Country Decorating Ideas, Harris Publications, 1115 Broadway, New York, NY 10160-0397. $14.97/8 issues.

Country Home, 1716 Locust Rd., P.O. Box 10635, Des Moines, IA 50380-0635. $17.97/6 issues.

Country Journal, P.O. Box 392, Mt. Morris, IL 61054-9957. $16.95/6 issues.

Country Living, P.O. Box 7137, Red Oak, IA 51591-0137. $17.97. Decorating, cooking, crafts, travel, real estate, antiques, gardens.

Country Sampler, Subscription Dept., P.O. Box 7598, Red Oak, IA 51591-0598. $19.96/6 issues.

Country Sampler's Decorating Ideas, Subscription Dept., P.O. Box 7598, Red Oak, IA 51591-0598. $19.95/6 issues. Home-decor crafts, remodeling, gardening, outdoor living.

Countryside, P.O. Box 7021, Red Oak, IA 51591-2021. 800-444-8783. $5.99 /6 issues. "Nature, houses, gardens, food, crafts, traditions."

Heritage Country, Keystone Publishing, P.O. Box 427, Shipshewana, IN 46565. $17.50/4 issues. "Amish and other rural lifestyles of the American Midwest."

Log Home Living, Home Buyer Publications, Inc., P.O. Box 5361, Pittsfield, MA 01203-9881. $19.95/6 issues.

Mother Earth News, P.O. Box 56304, Boulder, CO 80323-6304. $17.95.

Crafts
(see also *Magazines: Arts & Antiques; Handyman & Hobbyist; Metalworking; Model Building;* and *Woodworking*)

Bridal Crafts, 701 Lee St., Ste. 1000, Des Plaines, IL 60016-4570. 800-CRAFTS1. $14.97/4 issues.

Butterick, P.O. Box 569, Altoona, PA 16603-9974. $8.95/4 issues. Sewing.

Celebrations to Cross Stitch and Crafts, P.O. Box 420207, Palm Coast, FL 32142-0207. 800-829-9154. $17/6 issues. Patterns, instructions.

Country Folk Art Magazine, Subscription Dept., 8393 E. Holly Rd., Holly, MI 48442. 800-437-1218. $14.95/4 issues.

Country Handcrafts, 5925 Country Ln., P.O. Box 996, Greendale, WI 53129-0996. $16.98/6 issues.

Country Sampler, P.O. Box 7598, Red Oak, IA 51591-0598. 708-377-8399. $19.96/6 issues.

Country Stitch, P.O. Box 83620, Birmingham, AL 35282-9346. $19.97/6 issues.

Crafting Today, P.O. Box 517, Mt. Morris, IL 61054-7993. $15.97/6 issues.

Crafts, P.O. Box 3117, Harlan, IA 51593-2183. $19.98. "Creative woman's choice."

Crafts 'n Things, P.O. Box 7519, Red Oak, IA 51591-0519. $16.97/10 issues.

Craftworks for the Home, P.O. Box 413, Mt. Morris, IL 61054-9820. $35.40.

Creative Machine, The, Open Chain Publishing, P.O. Box 2634, Menlo Park, CA 94026. $12/4 issues. "For people who love their sewing machines and sergers the way others love their computers and cars."

Creative Needle, 1 Apollo Rd., Lookout Mtn., GA 30750. 800-443-3127. $19/6 issues. Heirloom sewing by machine, hand sewing, sewing machine tips, embroidery, sergers.

Creative Quilting, P.O. Box 7074, Red Oak, IA 51591-0074. $21/6 issues.

Cross Stitch Magazine, 23 Old Pecan Rd., Big Sandy, TX 75755. $14.95/6 issues.

Cross Stitch Sampler, P.O. Box 7040, Red Oak, IA 51591. 800-666-2255. $13.98/4 issues.

Cross Stitcher, The, P.O. Box 7521, Red Oak, IA 51591-0521. $14.97/6 issues.

Decorative Artist's Workbook, P.O. Box 3284, Harlan, IA 51593. 800-333-0888. $18/6 issues.

Dollmaking Projects and Plans, P.O. Box 1921, Marion, OH 43306-1921. $14.95/4 issues.

Fashion Knitting, P.O. Box 173, Mt. Morris, IL 61054-9823. $23.70/6 issues.

Folkart Treasures Country Marketplace, P.O. Box 1823, Sioux City, IA 51102. $12/4 issues. Photos of handcrafts for sale.

Just CrossStitch, P.O. Box 420319, Palm Coast, FL 32142-9698. $15.95/6 issues.

Knitter's, P.O. Box 1525, Sioux Falls, SD 57101-9804. $16/4 issues.

Lapidary Journal, Circulation Dept., P.O. Box 1100, Devon, PA 19333-9935. $24.

Leisure Arts: The Magazine, P.O. Box 420222, Palm Coast, FL 32142-0222. 800-829-9157. $17/6 issues. Cross-stitch, knit, crochet, crafts.

Make-It, The Craft Magazine, P.O. Box 993, Altoona, PA 16603-9800. $9.95 /4 issues. Knitting, crochet, fabric painting, embroidery, appliqué, quilting, soft sculpture, woodcraft, mosaics, jewelry, etc.

McCall's Crochet Patterns, P.O. Box 5082, Harlan, IA 51593-2582. $17.70/6 issues.

McCall's Needlework and Crafts, P.O. Box 3217, Harlan, IA 51593-2397. $13.97/6 issues. Quilts, cross-stitch, crochet, knitting, crafts, painting.

Miniature Quilts, P.O. Box 1762, Riverton, NJ 08077-9762. $9.95/4 issues.

Miniatures Showcase, P.O. Box 1612, Waukesha, WI 53187-9950. $19.95/6 issues. "Decorating and design in miniature."

Needlepoint Plus, 3300 Walnut Ave., P.O. Box 54223, Boulder, CO 80323-4223. $23.70/6 issues.

Nutshell News, P.O. Box 1612, Waukesha, WI 53187-9950. $29.95. Crafting miniatures and decorating dollhouses.

Old-fashioned Patchwork, Harris Publications, Inc., 1115 Broadway, New York, NY 10160-0397. $16.97/8 quarterly issues.

Ornament, P.O. Box 2349, San Marcos, CA 92079-9806. $25/4 issues. "Quarterly of personal adornment."

PaintWorks, P.O. Box 388, Mt. Morris, IL 61054-7948. $15.97/6 issues. "Discovery magazine for decorative painters."

Quick & Easy Crafts, P.O. Box 11309, Des Moines, IA 50340-1309. $12.97/6 issues.

Quick and Easy Needlecraft, 23 Old Pecan Rd., Big Sandy, TX 75755-9972. $14.95/6 issues.

Quick and Easy Plastic Canvas, 23 Old Pecan Rd., Big Sandy, TX 75755-9972. $14.95/6 issues.

Quilting International, P.O. Box 460, Mt. Morris, IL 61054. $16.97/6 issues.

Quiltmaker, P.O. Box 58358, Boulder, CO 80321-8358. $14.95/4 issues. "Pattern magazine for today's quilters."

Sew Beautiful, 518 Madison St., Huntsville, AL 35801-4286. $23/5 issues.

Sew News, Box 3134, Harlan, IA 51537-3134. 800-289-6397. $19.94. Fashion, fabric, technique, sources.

SourceLetter, The, 7509 7th Place SW, Seattle, WA 98106. $18 each (specify either crafter's, sewer's, or stitcher's edition). Supply sources for decorative painters, wearable artists; products.

Stoney Creek Cross Stitch Collection Magazine, 4336 Plainfield NE, Grand Rapids, MI 49505. $17/3 issues.

Threads, Taunton Press, 63 S. Main St., P.O. Box 5506, Newton, CT 06470-9977. $26/6 issues. Sewing, embroidery, quilting, etc.

Tole World, 3300 Walnut Ave., P.O. Box 52995, Boulder, CO 80323-2995. $23.70/6 issues. "Creative designs for decorative painting."

Traditional Quilter, P.O. Box 507, Mt. Morris, IL 61054-7939. $16.97/6 issues. "Leading teaching magazine for creative quilters."

Traditional Quiltworks, P.O. Box 1737, Riverton, NJ 08077-9837. $15.95/7 issues. "Pattern magazine for creative quilters."

Vogue Knitting International, P.O. Box 1072, Altoona, PA 16603-9972. $15.50/3 issues.

Vogue Patterns, P.O. Box 751, Altoona, PA 16603-9979. $11.95/6 issues.

Wildfowl Carving and Collecting, P.O. Box 1831, Harrisburg, PA 17105-9912. $29.95/4 issues.

Electronics, Audio, Video

Audio, P.O. Box 51011, Boulder, CO 80323-1011. $24. Stereos, components.

Car Audio and Electronics, P.O. Box 50267, Boulder, CO 80321-0267. 800-759-9557. $16.66/9 issues. Latest products, comparison test reports.

CD Review, P.O. Box 588, Mt. Morris, IL 61054-7911. $19.97. New recordings and equipment.

CQ Amateur Radio, 76 N. Broadway, Hicksville, NY 11801-7626. $22.95.

EQ, Creative Data Center, 650 S. Clark St., Chicago, IL 60605-9960. $19.97/6 issues. "The recording and sound magazine — for project recording, sound techniques, production tips and latest technology."

High Performance Review, P.O. Box 346, Woodbury, CT 06798. $20.97/4 issues. "Reviews of audio components and music."

Home and Studio Recording, Music Maker Publications, Inc., Subscription Service, P.O. Box 986, Julian, CA 92036-0986. $20. "Magazine for the recording musician."

Intelligent Decisions, 2132 Greenbay Rd., Highland Park, IL 60035-9952. $14/4 issues. "Guide to audio and video entertainment."

Mix, P.O. Box 41525, Nashville, TN 37204. $46. "Professional recording, sound and music production."

Motor, Att: E. Donnellan, 645 Stewart Ave., Garden City, NY 11530. $18. "Technical advice on how to cope with electronic controls, CV joints and other real-life problems for technicians and shop owners."

Popular Communications, 76 N. Broadway, Hicksville, NY 11801-9962. $19.95. For short-wave listening and scanner monitoring.

Popular Electronics, Gernsback Publications, Inc., 500-B, Bi-County Blvd., Farmingdale, NY 11735-3918. $19.

Radio Electronics and Electronics Now, Subscription Services, P.O. Box 51866, Boulder, CO 80321-1866. $19.97.

Radio Fun, P.O. Box 4926, Manchester, NH 03108-9839. 800-257-2346. $12.97.

73 Amateur Radio Today, P.O. Box 58866, Boulder, CO 80322-8866. 800-289-0388. $24.97.

Stereo Review, P.O. Box 55627, Boulder, CO 80322-5627. $13.94. Equipment and music.

Video Magazine, Reese Communications, 460 W. 34th St., New York, NY 10001. $12. "For the home video user."

Entertainment World

Cinefex, P.O. Box 20027, Riverside, CA 92516. $22/4 issues. "Journal of cinematic illusions."

Entertainment Weekly, P.O. Box 60001, Tampa, FL 33660. 800-828-6882. $51.48/52 issues. "Movies, TV, books, music, videos."

Film Comment, P.O. Box 3000, Denville, NJ 07834-9868. $19.95/6 issues. Spans past, present, future of moviemaking, insider news.

Film Quarterly, Journals Dept., University of California Press, 2120 Berkeley Way, Berkeley, CA 94720. $19/4 issues.

On Production, 17337 Ventura Blvd., Ste. 226, Encino, CA 91316. $36/8 issues. "Feature films, TV, commercials, corporate and computer graphics."

People, P.O. Box 61390, Tampa, FL 33661-1390. $84.27/53 issues.

Premiere, P.O. Box 55752, Boulder, CO 80322-5752. 800-289-2489. $18. Behind the scenes, business and art of moviemaking.

TV Guide, P.O. Box 400, Radnor, PA 19088-0400. $41/52 issues.

US, P.O. Box 50414, Boulder, CO 80321-0414. 800-677-4553. $23.95.

Ethnic Interests

American Visions, P.O. Box 37049, Washington, DC 20078-4741. $18/6 issues. "Magazine of Afro-American culture."

BE (Black Elegance), 475 Park Ave. S, New York, NY 10016. $16.99/9 issues. "Lifestyles of today's black women."

Class, P.O. Box 379, Mt. Morris, IL 61054-1473. $15/9 issues "Most comprehensive black magazine—Caribbean, Latin, African (Amer.) sights and sounds."

Colors, 50 W. 17th St., New York, NY 10011. $30/4 issues. "A magazine about the rest of the world."

Dollar and Sense, National Plaza, 1610 E. 79th St., Chicago, IL 60649. 800-858-8044. $17.95/12 bimonthly issues. Black politics, business, arts and entertainment, people in the news.

Ebony, P.O. Box 690, Chicago, IL 60690-9983. $16. Black women's beauty, fashion, etc.

Emerge, Subscription Dept., P.O. Box 7127, Red Oak, IA 51591-2127. $16.97/11 issues. Business, books, home entertainment, travel, life styles, sports, etc.

Essence, P.O. Box 51300, Boulder, CO 80321-1300. $12.96. Beauty, fashion, health, contemporary living for black women.

Hispanic, 111 Massachusetts Ave. NW, Ste. 410, Washington, DC 20077-0253. 800-338-2590. $24/11 issues. Music, travel, career, money, etc.

Jet, P.O. Box 538, Chicago, IL 60690-9983. $36/52 issues. Black newsmakers, sports, entertainment, national report.

Upscale, P.O. Box 10798, Atlanta, GA 30310. 800-UPSCALE. $19.95. "The successful black magazine."

Family Life
(see also *Magazines: Women*)

Child, P.O. Box 3176, Harlan, IA 51593-0367. 800-777-0222. $15.94/10 issues.

Christian Parenting Today, P.O. Box 545, Mt. Morris, IL 61054-7721. $14.97 /6 issues. Covers child development from birth through the teen years.

Family Circle, P.O. Box 3153, Harlan, IA 51593-2344. $15.97/17 issues.

Good Housekeeping, P.O. Box 7186, Red Oak, IA 51591-0186. 800-888-7788. $17.97. Nutrition, features, medical, book reviews.

Home Education Magazine, P.O. Box 1083, Tonesket, WA 98855. $24/6 issues.

Home Sweet Home, P.O. Box 1254, Milton, WA 98354. $20/4 issues. Home businesses, management, education, and medicine.

Joyful Child Journal, P.O. Box 5506, Scottsdale, AZ 85261-5506. $18/4 issues. Parenting ideas, innovations in education, stories for children.

Ladies' Home Journal, Customer Service, P.O. Box 53940, Boulder, CO 80322-3940. 800-374-4545. $12.

Marriage Partnership, Subscription Services, P.O. Box 11630, Des Moines, IA 50340-1630. $17.95/4 issues. "For couples who want Christ at the center of their marriage."

McCall's, P.O. Box 3191, Harlan, IA 51593-2382. $17.97.

Mickey Mouse Magazine, Welsh Publishing Group, 300 Madison Ave., 8th Fl., New York, NY 10017. $11.70/6 issues. Interactive magazine.

Mothering, P.O. Box 532, Mt. Morris, IL 61054-7856. $22/4 issues.

Parent Sports, 8 Wallacks Ln., P.O. Box 110141, Stanford, CT 06913-1025. $12.95/6 issues.

Parenting, Subscription Dept., Box 52424, Boulder, CO 80321-2424. $18/10 issues.

Parents, P.O. Box 3055, Harlan, IA 51593-2119. 800-727-3672. $12.97. Health, books, fashion, food, job issues, etc.

Play, 3620 NW 43rd St., Gainesville, FL 32606. $12/4 issues. "Quality entertainment for your children."

Pre-K Today, P.O. Box 54813, Boulder, CO 80323-4813. $29.95/8 issues.

Redbook, P.O. Box 7188, Red Oak, IA 51591-2188. $14.97.

Today's Family, 27 Empire Dr., St. Paul, MN 55103. $10.97/6 issues.

Woman's Day, P.O. Box 56061, Boulder, CO 80322-6061. 800-234-2960. $15.97/17 issues.

Working Mother, P.O. Box 51446, Boulder, CO 80323-1446. $7.97.

Financial & Business

Audacity, Subscription Office, P.O. Box 6606, Syracuse, NY 13217. 800-825-0061. $15/4 issues. Lessons of the past in business industry. By Forbes and American Heritage.

Business Ethics, 1107 Hazeltine, Ste. 530, Chaska, MN 55318. $49/6 issues. "Magazine of socially responsible business."

Business Week, McGraw-Hill Publishing Co., P.O. Box 421, Hightstown, NJ 08520-9493. $24.95/28 issues.

Economist, The, Subscription Dept., P.O. Box 50400, Boulder, CO 80321-0400. $98/51 issues. "Authoritative, but not boorish. Literate, but never long-winded. Witty, but rarely waggish. And consistently international."

Entrepreneur, Subscription Dept., P.O. Box 50368, Boulder, CO 80321-0368. $19.97. Franchise opportunities, advertising, management, etc.

Financial World, P.O. Box 7097, Red Oak, IA 51591-2097. 800-666-6639. $37.50/24 issues.

Forbes, P.O. Box 10734, Des Moines, IA 50347-0734. 800-888-9896. $52/27 issues.

Fortune, P.O. Box 61482, Tampa, FL 33661-1482. $52.95/27 issues.

Futures, The, 219 Parkdale, P.O. Box 6, Cedar Falls, IA 50613-9976. 800-221-4352. $39/15 issues. "Commodities, options and derivatives."

Harvard Business Review, Subscription Service Dept., P.O. Box 51038, Boulder, CO 80323-1038. $75/6 issues. Business issues, case studies, finance, management.

Inc., Subscription Service Dept., P.O. Box 54103, Boulder, CO 80321-4103. 800-336-5679. $19. "Magazine for growing companies."

Income Plu$, P.O. Box 420274, Palm Coast, FL 32142-0274. $19.95. "Money-making ideas and small business opportunities."

Kiplinger's Personal Finance Magazine, Editors Park, MD 20782-9960. $18. Family finances, taxes, investments, etc.

Minorities and Women in Business, Subscription Dept., P.O. Drawer 210, Burlington, NC 27216-9965. $15/6 issues.

Money, P.O. Box 61792, Tampa, FL 33661-1792. 800-338-1400. $33.95/13 issues.

Nation's Business, U.S. Chamber of Commerce, P.O. Box 51062, Boulder, CO 80321-1062. $22.

Worth, P.O. Box 55424, Boulder, CO 80323-5424. $15/6 issues. Banking, investment trends, global business.

Your Money, P.O. Box 3083, Harlan, IA 51593-2147. $15.97/6 issues. Mutual funds, taxes, trends, retirement, etc.

Fishing

American Angler, P.O. Box 434, Mt. Morris, IL 61054-7702. $23.95/6 issues. "Magazine of fly fishing and fly tying."

Bassin', P.O. Box 55739, Boulder, CO 80322-5739. $13.95/6 issues.

Fishing Facts, P.O. Box 331, Milwaukee, WI 53201-9362. $14.97/7 issues.

Fishing World Magazine, 51 Atlantic Ave., Floral Park, NY 11001-9984. $11.97/6 issues.

Flyfishing, P.O. Box 82112, Portland, OR 97282. $15.95/5 issues.

In-Fisherman, The, 2 In-Fisherman Dr., Brainerd, MN 56401-9908. $13.97/7 issues. "Journal of freshwater fishing."

Marlin, Subscription Service Dept., P.O. Box 8600, Winter Park, FL 32970. $24.95/6 issues. "International sport fishing."

Salt Water Sportsman, P.O. Box 11357, Des Moines, IA 50347-1357. $19.95.

Scientific Angler's Fly Fishing Quarterly, P.O. Box 3000, Dept. SAF, Denville, NJ 07834. $12.95/4 issues.

Sport Fishing, World Publishing Co., P.O. Box 8600, Winter Park, FL 32790-9849. $14.97/9 issues. "Magazine of offshore fishing."

Trout, Trout Unlimited Membership Service, 800 Follin Ln. SE, Ste. 250, Vienna, VA 22180. 703-281-1100. $25/4 issues. Includes membership in Trout Unlimited.

Food & Entertaining

All About Beer, Bosak Publishing, Inc., 4764 Galicia Way, Oceanside, CA 92056. $20/6 issues.

American Brewer, P.O. Box 510, Hayward, CA 94543-0043. $18/4 issues. Festivals and new brews.

Best Recipes, 208 W. 3rd St., Williamsport, PA 17701. $15/6 issues.

Bon Appetit, P.O. Box 7196, Red Oak, IA 51591-2196. 800-876-3663. $13.97. Recipes, wine, entertaining, restaurants.

Chili Pepper, P.O. Box 15308, N. Hollywood, CA 91615-5308. 800-9595-HOT. $15.95/6 issues. "Spicy world cuisine."

Chocolatier, P.O. Box 333, Mt. Morris, IL 61054. $19.95/6 issues. "Taste of the good life."

Cook's Illustrated, Subscription Dept., P.O. Box 59047, Boulder, CO 80323-9047. $24.95/6 issues. Cookbook, cooking school, consumer's guide, etc.

Cooking Light, P.O. Box 830656, Birmingham, AL 35282-9086. $20/7 issues.

Food and Wine, P.O. Box 3003, Harlan, IA 51593-2022. $26.

Gourmet, P.O. Box 51422, Boulder, CO 80321-1422. $18. "Magazine of good living." Menus, worldwide restaurant guide, entertaining in style.

Herb Companion, The, Interweave Press, 201 E. 4th St., Loveland, CO 80537. $21/6 issues.

Quarterly Review of Wines, P.O. Box 591, Winchester, MA 01890. 800-752-2587. $13.95/4 issues.

Quick 'N Easy Country Cookin', P.O. Box 66, Davis, SD 57021-0066. $12.95/6 issues.

Vegetarian Gourmet, P.O. Box 7641, Riverton, NJ 08077-9141. $9.95/4 issues.

Wine Enthusiast, Dept. W6, P.O. Box 39, Pleasantville, NY 10570-0039. $14.95/6 issues.

Wine Spectator, The, P.O. Box 1960, Marion, OH 43305-1960. 800-347-6969. $40/22 issues.

Gardening

African Violet, P.O. Box 3609, Beaumont, TX 77704. $15/6 issues. Includes membership in African Violet Society of America.

American Horticulturist, 7931 E. Boulevard Dr., Alexandria, VA 22308-9800. $15/6 issues. By American Horticultural Society.

Avant Gardening, Box 489C, New York, NY 10028. $18. New plants, products, techniques.

Gardendesign, P.O. Box 55455, Boulder, CO 80323-5455. $21/6 issues.

Green Prints, P.O. Box 1355, Fairview, NC 28730. "The Weeder's Digest."

Growing Edge, The, P.O. Box 1027, Corvallis, OR 97339. 800-888-6785. $17.95/4 issues. "Indoor and outdoor gardening for today's grower."

Horticulture, P.O. Box 51455, Boulder, CO 80323-1455. $18/10 issues. "Magazine of American gardening."

House Plant Magazine, P.O. Box 1638, Elkins, WV 26241-9909. $19.95/4 issues.

National Gardening, P.O. Box 51106, Boulder, CO 80321-1106. $18/6 issues. "For America's most devoted gardeners."

New Farm, P.O. Box 7596, Red Oak, IA 51591-2596. $14.97/7 issues. "Magazine of regenerative agriculture."

Organic Farmer, 15 Barre St., Montpelier, VT 05602. 800-223-7222. $15/4 issues.

Organic Gardening, Rodale Press, 33 E. Minor St., Emmaus, PA 18098-0682. $25/9 issues.

Taunton's Fine Gardening, Subscriptions, 63 S. Main St., P.O. Box 5506, Newtown, CT 06470-5506. $26/6 issues.

General Interest

Americana, P.O. Box 1950, Marion, OH 43306-2050. 800-347-6969. $18/6 issues. "The best of the past."

Change, 1319 18th St. NW, Washington, DC 20077-6117. $28/6 issues. "Magazine of higher learning."

Life, P.O. Box 61592, Tampa, FL 33661-1592. 800-634-4900. $23.97/14 issues.

National Geographic, P.O. Box 2895, Washington, DC 20077-9960. $21. Natural science, peoples, travel, etc.

Natural History, Membership Services, P.O. Box 3030, Harlan, IA 51593-2091. 800-234-5252. $25. Published by American Museum of Natural History.

Our Times, Ourselves, Special Report, Whittle Communications, P.O. Box 59026, Knoxville, TN 37950-9973. 800-848-8145. $15/6 issues. Wonderful photos, food, travel, kids, health, fashion, home, etc.

Reader's Digest, Subscription Data Processing Dept., P.O. Box 111, Pleasantville, NY 10571-2111. $17.97 (also has a large-type edition).

Robb Report, One Acton Place, Acton, MA 01720-9988. 800-229-7622. $65. "For the affluent lifestyle"—art, leisure, food, and people.

Saturday Evening Post, P.O. Box 7075, Red Oak, IA 51591-2075. $13.97/6 issues.

Smithsonian, Membership Data Center, P.O. Box 55583, Boulder, CO 80321-5583. $22. Includes membership in Smithsonian Institution with travel opportunities, discounts. History, science, art, discoveries, etc.

Southern Living, P.O. Box 830119, Birmingham, AL 35282-9562. 800-999-1750. $24. Entertaining, travel, gardening, decorating, recipes.

Southwest Sampler, Subscription Dept., P.O. Box 7598, Red Oak, IA 51591-0598. $13.96/4 issues. Decorating, SW architecture.

Sunset, P.O. Box 2041, Harlan, IA 51593-2004. $15. "Magazine of Western living."

Town and Country, P.O. Box 7180, Red Oak, IA 51591-2180. $24. Fashion, food, travel, avocations, and leisure.

Vanity Fair, P.O. Box 51333, Boulder, CO 80321-1333. $12. General editorial, interviews, books, society.

Victoria, P.O. Box 7150, Red Oak, IA 51591. $15.97.

World Press, P.O. Box 1997, Marion, OH 43305. $24.97. "News and views from around the world, business, environment, politics, leisure, etc."

Good Reading

Alfred Hitchcock Mystery Magazine, P.O. Box 7055, Red Oak, IA 51591. 800-333-3311. $20.95/15 issues.

American Scholar, The, Phi Beta Kappa Society, 1811 Q St. NW, Washington, DC 20077-3632. $21/4 issues. Contemporary thoughts and writing.

Analog, P.O. Box 7061, Red Oak, IA 51591. $34.95/every 28 days. "Science fiction and fact."

Asimov's Science Fiction, P.O. Box 7058, Red Oak, IA 51591. $34.95/every 28 days.

Atlantic, The, Subscription Dept., Box 51044, Boulder, CO 80321-1044. $15.94. Humor, fiction, poetry, arts and leisure, books.

Ellery Queen, P.O. Box 7052, Red Oak, IA 51591-2052. $19.97. Mysteries.

Fantasy and Science Fiction, Mercury Press, P.O. Box 56, Cornwall, CT 06753. $26/11 issues.

Gold Prospector, P.O. Box 507, Bonsall, CA 92003-0507. $15/6 issues.

Good Old Days, P.O. Box 11302, Des Moines, IA 50340-1302. $12.97. "America's premier nostalgia magazine."

New York Review of Books, P.O. Box 420384, Palm Coast, FL 32142-0384. 800-829-5088. $45/21 issues.

New Yorker, P.O. Box 56447, Boulder, CO 80322. 800-825-2510. $32/50 issues. Literary magazine.

P.I., 755 Bronx, Toledo, OH 43609. $16/4 issues. "Fact and fiction about the world of private investigators."

Reminisce, 5927 Memory Ln., P.O. Box 998, Greendale, WI 53129-0998. $16.98/6 issues. "The magazine that brings back the good times."

Science Fiction Age, P.O. Box 749, Herndon, VA 22070-9893. $14.95/6 issues.

Southwest Review, 307 Fondren Library West, SMU, Dallas, TX 75275. $20/4 issues. Essays, fiction, poetry.

Storytelling Magazine, P.O. Box 309, Jonesborough, TN 37659. $40/4 issues. Includes membership in National Association for the Preservation and Perpetuation of Storytelling.

Treasure Quest, P.O. Box 10030, McLean, VA 22102-8030. $16/4 issues. "Journal of lost treasure, shipwrecks and recovery."

Handyman & Hobbyist
(see also *Magazines: Crafts; Metalworking;* and *Woodworking*)

Family Handyman, The, P.O. Box 1956, Marion, OH 43305. $26/10 issues.

Home Mechanix, P.O. Box 54320, Boulder, CO 80322-4320. $13.94.

Live Steam, P.O. Box 1810, Traverse City, MI 49685. 800-447-7367. $31/6 issues. "Locomotive, marine, automotive, traction and stationary steam engines; shop tips, building working models."

Mecanica Popular, Editorial America, S.A., Subscription Dept., P.O. Box 10951, Des Moines, IA 50350-0951. $24. *Popular Mechanics* in Spanish.

Popular Mechanics, P.O. Box 7170, Red Oak, IA 51591. $15.94. Autos, home improvement, boating, electronics, science, technology, aviation.

Health & Fitness

Changes, Subscription Service, U.S. Journal, Inc., 3201 SW 15th St., Deerfield Beach, FL 33442-9879. 800-851-9100. $20/6 issues. "Magazine for personal growth."

East West Natural Health, P.O. Box 57320, Boulder, CO 80322-7320. $24/6 issues.

Eating Well, Ferry Road, P.O. Box 1001, Charlotte, VT 05445-9977. $18/6 issues.

Health, P.O. Box 56863, Boulder, CO 80322-6863. 800-274-2522. $18/6 issues.

HealthWorld, 1540 Gilbreath Rd., Burlingame, CA 94010. $12/4 issues. "For people who want to lead a healthy life."

Ironman, P.O. Box 12009, Marina del Rey, CA 90295-3009. 800-447-0008, ext. 2. $29.95.

Let's Live, P.O. Box 2030, Marion, OH 43305. 800-347-6969. $19.95. "America's foremost health and preventive medicine magazine."

Longevity, P.O. Box 3226, Harlan, IA 51593-2406. $17.97.

Men's Fitness, P.O. Box 560, Mt. Morris, IL 61054-7802. 800-423-5713. $19.97.

Men's Health, P.O. Box 7571, Red Oak, IA 51591-0571. 800-441-7761. $17.70/6 issues.

Muscle & Fitness, P.O. Box 562, Mt. Morris, IL 61054-7798. 800-423-5713. $34.97.

Muscular Development, P.O. Box 765, Medford, NY 11763-9881. $24. Bodybuilding.

Nautilus, P.O. Box 708, Independence, VA 24348-9989. 800-628-8458. $14.95/6 issues. "America's fitness magazine."

Pathways, 8 King St. E, Ste. 1000, Toronto, Ontario, Canada M5C 9Z9. $23.95/6 issues. "Guide to health through balanced living."

Prevention, P.O. Box 7305, Red Oak, IA 51591-2305. $13.97.

Psychology Today, P.O. Box 51844, Boulder, CO 80321-1844. $17.95/6 issues.

Shape, P.O. Box 563, Mt. Morris, IL 61054-7796. $17.97. "Fitness monthly for mind, body and spirit."

Today's Better Life, P.O. Box 1924, Marion, OH 43306-2024. $19.80/4 issues. "Magazine of spiritual, physical and emotional health" from a Christian perspective.

Total Health, 6001 Topanga Canyon #300, Woodland Hills, CA 91368. $13/6 issues.

Vegetarian Times, P.O. Box 446, Mt. Morris, IL 61054-8081. 800-435-9610. $24.95.

Walking, Customer Service Dept., P.O. Box 56561, Boulder, CO 80322-6561. 800-678-0881. $14.95.

Weight Watchers, P.O. Box 52200, Boulder, CO 80323-2200. 800-876-8441. $15.97.

Women's Sports & Fitness, P.O. Box 472, Mt. Morris, IL 61054-9908. $19.78 /8 issues.

History & Military

American Heritage Civil War Chronicles, P.O. Box 6903, Syracuse, NY 13217-7989. $10/4 issues.

American Heritage of Invention & Technology, Subscription Office, P.O. Box 52606, Boulder, CO 80321-2606. $15/4 issues. History of inventions.

American History Illustrated, P.O. Box 1776, Mt. Morris, IL 61054. 800-435-9610. $20/6 issues. American culture, politics, social and military history.

Blue and Gray, P.O. Box 28685, Columbus, OH 43228. 800-541-0956. $19/6 issues. "For those who still hear the guns."

Christian History, Subscription Services, P.O. Box 11633, Des Moines, IA 50340-1633. $16/4 issues.

Civil War, Civil War Society, P.O. Box 770, Berryville, VA 22611. $19.97/6 issues.

Civil War Times, P.O. Box 1863, Mt. Morris, IL 61054-9947. $16/6 issues.

Command Magazine, P.O. Box 4017, San Luis Obispo, CA 93403. 800-488-2249. $17.95/6 issues. "Military history, strategy and analysis."

Confederate Veteran, P.O. Box 59, Columbia, TN 38401-0059. $13/6 issues.

Great Battles, P.O. Box 417, Mt. Morris, IL 61054-8021. $16.95/6 issues.

Military History, P.O. Box 373, Mt. Morris, IL 61054-7967. $16.95/6 issues.

Naval Institute Naval History, New Member Services, 2062 Generals Hwy., Annapolis, MD 21401-9921. $28.

Quarterly Journal of Military History, Subscription Office, P.O. Box 2054, Marion, OH 43306-2054. 800-347-6969. $60/4 issues.

Sea History, National Maritime Historical Society, P.O. Box 68, Peeksill, NY 10566. $30 regular/$40 family/$15 student or retired/4 issues. Membership in society "to save America's seafaring heritage."

Warbirds International, P.O. Box 16149, N. Hollywood, CA 91615. 800-562-9182. $13.95/6 issues. "Only magazine completely devoted to aircraft of past military conflicts that are still flying or located in museums."

Wild West, P.O. Box 385, Mt. Morris, IL 61054-7943. $16.95/6 issues.

Homes & Decorating

Audio/Video Interiors, Subscription Dept., P.O. Box 51604, Boulder, CO 80321-1604. $19.95.

Better Homes and Gardens, 17 Locust St., P.O. Box 511, Des Moines, IA 50380-0511. 800-374-4244. $17.

Better Homes and Gardens Traditional Homes, 1716 Locust St., P.O. Box 11445, Des Moines, IA 50380-1445. $17.97/12 bimonthly issues.

Colonial Homes, P.O. Box 7142, Red Oak, IA 51591. $14.97/6 issues.

Country Sampler's Decorating Ideas, Subscription Dept., P.O. Box 7309, Red Oak, IA 51591-2309. 708-377-8399. $19.95/6 issues.

Country Victorian Accents, P.O. Box 508, Mt. Morris, IL 61054-7995. $14.97/6 issues.

House & Garden, P.O. Box 51466, Boulder, CO 80321-1466. $19.97.

House Beautiful, P.O. Box 7124, Red Oak, IA 51591-4124. $14.97.

Interior Design, 44 Cook St., Denver, CO 80206-5800. 800-542-8138. $34.95/16 issues.

Log Home Guide, Muir Publishing Co., 164 Middle Creek Rd., Cosby, TN 37722. 800-345-LOGS. $12/4 issues. For builders and buyers.

Metropolitan Home, 6060 Spine Rd., P.O. Box 54538, Boulder, CO 80323-4538. 800-374-4638. $19.95.

Old House Journal, P.O. Box 50214, Boulder, CO 80321-0214. $24/6 issues. Restoration ideas.

Unique Homes, P.O. Box 441, Mt. Morris, IL 61054. 800-827-0660. $30.97/6 issues. "National magazine of luxury real estate."

Victorian Homes, P.O. Box 61, Millers Falls, MA 01349-9901. $18/6 issues.

Victorian Sampler, Subscription Dept., P.O. Box 7598, Red Oak, IA 51591-0598. $13.96/4 issues. Houses, gardens, menus, antiques, and arts of years gone by.

Hunting & Guns

Black Powder Times, P.O. Box 842, Mt. Vernon, WA 98273. $15.

Bowhunter, P.O. Box 350, Mt. Morris, IL 61054-8029. $15.95/8 issues.

Bowhunting World, P.O. Box 362, Mt. Morris, IL 61054-0362. 800-877-6118. $20/8 issues.

Deer and Deer Hunting, 700 E. State St., Iola, WI 54990-0001. $17.95/8 issues.

Game Journal, Circulation Dept., P.O. Box 1208, Williamsport, PA 17701-1208. 800-225-7949. $24.95/6 issues. "Best of big game hunting."

Game Manager, The Multiple Use Managers, Inc., P.O. Box 1330, West Point, CA 95255-1330. 209-293-7087. $45. Newsletter about game management techniques and issues for private landowners and game managers.

Gray's Sporting Journal, P.O. Box 51098, Boulder, CO 80321-1098. $34.95/6 issues.

Guns & Ammo, P.O. Box 51214, Boulder, CO 80323-1214. 800-800-AMMO. $15.95.

Guns & Hunting, Harris Publications, Inc., 1115 Broadway, New York, NY 10160-0397. $12.47/6 issues.

Guns Magazine, P.O. Box 85201, San Diego, CA 92186-9911. $19.95.

Hunt, P.O. Box 58069, Renton, WA 98058. $19.97/6 issues. "Action hunting."

Hunting Horizons, 6471 Airpark Dr., Prescott, AZ 86301. $17/2 issues.

International Bowhunter, P.O. Box 67, Pillager, MN 56473-0067. $12/6 issues.

Petersen's Hunting, P.O. Box 56297, Boulder, CO 80322-6297. 800-800-4AIM. $12.97.

Shooting Times, P.O. Box 5004, Harlan, IA 51593-0504. $19.97.

Sporting Classics, Subscription Service Center, P.O. Box 1017, Camden, SC 29020. $28.96/6 issues. Hunting, fishing, wildlife art, guns, etc.

Traditional Bowhunter, P.O. Box 15583, Dept. MM, Boise, ID 83715. $16/6 issues.

Turkey and Turkey Hunting, 700 E. State St., Iola, WI 54990-0001. $9.95/4 issues.

Women & Guns, Second Amendment Foundation, P.O. Box 488, Station C, Buffalo, NY 14209-9930. $24.

Metalworking

Home Shop Machinist, P.O. Box 1810, Traverse City, MI 49685. 800-447-7367. $24.50/6 issues. "Precision metalworking."

Metalsmith, Bob Mitchell, SNAG, 5009 Londonderry Dr., Tampa, FL 33647. $45/4 issues. Includes membership in Society of North American Goldsmiths.

Projects in Metal, P.O. Box 1810, Traverse, MI 49685. 800-447-7367. $19/6 issues. "For serious machinist/metalworkers; not for hobbyists."

Tole World, 3300 Walnut Ave., P.O. Box 52995, Boulder, CO 80323-2995. $14.97/6 issues.

Model Building

Fine Scale Modeler, 21027 Crossroads Circle, P.O. Box 1612, Waukesha, WI 53187-1612. 800-533-6644. $14.95/8 issues. Cars, airplanes, military vehicles and figures.

High Power Rocketry, P.O. Box 96, Orem, UT 84059-0096. $25/6 issues.

Kitplanes, Subscription Dept., P.O. Box 487, Mt. Morris, IL 61054-8036. $26.97. "For designers, builders and pilots of experimental aircraft."

Model Airplane News, P.O. Box 428, Mt. Morris, IL 61054-9859. $17.70.

Model Railroader, P.O. Box 1612, Waukesha, WI 53187-1612. $28.95.

O-Gauge Railroading, P.O. Box 239, Nazareth, PA 18064. $19/6 issues.
Radio Control Boat Modeler, P.O. Box 427, Mt. Morris, IL 61054. 800-435-0715. $8.25/4 issues.
Radio Control Car Action, P.O. Box 427, Mt. Morris, IL 61054. 800-435-0715. $24.95.
RC Modeler, P.O. Box 487, Sierra Madre, CA 91025. $24. "World's largest publication for the radio control enthusiast."
Scale Auto Enthusiast, P.O. Box 10167, Milwaukee, WI 53210. $15/6 issues.
Scale R/C Modeler, 7950 Deering Ave., Canoga Park, CA 91304-9980. $19.95.
Scale Ship Modeler, 7950 Deering Ave., Canoga Park, CA 91304-9980. $19.95.

Motorcycles

Classic Cycle Review, 643 Seneca St., Harrisburg, PA 17110-9857. $24/6 issues. Classic motorcycles.
Classic MotorCycle, The, Motorsport, RR1, Box 200D, Jonesburg, MO 63351-9600. $42.
Cycle World, 853 W. 17th St., Costa Mesa, CA 92627. $17.94. Street, dirt, dual-purpose, all-terrain motorcycles.
Iron Works, Dennis Stemp Publishing, Inc., P.O. Box 8679, Pittsburgh, PA 15221. $16/6 issues. "American motorcycle riding experience."
Motorcycle Collector, Info Sport, 30011 Ivy Glenn Dr., Ste. 114, Laguna Niguel, CA 92677-9929. $20/6 issues.
Rider, P.O. Box 51901, Boulder, CO 80321-1901. $15.98. "Motorcycling at its best."

Music

Acoustic Guitar, P.O. Box 767, San Anselmo, CA 94979-0767. $23.95/6 issues.
American Organist, The, American Guild of Organists, 475 Riverside Dr. #1260, New York, NY 10115. $40. For organists and choral directors.
Bass Player, P.O. Box 57324, Boulder, CO 80323-3063. $29.95/8 issues.
Beat, The, Bongo Productions, P.O. Box 65856, Los Angeles, CA 90065. $12/6 issues. "Reggae, African, Caribbean world music."
Blues Access, 1514 North St., Boulder, CO 80304-3514. $12. Reviews, festival news, and news of the blues world.
Blues Review Quarterly, Rt. 2, Box 118, West Union, WV 26456. $12/4 issues.
Chorister's Guild Letters, 2834 W. Kingsley Rd., Garland, TX 75041. $40/11 issues. Technique, sample music for Christian choral musicians.
Contemporary Christian Music, P.O. Box 559960, Boulder, CO 80321-5996. $19.95.
Country Fever, P.O. Box 16598, N. Hollywood, CA 91615. $9.95/6 issues. Country music.
Country Music, One Country Music Rd., P.O. Box 2000, Marion, OH 43306. $15.98/6 issues.
Country Sounds, 5060 W. Albatross Place, Tucson, AZ 85741-5121. $37.50/13 issues. Country, western, folk, and bluegrass music.
Down Beat, P.O. Box 1071, Skokie, IL 60076. 800-535-7496. $26. "Jazz, blues and beyond."
Electronic Musician, P.O. Box 41525, Nashville, TN 37204-9830. $24.

Gramophone, General Gramophone Publication, Ltd., 177-179 Kenton Rd., Harrow, Middlesex, Great Britain HA3 0HA. $75. "Review of new classical recordings."

Guitar, P.O. Box 53063, Boulder, CO 80323-3063. $27.95.

Guitar World, P.O. Box 58660, Boulder, CO 80323-8660. $19.94.

Jazz Times, 7961 Eastern Ave., Ste. 303, Silver Spring, MD 20910-4898. 800-866-7664. $21.95/10 issues.

Journal of Country Music, The, 4 Music Sq. E., Nashville, TN 37203. $15/3 issues.

Keyboard, Box 58528, Boulder, CO 80322-8528. $29.95.

Living Blues, Circulation Dept., University of Mississippi, University, MS 38677. $18/6 issues.

Modern Drummer, P.O. Box 480, Mt. Morris, IL 61054. $27.95. Feature articles on world's great jazz drummers.

Opera News, Circulation Dept., 70 Lincoln Center Plaza, New York, NY 10023-6593. $30/17 issues. By Metropolitan Opera Guild.

Piano Quarterly, P.O. Box 767, San Anselmo, CA 94979-0767. $28/4 issues.

Saxophone Journal, P.O. Box 206, Medfield, MA 02052. $25/6 issues.

Strings, P.O. Box 767, San Anselmo, CA 94979-9938. $36/6 issues. "For players and makers of bowed instruments."

Wind Player, P.O. Box 15753, N. Hollywood, CA 91615-9913. $14.95/6 issues. "For woodwind and brass musicians."

Outdoors

American Forests, P.O. Box 2000, Washington, DC 20013. 800-368-5748. $24/6 issues.

Backpacker, P.O. Box 7580, Red Oak, IA 51591-2580. $24/8 issues. Wilderness travel, hiking, camping, paddle sports, off-road bicycles.

Backwoodsman Magazine, P.O. Box 637, Westcliffe, CO 81252. $14/6 issues. Woods lore, how-to projects, history, primitive weapons, etc.

Barron's Outdoor Guide, 4246 Linchmore Dr., Dayton, OH 45415-1860. $9.95/4 issues. Budget fishing and hunting.

Bird Watcher's Digest, P.O. Box 110, Marion, OH 45750-0110. $17.95/6 issues.

Birder's World, Subscription Dept., P.O. Box 1347, Elmhurst, IL 60126-9980. $25/6 issues. "Exploring wild birds and birding."

Field & Stream, P.O. Box 52044, Boulder, CO 80321-2044. $15.94.

Fur-Fish-Game, 2878 E. Main St., Columbus, OH 43209-2698. $13.95.

Ocean Realm, Subscription Dept., P.O. Box 6953, Syracuse, NY 13217-7955. $29.95.

Outdoor Life, P.O. Box 54733, Boulder, CO 80322-4733. $15.94. Hunting, guns, fishing, camping, sport vehicles, bowhunting, boating, hunting dogs, regional news.

People & Nature, Subscription Dept. ORN, P.O. Box 3000, Denville, NJ 07834-9797. $18/4 issues. "Published by Orion Society to cultivate a generation of citizen-leaders whose wisdom is grounded in and guided by nature literacy."

Rock & Ice, P.O. Box 3595, Boulder, CO 80307. $24. Outdoor adventure—mountain climbing, rock climbing, alpine ascents.

Sierra, P.O. Box 2674, Boulder, CO 80328-2674. $15/6 issues (for non-members).

Sport Climbing Magazine, P.O. Box 82158, Las Vegas, NV 89180-2158. $17.50/4 issues.

Summit, Dept. SUM, P.O. Box 3000, Denville, NJ 07834. $22.95/4 issues. Mountain climbing.

Trilogy, 310 Old E. Vine, Lexington, KY 40507. $14.95/6 issues. About preserving and enjoying the out-of-doors.

Warp, P.O. Box 469019, Escondido, CA 92046-9984. $14.95/8 issues. "Surf-skate-snow experience."

Whole Earth Review, P.O. Box 38, Sausalito, CA 94966-9932. $27/4 issues. Environment, community, land use, nomadics, etc.

Wildlife Conservation, Subscription Service, P.O. Box 56696, Boulder, CO 80323-6696. $13.95/6 issues.

Photography

American Cinematographer, P.O. Box 2230, Hollywood, CA 90078. $24.

American Photo, P.O. Box 51033, Boulder, CO 80322-1033. $19.90/6 issues.

Camera and Darkroom, Subscriber's Dept., P.O. Box 16928, N. Hollywood, CA 91615-9960. $24.95. "For creative photographers."

Darkroom and Creative Camera Techniques, P.O. Box 585, Mt. Morris, IL 61054-7686. $16.95/6 issues.

International Photographer, IFPO-S2, P.O. Box 18205, Washington, DC 20036-8205. $39/12 bimonthly issues.

Photo District News, P.O. Box 1983, Marion, OH 43306-4083. $36. "International publication for the professional photographer."

PhotoPro, P.O. Box 3088, Titusville, FL 32781-9912. 800-677-5212. $14.95/6 issues. "Magazine written for and by working professionals."

Shutterbug, P.O. Box 1209, Titusville, FL 32781-9910. $18.

Videography, P.O. Box 0513, Baldwin, NY 11510-9830. $30.

Videomaker, Subscription Fulfillment, P.O. Box 469026, Escondido, CA 92046-9938. $14.97. "Video camera user's magazine."

Politics & Opinions

American Spectator, 2020 N. 14th St., P.O. Box 549, Arlington, VA 22216-9851. 800-783-6707. $35. Investigative reporting.

Brookings Review, The, Attn: A. Lofton, 1775 Massachusetts Ave., Washington, DC 20077-5896. 800-257-1447. $17.95/4 issues. "Nonprofit organization devoted to nonpartisan research, education and publication in economy, government, foreign policy and social sciences."

Buzzworm — The Environmental Journal, P.O. Box 6853, Syracuse, NY 13217-7930. $21/6 issues.

Chronicles, P.O. Box 800, Mt. Morris, IL 61054. $24. "Magazine of American culture." By Rockford Institute.

Columbia Journalism Review, P.O. Box 1943, Marion, OH 43306-2043. $19.95/6 issues. "To assess the performance of journalism and to speak out for what is right, fair and decent."

Common Cause Magazine, P.O. Box 220, Washington, DC 20077-1275. $20 regular membership/$30 family/$10 student/4 issues. "Non-profit citizens' lobby that works to improve the way federal and state governments operate."

CovertAction Quarterly, 1500 Massachusetts Ave. NW #732, Washington, DC 20005. $19/4 issues. "Cutting-edge investigative journalism, exposing and challenging covert operations."

E, The Environmental Magazine, P.O. Box 6667, Syracuse, NY 13217-7934. $20/6 issues.

Earthwatch, 680 Mt. Auburn St., Box 403, Watertown, MA 02272. 800-776-0188. $25/6 issues. "To improve human understanding of the planet, the diversity of its inhabitants and the processes that affect the quality of life on earth."

Environment, Heldref Publications, Dept. W, 1319 18th St. NW, Washington, DC 20036. $29/10 issues. Environmental issues by scientists and policy-makers.

Foreign Policy, P.O Box 56616, Boulder, CO 80321-6616. $33/4 issues. By Carnegie Endowment for International Peace.

Futurist, The, 7910 Woodmont Ave., Ste. 450, Bethesda, MD 20897-1405. $30/6 issues. Includes membership in World Future Society. "Journal of forecasts, trends, ideas about future."

Harvard International Review, P.O. Box 401, Cambridge, MA 02238-9990. $14/4 issues. Politics, economy, foreign aid and policy, etc.

Insight on the News, P.O. Box 96067, Washington, DC 20090-6067. 800-356-3588. $39/52 issues.

Mother Jones, P.O. Box 50032, Boulder, CO 80322-0032. $12/6 issues. "Progressive politics, opinion and social activism."

National Interest, Subscription Dept. NI, P.O. Box 3000, Denville, NJ 07834-9831. $21/4 issues. Essays, politics, international issues.

National Review, P.O. Box 96636, Washington, DC 20078-7471. $57/25 issues.

New Republic, P.O. Box 52333, Boulder, CO 80321-2333. $69.97/weekly. Politics, ideas, culture.

Policy Review, Heritage Foundation, 214 Massachusetts Ave. NE, Washington, DC 20002-4999. $18/4 issues. Domestic and international policies analyzed.

Public Interest, The, Subscription Dept., P.O. Box 3000, Dept. PI, Denville, NJ 07834-9861. $21/4 issues. Issues from welfare reform to public art.

Southern Exposure, Institute for Southern Studies, P.O. Box 531, Durham, NC 27702. $24/4 issues. Includes membership in ISS. "A journal of politics and culture."

21st Century Science & Technology, P.O. Box 16285, Washington, DC 20041. $20/4 issues. "Campaign to revive progress and make environmentalist hoaxes extinct."

Vegetarian Journal, Vegetarian Resource Group, P.O. Box 1463, Baltimore, MD 21203. $20/6 issues. Includes membership in VRG. "Health, ecology, ethics."

Washington Journalism Review, Subscription Dept., P.O. Box 561, Mt. Morris, IL 61054. 800-827-0771. $24. Media watch.

Washington Monthly, The, P.O. Box 587, Mt. Morris, IL 61054-7928. $35. Politics, opinion, issues.

Washington Quarterly, 55 Hayward St., Cambridge, MA 02142. $32/4 issues. By MIT Center for Strategic and International Studies.

Wilson Quarterly, Subscriber Service, P.O. Box 420406, Palm Coast, FL 32142-0406. 800-829-5108. $24/4 issues. Articles on society, politics, government, etc. By Woodrow Wilson International Center for Scholars.

World Policy Journal, New School for Social Research, 65 5th Ave., Ste. 413, New York, NY 10211-0655. $26/4 issues.

World Watch, P.O. Box 6991, Syracuse, NY 13217-9942. $15/6 issues. "Keeps global vigil on declining health of the Earth, making clear connections between environmental stability and economic sustainability." In English, Japanese, Italian, and Russian.

Religious

Bible Review, P.O. Box 7027, Red Oak, IA 51591-2027. 800-678-4444. $24/6 issues.

Campus Life, Subscription Services, P.O. Box 11624, Des Moines, IA 50347-1624. $14.95/10 issues. Christian articles for college age.

Christianity Today, Subscription Services, P.O. Box 11617, Des Moines, IA 50340-1617. 800-999-1704. $24.95/15 issues.

Discipleship Journal, Subscription Services, P.O. Box 54479, Boulder, CO 80321-4479. $18.97/6 issues. Bible teaching on practical issues.

Guideposts, P.O. Box 858, Carmel, NY 10512-9968. $10.97. Inspirational.

Moment Magazine, 3000 Connecticut Ave. NW, Ste. 300, Washington, DC 20008-2509. $27/6 issues. Interests of the Jewish community.

Tikkun, P.O. Box 460926, Escondido, CA 92046. $19.85/6 issues. "Jewish critique of politics, culture and society."

Young Israel Viewpoint, National Council of Young Israel, 3 W. 16th St., New York, NY 10011. $25/4 issues. Jewish interests.

Science

Archaeology, Subscription Service, P.O. Box 420425, Palm Coast, FL 32142-9808. $19.97/6 issues.

Astronomy, P.O. Box 1612, Waukesha, WI 53187-1612. 800-533-6644. $17.70.

Biblical Archaeology Review, P.O. Box 7026, Red Oak, IA 51591-2026. $24/6 issues.

Cosmos, Ediciones KST, Abadia No. 3, 46700 Gandia (Valencia), Spain. $97.50 by international money order. *Sky & Telescope* in Spanish.

Discover, The World of Science, P.O. Box 420105, Palm Coast, FL 32142-0105. 800-829-9132. $29.95.

Earth, P.O. Box 1612, Waukesha, WI 53187-9950. 800-533-6644. $19.95. "Explore the science of our planet through comprehensive editorials and stunning visuals."

Final Frontier, 1516 W. Lake St., Ste. 102, Minneapolis, MN 55408. 800-24-LUNAR. $17.95/6 issues. "Magazine of space exploration."

Issues in Science and Technology, National Academy of Sciences, 2101 Constitution Ave. NW, Washington, DC 20077-5576. $36/4 issues. By National Academy of Sciences, National Academy of Engineering, and Institute of Medicine.

Popular Science, P.O. Box 5099, Harlan, IA 51593-2599. 800-228-8828. $13.94.

Rock and Gem, P.O. Box 6935, Ventura, CA 93006-9878. $18.

Rocks and Minerals, 1319 18th St. NW, Washington, DC 20077-6117. $32/6 issues. Also fossils.

Science, American Association for the Advancement of Science, 1333 H St. NW, Washington, DC 20005. $87/51 weekly issues. Research news, technical articles.

Science News, P.O. Box 1925, Marion, OH 43305. 800-247-2160. $39.50. "Weekly newsmagazine of science."

Science Probe!, Subscription Dept., P.O. Box 54098, Boulder, CO 80321-
4098. $13.95/4 issues. "Amateur scientist's journal." High school ages up.
Sciences, The, Subscription Dept., 2 E. 63rd St., New York, NY 10131-0164.
800-843-6927. $18/6 issues. By the New York Academy of Science.
Scientific American, P.O. Box 3186, Harlan, IA 51593-2377. 800-333-1199.
$36. Science, business, and the citizen.
Sea Frontiers, P.O. Box 498, Mt. Morris, IL 61054-8004. $24/6 issues.
"Official magazine of the International Oceanographic Foundation." Ma-
rine life: photos, research, etc.
Sky & Telescope, P.O. Box 9111, Belmont, MA 02178-9918. $27.
Spectrum, Attn: Circulation Manager, 345 E. 47th St., New York, NY
10164-0621. $29.95. Fast-breaking technology.
Technology Review, P.O. Box 489, Mt. Morris, IL 61054-8019. $24/8 issues.
Latest technology in all areas: sports, science, business, etc.
Wall Street and Technology, P.O. Box 7626, Riverton, NJ 08077-7626. 800-
964-9494. $65.
Weatherwise, 1319 18th St. NW, Washington, DC 20077-6117. $28/6 issues.

Senior Citizens
Golden Years, P.O. Box 537, Melbourne, FL 32902-0537. $12.95/12 bi-
monthly issues. Healthy living, travel, money matters, relationships.
New Choices, P.O. Box 2037, Marion, OH 43306-2137. $15.97/10 issues.
"New choices for retirement living." Travel, health, feelings, money.
Successful Retirement, P.O. Box 7321, Red Oak, IA 51591. $13.97/5 issues.
Travel 50 and Beyond, 1502 Augusta Dr., Ste. 415, Houston, TX 77057.
$11.80/4 issues. "Discounts, bargains, tips for travelers over 50."
Where to Retire, 1502 Augusta Dr., Ste. 415, Houston, TX 77057. $11.80/4
issues. Taxes, climate, and more on retirement options.

Special Needs
Ability Magazine, P.O. Box 4140, Irvine, CA 92716-9919. $23.70/6 issues.
"Information resource on disability issues."
Deaf American, National Association of the Deaf, 814 Thayer Ave., Silver
Spring, MD 20910. 301-587-1788. $10/8 issues.
Disability Rag, Box 145, Louisville, KY 40201. $17.50/6 issues. Legislation,
issues on disabilities.
Exceptional Parent, P.O. Box 3000, Dept. EP, Denville, NJ 07834. $18/8 is-
sues. "Parents of a child with a disability."
Guideposts (Large print), P.O. Box 858, Carmel, NY 10512-9968. $10.97.
Inspirational.
Jewish Braille Review, Jewish Braille Institute, 110 E. 30th St., New York,
NY 10016. Free/10 issues.
Mainstream, P.O. Box 370598, San Diego, CA 92137-9894. $20/10 issues.
"Magazine of the able-disabled."
New Mobility, P.O. Box 4162, Boulder, CO 80306-9906. $18/6 issues.
Reader's Digest Large Type Edition, Reader's Digest Fund for the Blind,
Pleasantville, NY 10570. $17.97.

Sports
(see also *Magazines: Outdoors*)
Action Pursuit Games, CFW Enterprises, Inc., P.O. Box 405, Mt. Morris, IL
61054-8065. 800-877-5528. $24.50. Paintball, etc.

American Kite, 480 Clementine St., San Francisco, CA 94103-9931. $14/4 issues.

Baseball Digest, Century Publishing Co., 990 Grove St., Evanston, IL 60201-4370. $22. Major league baseball action.

Basketball Digest, Century Publishing Co., 990 Grove St., Evanston, IL 60201-4370, $22/8 issues. Pro basketball news.

Bicycle Guide, P.O. Box 21130, Lehigh Valley, PA 18003-9928. $12.95/9 issues.

Bicycling, P.O. Box 7592, Red Oak, IA 51591-2592. $15.97/11 issues.

Bowling Magazine, 5301 S. 76th St., Greendale, WI 53129. $10/6 issues.

Boxing Illustrated, P.O. Box 304, Pleasantville, NY 10570-9915. $18.92.

Football Digest, Century Publishing Co., 990 Grove St., Evanston, IL 60201-4370. $22/10 issues. Pro football scene.

Golf Digest, P.O. Box 3102, Harlan, IA 51593-2036. $23.94.

Golf for Women, 6060 Spine Rd., P.O. Box 54877, Boulder, CO 80323-4877. $14.97/6 issues.

Golf Illustrated, P.O. Box 10156, Des Moines, IA 50347-0156. $23.95.

Golf Magazine, P.O. Box 51413, Boulder, CO 80321-1413. $13.97.

Hang Gliding, United States Hang Gliding Association, P.O. Box 8300, Colorado Springs, CO 80933-8300. $49. Includes membership in USHGA.

Hockey Digest, Century Publishing Co., 990 Grove St., Evanston, IL 60201-4370. $22/8 issues. Professional hockey world.

Hockey News, P.O. Box 904, Buffalo, NY 14240-9947. $49.95/42 issues.

Hoop, P.O. Box HOOP, Lowell, MA 01852. $20.95/8 issues. Basketball.

Inside Hockey, P.O. Box 904, Buffalo, NY 14240-9947. $24.95.

Inside Karate, Subscription Dept., P.O. Box 404, Mt. Morris, IL 61054. $18.

Inside Sports, P.O. Box 346, Mt. Morris, IL 61054-7785. $9.97/10 issues.

International Gymnast, P.O. Box 2450, Oceanside, CA 92051-2450. $20/10 issues.

Mountain Biking, 7950 Deering Ave., Canoga Park, CA 91304-9980. $13.95.

Paintball Sports Magazine, 295 Main St., Mt. Kisco, NY 10549. $24.75.

Parachutist, 1440 Duke St., Alexandria, VA 22314. $21.50.

Racquet, P.O. Box 3000, Dept. FF, Denville, NJ 07834. $18/6 issues.

Ring, The, Box 768, Rockville Center, New York, NY 11571-9905. $21.95. Boxing.

Runner's World, P.O. Box 7594, Red Oak, IA 51591-2594. $17.94.

Soccer Digest, Century Publishing Co., 990 Grove St., Evanston, IL 60201-4370. $22/6 issues.

Soccer International, P.O. Box 246, Artesia, CA 90702-0246. $33.

Sport, P.O. Box 51541, Boulder, CO 80323-1541. $9.97. Varied sports.

Sports Illustrated, P.O. Box 61292, Tampa, FL 33661-1292. 800-521-3474. $80.46/54 issues.

Sports Spectrum, P.O. Box 3566, Grand Rapids, MI 49501. 800-653-8333. $11.97/6 issues. Christian perspective on sports.

Tennis, P.O. Box 3202, Harlan, IA 51593-2048. $11.97.

Track & Field News, Box 5013, Fremont, CA 94537. $33.

Triathlete Magazine, 744 Roble Rd., Ste. 190, Allentown, PA 18103-9838. $9.99/5 issues.

Volleyball Monthly, P.O. Box 3137, San Luis Obispo, CA 93403-9984. $19.95.

Wind Surfing, P.O. Box 8500, Winter Park, FL 32790-9825. 800-394-6006. $11.97/8 issues.

Women's Sports & Fitness, 1919 14th St., Ste. 421, Boulder, CO 80302. $19.97/8 issues.

Teaching

Challenge, Good Apple, 1204 Buchanan St., Box 299, Carthage, IL 62321-9988. $29.95/5 issues. For preschool to grade 8. Ideas to challenge the academically, physically, mechanically, and artistically gifted child: games, creative and critical thinking activities, etc.

Creative Classroom, P.O. Box 51139, Boulder, CO 80321-1139. $15.97/6 issues. From Children's Television Workshop. Over 25 reproducibles and activity sheets, seasonal activities, education news, plays, short stories.

Educational Oasis, Good Apple, 1204 Buchanan St., Box 299, Carthage, IL 62321-9988. $21.95/5 issues. For grades 5-9. Tips, posters, calendars, etc.

Horn Book Magazine, The, Circulation Dept., 14 Beacon St., Boston, MA 02108. $38/6 issues. About books for children and young adults.

Instructor, Scholastic, Inc., P.O. Box 53895, Boulder, CO 80323-3895. $19.95/9 issues. Teacher-ready pages, product reviews, ideas.

Mailbox, The, 1607 Battleground Ave., P.O. Box 9753, Greensboro, NC 27499-0123. $19.95/6 issues. Choose from three levels: preschool/kindergarten, primary (grades 1-3), intermediate (grades 4-6).

Schooldays, Frank Schaffer Publications, P.O. Box 2853, Torrance, CA 90509-9943. $17.95/4 issues. For grades K-3. Ready-to-go science, teacher idea exchange, bulletin boards, thematic units, etc.

Trains
(see also *Magazines: Model Building*)

Classic Toy Trains, Kalmbach Publishing Co., P.O. Box 1612, Waukesha, WI 53187. 800-533-6644. $19.95/6 issues.

Train Collector's Quarterly, Paradise Lane, Ronks, PA 17572. $12.

Trains, P.O. Box 1612, Waukesha, WI 53187-9950. 800-533-6644. $28.95.

Travel

Arizona Highways, 2039 W. Lewis Ave., Phoenix, AZ 85009. $17.

Baja Explorer, P.O. Box 81323, San Diego, CA 92138-1323. $16/6 issues.

British Heritage, P.O. Box 1066, Mt. Morris, IL 61054-9946. $30/6 issues.

Caribbean Travel and Life, Circulation, Box 2054, Marion, OH 43305. $19.95/6 issues.

Conde Nast Traveler, Box 57018, Boulder, CO 80322-7018. 800-777-0700. $15.

Country Inns, P.O. Box 457, Mt. Morris, IL 61054-9855. $17.95/6 issues. "Lifestyle magazine for sophisticated traveler"—bed and breakfasts.

Cruises and Tours, 1502 Augusta Dr., Ste. 415, Houston, TX 77057. $11.80 /4 issues. "Comprehensive listing of cruise lines, ships and destinations."

Eco Travel Magazine, 8533 83rd Ave., Edmonton, Alberta, Canada T6C 1A9. $26/4 issues. "Written for the socially responsible and environmentally conscious traveller."

Great Expedition, P.O. Box 18036, Raleigh, NC 27619. 800-743-3639. $18/ 4 issues. Adventure travel.

Ireland of the Welcomes, P.O. Box 51544, Boulder, CO 80321-1544. $21/6 issues.

Islands, Subscribers Service Dept., P.O. Box 51303, Boulder, CO 80321-1303. $19.95/6 issues.

Italy, Italian American Multimedia Corp., 138 Wooster St., New York, NY 10012. $30/6 issues.

Kauai Magazine, 976 Kuhio Hwy., Kapaa, HI 96746. $16/4 issues.

Mexico Events, P.O. Box 475, Mt. Morris, IL 61054. $11/6 issues.

National Geographic Traveler, P.O. Box 37054, Washington, DC 20078-9961. 800-638-4077. $17.95/6 issues.

National Parks, National Parks and Conservation Association, 1776 Massachusetts Ave., P.O. Box 96786, Washington, DC 20078-7463. $25 annual membership/$18 student/6 issues. "Defending, promoting and improving our country's National Park System."

Nevada, Subscription, P.O. Box 345, Mt. Morris, IL 61054-7716. $14.95/6 issues. "Magazine of the real West."

New Mexico, 495 Old Santa Fe Trail, Santa Fe, NM 87503. 800-334-8152. $19.95.

Realm, P.O. Box 215, Landisburg, PA 17040-9988. $27/6 issues. "Magazine of Britain's history and countryside."

Southwest Profile, Subscription Fulfillment Dept., P.O. Box 8504, Santa Fe, NM 87504-8504. $25/10 quarterly issues.

Texas Highways, Circulation Customer Service, Box 5016, Austin, TX 78763-5016. 512-483-3689. $12.50.

Trailer Life, P.O. Box 55793, Boulder, CO 80322-5793. $22. "Motorhomes, trailer, truck campers, folding trailers."

Transitions Abroad, Subscription Dept. TRA, P.O. Box 3000, Denville, NJ 07834-9767. $18/6 issues. "Guide to learning, living and working overseas."

Travel and Leisure, P.O. Box 2093, Harlan, IA 51593-2031. $32.

Travel Holiday, P.O. Box 2036, Marion, OH 43305. $11.97/10 issues.

Turista, Ragon International Publishing, Subscription Dept., 3033 Chimney Rock, Ste. 300, Houston, TX 77056. $18.95. International, bi-lingual.

Up-Here, P.O. Box 1350, Yellowknife, NWT, Canada X1A 2N9. $22.50/6 issues. "Life in Canada's north."

Vacations, 1502 Augusta Dr., Ste. 415, Houston, TX 77057. $11.80/4 issues. "Vacation ideas, tips and insider advice on best travel deals."

Vermont Life, 6 Baldwin St., Montpelier, VT 05602-9891. $11.95/4 issues.

Vermont Magazine, Subscription Dept., P.O. Box 389, Bristol, VT 05443-9986. $16.95/6 issues.

Water Sports

Canoe, P.O. Box 3146, Kirkland, WA 98083. $18/6 issues. Canoeing, kayaking, camping, outdoor activities.

Discover Diving, Watersport Publishing, P.O. Box 83727, San Diego, CA 92138. $14.50/6 issues.

Dive Travel, P.O. Box 1388, Soquel, CA 95073. $11.97/6 issues.

Rodale's Scuba Diving, P.O. Box 7589, Red Oak, IA 51591-0589. $14.97/6 issues.

Scuba Times, P.O. Box 40702, Nashville, TN 37204-9905. $11.95/6 issues. "Active diver's magazine."

Sea Kayaker, 6327 Seaview Ave. NW, Seattle, WA 98107-2664. $13/4 issues.
skin diver, P.O. Box 51473, Boulder, CO 80323-1473. $21.94.
Splash, Subscription Dept., McMullen & Yee Publishing, P.O. Box 70015, Anaheim, CA 92825-0015. $19.95. Watercraft.
Water Scooter, P.O. Box 524, Mt. Morris, IL 61054-0524. $15.97/9 issues. "Flagship magazine of personal water vehicles."
Waterski, P.O. Box 8400, Winter Park, FL 32790. $18.97/10 issues.

Winter Sports
(see also *Magazines: Outdoors*)
Ski, P.O. Box 52011, Boulder, CO 80321-2011. $9.97/8 issues.
Skiing, P.O. Box 51557, Boulder, CO 80321-1557. $11.94/7 issues.
Snow Country, P.O. Box 2072, Harlan, IA 51593. 800-333-2299. $13.97/8 issues. "Year-round magazine of skiing, mountain sports and living."
Transworld Snowboarding, P.O. Box 469019, Escondido, CA 92046-9984. $14.95/7 issues.

Women
(see also *Magazines: Family Life*)
Allure, P.O. Box 50025, Boulder, CO 80321-0025. $15. "Only magazine all about beauty."
Belles Lettres, P.O. Box 372068, Satellite Beach, FL 32937-0068. $20/4 issues. Reviews of books by women.
Brides Today, 3400 Dundee Rd., Ste. 300, Northbrook, IL 60062. $12/4 issues. "For brides of color."
Country Woman, 5925 Country Ln., P.O. Box 995, Greendale, WI 53129-0995. $16.98. "Down-home recipes, decorations, crafts and more."
Glamour, Box 53716, Boulder, CO 80322. 800-274-7410. $15.
Harper's Bazaar, P.O. Box 7176, Red Oak, IA 51591-2176. $17.94.
Mademoiselle, P.O. Box 51611, Boulder, CO 80321-1611. $12. Fashion, beauty.
Modern Bride, P.O. Box 51622, Boulder, CO 80321-1622 $17.97/6 issues.
Ms., P.O. Box 57132, Boulder, CO 80322-7132. $45/6 issues. On arts, books, women's issues.
New Woman, P.O. Box 52233, Boulder, CO 80323-2233. $12.97. Relationships, career, food.
SELF, Conde Nast Publications, 350 Madison Ave., New York, NY 10017. $15. Sourcebook for contemporary women.
Today's Christian Woman, Subscription Services, P.O. Box 11621, Des Moines, IA 50340-1621. $14.95.
Victoria, P.O. Box 1750, Red Oak, IA 51591. $15.97. "For contemporary women who wish to incorporate the elegance of the past into their personal life style." Fashion, beauty, home, entertaining.
Vogue, P.O. Box 52155, Boulder, CO 80321-2155. $24. High fashion.
Woman's Own, Harris Publications, Inc., 1115 Broadway, New York, NY 10160-0397. $10.79/8 issues.
Working Woman, P.O. Box 3276, Harlan, IA 51593-2456. 800-234-9675. $9.97.

Woodworking
Creative Woodworks & Crafts, P.O. Box 518, Mt. Morris, IL 61054. $15.97/6 issues.

Fine Woodworking, P.O. Box 5506, 63 S. Main St,. Newtown, CT 06470-9971. 800-888-8286. $29/6 issues.

Popular Woodworking, 3300 Walnut Ave., P.O. Box 58279, Boulder, CO 80323-8279. $19.97/6 issues.

Rodale's American Woodworker, P.O. Box 7579, Red Oak, IA 51591. $19.97/6 issues.

Shop Notes, P.O. Box 10930, Des Moines, IA 50347-0930. $19.95/6 issues. Tips, tools, techniques.

Today's Woodworker, P.O. Box 44, Rogers, MN 55374. $18.95/6 issues. Projects, tips, techniques.

Weekend Woodcrafts, 3300 Walnut Ave., P.O. Box 59006, Boulder, CO 80323-9006. $14.97/6 issues.

Woodcarving, Guild of Master Craftsmen Publications, Ltd., 166 High St., Leves, E. Sussex, BN7 1XU England. 800-225-9262. $27.50/4 issues. "Worldwide woodcarving."

Woodturning, Guild of Master Craftsmen Publications, Ltd., 166 High St., Leves, E. Sussex, BN7 1XU England. 800-225-9262. $34.95/6 issues.

Woodwork, Circulation Dept., P.O. Box 1529, Rosa, CA 94957. $15/6 issues.

Woodworker Projects & Techniques, P.O. Box 10127, Des Moines, IA 50350-0127. $19.97/6 quarterly issues.

Woodworker's Journal, P.O. Box 1629, New Milford, CT 06776. $17.95/6 issues.

Writing

Armchair Detective, The, 129 W. 56th St., New York, NY 10019. $26/4 issues. About writing detective stories.

Writer, The, 120 Boylston St., Boston, MA 02116-4615. $27.

Writer's Digest, P.O. Box 2124, Harlan, IA 51593-2313. $24. "Monthly guide to getting published."

Writer's Journal, 27 Empire Dr., St. Paul, MN 55103. $14.97/6 issues.

᪣ CATALOGS ᪣

What fun is in store for you in these catalogs! You'll find products for everyone on your gift list in whatever price range you prefer. Catalog shopping saves time, gas, and sales tax and you can shop any time that is convenient for you. To request a catalog, simply send a postcard or call the company. Some catalogs cost a few dollars, but quite a few of those give refunds on your first order. A few smaller companies request an SASE (self-addressed, stamped envelope). Don't let the cost deter you from ordering a catalog if the merchandise sounds like something you'd like to look at. Even in major metropolitan areas, you could easily spend more than the cost of the catalog driving around trying to find a specialty item. Some of these catalogs are slick and beautiful; some are copied on a copier, but don't judge the merchandise by the catalog. Some of the most wonderful handcrafts are described on copied pages because the artists run a one-person business and are keeping costs down so you can afford their creations.

Another advantage of catalog shopping is that often the companies will share your name with other companies with similar products so you have a continuing supply of gift sources. (Most companies have a place on their order form for you to check if you do *not* want your name given out.) The catalogs here are just a small sampling of those available. If you want more options in a particular area, go to a library or newstand and look through a magazine in the interest area. You'll find dozens more catalogs to request.

Many catalogs offer a wide variety of gifts and could logically be listed in several categories. Be sure to check the other categories referenced at the beginning of each section or browse through categories you might not think you are interested in and you'll be surprised at what you find. Catalogs of books and videos are generally listed under the special interest area such as *Gardening* or *Outdoors*. Companies carrying books (on paper and on audio or video cassette) on many topics are listed under *Books & More. Music & Movies* are combined into one category since many companies offer anything audio- or video-related in the same catalog.

The information listed is subject to constant change. Companies may publish one major and several smaller sale catalogs throughout the year, so the number of pages will vary (these have the number of pages listed as "various"). The number of pages listed is for the catalog I reviewed, but the catalog you receive may be a newer one and have a different number of pages. *Brochure* refers to a brochure or several loose sheets of information. Merchandise will vary from season to season, but the emphasis of the catalog will normally be constant. Assume that an "etc." appears at the end of each sentence in the descriptions. The products described or categories of merchandise given are merely examples of the items offered and are not complete listings.

I have not had personal experience with all of these companies. Before ordering, be sure to read return policies carefully. Always save the packing slip for several months after ordering in case you have any problem with the merchandise. Most companies have toll-free numbers for ordering with a credit card. Many have gift wrapping services, and most will send gifts directly to the person for whom you are buying. Gift buying can't get much more convenient!

Animals, Birds, Fish (and Lovers of Same!)
(see also *Environmentally Friendly* and *Outdoors* for other wildlife-inspired gifts)

AQUARISTS SUPPLY MANUAL, THE, Daleco Master Breeder Products, 3340 Land Dr., Ft. Wayne, IN 46809. $4, 36 pp. Fresh and salt water support systems, medications and water conditioners, lighting and temperature controls, biological purification devices, power filtration system, and live food cultures.

ART STUDIO WORKSHOPS, 518 Schilling, Forest Lake, MN 55025. $1, 16 pp. For cat lovers — cats on original greeting cards, limited edition prints, notecards, rubber stamps, recipe cards, stickers, and other paper products.

ARTFUL FISH, P.O. Box 40, Santa Cruz, CA 95063-0040. Free, 36 pp. Gifts for those who love to admire or consume fish—artwork, books, jewelry, educational toys, fish cooking equipment, housewares with fish motifs.

ARTGAME, THE, 11561 Shelly Vista Dr., Dept. C, Tujunga, CA 91042. 818-352-9966. Free, brochure. Colorful art prints of animals.

AUDUBON WORKSHOP, 1501 Paddock Dr., Northbrook, IL 60062. Free, 32 pp. All about wild birds—houses, videos, books, feeders, seeds, baths.

BUSH HERPETOLOGICAL SUPPLY, 4869 S. Bradley Rd., Ste. 18 B-180, Santa Maria, CA 93455. $1, 17 pp. Dry goods for reptile and amphibian needs —bedding, heating, books, videos, cages.

C&C ON THE ROCKS, 4882 Hamer Dr., Placentia, CA 92670. 714-731-6767. $1, 10 pp. Gifts for cats and cat lovers.

CAT CLAWS, P.O. Box 1774, Des Plaines, IL 60018. Free, 6 pp. Toys, cat tree, scratching pad, catnip, other treats for cats.

CATSFIRST, 1701 N. Market St., Ste. 125, Dallas, TX 75202. 800-548-2776. $.99, 9 pp. Fun-loving cats on picture frames, earrings, key chains, welcome mats, rubber stamps, videos.

CRAZY ABOUT CATS, 7000 Juneberry, Austin, TX 78750. Free, brochure. Whimsical accessories with cats on them.

DROLL YANKEES BIRD FEEDERS, 27 Mill Road, Foster, RI 02825-1366. 401-647-3324. Free, 24 pp. Lots of styles of bird feeders.

DUNCRAFT, Penacook, NH 03303-9020. Free, 36 pp. Bird feeders, houses, seeds, and accessories.

EVERYTHING COWS, P.O. Box 1019, Stowe, VT 05672. 800-639-2690. Free, 12 pp. Cows on literally everything—mugs, spoon rest, shopping list, boxer shorts, throws, pens, etc.

FAZO-CORP PRODUCTS, INC., P.O. C.P. 69007, Ste. Dorothee, Laval, Quebec, Canada H7X 3M2. Free, 40 pp. Books on pet care—birds, amphibians, cats, dogs.

HEAD TO TAIL, P.O. Box 3019, E. Hampton, NY 11937. 800-626-7817. Free, 14 pp. Cat, dog, and horse treats; herbal flea treatments; personalized gifts for pets and pet owners including invisible fencing.

HEP CAT CAT-ALOG, P.O. Box 40223, Nashville, TN 37204. Free, 32 pp. Fun fashions for feline fanciers—nightshirts, T-shirts, sweatshirts for women.

HERB GATHERING, INC., 5742 Kenwood, Kansas City, MO 64110. 816-523-2653. Free, brochure. Handmade catnip toys.

MASTER ANIMAL CARE, Humboldt Industries, Inc., Lake Rd., P.O. Box 3333, Mountaintop, PA 18707-0330. 717-384-3600. $2, 64 pp. Unique gifts for dogs and cats—toys, treat jars, training aids, books, beds, feeders.

NATIONAL WILDLIFE, National Wildlife Federation, Order Dept., 8925 Leesburg Pike, Vienna, VA 22184-0001. 800-822-9919. Free, 64 pp. Animal motifs on everything—clothing, cards, mugs, garden accessories.

NOAH'S ANIMALS, Dept. 4, 17150 Newhope #805, Fountain Valley, CA 92708. $2 refundable, 23 pp. 240 animal designs reproduced on quality products and notecards, scribble pads, jewelry, and framed prints.

PARROT MOUNTAIN CO., P.O. Box 2037, Ocean, NJ 07712. 800-362-8183. Free, 20 pp. Many books, supplies for pet birds.

PEDIGREES, 1989 Transit Way, Box 905, Brockport, NY 14420-0905. Free, 40 pp. All-around ideas for pet gifts from treats to Santa.

PET BOOK SHOP, THE, P.O. Box 507, Oyster Bay, NY 11771. 516-922-1169. Free, 64 pp. Hundreds of books on amphibians, cage birds, cats, dogs, fish, reptiles, spiders; care, diseases, training, careers with.

PET FURNITURE, Abeta Products, 503 Miltwood Dr., Dept. GG, Greensboro, NC 27455. 919-288-5391. $1, 18 pp. Cat scratching posts, beds, playgrounds, toys.

PET WAREHOUSE, Dept. C12, P.O. Box 20250, Dayton, OH 45420. 800-443-1160. Free, 106 pp. Large selection of supplies for cats, dogs, birds, fish.

SERENGETI, P.O. Box 349, Estero, FL 33928-0349. Free, 52 pp. Nice assortment and quality of wildlife gifts and apparel. 10% of the profits are donated to wildlife organizations. Moon and wolf earrings, jungle jigsaw puzzle, animals on baby's dinnerware, tote bags with endangered species.

WILDLIFE NURSERIES, INC., P.O. Box 2724, Oshkosh, WI 54903. 414-231-3780. Free, 34 pp. Plants and seeds which provide natural food and habitat for wildlife.

WORLD WILDLIFE FUND, P.O. Box 224, Peru, IN 46970. Free, 40 pp. A portion of each dollar goes to protect endangered wildlife, preserve threatened wetlands, and meet human needs without destroying natural resources. Featuring endangered species and other wildlife on clothing, calendars, home accessories, artwork, even wrapping paper and greeting cards.

Art & Special Treasures

(see also *Handcrafts* and *Craft Supplies*, which includes some finished pieces)

ALBERT S. SMYTH CO., INC., 29 Greenmeadow Dr., Timonium, MD 21093. 800-638-3333. Free, 8 pp. Special values on name-brand china, flatware, crystal, jewelry, pewter.

BIBLICAL ARCHAEOLOGY SOCIETY COLLECTION, 3000 Connecticut Ave. NW, Ste. 300, Washington, DC 20008. Free, 16 pp. Replicas of ancient (mainly Israeli, Egyptian, Turkish) jewelry, artifacts, artwork, toys.

COLONIAL WILLIAMSBURG, Dept. 023, P.O. Box 3532, Williamsburg, VA 23187-3532. Free, 22 pp. Fine reproductions from the colonial period.

FINE ART PRINTS, LTD., P.O. Box 3369, Newport, RI 02840-9869. Free, 20 pp. Diverse group of framed prints on regional, hunting, floral, nautical, Afro-American, sports, American West, classic themes.

HAMPSHIRE PEWTER, P.O. Box 1570, Wolfeboro, NH 03894. 603-569-4944. $2, 18 pp. Lovely colonial-style pewter vases, goblets, tankards, Christmas ornaments, bells, and other items handcrafted in New Hampshire.

HUNTINGTON BRONZES, E.M.I., 401 E. Cypress Ave., Visalia, CA 93277-2834. 800-777-8126. Free, 52 pp. Fine bronze castings of equestrian, Western, classic, wildlife, contemporary subjects.

J. PETERMAN CO., 2444 Palumbo Dr., Lexington, KY 40509-9966. 800-874-4616. Free, 74 pp. "Booty, spoils and plunder"—reproductions and actual ancient and antique works of art such as silver, pottery, furniture, English whistles, Italian leather boxes, other intriguing items. Some are one-of-a-kind. They also have a catalog of clothing from around the world.

MINNEAPOLIS INSTITUTE OF ARTS, 2400 3rd Ave. S, Minneapolis, MN 55404. Free, 14 pp. Items influenced by the art world—silk scarves, 8th century reproduction jewelry, mummy tins, photography books.

MONTICELLO CATALOG, P.O. Box 318, Charlottesville, VA 22902-0318. Free, 32 pp. Gifts from the time of Thomas Jefferson such as garnet necklace, boxwood topiary, medallion throw, fleur-de-lis demitasse set, pennywhistle with book and tape, other special items.

MUSEUM COLLECTIONS, Midwest Distribution Center, 4555 Lyman Dr., Hilliard, OH 43026-1282. 800-442-2460. Free, 55 pp. Museum replicas and reproductions from museums around the world.

NATIONAL ARCHIVES TRUST FUND, P.O. Box 100793, Atlanta, GA 30384-0001. 800-788-6282. Free, 20 pp. Reproductions of historic or patriotic items—George Washington teapot, Greek architecture building blocks.

NATIONAL GALLERY OF ART, Publications Mail Order Dept., 2000B S. Club Dr., Landover, MD 20785. 301-322-5900. Free, 64 pp. Prints and postcards of famous works of art.

ROSS-SIMONS, 9 Ross Simons Dr., Cranston, RI 02920-9848. 800-556-7376. Free, 36 pp. Fine jewelry, watches, English china, crystal stemware, sterling silver and stainless flatware, a few decorative items—all at discounts off retail.

SMITHSONIAN CATALOGUE, Dept. 0006, Washington, DC 20073-0006. Free, 60 pp. Reproductions and other beautiful items that reflect the rich diversity of the Smithsonian Institution, the world's largest complex of museums, art galleries, and research facilities. Examples—seven-drawer chest painted like a country manor house, musical pocket watch, lead Civil War soldiers, Renaissance silk/wool floral scarf—all are works of art.

TIFFANY & CO., 801 Jefferson Rd., P.O. Box 5477, Parsippany, NJ 07054-9957. 800-452-9146. Free, 35 pp. Classic jewelry, perfume, serving pieces, vases, sterling silver baby gifts, lead crystal.

WINGS FINE ARTS, 221 Randall St., Oakville, Ontario L6J IP5 Canada. 800-545-9464. Free, 24 pp. Aviation and naval art prints by Robert Taylor.

WINTERTHUR, Winterthur Museum and Garden, Catalogue Div., 100 Enterprise Pl., Dover, DE 19901. 800-767-0500. Free, 48 pp. "World's premier collection of American decorative arts."

Books & More

(This includes books on tape. See also *For Children Only* and other categories for books on specific topics.)

AIDS FOR GENEALOGICAL RESEARCH, National Archives Trust Fund, NEPS Dept. 735, P.O. Box 100793, Atlanta, GA 30384. Free, 29 pp. Books on genealogical research, Pennsylvania Dutch style family tree, many catalogs of specific records available at National Archives.

AMERICAN HERITAGE BOOKS, P.O. Box 10934, Des Moines, IA 50350-0934. Free, 6 pp. Books, videos, calendars on historical events and figures.

AUDIO DIVERSIONS, 306 Commerce St., Occoquan, VA 22125. 800-628-6145. Free, brochure. More than 1,300 titles to rent or buy on audio tape —classics, best sellers, self-help.

AVIATION BOOKS, 25133 Anza Dr., Santa Clarita, CA 91355-3412. 805-294-0101. Free, 74 pp. Books, video cassettes (air shows, military, piloting, building your own airplane), pilot supplies.

BARNES & NOBLE, 126 5th Ave., New York, NY 10011-5666. Free, 56 pp. Book bargains—science, foreign language, world history, etc.; videos.

BELLEROPHON BOOKS, 36 Anacapa St., Santa Barbara, CA 93101. 805-965-7035. Free, 11 pp. Appealing (to the eyes and the pocketbook) paperback art and coloring books for children. Subjects such as great explorers, presidents, Vikings, medieval times and societies, old cars, historical events and persons.

BOOKS FOR COOKS, NightinGale Resources, P.O. Box 322, Cold Spring, NY 10516. $3, 8 pp. Hundreds of cookbooks pleasantly priced from classic French chefs to vegetarian, special diet, ethnic, historic, camper's recipes.

CHARLES C. THOMAS PUBLISHER, 2600 S. 1st St., Springfield, IL 62794-9265. 217-789-8980. Free, 160 pp. Over 1,300 books on social, behavioral, and biological sciences. Also special education, criminal justice, and rehabilitation.

CLASSIC MOTORBOOKS, P.O. Box 1, Osceola, WI 54020. 800-826-6600. Free, 104 pp. Large selection of automotive, motorcycle, racing, restoration, truck and tractor books and videos.

COLUMBIA TRADING CO. NAUTICAL BOOKS, 504 Main St. (Rt. 6A), W. Barnstable, MA 02668. 800-362-8966. Free, 24 pp. Pirates, maritime law, yacht designs, maritime history, how-to.

DÆDALUS BOOKS, P.O. Box 9132, Hyattsville, MD 20781-0932. Free, 48 pp. Wide selection of remainders and new books from trade publishers and university presses.

DOVE AUDIO, 301 N. Canon Dr., Ste. 203, Beverly Hills, CA 90210-4724. $4, 35 pp. Books on tape—from National Public Radio, mysteries, best sellers, classics, biographies, sports, humor, children.

DOVER PUBLICATIONS, INC., 31 E. 2nd St., Mineola, NY 11501. Free, 82 pp. Over 5,200 high-quality paperback books (most under $6) on a wide variety of subjects such as puzzles, anthropology, chess, folklore, languages, plants, stickers. Some activity books.

ECONO-CLAD BOOKS, P.O. Box 1777, Topeka, KS 66601. 800-255-3502. Free, 544 pp. Thousands of books for preschool through adult—nonfiction, early learning, crafts, science, fiction, humor, all interest areas.

EDWARD R. HAMILTON, Falls Village, CT 06031-5000. Free, 32 pp. Publishers' closeouts, overstocks, remainders, but all new — biographies, history, crafts, business, reference, children's books, art books.

ELP (Essential Learning Products), Division of Highlights for Children, 2300 W. 5th Ave., P.O. Box 2607, Columbus, OH 43272-4247. 614-486-0762. Free, 16 pp. Educational books, games, workbooks, classroom motivational products through grade 8.

F&W Publications, Inc. 1507 Dana Ave., Cincinnati, OH 45207-1005. 800-289-0963. Free, 65 pp. Practical books on writing, photography, art, home building and remodeling, theater, hobbies, sports, for young readers. Writer's Digest Books, North Light Books, and Betterway Books.

HARBINGER HOUSE, P.O. Box 42948, Tucson, AZ 85733-2948. Free, 32 pp. Books for children, geoscience, outdoor topics, poetry, self-help, nature series, earth sciences and travel (including bed and breakfast guides).

HARCOURT BRACE JAVONOVICH PUBLISHERS, Trade Sales Dept., 1250 6th Ave., San Diego, CA 92101. 800-543-1918. Free, various. Several catalogs for adult and children's books.

HOME EDUCATION PRESS, P.O. Box 1083, Tonasket, WA 98855. 509-486-1351. Free, 24 pp. Books about home schooling and curriculum aids for home schoolers.

J. TUTTLE MARITIME BOOKS, 1806 Laurel Crest, Madison, WI 53705. Free, 61 pp. Adventure, history, people of the sea.

LISTENING LIBRARY, One Park Ave., Old Greenwich, CT 06870-1727. 800-243-4504. Free, 40 pp. Favorites in print and on tape.

MCGOWAN BOOK CO., P.O. Box 16325, Chapel Hill, NC 27516-6325. 919-968-1121. Free, 32 pp. Americana and Civil War books.

MEADOWBROOK PRESS, 18318 Minnetonka Blvd., Deephaven, MN 55391. 800-338-2232. Free, 30 pp. Family books—children's activities, entertaining, humor, baby care and albums.

MIDLAND COUNTIES PUBLICATIONS, Unit 3 Maizefield, Hinckley, Leics LE10 1YF United Kingdom. Free, various. Aviation and military books and videos.

NOBLE PRESS, 213 W. Institute Pl., Ste. 508, Chicago, IL 60610. 800-486-7737. Free, 25 pp. Serious subjects like discrimination, social justice, environmental issues.

OLDE SOLDIER BOOKS, 18779 B N. Frederick Ave., Gaithersburg, MD 20879. 301-963-2929. Free, 24 pp. Many original letters, documents, manuals, photos from Civil War.

PENGUIN USA, P.O. Box 999 - Dept. 17109, Bergenfield, NJ 07621. Free, 78 pp. Catalogs for trade paperbacks and for hardbacks. Over 50 categories of books from anthropology to mystery to sports and recreation.

Q.M. DABNEY & CO., Inc., P.O. Box 42026, Washington, DC 20015. 301-881-1470. Free, 232 pp. Old, rare, used, and out-of-print books on military history.

RECORDED BOOKS, INC., 270 Skipjack Rd., Prince Frederick, MD 20678. 800-638-1304. Free, 20 pp. Unabridged current titles on audio cassettes for rent.

RIZZOLI INTERNATIONAL, INC., 300 Park Ave. S, New York, NY 10010. 212-387-3528. $2, 56 pp. Books on art, architecture, culinary arts, decorative arts, photography, fashion; separate catalog of children's books and paper products.

RODALE PRESS, Catalog Sales Dept., 33 E. Minor St., Emmaus, PA 18098. 800-527-8200. Free, 76 pp. Practical books on gardening, health, bicycling, crafts, cookbooks, "books that empower people's lives."

SELECTIONS, READER'S DIGEST, Order Dept., Pleasantville, NY 10570. Free, 52 pp. Family books, videos, and music.

SOUNDVIEW EXECUTIVE BOOK Summaries, 5 Main St., Bristol, VT 05443-1398. 800-521-1227. Free, various. Catalog of back issues of their summaries of business books. Can subscribe to the monthly service also which summarizes two to three business books a month in eight-page summaries for the busy businessman.

SOZO'S CREATIVE LEARNING CO., P.O. Box 311, Boulder, CO 80306-0311. 303-444-1745. Free, 24 pp. Family learning made fun—music, science, art, games, storytelling.

SPOKEN ARTS, 10100 SBF Dr., Pinellas Park, FL 34666. 800-326-4090. Free, 48 pp. Books and books on audio tape for children, youth, adults.

STACKPOLE BOOKS, P.O. Box 1831, Cameron & Kelker Sts., Harrisburg, PA 17105. 800-732-3669. Free, 48 pp. Nice variety of topics from outdoors to crafts, carving, hunting, military history, sporting literature.

STOREY'S BOOKS FOR COUNTRY LIVING, Dept. 46, P.O. Box 38, Pownal, VT 05261-9989. Free, 36 pp. Books on small-scale farming, animals, nature, energy, building, home improvement, crafts, children, cooking, gardening, herbs, country business.

TRAFALGAR SQUARE BOOKS, P.O. Box 257, N. Pomfret, VT 05053. 800-423-4525. Free, 90 pp. Multitude of topics from crafts, dogs, and poetry to hunting, humor, and psychology.

U.S. NAVAL INSTITUTE PRESS, Customer Service, Operations Center, 2062 General's Hwy., Annapolis, MD 21401-6780. 800-233-USNI. Free, 47 pp. Books on seamanship, naval history and literature, biographies, ship and aircraft references. Also fine color reproductions and museum prints of naval scenes.

VESTAL PRESS, 320 N. Jensen Rd., P.O. Box 97, Vestal, NY 13851-0097. 607-797-4872. Free, 15 pp. Books on unusual subjects including carousels, cinema history, mechanical music, piano and player pianos, picture postcard histories, radio and phonograph collecting, reed organ, jukeboxes and slot machines, with a little woodcarving thrown in. Lots of nostalgia here!

WHOLE MIRTH CATALOG, THE, 1034 Page St., San Francisco, CA 94117. 415-431-1913. $1, 12 pp. All in fun! Jokes books, books about inner joy, fun and games, and laughter.

WINTERTHUR BOOK CATALOGUE, Winterthur Museum and Garden, Catalogue Division, 100 Enterprise Pl., Dover, DE 19901. 800-767-0500. $1, 48 pp. 1,800 books on decorative arts—furniture, architecture, woodworking, textiles, interior design, gardening, painting, and graphic arts.

WORKMAN PUBLISHING, 708 Broadway, New York, NY 10003. 800-722-7202. Free, 104 pp. Page-a-day calendars, gardening, cooking, health, child care, sports, Shakespeare, science, fun and games. hobbies, reference, more!

ZENITH BOOKS, P.O. Box 1, Osceola, WI 54020. 800-826-6600. Free, 56 pp. Aviation books — on combat, weaponry, military history, museums, racing, aviation milestones.

Clothing—Children Thru Teens
(see also *For Children Only* and *Infant/Maternity Supplies*)

BIOBOTTOMS FRESH AIR WEAR, P.O. Box 6009, Petaluma, CA 94953. 800-766-1254. Free, 56 pp. Irresistible children's fashions up through preteen —party dresses, casual, and in-between.

BRIGHTS CREEK, Bay Point Pl., Hampton, VA 23653-3122. Free, 48 pp. Adorable designs for babies through preteens at affordable prices.

GOOSE-EYE ORIGINALS, 8895 N. Archie, Fresno, CA 93720. 209-323-8317. Free, 10 pp. Small children's clothing—even a small size umbrella.

KIDS AT LARGE, Bldg. 32, Endicott St., Norwood, MA 02062. Free, 16 pp. Right-now styles for large-sized child, size 4-14. You'll like the prices.

Clothing—General
(see also other *Clothing* categories; *Animals, Birds, Fish (and Lovers of Same!); Infant/Maternity Supplies; Environmentally Friendly; Smorgasbord; Western & Equestrian;* and *Outdoors*)

BROOKS BROTHERS, 350 Campus Plaza, P.O. Box 4016, Edison, NJ 08818-4016. 800-274-1816. Free, 60 pp. Tailored clothing for men, women, children.

DAMART, 3 Front St., Rollinsford, NH 03805. 800-258-7300. Free, 40 pp. Lightweight but warm thermal under and outer garments for men, women, children.

DEERSKIN, 119 Foster St., P.O. Box 6008, Peabody, MA 01961-6008. 508-532-4040. Free, 64 pp. Leather fashions for men and women — coats, dresses, shoes, jackets, bags, gloves, skirts, pants.

DEVA LIFEWEAR, Box S93, 303 E. Main St., Burkittsville, MD 21718-0438. Free, 40 pp. Natural fiberware garments. Comfortable styles for men and women.

GORSUCH, LTD., 263 E. Gore Creek Dr., Vail, CO 81657. Free, 40 pp. High fashion ski wear and clothes for back at the lodge.

LANDS' END, 1 Lands' End Ln., Dodgeville, WI 53595-0001. 800-356-4444. Free, 260 pp. Casual clothes for men, women, and children; cotton and wool bed, bath, and kitchen linens; luggage. Good values.

NAMELY YOURS, 5024 W. Nassau St., Tampa, FL 33607-8315. Free, 35 pp. Personalize a polo, rugby, or golf shirt or Turkish towel or warm-up jacket with your choice of design and lettering (many to choose from).

PAMBÉ, Abtahi Enterprises, P.O. Box 802613, Santa Clarita, CA 91380-9959. Free, 13 pp. Natural fabric underclothing—wool, silk, cotton—for women and children.

RED FLANNEL FACTORY, THE, P.O. Box 370, 157 W. Beech, Cedar Springs, MI 49319. Free, 12 pp. The name says it! Red and plaid flannel Christmas stockings, gowns and robes, lumberjack shirts, boxer shorts, long johns.

SICKAFUS SHEEPSKINS, Rt. 78, Exit 7, Strausstown, PA 19559. 215-488-1782. $.50, 16 pp. Sheepskin coats, slippers, gloves; leather jackets, purses; fur coats.

SIMPLY DIVINE, 1606 S. Congress, Austin, TX 78704. 512-444-5546. Free, 16 pp. All cotton clothing for women and children—pants, jumpers, dresses, socks.

WOODEN SOLDIER, THE, P.O. Box 800, N. Conway, NH 03860-0800. 603-356-7041. Free, 56 pp. A great idea! Mother/child matching ensembles and other fanciful designs for children.

TUTTLE GOLF COLLECTION, P.O. Box 941, Meriden, CT 06450-0941. Free, 40 pp. Distinctive sportswear for men and women.

TWEEDS, ONE AVERY ROW, Roanoke, VA 54012-8528. Free, 68 pp. Classic looks for men and women. Mostly casual attire.

WINTER SILKS, 2700 Laura Ln., P.O. Box 130, Middleton, WI 53562-0130. 800-621-3229. $2, 68 pp. Machine-washable silks for men and women —long johns, sleepwear, shirts, sweaters, ties, gloves.

Clothing—Men

(see also *Clothing—General; Outdoors;* and *Western & Equestrian*)

BACHRACH BY MAIL, P.O. Box 8740, Decatur, IL 62524-8740. 800-637-5840. Free, 68 pp. Fashionable men's clothing for play, work, and partying.

BULLOCK & JONES, P.O. Box 883124, San Francisco, CA 94188-3124. 800-358-5832. Free, 40 pp. Fine men's wear from the likes of Salvatore Ferragamo.

HITCHCOCK, Hingham, MA 02043-1596. Free, 48 pp. Wide shoes for men (sizes 5-13, EEE to EEEEE in most styles). Dress shoes, deck shoes, athletic shoes, canvas sneakers.

INTERNATIONAL MALE, Order Processing Center, Hanover, PA 17333-0075. 717-633-3300. Free, 52 pp. Bold looks from around the world for the office, a night on the town, or working out.

KING-SIZE CO., P.O. Box 9115, Hingham, MA 02043. 800-846-1600. Free, 96 pp. Clothing for tall and big men (5XL talls, 8XL bigs, 40-inch sleeves, 24-inch necks, 15 and EEEEE shoes), also extra-sized luggage, sleeping bag.

SHORT SIZES, INC., Southgate Shopping Ctr., 5385 Warrensville Ctr. Rd., Cleveland, OH 44137. 216-475-2515. $1, 16 pp. Distinctive apparel for the man under 5'8".

Clothing—Women

(see also *Clothing — General; Infant/Maternity Supplies; Outdoors;* and *Western & Equestrian*)

ALL WEEK LONG, P.O. Box 3700, Seattle, WA 98124-3700. Free, 64 pp. Festive, feminine, classic clothes from Eddie Bauer.

ANTHONY SICARI, Classic American Fashions, 32 W. State St., Sharon, PA 16146. 800-452-1667. Free, 19 pp. Limited styles, but all are elegant— for women size 6-16.

APPLESEED'S, 30 Tozer Rd., P.O. Box 1020, Beverly, MA 01915-0720. Free, 64 pp. Traditional clothing, sizes 6-18, some petites.

BEDFORD FAIR LIFESTYLES, 421 Landmark Dr., Wilmington, NC 28410-0001. Free, 104 pp. Reasonably priced fashions for misses and petites.

BLOOMINGDALE'S BY MAIL, LTD., 475 Knotter Dr., Cheshire, CT 06410-9927. Free, various. The latest styles for the office and afterwards. Other catalogs for home decorating, housewares.

CARROLL REED, 1777 Sentry Pkwy. W, Dublin Hall, Ste. 300, Blue Bell, PA 19422-2203. Free, 64 pp. Ivy League, classic styles for young women.

CARUSHKA BODYWEAR, 7716 Kester Ave., Van Nuys, CA 91405. Free, 36 pp. Fashionable, lightweight bodywear—leotards, racer tops, original styles.

CHADWICK'S OF BOSTON, LTD., One Chadwick Pl., Box 1600, Brockton, MA 02403-1600. Free, 72 pp. "Off-price" fashions for all occasions.

FITNESS STUFF, 338 NE 219th Ave., Gresham, OR 97030. Free, 16 pp. Aerobic and dance workout attire.

GENE'S SHOES DISCOUNT CATALOG, 126 N. Main St., St. Charles, MO 63301. Free, 18 pp. Women's comfortable and walking shoes from Selby, Soft Spots, Hush Puppies.

LANE BRYANT, P.O. Box 8303, Indianapolis, IN 46283-8303. 800-477-0448. Free, 124 pp. Comfortable clothing for women sizes 14-56.

NEWPORT NEWS, Avon Lane, Hampton, VA 23630. 800-688-2830. Free, 88 pp. Young women's styles at discount prices.

NICOLE SUMMERS, Catalog Request Dept., P.O. Box 3003, Winterbrook Way, Meredith, NH 03253-3003. 800-642-6786. Free, 56 pp. Casual to cocktail dresses for sizes 6-20. Selected petite styles also.

ROAMAN'S, P.O. Box 8360, Indianapolis, IN 46283-8360. Free, 100 pp. Affordable, comfortable clothing for sizes 14 up.

SILHOUETTES, Hanover, PA 17333-0256. Free, 56 pp. Clothes for work, party, or play for women sizes 14W to 26W.

TALBOTS, 175 Beal St., Hingham, MA 02043. 800-8-TALBOT. Free, 132 pp. Sophisticated, tailored fashions for women — from bathing suits to evening wear. A few children's clothes.

TALL CLASSICS, P.O. Box 15024, Shawnee Mission, KS 66285. Free, 12 pp. Classic styles for women over 5'10"—from Pendleton jackets and skirts to a stretch lace teddy.

TOG SHOP, THE, Lester Sq., Americus, GA 31710-0025. 912-924-4800. Free, 128 pp. Sizes 4-18. Lots of casual styles and pages of shoes.

VERY THING, THE, P.O. Box 3005, Winterbrook Way, Meredith, NH 03253-3005. Free, 64 pp. Upscale clothes for women, bathing suits to business suits. Overnight delivery for no extra charge. Some petites.

VICTORIA'S SECRET, P.O. Box 16589, Columbus, OH 43216-6589. 800-888-8200. $2 refundable, 24 pp. Ultra-feminine lingerie, high fashion separates, romantic evening dresses, English country style bed linens.

WILLOW RIDGE, 421 Landmark Dr., Wilmington, NC 28410. 919-763-7500. Free, 103 pp. Reasonably priced fashions for misses and petites.

Collectibles

(see also *Art & Special Treasures; Handcrafts;* and *Smorgasbord*)

AMERICAN GIRLS COLLECTION, Pleasant Co., P.O. Box 497, Middleton, WI 53562-9940. 800-845-0005. Free, 50 pp. Collector-quality dolls (most 18") with historically accurate accessories, storybooks, furniture.

ANNE OF GREEN GABLES, Avonlea Traditions, Inc., #1-9030 Leslie St., Richmond Hill, Ontario, Canada L4B 1G2. Free, 18 pp. Fine Victorian goods, books, and paraphernalia celebrating the work of Lucy Maud Montgomery's book series. Porcelain dolls, figurines, books, taffeta accessories, stationery, paper dolls.

ATLANTIC BRIDGE, Dept. GGG, Ballybane, Galway, Ireland. $2, 32 pp. Collectibles from Belleek, Waterford, Royal Doulton, Lladró, Lilliput Lane, Irish Dresden, and other respected names in collectibles.

BEAR-IN-MIND, 53 Bradford St., W. Concord, MA 01742. 508-369-1167. $1, 48 pp. Adorable collectible bears such as Grrruff, Gund, and Muffy. Plus other accessories with bears such as photo frame, bank, bookends.

COLLECTOR BOOKS, P.O. Box 3009, Paducah, KY 42002-3009. 800-626-5420. Free, 28 pp. Books for collectors of antiques, dolls, watches, trading cards, hat pins, country baskets.

COLLECTOR'S HERITAGE, Inc., P.O. Box 355, Bernardsville, NJ 07924. 088-374-2696. $5, 42 pp. Exact reproductions of some of the most famous edged weapons in the history of warfare. Hand-forged with fully tempered blades. Very handsome.

HAKE'S AMERICANA & COLLECTIBLES, P.O. Box 1444, York, PA 17405. 717-848-1333. $5, 206 pp. Collectibles by mail and telephone bids—mostly one-of-a-kind items—toys, buttons, coloring books, campaign items.

INTERGALACTIC TRADING CO., P.O. Box 1516, Longwood, FL 32752. 407-831-8344. $1, 70 pp. Sci-fi related products — comics, toys, videos, posters, hats, games, books.

INTERNATIONAL COINS & CURRENCY, INC., 11 E. State St., P.O. Box 218, Montpelier, VT 05601. 802-223-6331. $2, various. Vintage coins and currency and other collectibles such as country oak wall telephones, baseball cards, ancient artifacts.

JAMESTOWN STAMP CO., INC., Dept. GG, 341 E. 3rd St., Jamestown, NY 14701-9974. 716-488-0763. Free, 64 pp. Stamps of all kinds—mint and used, American and foreign, etc.; also albums and supplies.

JAN HAGARA COLLECTIBLES, The B&J Co., P.O. Box 67, Georgetown, TX 78627. $5, 40 pp. Limited edition Victoriana dolls, prints, porcelain figurines and bells, notecards and paper products.

KAPLAN'S-BEN HUR, P.O. Box 7989, Houston, TX 77270-7989. Free, 48 pp. Keepsakes from Lladró porcelains, Madame Alexander dolls, Wedgwood, Lenox, Hummel, Belleek, Royal Copenhagen, Sabino glass, Baccarat, and other well-known suppliers of fine giftware.

L&C COINS, 3700 Katella Ave., Ste. D, Los Alamitos, CA 90720. 310-795-0560. Free, 50 pp. Wide selection of U.S. coins, type coins, gold coins, proof sets and singles, brilliant, uncirculated singles and sets.

M.C. ARTS, 3312 S. Cedar, Lansing, MI 48910. Free, various. Bicycle, motorcycle, tattoo collectibles.

NORTH AMERICAN BEAR CO., 401 N. Wabash St., Ste. 500, Chicago, IL 60611. 312-329-0020. Free, 54 pp. Collectible bunnies, bears, monkeys including the famous Muffy Bear.

OCCIDENTAL WESTERN MARKETING CO., 136 E. 7th Dr., Mesa, AZ 85210. 602-964-0794. $3, 88 pp. International insignia—mostly military.

ONE OF A KIND COLLECTIBLES OF AMERICA, P.O. Box 430451, Miami, FL 33243-0451. 305-595-0118. $3, 24 pp. Autographed memorabilia from the worlds of sports, movies, history, war, music stars.

SAFE COLLECTING SYSTEMS, P.O. Box 263, Southampton, PA 18966. 215-357-9049. $1, 56 pp. Fine collecting systems for stamps, coins, covers, postcards, and buttons as well as examining equipment.

UNITED STATES MINT, Customer Service Ctr., 10001 Aerospace Rd., Lanham, MD 20706. 301-436-7400. Free, brochure. Medals, proof coin sets, commemoratives from the U.S. Dept. of the Treasury.

VILLAGE COIN SHOP, INC., P.O. Box 207, Plaistow, NH 03865-1101. 603-382-5492. Free, 30 pp. Coins, currency, supplies for the numismatist.

Computing

(check also the particular area of interest for specialty software)

BABBAGE'S, 10741 King William Dr., Dallas, TX 75220. Free, 36 pp. Computer software, video games, accessories.

COLLECTOR SOFTWARE, 436 W. 4th St., Ste. 222, Pomona, CA 91766. 714-620-9014. Free, 16 pp. Computer clip art—mostly school subjects.

COMPUTEACH, P.O. Box 9515, New Haven, CT 06534. 800-44-TEACH. Free, brochure. Educational software for kids and adults.

DISNEY SOFTWARE, Catalog Order, P.O. Box 290, Buffalo, NY 14207-0290. Free, 16 pp. IBM and Amiga-compatible software.

DR. MAC, 11050 Randall St., Sun Valley, CA 91352. 800-825-6227. Free, 30 pp. Variety of software for the Macintosh.

EDUCATIONAL RESOURCES, 1550 Executive Dr., Elgin, IL 60123. 800-624-2926. Free, 188 pp. Lots and lots of software for school subjects, art, SAT preparation, plus hardware and accessories.

HI TECH EXPRESSIONS, 1800 NW 65th Ave., Plantation, FL 33313. 800-447-6543. Free, brochure. Educational, creative, entertainment software.

LEARNING CO., 6493 Kaiser Dr., Fremont, CA 94555. 510-792-2101. Free, 12 pp. Educational software for ages 3-17.

MAC ZONE, Multiple Zones International, Inc., 1741 NE Union Hill Rd., Redmond, WA 98052. Free, 96 pp. Full of software for Macintosh computers for illustration, personal management, games, education. Also hardware and accessories.

MACCONNECTION, 14 Mill St., Marlow, NH 03456. 800-800-2222. Free, 81 pp. Software and peripherals for Macintosh computers.

MACWAREHOUSE, P.O. Box 3013, 1720 Oak St., Lakewood, NJ 08701-3013. 800-925-6227. Free, 152 pp. Software, accessories, hardware for the Macintosh.

MICROPROSE ENTERTAINMENT SOFTWARE, 180 Lakefront Dr., Hunt Valley, MD 21030-2245. 800-879-PLAY. Free, 24 pp. Computer games for older teens and adults.

MICROSHOPPER, 1720 Oak St., P.O. Box 341, Lakewood, NJ 08701-9936. Free, 16 pp. Softkey software for clip art, desktop publishing, calendars, and other popular applications.

MICROWAREHOUSE, 1690 Oak St., P.O. Box 3014, Lakewood, NJ 08701-9823. 800-285-7080. Free, 90 pp. Chock full of software and computer accessories.

PARSONS TECHNOLOGY, One Parsons Dr., P.O. Box 100, Hiawatha, IA 52233-9904. Free, 46 pp. IBM-compatible software for family finances, genealogy, legal, church and Bible study, writing, personal improvement.

PC CONNECTION, 6 Mill St., Marlow, NH 03456. 800-800-5555. Free, 70 pp. Software, hardware, and accessories.

PC TECHNIQUES BOOKSTREAM, 7721 E. Gray Rd., Ste. 204, Scottsdale, AZ 85260-6912. 602-483-0192. Free, 8 pp. Technical books about PCs.

POWER UP! DIRECT, P.O. Box 7600, San Mateo, CA 94403-7600. Free, 60 pp. Software programs for personal organization, publishing, business, home fun.

PUBLIC BRAND SOFTWARE, P.O. Box 51315, Indianapolis, IN 46251. 800-426-3475. $2, 100 pp. Over 2,000 shareware software programs—utilities, games, applications, desktop publishing, educational software.

REASONABLE SOLUTIONS COMPUTER SOFTWARE, 1221 Disk Dr., Medford, OR 97501-6639. 503-776-5777. Free, 38 pp. Software for IBM PCs and compatibles—clip art, education, games, type fonts, more.

SOFTSHOPPE, P.O. Box 19069, Irvine, CA 92714. $.50, 29 pp. IBM-compatible public domain software, shareware—clip art, desktop publishing, games, Windows applications, financial, business, animation, more.

SOFTWARE EXCITEMENT!, Inc., 6475 Crater Lake Hwy., Central Point, OR 97502. $2, 34 pp. Wide range of software for IBM-compatible computers—business, education, database, games, graphics, more.

T/MAKER CO., 1390 Villa St., Mountain View, CA 94041. 800-937-5530. Free, 20 pp. Software, especially "click art."

Cookware
(see also *Housewares*)

CAKE DECORATING!, Wilton Enterprises, Caller Service No. 1604, 2240 W. 75th St., Woodridge, IL 60517-0750. 708-963-7100. Free, 192 pp. Most complete source of cake, cookie, and candy decorating—molds, baking equipment, videos, books; decorations, ornaments, candles, and toppers for weddings, birthdays, showers, every occasion.

CHAR-BROIL, P.O. Box 1300, Columbus, GA 31993-2499. Free, 32 pp. Everything for the grilling enthusiast—smoker, BBQ grill, BBQ sauce, slicing tongs, steak, other utensils for a grilling party.

COOKIE CRAFT, P.O. Box 295, Hope, NJ 07844. Free, 15 pp. Cookie cutters for special occasions.

KITCHEN KRAFTS, P.O. Box 805, Mt. Laurel, NJ 08054-0805. $1, 32 pp. Quality food crafting supplies for candy making (dozens of chocolate molds), cake decorating, baking; also books and videos.

WOODEN SPOON, P.O. Box 931, Clinton, CT 06413. 203-664-0303. Free, 47 pp. Specialty cookware.

WILLIAMS-SONOMA, Mail Order Dept., P.O. Box 7456, San Francisco, CA 94120-7456. Free, 70 pp. Unusual items for cooks; bay leaf wreath, gingerbread house mold, professional baking equipment, serving dishes, etc.

Craft Supplies—Assorted
(see also other *Craft Supplies* categories and *Handcrafts*)

CANDLE MAKING SUPPLIES, Barker Enterprises, 15106 10th Ave. SW, Seattle, WA 98166. 206-244-1870. $2, 34 pp. Everything for making quality candles—wide selection of molds, wax, scents, candle holders, instruction books.

CAPRI ARTS & CRAFTS BOOK CATALOG, 866 S. McGlincey Ln., Campbell, CA 95008. 408-377-3833. Free, 80 pp. How-to and pattern books for many crafts (most under $10)—decorative painting, stenciling, fabric painting, jewelry, bridal and wedding, pine cone and clothespin art, doll crafting, lots more.

CHELSEA SQUARE, 19001 Bronco Dr., Germantown, MD 20874. Free, brochure. Instructions for making your own home accessories — hat boxes, Victorian picture bows, topiary trees, fireplace fans, fabric covered desk sets, more.

CRAFT GALLERY, P.O. Box 145, Swampscott, MA 01907. 508-744-2334. $2, 63 pp. Thread, books, fabrics, canvas, kits, home study programs; accessories for stitchers, quilters, tatters, miniaturists; smocking, lace work, knitting, crochet, "and sew on."

CREATIVE ARTS NETWORK, Vision Video Productions, Inc., 3932 RCA Blvd., Ste. 3209, Palm Beach Gardens, FL 33410. 407-775-0406. Free, brochure. Video teaching tapes on oil painting, watercolor, earth pottery; also oil painting books.

DESIGN FACTORY, P.O. Box 1088, Hughes Springs, TX 75656-1088. 800-657-1823. Free, various. Several small catalogs—one with patterns for the cutest elves, angels, and rag-a-muffin kid dolls; another with indoor/outdoor Christmas displays.

DESIGN ORIGINALS, 2425 Cullen St., Fort Worth, TX 76107-1411. 817-877-0067. $2, 18 pp. Over 200 books, folders, patterns for doll making, fabric crafts, ribbons and lace, plastic canvas, wearables, wood crafts, beading, clay, cross-stitch, florals, kids' crafts, leather, and how-to-make-money books.

FABRIC LABEL CO. OF KDI, KDI, INC., 7746 Arjons Dr., San Diego, CA 92126. 619-566-4461. Free, brochure. Fabric labels for seamstresses—your design.

FERN CLIFF HOUSE, P.O. Box 177, Tremont City, OH 49372. 513-390-6420. Free, 22 pp. Coatings, molds, supplies for making chocolate candy.

GRAMMA'S GRAPHICS, INC., Dept. GGGE-P3, 20 Birling Gap, Fairport, NY 14450. $1 + SASE, brochure. Sunprint cards, invitations, and gift tags in your own backyard—dry processing, easy for all ages. Or print photographs, college seals, engravings, natural objects such as shells, or magazine illustrations on fabric for quilts, pillows, placemats, doll faces, banners, handbags, fashions, pictures to embroider.

GREY OWL INDIAN CRAFT SALES CORP., 132-05 Merrick Blvd., P.O. Box 468, Jamaica, NY 11434-0468. 718-341-4000. $3, 210 pp. Complete line of supplies for Indian crafts; books on Indian medicine, religion, history; ready-made Indian-design blankets.

HUDSON GLASS CO., Inc., 219 N. Division St., Peekskill, NY 10566-2700. $3, 173 pp. Supplies for stained glass including lamp kits, tools, patterns.

KLOCKIT, P.O. Box 636, Lake Geneva, WI 53147-0636. Free, 68 pp. All you need for clock making—clock and weather inserts, quartz movements, dials, music and mechanical movements, supplies and tools, books, kits, plans, and finished clocks and watches. All styles from fretwork to cuckoo to a '64 Mustang!

LEISURE ARTS, P.O. Box 5595, Little Rock, AR 72215. 501-868-8800. Free, brochure. Very attractive crafts book series — *Spirit of Christmas* (decorating, entertaining, and gift-giving sections), *Christmas Remembered* (nostalgic pictures and portraits charted for cross-stitch), *Memories in the Making* (country cooking, decorating, gift-giving for holidays and special occasions).

MAPLEWOOD CRAFTS, Humboldt Industrial Park, 1 Maplewood Dr., P.O. Box 2010, Hazelton, PA 18201-0676. $2, 64 pp. A smattering of all kinds of craft supplies, kits—plastic canvas, doll making, needlepoint, beadcraft, ornaments, wearable art, more!

MARY MAXIM, 2001 Holland Ave., P.O. Box 5019, Port Huron, MI 48061-5019. $2, 70 pp. Needlework and crafts—plastic canvas, pompom, knitting, crochet, counted cross-stitch, plaster crafts, more.

OTT'S DISCOUNT ART SUPPLY, 714 Greenville Blvd., Greenville, NC 27858. $2, 145 pp. Save up to 75% on supplies for fine, graphic, and decorative artists. Over 2,000 new products—art papers, drafting materials, clays, wood burners, Dremel tools, paints, canvas, and on and on.

PAPERCUTTINGS BY ALISON, 404 Partridge Cir., Sarasota, FL 34236. 813-957-0328. $2.25, 26 pp. Patterns, kits, videos, books on papercutting, 3-D cuttings, stand-up Christmas cards.

PASTIMES, 4944 Commerce Pkwy., Cleveland, OH 44128-5985. Free, 62 pp. Kits, supplies for HO railroad scenes, die-cast car and plane models, ship models, scrimshaw, wooden puzzles, miniatures, clocks, folk instruments, marquetry, doll houses, stenciling, embossing, metalcraft, country baskets, carving, stained glass.

PIPKA'S FOLK ART GALLERY AND STUDIO, P.O. Box 348, Hwy. 42, Nordic Dr., Sister Bay, WI 54234. 414-854-4392. Free, 25 pp. Folk art packets, supplies, and wood; books, hearts to wear, music to paint by.

PRO CHEMICAL & DYE INC., P.O. Box 14, Somerset, MA 02726. 508-676-3838. Free, 18 pp. Dyes for fibers and fabrics.

RIBBONS & LACE, P.O. Box 30070, Mesa, AZ 85275-0070. 800-358-LACE. Free, 34 pp. Ruffled or flat ribbons and imported lace, ribbon roses, etc.

S&S ARTS AND CRAFTS, P.O. Box 513, Colchester, CT 06415-0513. 800-937-3482. Free, various. Myriad packs of inexpensive but cute craft projects for children.

SCHACHT SPINDLE CO., 6101 Ben Pl., Boulder, CO 80301. 303-442-3212. Free, 27 pp. Equipment for the serious weaver—looms of all kinds, accessories.

SHARIN-A-LITTLE-BIT, 139 Berry Creek Dr., Folsom, CA 95630. 916-989-0288. $2 refundable, brochure. Kits for adorable country-look dolls and plaques.

SOUTHWEST SAVVY, P.O. Box 1361-G, Apple Valley, CA 92307. 619-247-5680. Free, brochure. Plans for making delightful Southwest crafts from wood or fabric (some require no sewing!). Low prices on very stylish home decorating accents.

TANDY LEATHER CO., Dept. GGGE93, P.O. Box 2934, Fort Worth, TX 76113. 817-551-9620. $2.50, 108 pp. Books, materials for making fashion leather garments and accessories such as moccasins, vests, belts, wallets, holsters, Indian crafts.

TREE TOYS, P.O. Box 492, Hindale, IL 60522-0492. 708-323-6505. $1, 12 pp. Books, patterns, supplies for paper snipping, silhouette, and quilling.

UNICORN STUDIOS, P.O. Box 370, Seymour, TN 37865. Free, 40 pp. Musical movements and accessories—clock movements, porcelain bisque carousel animals, plastic canvas pattern books that can be adapted for musical movements.

Craft Supplies—Caning/Basketry

FRANK'S CANE AND RUSH SUPPLY, 7252 Heil Ave., Huntington Beach, CA 92647. 714-847-0707. Free, 39 pp. Supplies, instruction books for chair caning, seat weaving, wicker repair, upholstery, basketry, fiber arts, wood furniture.

ROYALWOOD, LTD., 517 Woodville Rd., Mansfield, OH 44907. 419-526-1630. $1.50, 22 pp. Basket weaving and caning supplies, patterns, books.

Craft Supplies—Jewelry Making

CGM, INC., 19562 Ventura Blvd., Ste. 231, Tarzana, CA 91356. 800-426-5CGM. Free, 28 pp. 14K, sterling silver and gold-filled findings and gemstones.

HARDIES, P.O. Box 1920, Quartzsite, AZ 85346. 602-927-6381. $3, 48 pp. Supplies for making Indian and other jewelry; pewter miniatures.

KUMACO, Dept. KA2, P.O. Box 2719, Glenville, NY 12325. 518-384-0110. $2 refundable, various. High quality beads and jewelry supplies for artists and hobbyists. Gemstone beads, carved and unusual beads from around the world, findings, tools, books.

TSI, INC., 101 Nickerson St., P.O. Box 9266, Seattle, WA 98109. 206-282-3040. Free, 100 pp. Lots of choices of chains, clasps, books, videos, beads, settings, gems for jewelry making.

Craft Supplies—Needlework

AARDVARK ADVENTURES, P.O. Box 2449, Livermore, CA 94551. Free, 20 pp. Chatty newspaper format with books, supplies, new products for needleworkers.

AMAZON DRYGOODS, 2218 E. 11th St., Davenport, IA 52803. $7, 120 pp. Over 1,000 patterns from the past and a few hard-to-find ones from the present—Victorian attire for men and women, desert caravan garb and belly-dancing costumes, square dancing dresses, 18th and 19th century fashions, Amish clothing, more; custom-made footwear from prehistoric times to clown boots; also clothing research fashion books, books on children's games, women's hats, just as entertaining as a country store.

AMERICAN NEEDLEWOMAN, THE, P.O. Box 6472, 2944 SE Loop 820, Fort Worth, TX 76115. 817-551-1221. $2, 80 pp. Designs from Europe and the U.S. in kits for needlepoint, weaving, crochet, cross-stitch, felt.

ANNE POWELL LTD., P.O. Box 3060, Stuart, FL 34995-3060. 800-622-2646. Free, 22 pp. Victorian samplers, collectible thimbles, handpainted enamel pincushions, antique needlework tools, other fine gifts for needleworkers.

ATLANTA THREAD & SUPPLY CO., 695 Red Oak Rd., Stockbridge, GA 30281. Free, 64 pp. Sewing supplies for the serious seamstress—threads, dress forms, basic supplies, irons, sewing machines, drapery supplies, press boards and pads, books.

BEAR CLAWSET, 27 Palermo Wk., Long Beach, CA 90803. 310-434-8077. $2, 23 pp. Bear making patterns, supplies, accessories.

BIRCH STREET CLOTHING, P.O. Box 6901, San Mateo, CA 94403. Free, 8 pp. Unique designs for children and adults that use only a few pattern pieces (like a jacket with three pieces!). Patterns to transform old sweatshirts into cute jumpsuits.

CLOTILDE, 1909 SW 1st Ave., Ft. Lauderdale, FL 33315-2100. $2, 80 pp. Supplies, accessories, books, videos for sewing, quilting, needlework, crafts.

COUNTED CROSS STITCH, 120 N. Meadows Rd., Medfield, MA 02052-1555. $2, 36 pp. Pictures, pillows, coasters, sweatshirts, clocks, afghans, ornaments in nice variety of designs.

CR's CRAFTS, Box 8, Leland, IA 50453. 515-567-3652. Free, 96 pp. Kits, patterns, parts for dolls and bears.

CRAFTERS' GALLERY, 2001 Holland Ave., P.O. Box 5019, Port Huron, MI 48061-5019. $1, 64 pp. Mostly needlecrafts such as plastic canvas, needlepoint, cross-stitch, smocking, quilts, dolls to sew.

CROSS STITCH & COUNTRY CRAFTS, Catalog Dept., 111 10th St., P.O. Box 11447, Des Moines, IA 50336-1447. $2, 64 pp. Lots of accessories and kits for cross-stitch, fancywork, wool-work, tatting, Hardanger embroidery, quilling, and other "old" crafts.

DONNA SALYERS' FABULOUS-FURS, 700 Madison Ave., Covington, KY 41011. 606-291-3300. $1, 16 pp. "The luxurious alternative to animal furs." Patterns, exquisite man-made furs and ready-made coats. Also Ultraleather with "memory" for returning to original shape after sitting.

EMBROIDERY STOP, Harriet Segal, 1042 Victory Dr., Yardley, PA 19067. 215-493-1640. $3, various. Immense collection of threads, books, and kits for needlepointers (or canvas embroiderers, as she prefers it).

FULL HOOKUPS INCLUDED, Crafts for Campers, 9 Peters Path, Setauket, NY 11733. 800-524-3690. Free, brochure. Cross-stitch kits of RV campers for key ring, photo frame, pictures.

GINSCO TRIMS, 242 W. 38th St., New York, NY 10018. 212-719-4871. Free, 12 pp. Braids, trims, frogs, press-on embroidery—many have metallic threads.

GRANNIES HEARTSTRINGS, P.O. Box 1756, Morgan Hill, CA 95038-1756. 408-779-3287. Free, 12 pp. Patterns for baby dresses, bonnets, pillowcases, and collars from antique hankies, tea towels, or tablecloths.

HANDWORKS, Rt. 1, Box 138, Afton, VA 22920. 703-456-6596. Free, 2 pp. Choice of eight simple sewing projects for children plus a child's first knitting or sewing basket complete with supplies and a booklet of ideas for several projects. Reasonable prices.

HISTORIC PATTERNS AND OTHER TREASURES, Campbell's, P.O. Box 400, Gratz, PA 17030-0400. 717-425-2045. $4.50, 70 pp. Historic clothing patterns, books on fashion in the past.

JEHLOR FANTASY FABRICS, 730 Andover Pk. W, Seattle, WA 98188. Free, various. Constantly changing selection of over 1,000 specialty fabrics (sequined, cracked ice, metallic sheers, sparkle knits) and 1,000 trims (turkey feather boas, stretch sequins, beaded and jeweled braids, imported crystals).

JUDI'S DOLLS, P.O. Box 607, Port Orchard, WA 98366. 206-895-2779. $2, 34 pp. Catalog is a coloring book showing available cloth doll patterns and supplies—variety of styles including dew drop fairy, ballerina, Shirley Temple patterns.

KEEPSAKE QUILTING, Rt. 25, P.O. Box 1618, Centre Harbor, NH 03226-1618. Free, 110 pp. Huge selection of books, supplies, tools, fabrics for doll making and quilting.

LACE HEAVEN, 2524 Dauphin Island Pkwy., Mobile, AL 36605. 205-478-5644. $3, 58 pp. Lingerie and dress fabrics, Lycra, knits, velour, terrycloth, cone thread, ribbon, notions, lace.

LACIS, 2982 Adeline St., Berkeley, CA 94703. 510-843-7178. $4, 60 pp. Supplies, books, notions for lace making, embroidery, and costumes.

LEDGEWOOD STUDIO, 6000 Ledgewood Dr., Forest Park, GA 30050. 404-361-6098. Free, 22 pp. Patterns for doll clothes; also braids and lace.

NANCY'S NOTIONS, 333 Beichl Ave., P.O. Box 683, Beaver Dam, WI 53916-0683. 800-833-0690. Free, 160 pp. Notions, sewing videos, supplies, fabric, patterns. Very complete selection.

NEEDLECRAFT SHOP, THE, 23 Old Pecan Rd., Big Sandy, TX 75755-2219. Free, 32 pp. Books, kits, patterns for plastic canvas, crochet—ideas like Barbie dream camper, afghans, bookmarks, Victorian Christmas tree ornaments.

NEWARK DRESSMAKER SUPPLY, 6473 Ruch Rd., P.O. Box 20730, Lehigh Valley, PA 18002-0730. 215-837-7500. Free, 60 pp. Sewing, craft, and needlework supplies; books.

OPPENHEIM'S LADIES' BOOK, 120 E. Main St., N. Manchester, IN 46962-0052. $2, 48 pp. Fabric (remnants), patterns, supplies for the fabric crafter.

PEACOCK ALLEY NEEDLEPOINT, 650 Croswell St. SE, Grand Rapids, MI 49506. 616-454-9898. $3, 41 pp. Traditional needlepoint pillows, eyeglass cases, Christmas ornaments, pictures. A variety of subjects from Raggedy Ann to birds.

PLATYPUS, Box 396, Planetarium Station, New York, NY 10024. $2, 30 pp. Catalogs always include a complimentary pattern. Patterns and instructions for dolls, stuffed animals, other handsewn gifts.

PURCHASE FOR LESS, 231 Floresta GGG, Portola Valley, CA 94028. $2, 27 pp. Quilt, sewing, and other fiber arts books at discounted prices.

QUILTER'S BOOKSHELF, Dover St. Booksellers, Ltd., 8673 Commerce Dr. #13, P.O. Box 1563, Easton, MD 21601. 410-822-9329. $2, 52 pp. Only books on quilting! Miniature quilts, getting kids interested in quilting, patterns from past and present and around the world, how-to.

RAIMENTS, P.O. Box 6176, Fullerton, CA 92634-6176. $5, 111 pp. Hundreds of historical and ethnic clothing patterns, costume books and supplies, underpinnings and accessories.

SCHOOLHOUSE PRESS, 6899 Cary Bluff, Pittsville, WI 54466. 715-884-2799. $3, samples, brochure. Tools, books, patterns, yarn for knitting.

SEATTLE FABRICS, 3876 Bridge Way N, Seattle, WA 98103. 206-632-6022. $3, 15 pp. Outdoor and recreational fabrics, hardware, and patterns for such items as gaiters, parkas, duffel bags, ski bags, and cycling jerseys.

SEW SPECIAL, 9823 Old Winery Pl., Ste. 20, Sacramento, CA 95827. $2, 20 pp. Patterns and kits for adorable dolls, wreaths, decorative arts.

SMOCKING ETCETERAS, 7310 Bucknell Dr., Austin, TX 78723. 512-928-3217. Free, brochure. International smocking books.

SPECIALTIES, 4425 Cotton-Hanlon Rd., Montour Falls, NY 14865. 607-594-2021. $2, 28 pp. Fabrics, notions, patterns.

STITCHERY, THE, 120 N. Meadows Rd., Medfield, MA 02052-1592. 800-359-5440. $2, 64 pp. Nice variety of subjects for needlepoint, counted cross-stitch kits.

STRETCH & SEW, INC., 3895 E. 19th, P.O. Box 185, Eugene, OR 97440. 503-726-9000. $2, 32 pp. Patterns, well-illustrated books, and notions for sewing with stretch fabrics.

SUNDANCE DESIGNS, INC., 4500 E. Speedway Blvd., Ste. 93, Tucson, AZ 85712. 602-795-3800. $5, 14 pp. Exquisite handpainted needlework canvases that capture the spirit of the Southwest and the Indian.

THREADS, Taunton Press, 63 S. Main St., Box 5506, Newtown, CT 06470-9959. 800-888-8286. Free, brochure. Books and videos on various needlecrafts.

Craft Supplies—Painting/Decorative Arts

CHATHAM ART DISTRIBUTORS, INC., 11 Brookside Ave., Chatham, NY 12037. 800-822-4747. Free, 94 pp. Wealth of supplies for the decorative artist—including bentwood boxes, brass stencils, stoneware, wood ornaments, toys, peg racks, home decor; canvas photo albums, scrapbooks, picture frames, placemats; whatever it is, you'll probably find it here.

CRAFT TIME, 211 S. State College Blvd., Ste. 341, Anaheim, CA 92806. 714-671-1639. $2, 29 pp. Unfinished plastercraft and supplies in wide variety of themes.

CRIDGE, INC., P.O. Box 210, Morrisville, PA 19367. 215-295-3667. $2, 60 pp. Unique jewelry settings and gift ideas for china painters, decorative painters, hobby and professional artists—puffed porcelain heart or star, lockets, switch plates, pins, cameos, collector spoons, holiday ornaments, belt buckles, porcelain inserts in styles from Victorian to Southwestern.

CUPBOARD DISTRIBUTING, 114 S. Main St., P.O. Box 148, Urbana, OH 43078. 513-390-6388. Free, 32 pp. Unfinished wood products including game boards and pieces, spool doll kits, carousels, pull toys, candlesticks, more.

DECORATIVE ART DESIGNS, 468 W. 43rd St., Loveland, CO 80538. 303-667-1006. $1, 8 pp. Packets with a colored photograph, inked pattern, and instructions with painting tips for painted decorative objects. The objects (clock, tray, band boxes, frosted glass ornaments) are also available.

STAN BROWN ARTS AND CRAFTS, 13435 NE Whitaker Way, Portland, OR 97230. 800-547-5531. Free, 288 pp. Numerous design books and wealth of supplies for painting, decorative arts, folkart, oils, watercolor.

SURMA, 11 E. 7th St., New York, NY 10003. Free, brochure. Ukrainian Easter egg painting supplies, books.

Craft Supplies—Rubber Stamping

HIPPO HEART RUBBER STAMPS, P.O. Box 4460, Foster City, CA 94404. 415-347-HIPP. $2, 72 pp. Hundreds of delightful rubber stamp designs and accessories.

PAPER ANGEL, P.O. Box 1336, Santa Cruz, CA 95061. 408-423-5115. Free, 30 pp. Fun with rubber stamps—kits, ink pads, stamps, personalized round stamps.

STAMP FRANCISCO, 466 8th St., San Francisco, CA 94103. 415-252-5975. Free, 133 pp. Over 1,800 rubber stamps.

STAMP PAD CO., Inc., P.O. Box 43, Big Lake, MN 55309. $2, 48 pp. Thousands of designs of rubber stamps, accessories.

Craft Supplies—Woodworking

(see also *Models & Miniatures*)

AMERICAN TOOLMAKER, P.O. Box 369, 1801 Vine St., Harrisonville, MO 64701. Free, 32 pp. Woodworking tools and accessories.

ARMOR PRODUCTS, Box 445, E. Northport, NY 11731-0445. 516-462-6228. Free, 72 pp. Clock movements, darling wood toy plans and parts, door harp parts, furniture plans, doll house kits.

BRIDGEWATER SCROLLWORKS, Rt. 1, Box 585, Osage, MN 56570. $5, 80 pp. Dream book for folkart and tole painters. Fantastic variety of wood cutouts—seasonal, wheel toys, shelves, miniatures, circus train—choose thick or thin.

CHERRY TREE TOYS, INC., P.O. Box 369, Belmont, OH 43718-9989. $1, 68 pp. Plans, parts, kits, tools, supplies for woodworking crafts—door harps, musical movements, clock kits, whirligigs, outdoor cutouts, doll houses.

CRAFTER'S HOME OF FINE ARTS, 11840 N. US 27, Dewitt, MI 48820. $1, 10 pp. Woodcraft patterns for lawn and garden, bird houses, whirligigs.

CUSTOM WOOD CUT-OUTS UNLIMITED, P.O. Box 518, Massillon, OH 44648. 216-832-2919. Free, 20 pp. Reasonably priced wood cutouts in many shapes and for many purposes from ornaments to pencil tops to wall decorations—lots of seasonal, children's, country themes.

FINE WOODWORKING, Taunton Press, 63 S. Main St., P.O. Box 5506, Newtown, CT 06470-9959. Free, 16 pp. Books and videos on all aspects of fine woodworking — with your kids, hand tools, identifying wood, turning projects, carving.

LL ENTERPRISES, P.O. Box 908, Cornville, AZ 86325. $1, 20 pp. Woodworking plans for outdoor furniture, toys, children's play furniture, work benches, storage shelves, home decorations, den furniture.

UNFINISHED BUSINESS, P.O. Box 246, Wingate, NC 28174. 704-233-4295. $3, 76 pp. Heartwarming assortment of unfinished wood products (with examples of how to finish them) — seasonal, doll house accessories, whimsical bird houses, folkart designs.

VAN DYKE'S RESTORERS, P.O. Box 278, Woonsocket, SD 57385-0278. $1, 266 pp. Supplies galore for upholstery, cabinet making, woodworking, antique restoration, and related trades—gingerbread, trim, color wildlife photographs, electric or oil burning lamps, much more.

WINFIELD COLLECTION, THE, 1450 Torrey Rd., Fenton, MI 48430. 313-629-4559. Free, 48 pp. Full-size woodcraft patterns that will have you grinning. Country charm in furniture, folkart, layered animals, yard ornaments, wheeled toys, yard swingers, whirligigs, more.

WOODCARVERS HOME-STUDY UNIVERSITY, Fox Books, Box 7948G, Lancaster, PA 17604. $2, 12 pp. Woodworking books and materials for the home crafts person. Free patterns with each issue.

WOODCRAFT DESIGNS, Accents in Pine, P.O. Box 7387, Gonic, NH 03839. Free, 18 pp. Over 1,500 plans and blueprint patterns for pencil holders to picnic tables, wall plaques to whirligigs, toys to yard ornaments.

WOODCRAFT, 210 Wood County Industrial Pk., P.O. Box 1686, Parkersburg, WV 26102-1686. 800-535-4482. Free, 143 pp. Tools, books, project supplies for woodworking, wood burning, carving.

WOODWORKING, Garrett Wade, 161 Ave. of the Americas, New York, NY 10013-1299. $4, 216 pp. Huge assortment of tools, machines, project supplies, stains.

Electronics
(see also *Computing*)

CAMBRIDGE SOUNDWORKS, 154 California St., Newton, MA 02158-9954. Free, 62 pp. Stereo, CD, audio, video systems.

COMPLETE CRUTCHFIELD, THE, 1 Crutchfield Park, P.O. Box 9041, Charlottesville, VA 22906-9041. 800-955-9009. Free, 151 pp. Discount prices on audio/video and car stereo accessories and their own brand of computers.

Environmentally Friendly
(see also *Infant/Maternity Supplies; Gardening;* and *Health & Beauty*)

AERIE DESIGN, 141 Blackberry Inn Rd., Weaverville, NC 28787. Free, brochure. Wildlife graphics hand screenprinted on T-shirts.

AMERICAN ENVIRONMENTAL OUTFITTERS, 242 Noble Rd., Clarks Summit, PA 18411. Free, brochure. Environmental and nature T-shirts—humorous, thought-provoking, educational, off-beat.

ATLANTIC RECYCLED PAPER CO., P.O. Box 39179, Baltimore, MD 21212. 410-323-2676. Free, 10 pp. Copier paper, FAX paper, envelopes, toilet paper, napkins, memo pads, paper cups and plates, notecards, unbleached coffee filters all from recycled paper. Also recycling equipment.

BLUE OCEANS, P.O. Box 81, Stonington, CT 06378. 800-747-7757. Free, 8 pp. "Ecologically preferred" products for your boat—say good-bye to toxic chemicals with their environmentally safe cleaners. Waterproof bags, inflatable underwater viewer, clever replacements for ordinary things.

CORNUCOPIA NATURALS, Ste. 285, 2400 E. Main St. #103, St. Charles, IL 60174-2414. 708-208-0701. $1, 10 pp. Natural foods (jams, spreads, cookies, pancake mix, syrups, tea, coffee) and personal care products (soap, shampoo, bath oil, moisturizers). Available also in gift baskets.

DR. POSSUM, P.O. Box 4183, Mountain View, CA 94040. Free, 38 pp. Natural alternatives to everyday healthcare products for baby and mother—lotions, powders, diapering needs; home cleaning products; herbal pet treatments; baby sleep comforters; childbearing books; and lullabies on tape.

EXPLORE!, Box 71, Boulder, CO 80306. 303-449-2461. Free, 6 pp. Coffee mugs and bumper stickers with mostly environmental themes.

ISLAND PRESS ENVIRONMENTAL SOURCEBOOK, 1718 Connecticut Ave. NW, Ste. 300, Washington, DC 20009. 800-828-1302. Free, 50 pp. Books for better conservation and management—business and the environment, wetlands, forestry, hazardous waste, sustainable development, other hot topics.

JIM MORRIS ENVIRONMENTAL T-SHIRTS, 5660 Valmont, P.O. Box 18270, Boulder, CO 80308-1270. 800-788-5411. Free, 48 pp. Colorful, appealing artwork with environmental messages.

MEADOWBROOK HERB GARDEN, P.O. Box 578, Fairfield, CT 06430-0578. $1, 16 pp. Natural herbs, teas, seasonings, skin care, toiletries, pet care, books, and more.

PURE PODUNK, INC., Old Schoolhouse Center, P.O. Box 194, Sharon, VT 05065. Free, various. All-natural gift ideas; organic wool sweaters, hats, scarves, and blankets; organic futons; organic cotton clothes for women and children; unbleached towel sets; organic upholstery fabric by the yard; organic wool yarn; tagua nut buttons; toys, herb tea, many more natural products for "living lightly on the earth."

REAL GOODS, 966 Mazzoni St., Ukiah, CA 95482-3471. Free, 32 pp. Lots of solar powered, energy-saving devices for the home; recycled paper products.

REDDING'S COUNTRY CABIN, Rt. 1, Box 198-A, Ronda, NC 28670. 919-984-4070. $2, 22 pp. Herbs, dried flowers, handmade furniture, natural health care products, flavorings, spices.

SAVE ENERGY CO., The Planetary Store, 2410 Harrison St., San Francisco, CA 94110. 800-326-2120. Free, 39 pp. Dozens of products to save money, resources, and the environment — energy-saving light bulbs, household cleaners, composting equipment, solar-powered items, water savers, powerless tools, solar experiments for kids.

WALDEN'S, One American Way, Roanoke, VA 24016. 800-336-4460. Free, 32 pp. Delightful gifts that are kind to the environment.

WHOLE EARTH BOOKSTORE, P.O. Box 38, Sausalito, CA 94966-9932. Free, brochure. Books "to challenge your assumptions and give you keys to new skills and opportunities"—alternative energy sources, ecology, new housing concepts.

Floral Gifts
(see also *Gardening*)

CALYX & COROLLA, 1550 Bryant St. #900, San Francisco, CA 94103. 800-877-0998. Free, 32 pp. Fresh flowers in lovely arrangements (vases optional), dried flower wreaths, flowers-by-the-month service.

DOROTHY BIDDLE SERVICE, HC 01, Box 900, Greeley, PA 18425-9799. 717-226-3239. Free, 22 pp. Supplies for flower arrangers.

JACKSON & PERKINS, 11 Rose Ln., Medford, OR 97501-0705. Free, 32 pp. A flower-a-month club. Fashionable fresh and dried arrangements. Gift items with floral motifs.

SANTA BARBARA ORCHID ESTATE, 250 Orchid Dr., Santa Barbara, CA 93111. 805-967-1284. Free, brochure. Orchids cut and as seedlings, also books and orchid pottery.

Food—Assorted
(see also *International/Regional Specialties* and *Smorgasbord*)

800 SPIRITS, 800-BE-THERE. Free, 12 pp. Champagne, liqueurs, fresh fruit, specialty gift items such as crystal glasses, fresh roses, caviar—along with your personal message.

AMERICAN SPOON FOODS, 1668 Clarion Ave., P.O. Box 566, Petoskey, MI 49770-0566. 616-347-9030. Free, 40 pp. Preserves, marmalades, fruit butters, salad dazzlers, sauces and spreads, honey, regional favorites, and gift boxes.

BLUE HERON, 3221 Bay Shore Rd., Sarasota, FL 34234. 800-237-3920. Free, 14 pp. Citrus and tropical fruit in gift boxes.

CALEF'S FAMOUS COUNTRY STORE, Rt. 9, Box 57, Barrington, NH 03825. 800-462-2118. Free, 8 pp. Jellies, cheese, Vermont maple syrup, pancake mix, candies, and gift packs.

COMMUNITY KITCHENS, P.O. Box 2311, Baton Rouge, LA 70821-2311. 800-535-9901. Free, 40 pp. Gourmet Club that sends rare coffees, teas, or unique Creole and Cajun cuisine every month. Also "of-the-month" programs for coffee, dessert, preserves, sugarless fruit spread, pasta and sauce, rice, Louisiana dinner mix. These can be ordered individually along with colorful serving dishes and handy kitchen items.

DAT'L DO-IT, P.O. Box 4019, St. Augustine, FL 32085. 800-HOT-DATL. Free, brochure. Sauce, relish, jelly, vinegar from the datil pepper. Also clothing with the company's logo.

DIAMOND ORGANICS, P.O. Box 2159, Freedom, CA 95019. Free, brochure. Fresh organically grown lettuces, greens, herbs, roots, and fruits.

E PETAK AND CO., P.O. Box 171, Wyckoff, NJ 07481-0171. Free, brochure. Selections for gift baskets change monthly, but are always popular and nutritious, e.g., popcorn and pretzels, California dried fruit, cakes and biscuits, candies, cheese and crackers, soups and beverages. Boxed for the occasion and include a seasonal treat.

EARLY'S HONEY STAND, P.O. Box 908, Spring Hill, TN 37174-0908. Free, 24 pp. Country foods; honeys, ribs, smoked meats, cheese, breakfast favorites.

EXTENDED FAMILY HOME-COOKED MAIL-ORDER MEALS, Falls Rd., RD#3, Hudson, NY 12534. 800-235-7070. Free, 10 pp. Home-cooked dinners for two — 35 choices of entrees including Cornish hens, pot pies, Chicken Mandarin. Also 21 selections for the thrifty; single portions, including breads and desserts. Party packages and special holiday gift baskets also available.

FIGIS, 3200 S. Maple Ave., Marshfield, WI 54404-2000. Free, 100 pp. Wide assortment of gift boxes and baskets filled with cheese, sausage, nuts, candies, tortes. Plus a few gift items.

FRANK LEWIS' ALAMO FRUIT, 100 N. Tower Rd., Alamo, TX 78516-2577. 800-477-4773. Free, 14 pp. Ruby red grapefruit, oranges, dates, hickory smoked meats, cakes, dried fruits, honey spreads, fruit-a-month club.

GETHSEMANI FARMS, Trappist, KY 40051. Free, 16 pp. Chocolate and cheese gift assortments; raisins, nuts, cheese, and gourmet gift boxes made by monks of the Abbey of Gethsemani.

GOURMET MARCHÉ, 5405 Alton Pkwy., Ste. 640, Irvine, CA 92714. 800-428-0522. Free, 7 pp. Tins of flavored popcorn, gift assortments of nuts, confections, popcorn, even Alaskan smoked salmon.

HARRY AND DAVID, P.O. Box 712, Medford, OR 97501. 800-345-5655. Free, 53 pp. Fruit-of-the-month club; baskets of fruit, preserves, chocolates, cheese; seasonal arrangements.

HEARTY MIX CO., 1231 Madison Hill Rd., Rahway, NJ 07065. 908-382-3010. Free, 15 pp. Healthful mixes for breads, cakes, pancakes and waffles, muffins, bagels, biscuits, coffee cakes, pizza, pita, pie crusts, cookies, doughnuts, also salt-free mixes.

KNOTT'S BERRY FARM, P.O. Box 1989, Placentia, CA 92670-0989. Free, 16 pp. Renowned for their preserves and syrups. Also pancake mix, boysenberry cheesecake, selected gifts, and other foods.

KOINONIA PARTNERS, INC., 1324 Dawson Rd., Americus, GA 31709. 912-924-0391. Free, 15 pp. Self-help community offers pecans (shelled or unshelled, spiced hickory smoked), peach cake, granola, peanut crunch, pecan bark, Clarence Jordan tapes.

MAPLE'S FRUIT FARM, P.O. Box 167, Chewsville, MD 21721. 301-733-0777 Free, 16 pp. Down-on-the-farm quality in gift packs—nuts, coffees, fruit and nut mixes, dried fruits, teas, Arabica bean coffees, coffee-of-the-month club.

MISSION ORCHARDS CATALOGUE, 3501 Taylor Dr., P.O. Box 8505, Ukiah, CA 95482-8505. 800-333-1448. Free, 32 pp. Fruit-of-the-month and fruity-dessert-of-the-month clubs; boxes and gift baskets of fruit, dried fruit, fruit candies, fruity desserts.

NATURAL RESOURCES, 6680 Harvard Dr., Sebastopol, CA 95472. 707-823-4340. Free, brochure. Vegetarian main courses and side dishes with no sugar, hydrogenated fat, preservatives, artificial color or flavor, or MSG. Also herbal teas.

NUTS DIVINE, P.O. Box 589, Edenton, NC 27932-0589. Free, brochure. Peanuts—raw, cooked, or roasted; peanut sauce, peanut brittle.

OMAHA STEAKS INTERNATIONAL, 4400 S. 96th St., P.O. Box 3300, Omaha, NE 68103-0300. Free, 36 pp. Corn-fed beef steaks; poultry, pork, seafood, lamb. Entrees such as lasagna, beef stroganoff, calves' liver, sweet 'n sour chicken, others.

POPCORN FACTORY, Mail Order Dept., P.O. Box 4530, Lake Bluff, IL 60044. Free, 28 pp. Popcorn and other goodies in imaginative tins, chocolate pizza slices, chocolate chip cookies, seasonal and special occasion tins.

RANDALL'S FLAGSHIP, Catalog Div., 2901 Polk St., Houston, TX 77003. Free, 24 pp. Meats, sweets, Texas treats, and more in gift baskets — steaks, shrimp, salmon, ham, fruit, honey, coffees, dart/cheese board, bucket of chocolate golf balls, other creative presentations.

SCHAPIRA COFFEE CO., 117 W. 10th St., New York, NY 10011. 212-675-3733. Free, brochure. Roasted coffees, teas, hand grinders, espresso pots, coffee mills.

SQUIRE'S CHOICE, THE, 2000 W. Cabot Blvd., Ste. 110, Langhorne, PA 19047. 800-523-6163. Free, 40 pp. Decorative tins filled with nuts, candies, mixed snacks, pastries. Coffee-and-dessert-of-the-month club.

SUNNYLAND FARMS, INC., Jane and Harry Willson, Willson Rd. at Pecan City, P.O. Box 8200, Albany, GA 31706-8200. 912-883-3085. Free, 48 pp. Pecans, plain and fancy, and other nuts and fruits in candy, dried, or toasted.

SWISS COLONY, 1112 7th Ave., Monroe, WI 53566-1364. Free, 94 pp. Hundreds of gift boxes with cheese, sausage, candy, preserves, nuts, fruit; luscious tortes, chocolates, pastries; collectible gifts.

THEE DIET SHOPPE, Calco Co., P.O. Box 1343, Northbrook, IL 60065-1343. Free, 23 pp. Foods for those who are restricting their intake of sugar, salt, cholesterol, calories, or fat. Soup bases, drink mixes, candies, bakery mixes, freeze-dried fruits and vegetables, more.

VERMONT GENERAL STORE, F.H. Gillingham & Sons, 16 Elm St., Woodstock, VT 05091. 800-344-6668. Free, 24 pp. What you'd expect in a country store — maple syrup and candy, pancake mixes, cured meats, cheeses, pickles and preserves, dessert sauces and seasonings, plus a few regional gifts like maple wood bowls, soapstone griddle. Even a Vermont gift-a-month club.

WALNUT ACRES, Penns Creek, PA 17862. 800-433-3998. Free, 52 pp. Organic whole foods — every kind from beans to grains and granola to soups, muffin mixes, nut butters, juice and milk products.

WHISTLING WINGS FARM, 427 West St., Biddeford, ME 04005. Free, brochure. Handpainted oak and ash baskets crafted in Maine and filled with preserves, syrups; other decorative containers filled with sweets, vinegars, honeys.

WISCONSIN CHEESEMAN, P.O. Box 1, Madison, WI 53782-0001. 608-837-4100. Free, 112 pp. More than cheese! Gift boxes with meats, candy, nuts, preserves. Even a section of non-food gifts such as an abalone shell watch.

WOLFERMAN'S, One Muffin Ln., P.O. Box 15913, Shawnee Mission, KS 66285-5913. Free, 16 pp. Fine breads—English muffins, crumpets, tea breads, focaccia, bagels, cinnamon rolls. Gift-of-the-month club and gift baskets.

Food—International

BARONET COFFEE, P.O. Box 987, Hartford, CT 06143-0987. 800-253-7374. Free, 8 pp. Gourmet coffees from around the world.

DON ALFONSO FOODS, P.O. Box 201988, Austin, TX 78720. 512-335-2370. $1, 10 pp. Chilies, salsas, juices, specialties from Mexico; chili wreaths and seeds.

G.B. RATTO & CO., 821 Washington St., Oakland, CA 94607. 800-228-3515. Free, 32 pp. Products from around the world—grains, mixes, oils, teas, syrups, beans, coffee, mushrooms, the whole cafeteria!

GEVALIA KAFFE IMPORT SERVICE, Katalogvagen, P.O. Box 7045, Dover, DE 19903-9962. 800-438-4438. Free, brochure. Gevalia Swedish coffee flavors, coffeemakers.

HORTICULTURAL ENTERPRISES, P.O. Box 810082, Dallas, TX 75381-0082. Free, brochure. Over two dozen kinds of pepper seeds from sweet to hot.

SIMPSON & VAIL, INC., P.O. Box 309, Pleasantville, NY 10570-0309. Free, 22 pp. International teas (teapots, accessories), coffees, confections, baking mixes, honey, syrups, preserves, beans, rice, sauces, soups, oils, spices, specialties.

SULTAN'S DELIGHT, INC., 25 Croton Ave., Staten Island, NY 10301. 718-720-1557. Free, 13 pp. International delicacies, beans, cereals, spices, nuts, seeds, pickles, preserves, syrups, candy, dried fruit, and items such as Turkish coffee cups and belly dancing costumes.

Food—Meats
(see also *Food—Assorted; International;* and *Regional*)

AMANA MEAT SHOP & SMOKEHOUSE, P.O. Box 158, Amana, IA 52203-0158. 319-622-3111. Free, 22 pp. Fine smoked and fresh meats. Also sausage, preserves, and gift assortments.

NEW BRAUNFELS SMOKEHOUSE, P.O. Box 311159, New Braunfels, TX 78131-1159. 512-625-7316. Free, 24 pp. Hickory smoked turkey, ham, brisket, tenderloin, bacon, chicken, pork chops, sausages; gift assortments.

SCHALER & WEBER, 1654 2nd Ave., New York, NY 10028. 212-879-3047. Free, brochure. Sausages, liverwurst, salami, bacon, cold cuts, smoked meats.

Food—Regional

BAGELICIOUS, 1864 Front St., E. Meadow, NY 11554. 800-55-BAGEL. Free, brochure. Giant Bagel Heroes in shape of letters, numbers, or logo; cold salad platters, complete line of deli foods; homemade cream cheese.

BOUDIN GIFTS, P.O. Box 885421, San Francisco, CA 94188-5421. Free, 16 pp. Sourdough French bread, pizzas, French toast, rolls, baguettes; continental panettone breakfast; accessories, gift packs.

CALIFORNIA CUISINE, 3501 Taylor Dr., Ukiah, CA 95482. Free, 32 pp. Soup base, pastes, sauces, appetizers, desserts, sourdough bread, breakfast mixes, much more plus kitchen supplies.

CHILDREN'S CATALOG, THE, Children's Home Society of Washington, P.O. Box 15190, Seattle, WA 98115-0190. 800-456-3338. Free, 19 pp. Washington produce in gift packs. Profits benefit thousands of children and their families through the Children's Home Society. Also salmon, coffees, scone mix, and the children's clubs—seasonal deliveries of specified produce.

COLORADO SPICE CO., 5030 Nome St. Unit A, Denver, CO 80239. $1, 32 pp. Fresh spices, seasonings, and culinary herbs; baking kits, cookbooks, gift baskets, soups.

CREOLE DELICACIES, 533 St. Ann St., New Orleans, LA 70116. Free, 20 pp. A taste of New Orleans—praline topping, Creole fruitcake, Cajun dip mix, Cajun sauces, Louisiana cookbooks, French coffees, plantation rice, gift baskets.

DESERT MOUNTAIN TEA CO., Ltd., P.O. Box 328, Whitehorn, CA 95589. $1, 32 pp. Desert herbal teas based on the wild desert tea of the American West. Also teapots, canisters, gift boxes.

GAZIN'S CAJUN CREOLE CUISINE, 2910 Toulouse St., P.O. Box 19221, New Orleans, LA 70179-0221. 504-482-0302. $1 refundable, 36 pp. Totally Cajun from the appetizers to the desserts, including drink mixes from the French Quarter. Cajun-Creole meal-of-the-month club.

GRAFTON VILLAGE APPLE CO., RFD#1, Box 6D, Weston, VT 05161. Free, 22 pp. Vermont specials—sparkling cider, buttermilk and honey pancake mix, maple syrup, fruit butters, honey, apple cider jellies, apple-wood and cob-smoked meats, bird houses, and of course apples.

GREEN MOUNTAIN SUGAR HOUSE, RFD#1, Box 341, Ludlow, VT 05149. 800-643-9338. Free, 14 pp. Vermont by mail—maple syrup and fudge, cheese, maple nut brittle, corn-cob-smoked bacon, mincemeat, creamed honey, gift combinations.

HEGG & HEGG, 801 Marine Dr., Pt. Angeles, WA 98362. Free, brochure. Seafood from the Pacific Northwest—smoked salmon, tuna, shrimp, clams.

MANGANARO'S, 488 9th Ave., New York, NY 10018. Free, 12 pp. Italian foods—antipasto, oils, cheeses, meats, pastas, sweets, coffees.

MAUNA LOA, Mainland Expediting Ctr., 6523 N. Galena Rd., P.O. Box 1772, Peoria, IL 61656-1772. Free, 28 pp. The goodness of Hawaii — Macadamia nut treats, Kona coffee, tropical fruits and flowers.

NELSON CRAB, INC., P.O. Box 520, Tokeland, WA 98590-0520. 800-262-0069. Free, brochure. Sea treats in gift packs—salmon, crab, albacore tuna, shrimp, clams, river shad.

PEDRO'S TAMALES, P.O. Box 3571, Lubbock, TX 79452. 800-522-9531. Free, brochure. Tamales—that's it! This "sirloin in a shuck" can be shipped overnight anywhere in the U.S.

RENT MOTHER NATURE, 52 New St., P.O. Box 193, Cambridge, MA 02238. Free, 48 pp. Besides a tasty array of New England goodies and toys, this company lets you "rent" a maple, fruit, nut, or coffee tree; bee hive, lobster trap, or acre of red wheat. Recipient is sent a handsome "lease document" and all the produce of that source at harvest time (guaranteed minimum) plus progress reports on "his tree or trap" throughout the year.

2ND AVE. DELI, 225 Broadway, New York, NY 10007. Free, 8 pp. Just what you would expect — corned beef, pastrami, chicken soup, lox, beef goulash, rugelach, gefilte fish, and other deli specialties.

TEXAS TASTE BUDS, 216 Kirby Rd., Seabrook, TX 77586. 800-75-TASTE. Free, brochure. Cinnfull (cinnamon) and cinnfully picante pecans; fire and brimstone brittle and White Heat chocolate peanut cluster—separately or in gift packs.

WEATHERVANE SEAFOODS, Public Landing, Belfast, ME 04915. 207-338-1777. Free, brochure. Maine lobsters, clams, haddock, scallops, shrimp, and other sea specialties.

Food —Sweets

APLETS & COTLETS, Liberty Orchards, P.O. Box 179, Cashmere, WA 98815-0179. 800-888-5696. Free, 24 pp. Elegant fruit and nut candies.

BEAR TREATS, 14934 NE 31st Cir., Redmond, WA 98052. Free, 4 pp. Shaped chocolates you'll love to give—cellular telephone, baseballs, fun themes, holiday shapes.

CHOCOLATE HEAVEN, Pier 39, D-1, San Francisco, CA 94133. 800-858-CHOC. Free, 8 pp. Just about everything chocolate—bottles, cable cars, Band-Aids!, sardines, greeting cards, tennis racquets. Use your imagination; they've probably got it.

COOKIE BOUQUET, 6757 Arapaho Rd., Ste. 761, Dallas, TX 75248. 800-945-2665. Free, 20 pp. Adorable decorated shaped cookies with your personal message—in a bouquet. Special designs for baby, musician, computer enthusiast, graduate, bon voyage, holidays, other occasions.

CRYER CREEK KITCHENS, P.O. Box 9003, Corsicana, TX 75151-9003. 903-872-8411. Free, 16 pp. Homemade cakes, pies, cookies, and a few other treats.

DELECTABLE EDIBLES, 4442 Lovers Ln., Dallas, TX 75225. 800-233-8237. Free, brochure. Cookie bouquets for all occasions.

GHIRARDELLI, Mail Order, 900 N. Point St., Box 71, San Francisco, CA 94109. Free, 12 pp. The legendary chocolate in shapes, fudge sauce, hot chocolate mix, all kinds of gift boxes.

GODIVA CHOCOLATIER, Godiva Direct, P.O. Box 945, Clinton, CT 06413. Free, 32 pp. The famous chocolates in exquisite wrappings.

HERSHEY'S GIFT CATALOG, P.O. Box 801, Hershey, PA 17033-0801. Free, 14 pp. Chocolate in traditional kisses and bars and in innovative gifts such as chocolate checkers game, computer, and greeting cards.

LAMMES CANDIES, P.O. Box 1885, Austin, TX 78767. 800-252-1885. Free, 8 pp. Finest chocolates, chocolate-dipped pretzels, peanut brittle, pralines, nuts.

MARY OF PUDDIN HILL, P.O. Box 241, Greenville, TX 75403-9981. 800-545-8889. Free, brochure. Lovely chocolates in seasonal shapes, nut brittles, praline pecan pie, brandy and rum cakes.

MISS GRACE LEMON CAKE CO., Catalogue Sales, 16571 Ventura Blvd., Encino, CA 91436-2055. 800-367-2253. Free, 24 pp. Cookie-of-the-month plan; cakes, breads.

MRS. FIELDS EXPRESS GIFTS, P.O. Box 4000, Park City, UT 84060-4000. 800-344-CHIP. Free, 6 pp. Famous cookies, candy, bundt cakes, a cookie club for monthly giving.

ROCKY MOUNTAIN CHOCOLATE FACTORY, 265 Turner Dr., Durango, CO 81301-7941. 800-438-7623. Free, 23 pp. Hand-made chocolates—nutty, crunchy, creams; plus baskets with coffees, peanut brittle, and other mouth-watering treats.

TEUSCHER CHOCOLATIER, 620 5th Ave., New York, NY 10020. 800-554-0924. Free, brochure. Chocolates of Switzerland — assorted pralines and truffles.

TEXAS YA-HOO! Cake Co., 5302 Texoma Pkwy., Sherman, TX 75090-2112. Free, 8 pp. Texas-shaped pecan cake and other yummy flavors.

For Children Only
(see also *Clothing—Children thru Teens; Collectibles; Computing; Handcrafts; Models & Miniatures; Music & Movies;* and *Toys, Dolls, Games*)

GENTLE WIND SONGS AND STORIES FOR CHILDREN, P.O. Box 3103, Albany, NY 12203. 518-436-0391. Free, 12 pp. Merry children's songs and heartwarming stories on tape for ages 2-12.

ANIMAL TOWN, P.O. Box 485, Healdsburg, CA 95448-0485. Free, 48 pp. Co-operative and non-competitive games, outdoor playthings, environmental board games; children's tapes, books, puzzles; books on cooperation and family activities.

BIGTOYS, Northwest Design Products, Inc., 7717 New Market St., Olympia, WA 98501. 800-426-9788. Free, 15 pp. Commercial grade backyard play equipment.

BOOK LADY, INC., THE, 8144 Brentwood Industrial Dr., St. Louis, MO 63144. 314-644-3252. Free, 26 pp. Books for children.

BOOKS FOR OUR CHILDREN, 217 E. 85th St., Ste. 184, New York, NY 10028-3092. 212-249-2743. Free, 15 pp. Children's books; about famous black people, with illustrations of black people, about being black.

CEDAR HILL BOOKS, Rt. 8, Box 883, Tulsa, OK 74127. 918-425-2590. $2, 48 pp. Native American books for children of all ages—tribal history, biographies, fiction, nature; some videos and cassettes.

CHILD'S BOOKSHELF, Tri-mont, 17220 Newhope St., Ste. 222, Fountain Valley, CA 92708. Free, 16 pp. Favorite children's books (like Dr. Seuss, Richard Scarry, Mother Goose), children's classics at reduced prices and toys to match many of them.

COMMUNITY PLAYTHINGS, Box 901, Rifton, NY 12471-0901. 800-777-4244. Free, 62 pp. School quality wooden children's furniture, shelves, wheeled toys, blocks, play centers.

CREATE-A-BOOK, 3310 W. Bell Rd., Ste. 226, Phoenix, AZ 85023. 800-598-1044. Free, brochure. Over a dozen story lines into which your child's name is inserted as the main character.

CRITICS' GALLERY, P.O. Box 1777, Topeka, KS 66601. 800-255-3502. Free, 120 pp. More than 2,000 best-selling children's books, arranged by age.

CUISENAIRE CO. OF AMERICA, INC., P.O. Box 5026, White Plains, NY 10602-9926. Free, 120 pp. Materials, books, videos for learning or teaching mathematics and science to K-9 graders.

DAVIDSON & ASSOCIATES, INC., P.O. Box 2961, Torrance, CA 90509. Free, 20 pp. Software that makes learning fun—ages 2 to adult. Math, reading, science/ecology, social studies, writing, early learning.

DISNEY CATALOG, One Disney Dr., P.O. Box 29144, Shawnee Mission, KS 66201-9144. 800-237-5751. Free, 48 pp. Favorite Disney characters on nightshirts, videos, watches, bed linens, baby overalls, toys for kids from infant thru teens.

EDUCATIONAL INSIGHTS, 19560 S. Rancho Way, Dominguez Hills, CA 90220. 800-933-3277. Free, 34 pp. Products for teaching language arts, reading, math, science, geography; electronic teaching aids, books, manipulatives.

ENTERTAINMENT KIDS, P.O. Box 1760, Burbank, CA 91507. Free, brochure. Cassettes and CDs with songs, motion picture soundtracks, sing-alongs, lullabies, early learning concepts for children.

ENVIRONMENTS, EARLY CHILDHOOD EDUCATION DIV., P.O. Box 1348, Beaufort Industrial Park, Beaufort, SC 29901-1348. Free, 380 pp. Classroom quality furniture, books, dolls, indoor exercise equipment, wood blocks, art project and manipulative materials.

HARPER FESTIVAL, Order Dept., 1000 Keystone Industrial Pk., Scranton, PA 18512-4621. 800-242-7737. Free, 20 pp. Special projects, interactive books, character-based dolls, activity kits, books for children.

JENNY WREN PRESS, THE, P.O. Box 505, Mooresville, IN 46158. Free, 15 pp. "The magical world of Tasha Tudor." Stickers, dolls, paper dolls, stationery, cards, books, spice shelf, lithographs.

JUST FOR KIDS, P.O. Box 29141, Shawnee, KS 66201-9141. Free, 48 pp. Not your run-of-the-mill costumes, role play accessories, clothing, after-school fun for ages 3-12.

KIDVIDZ, 618 Centre St., Newton, MA 02158. 617-965-3345. Free, brochure. Four videos by and for children on moving, a new baby, art and creativity, and cooking for kids (nutrition, science experiments, art projects).

KIMBO EDUCATIONAL, P.O. Box 477R, Long Branch, NJ 07740. 908-229-4949. Free, 30 pp. Cassettes, records, filmstrips, videos, read-alongs for children on educational, storyline, foreign language, musical topics.

MACMILLAN CHILDREN'S BOOK GROUP, 866 3rd Ave., New York, NY 10022. Free, 105 pp. Fiction and non-fiction books for children of all ages.

MARBLESOFT, 12301 Central Ave. NE, Blaine, MN 55434. 612-755-1402. Free, 16 pp. Children's learning software—crossword puzzles, money skills, early learning.

MARVELOUS TOY WORKS, RR 1, Box 124A, Stillwater, PA 17878. Free, brochure. Simple designs in wooden toys that encourage a child's imagination. Also create your own set of wooden blocks from a wide variety of shapes.

MECC EDUCATION CATALOG, 6160 Summit Dr. N, Minneapolis, MN 55430. 612-569-1500. $3, 78 pp. Software for children's learning—math, science, social studies, thinking skills.

METROPOLITAN MUSEUM OF ART, Special Service Office, Middle Village, NY 11381-0001. Free, 32 pp. Wonderful and different entertainment for children—ancient games, children's classic books and matching dolls, Tangle movable sculpture, American slide whistle, punch-out masks.

MUSIC FOR LITTLE PEOPLE, Box 1460, Redway, CA 95560. Free, 60 pp. Audio cassettes, videos, child-size musical instruments in wonderful variety—stories, songs, folk tunes, children's classics, international music.

NATURAL CHILD, THE, 611 Ash Ave., Ames, IA 50010. 515-292-4471. $2, 18 pp. Children's clothes and toys made by craftspeople or small manufacturers representing traditional designs and quality that will last for years—white rabbit jack-in-the-box, corduroy overalls with embroidered bib, hand-knit cardigans and mitts, more. Clothing of natural materials.

NATURE'S CHILD, PLAYTHINGS FOR CHILDREN, P.O. Box 999, Ashland, OR 97520. Free, 10 pp. Original designs in wooden toys such as castle and knights, train whistle, several doll houses, flying machine, and other fine playthings.

NIÑOS, P.O. Box 3398, Livonia, MI 48151-3398. 800-634-3304. Free, 40 pp. Catalog in Spanish and English—Spanish and English children's books and book/audio cassette combo.

READER'S DIGEST KIDS CATALOG, P.O. Box 188016, Fairfield, OH 45018-8016. Free, 44 pp. Celebrating childhood with great books, toys, videos —porcelain tea sets, volcano kit, sit-down easel/blackboard, police officer pajamas, and more fun!

SCHOLASTIC, INC., P.O. Box 7502, Jefferson City, MO 65102. Free, 21 pp. Early childhood materials—books, videos, book/cassette combinations, play songs, and lullabies.

SENSATIONAL BEGINNINGS, P.O. Box 2009, Monroe, MI 48161. Free, 48 pp. Charming and whimsical toys for children—bed bug sleeping bags, soft sculpture animal barn, cuddly earth ball, books, cassettes, and doll sets— and that's just the beginning!

STORIES TO REMEMBER, Lightyear Entertainment, Empire State Bldg., 350 5th Ave., Ste. 501, New York, NY 10118. 212-563-4610. Free, brochure. Exquisitely animated videos and a corresponding line of high quality audio cassettes and CDs based on outstanding children's literature.

TOOLING AROUND, P.O. Box 720100, San Jose, CA 95172-0100. 408-286-9770. Free, 16 pp. Real tools for children — for gardening, cooking, sewing, building.

TOYS TO GROW ON, 2695 E. Dominguez St., P.O. Box 17, Long Beach, CA 90801-0017. Free, 48 pp. Toys that will please and entertain—make-believe and role play, travel games, arts and crafts, toddler toys, learning toys, young scientist supplies, personalized gifts.

TUNDRA BOOKS, P.O. Box 1030, Plattsburgh, NY 12901. 514-932-5434. Free, 24 pp. Children's books that are also works of art.

WIND RIVER PUZZLES, Wind River Products, Inc., P.O. Box 840, Carson, WA 98610-0840. Free, 8 pp. Wooden puzzles with simple designs on world peace themes for young children. Each piece is replaceable!

WOODPLAY, INC., P.O. Box 27904, Raleigh, NC 27611-7904. 800-982-1822. Free, 22 pp. Sturdy backyard play equipment.

Gardening
(see also *Environmentally Friendly;* and *Floral Gifts*)

A.C. BURKE & CO., 2554 Lincoln Blvd., Ste. 1058, Marina Del Rey, CA 90291. Free, 24 pp. "Intelligent tools for your garden." Videos, software, books, accessories on indoor and outdoor gardening, for kids, on landscaping.

ABBEY GARDEN CACTI AND SUCCULENTS, 4920 Carpinteria Ave., Carpinteria, CA 93013. 805-684-5112. $2, 56 pp. Pages of really interesting cacti and succulents.

BANANA TREE, INC., 715 Northampton St., Easton, PA 18042. 215-253-9589. $3, 36 pp. Rare seeds and books on them.

BONSAI TREE, 609 Shallowford Rd., Gainesville, GA 30504. 404-535-2991. Free, 10 pp. Bonsai trees, pottery, and tools.

BOUNTIFUL GARDENS, 18001 Shafer Ranch Rd., Willits, CA 95490-9626. Free, 63 pp. Presents the results of research into biointensive mini-gardening. They offer biological controls and supplies, seeds, books on organic gardening.

BRITTINGHAM PLANTS FARM, INC., P.O. Box 2538, Salisbury, MD 21802-2538. Free, 32 pp. All kinds of berry plants — strawberry, blackberry, raspberry, blueberry—plus grapes, asparagus, and rhubarb.

BURPEE & CO., 300 Park Ave., Warminster, PA 18974. Free, 148 pp. Thousands of plants and seeds.

CAPABILITY'S BOOKS FOR THE GARDENER, 2379 Hwy. 46, Deer Park, WI 54007. 800-247-8154. Free, 80 pp. Many books on gardening—making money from your garden, landscaping, weather, Japanese and British gardens as well as the traditional topics.

COOK'S GARDEN, THE, P.O. Box 535, Londonderry, VT 05148-0535. 802-824-3400. Free, 94 pp. Seeds and supplies for the kitchen garden.

GARDEN SPECIALTIES, P.O. Box 1774, New Port Richey, FL 34656. Free, 17 pp. Products for the display and care of garden and hanging plants.

GURNEY'S SEED & NURSERY CO., 110 Capital St., Yankton, SD 57079. 605-665-1930. Free, 64 pp. Vegetables, trees, herbs, fruits, perennials, garden supplies.

INDOOR GARDENING SUPPLIES, P.O. Box 40567, Detroit, MI 48240. 313-426-9080. Free, 32 pp. Seedling carts, fluorescent lamps, books, accessories for hydroponics.

J.L. HUDSON, SEEDSMAN, P.O. Box 1058, Redwood City, CA 94064. $1, 96 pp. Ethnobotanical catalog of seeds.

JACKSON & PERKINS ROSES AND GARDENS, 1 Rose Ln., Medford, OR 97501-0702. Free, 60 pp. Beautiful roses and perennials.

PARK SEED, Cokesbury Rd., Greenwood, SC 29647-0001. 803-223-7333. Free, 131 pp. Huge variety of flowers and vegetables for the garden.

R.H. SHUMWAY'S, P.O. Box 1, Graniteville, SC 29829-0001. Free, 56 pp. Vegetable and flower seeds.

SANTA BARBARA WATER GARDENS, 160 E. Mountain Dr., Santa Barbara, CA 93108. 805-969-5129. $2, 16 pp. Plants and supplies for the water garden.

SEEDS FOR THE WORLD, Vermont Bean Seed Co., Garden Ln., Fair Haven, VT 05743. 802-273-3400. Free, 96 pp. Seeds for vegetables and beans from around the world, including the habanero pepper, 1,000 times hotter than the jalapeño!

SISKIYOU RARE PLANT NURSERY, 2825 Cummings Rd, Medford, OR 97501. 503-772-6846. $2, 75 pp. Alpines and other dwarf, hardy plants for the woodland and rock garden.

SPRING HILL NURSERIES, 110 W. Elm St., Tipp City, OH 45371. $2, 52 pp. Plants, trees, shrubs.

ST. LAWRENCE NURSERIES, R.R. 5, Box 324, Potsdam, NY 13676. 315-265-6739. Free, 26 pp. Fruit and nut trees.

SUNRISE ENTERPRISES, P.O. Box 330058, W. Hartford, CT 06133-0058. 203-666-8071. $2, 28 pp. Specify English or Chinese catalog of Oriental vegetable and flower seeds, garden books and supplies, and Oriental cookbooks.

THOMPSON & MORGAN, INC., P.O. Box 1308, Jackson, NJ 08527-0308. 908-363-2225. Free, 210 pp. Hundreds of flower and vegetable seeds.

TOMATO SEED CO., P.O. Box 1400, Tryon, NC 28782. Free, 20 pp. Seeds for dozens of varieties and sizes of tomatoes.

VAN NESS WATER GARDENS, 2460 N. Euclid Ave., Upland, CA 91786-1199. 909-982-2425. $6, 56 pp. Plants, equipment, and books for water gardening.

WALT NICKE'S GARDEN TALK, Walt Nicke Co., 36 McLeod Ln., P.O. Box 433, Topsfield, MA 01983. 800-822-4114. $.50, 62 pp. Great assortment of tools and equipment for the gardener plus books and bird feeders.

WAYSIDE GARDENS, 1 Garden Ln., Hodges, SC 29695-0001. Free, 96 pp. Lots of flowers—bulbs and seedlings.

WILDSEED, INC., 1101 Campo Rosa Rd., P.O. Box 308, Eagle Lake, TX 77434-0308. $2, 46 pp. Wildflower seeds and culinary herbs.

WORM'S WAY, 3151 S. Hwy. 446, Bloomington, IN 47401-9111. 800-874-9676. $3, 64 pp. "Urban farmer's source book." Indoor/outdoor gardening equipment, hydroponics supplies, organic gardening supplies, seeds, plants, beer making kits and equipment.

Handcrafts
(see also *Art & Special Treasures;* various *Craft Supplies categories; International/Regional Specialties;* and *Jewelry*)

ANDERSEN DESIGN, Andersen Rd., E. Boothbay, ME 04544. 207-633-4397. Free, various. Fine stoneware bird and animal sculptures, decorative and useful bowls and vases.

BEREA COLLEGE CRAFTS, CPO 2347, Berea, KY 40404. 606-986-9341. Free, 32 pp. Beautiful handcrafts made by students and professionals in weaving, woodcraft, ceramics, broomcraft, and wrought iron—carved critters, wooden Christmas ornaments, toys, serving aids, wool couch throws, hand-forged fireplace accessories, dishwasher-, microwave-, and oven-safe pottery, seagrass stool, hand-braided hearthsweep, etc.

BEST OF MISSOURI'S HANDS, Missouri Artisans Business Development Association, Drawer A, T-16 Research Park, Columbia, MO 65211. 314-882-9889. $5, 85 pp. Handcrafts at their best representing rural artisans. You'll find collector dolls, woodcarvings, string puppets, baskets, wooden kaleidoscopes, leather sculptures, more creative crafts.

BLUE MOUNTAIN QUILTS, Shelly G. Callies, 4072 Scenic Rd., Campbellsport, WI 53010. 414-533-8813. $1, 6 pp. Made to order quilts or other patchwork gifts—vests, tote bags, placemats, table runners, jewelry.

CHRISTMAS TREASURES, P.O. Box 53, Dewitt, NY 13214. Free, 20 pp. Handcrafted holiday ornaments from around the world.

DICK SCHNACKE'S MOUNTAIN CRAFT SHOP, American Ridge Rd., Rt. 1, New Martinsville, WV 26155. 304-455-3570. Free, 8 pp. Handmade American folk toys like buckeye dolls, clothespin horse, jacks, ball and cup, and other old favorites.

ELWOOD TURNER, HCR Box 132, Morrisville, VT 05661. 802-888-3375. Free, 12 pp. Fine toys for children, including the famous Quackey the Duck, who walks and jumps from chairs!

FANCY FREE CREATIONS, P.O. Box 117, Brookville, OH 45309. 513-833-3907. Free, 20 pp. Sweet creatures (patterns or ready-made) to be used as dolls, toilet paper covers, doorstops, air freshener covers, wall hanging.

FOLKCRAFT INSTRUMENTS, P.O. Box 807, Winsted, CT 06098. 203-379-9857. Free, 4 pp. Solid wood, handcrafted mountain dulcimers, folk harps, psalteries, chord harps; books, recordings, instrument kits, accessories.

GAZEBO OF NEW YORK, 127 E. 57th St., New York, NY 10022. $6, 44 pp. Unbelievable array of handmade quilts, pillows, rag rugs, curtains plus soft sculpture collectible ornaments from series such as fairy tales, nursery rhymes, animals.

GINA SEKELSKY CALLIGRAPHY AND DESIGN, 3526 Girard Ave. S, Minneapolis, MN 55408. 612-824-2948. Free, 10 pp. Calligraphy and hand-painted journals, accordion calendar, book plates, sachets, cards.

GLAZE 'N IMAGE, P.O. Box 248, Hurst, TX 76053. 817-232-0433. Free, brochure. Have a favorite photo glazed onto a myriad of porcelain products—special occasion plates, key chains, sports bank, mug, jewelry.

GOD'S COUNTRY STORE, Box 1491, Eagle River, WI 54521. 715-479-6000. Free, brochure. Accent furniture from the past for today's living—bookshelves, cabinets with drawers, cupboards and hutches, drysink.

H.O.M.E. CRAFTERS' CATALOG, H.O.M.E., Box 10, Rt. 1, Orland, ME 04472. 207-469-7961. Free, 12 pp. Great prices on good variety of handcrafts—wood mittens, quilts, spice mug mat, pottery—plus Maine maple products and jams. H.O.M.E. is a cooperative community dedicated to helping the unemployed, the homeless, the unskilled.

HANGOUTS HAMMOCKS, 1328 Pearl St. Mall, P.O. Box 148, Boulder, CO 80306-9910. 800-HANGOUT. Free, brochure. Handwoven hammocks —colorful Mayan or Brazilian designs.

HERE'S MY HEART COUNTRY COLLECTIBLES, 53 E. Kings Hwy., Haddonfield, NJ 08033. 609-354-2064. $2, 20 pp. Country crafts at their best— collectible quality dolls with lots of character, decorating accents, afghans, braided heart rugs.

HISTORICAL PRODUCTS, P.O. Box 403, E. Longmeadow, MA 01028. 413-525-2250. Free, brochure. Portraits of famous people and a few designs (or you supply the picture!) silk screened onto T-shirts, sweatshirts, tote bags, chef's aprons.

HUMANE TROPHIES, Dianne Shapiro Soft-Sculpture, Inc., 19 Cedar St., BRattleboro, VT 05301. 802-254-8431. $3, 11 pp. Soft sculpture animal heads and "other ends" for wall mounting or rugs by Dianne Shapiro. Realistic fur. Part of each order goes to conservation organizations.

ITHACA GUITAR WORKS, 215 N. Cayuga St., Ithaca, NY 14850. 607-272-2602. Free, various. Beautiful handcrafted acoustic/electric string instruments developed by musicians to interface acoustic instruments with amplifiers or mixing consoles without losing the feel of fine instruments.

LAURA COPENHAVER INDUSTRIES, INC., P.O. Box 149, Marion, VA 24354. 800-227-6797. Free, 22 pp. Handcrafted furniture, coverlets, canopies, curtains, rugs, and quilts preserve traditional mountain crafts.

LITTLE COLORADO, 15866 W. 7th Ave., Golden, CO 80401. $2, brochure. Handcrafted children's furniture and accessories such as kitchen center, knick-knack shelves, rocking horse, bear lamp.

NORTH STAR TOYS, 617 N. Star Rt., Questa, NM 87556. Free, brochure. Beautiful in their simplicity—wooden rolling toys and puzzles with few pieces in bright colors. Very affordable and child-pleasing.

ROCKER SHOP OF MARIETTA, GA, 1421 White Circle NW, P.O. Box 12, Marietta, GA 30061. 404-427-2618. Free, brochure. Finely handcrafted wood furniture, hand-woven cane seats—several styles of rockers, occasional tables, footstools, child's rocker, porch swing, lap desks.

SHAKER WORKSHOPS, P.O. Box 1028, Concord, MA 01742-1028. 617-646-8985. Free, 56 pp. Practical and pure in design are these Shaker furniture pieces, baskets, trays, boxes, carriers, and accessories. Also chair and basket kits.

SKYFLIGHT MOBILES, P.O. Box 974, Woodinville, WA 98072. 800-766-8005. Free, 24 pp. Whimsical, colorful, 3-D handmade mobiles of birds and animals. A portion of each purchase benefits wildlife and conservation groups.

SOUTHWEST INDIAN FOUNDATION, P.O. Box 86, Gallup, NM 87302-0001. Free, 16 pp. Profits benefit the foundation that helps educate, feed, clothe, and rehabilitate Native Americans on the Navajo Reservation. All handcrafted turquoise and silver jewelry, dolls, baby spoons, coloring books, limited edition prints, pottery.

TOUCHING LEAVES INDIAN CRAFTS, 927 Portland Ave., Dewey, OK 74029. Free, 20 pp. Handmade Lenape (Delaware) Indian crafts. Also books on American Indian games, crafts, history, heritage.

TOYS OF YORE, 82264 Hillview Dr., Creswell, OR 97426. 800-572-PLAY. Free, 12 pp. Handmade wooden doll houses, stable, castles, and wiggle wands for the prince or princess of the house.

TOYS THAT TEACH, Innovations for Children, 1905 Green Willow, Fort Worth, TX 76134. 807-568-0226. Free, brochure. Handmade hardwood puzzles, toys, vehicles, more for children.

TRADE WIND, P.O. Box 380, 156 Drake Ln., Summertown, TN 38483. 615-964-2334. $1, 20 pp. Handmade shirts, tote bags, beadwork, pottery, baskets, poet's vest, tablecloths by Native Americans. Also a few books, videos, cassettes.

TRADITIONAL NORWEGIAN ROSEMALING, Pat Virch Inc., 1506 Lynn Ave., Marquette, MI 49855. 906-226-3931. $2, 16 pp. Kits and custom work for Norwegian rosemaling and bronze powder stenciling.

TWIN OAKS HAMMOCKS, Rt. 4, Box 169, Louisa, VA 23093. Free, brochure. Handcrafted hammocks, hammock pillows, hanging chairs.

WESTON BOWL MILL, Weston, VT 05161. Free, 28 pp. Hand-crafted bowls, lazy Susans, wooden fruit and vegetables, serving accessories, household furnishings, cutting and carving boards, stoneware, wooden toys, country store items, baskets.

WOODBURY PEWTERS, 860 Main St. S, P.O. Box 482, Woodbury, CT 06798. 203-263-2668. Free, 12 pp. Handmade pewter tableware, pitchers, candleholders, desk accessories, bells, magnets, Christmas ornaments.

WRIGHT MADE PRODUCTS, Dept. W.D., 415 17th Ave. S, Grand Forks, ND 58201. 701-772-6554. Free, brochure. Handcrafted wooden board games for all ages.

Handyman
(see also *Craft Supplies—Woodworking*)

FINE HOMEBUILDING, Taunton Press, 63 S. Main St., P.O. Box 5506, Newtown, CT 06470-9959. Free, 4 pp. Books and videos on construction and specific skills such as installing doors and windows, stair building, laying hardwood floors.

NORTHERN, P.O. Box 1499, Burnsville, MN 55337-0499. Free, 136 pp. Lots of ideas for the handyman—from automotive parts to fencing supplies to spotlights to hand tools.

WHOLE EARTH ACCESS, 822 Anthony St., Berkeley, CA 94710. 800-829-6300. Free, 48 pp. Woodworking and construction supplies, tools, books, accessories.

WOMANSWORK, P.O. Box 543, York, ME 03909-0543. Free, 12 pp. Pigskin and cowhide work gloves for women plus other helpful items such as work aprons, work boots, tote bags, and sweatshirts.

Health & Beauty
(see also *Environmentally Friendly*)

AEROBICS MUSIC, Power Productions, P.O. Box 550, Gaithersburg, MD 20884-0550. Free, 41 pp. Exercise to your choice of music on cassette— Latin, rap, instrumental, Christian, blues, funk, you name it!

BODY SHOP BY MAIL, THE, 45 Horsehill Rd., Cedar Knoll, NJ 07927-2014. 800-541-2535. Free, various. Environmentally friendly cosmetics and bath products. No animal testing or rainforest destruction.

COLLAGE VIDEO SPECIALTIES, INC., 5390 Main St. NE, Dept. 1, Minneapolis, MN 55421. 800-433-6769. $2, 54 pp. All kinds of exercise videos for step-bench, mini-trampoline, aerobics, muscle toning, relaxation, dance, ski-machine, kids, pregnancy, backpain relief, mature viewers, large size viewers, and special disabilities. Also some accessories.

COUNTRY DOCTOR, 103 Greenleaf Rd., Fort Worth, TX 76107. $2.95, 32 pp. Health care products—pill reminders, no-slip grip doorknob, back massager for your car, other practical helps.

CRABTREE & EVELYN, Mail Order Dept., P.O. Box 167, Woodstock, CT 06281-0167. $3.50, 24 pp. Fine toiletries and comestibles—dozens of romantic scents of soap, shampoo, body lotion, bath gel, massage oil, talc, and cologne. Also a few discriminating gift items.

DR. LEONARD'S HEALTH CARE CATALOG, 74 10th St., Brooklyn, NY 11232-1100. 718-768-2620. Free, 48 pp. Items for easier, healthier living such as pine tar soap, no-hands magnifier, wigs, step exerciser.

DYNAMIX MUSIC SERVICE, 711 W. 40th St., Ste. 428, Baltimore, MD 21211. 800-843-6499. Free, 15 pp. Audio, video cassettes for aerobics.

EARTH REVERENCE, P.O. Box 12243, St. Petersburg, FL 33733-2243. 813-866-2602. Free, 12 pp. Organic bath and massage oils, sachet bags, scented light bulb rings, essential oils, bottles, books on aromatherapy.

EVERYBODY, 1738 Pearl St., Boulder, CO 80302. 303-440-0188. Free, 10 pp. Body care products. They can blend your choice of 120 essential perfume oils into lotion, bubble bath, massage oil, shampoo, hair rinse, or after-shave lotion.

GOLD MEDAL HAIR PRODUCTS, One Bennington Ave., P.O. Box 815, Freeport, NY 11520-0815. Free, 80 pp. Special hair care and health products, wigs and hair pieces for black women. Also hats, jewelry, books, videos, and puzzles for children; gospel, blues, and Motown cassettes and videos.

HEALTHHOUSE USA, Box 9034, Jericho, NY 11753. Free, 32 pp. Health aids for exercise, monitoring; handy helps.

INTERNATIONAL YOGURT CO., 628 N. Doheny Dr., Los Angeles, CA 90069. 213-274-9917. Free, brochure. Yogurt shampoo, face cream, body powder; yogurt, buttermilk, sour cream, acidophilus milk, and kefir cultures.

MUSCLE MIXES MUSIC, P.O. Box 533967, Orlando, FL 32853. 800-52-MIXES. Free, brochure. Choose your kind of music for your aerobic session—Latin, Motown, rock 'n roll, big band, rock.

SIMMONS HANDCRAFTS, 42295 Hwy. 36, Bridgeville, CA 95526. Free, 26 pp. Pure soaps, hard-to-find natural bath and bodycare products, recycled paper products, puppet washcloths, and vinyl foam shapes that stick to (and peel off) the bathtub or the child!

SPORTS MUSIC, Box 769689, Roswell, GA 30076. 800-878-4764. Free, various. Tapes to enjoy while walking, running, doing aerobics, cycling, using treadmill or ski machines.

WOODS OF WINDSOR, 125 Mineola Ave., Ste. 304, Roslyn Heights, NY 11577. 800-969-SCENT. Free, 26 pp. Home fragrances and toiletries for men and women, made from recipes popular in 18th and 19th century England. Packaging typical of an English country garden.

Home Furnishings
(see also *Art & Special Treasures; Collectibles; Handcrafts; International/Regional Specialties;* and *Smorgasbord*)

ALEX & IVY COUNTRY, 550 Bailey, Ste. 660, Fort Worth, TX 76107. Free, 24 pp. Country simplicity, instant heirlooms, furniture, quilts, accessories.

ANTICIPATIONS, Ross-Simons Jewelers, 9 Ross-Simons Dr., Cranston, RI 02920-9848. 800-521-7677. Free, 48 pp. Lovely home furnishings and tabletop designs—china, flatware, rugs, linens, art prints, gifts.

BOMBAY CO., P.O. Box 161009, Fort Worth, TX 76161-1009. Free, 32 pp. Quality reproductions of elegant 18th and 19th century antique English furniture, accessories.

CAPE COD CUPOLA CO., INC., 78 State Rd., Rt. 6, N. Dartmouth, MA 02747. 508-994-2119. $2, 43 pp. Weathervanes, cupolas, sundials, lawn and mailbox signs, flagpole eagles, weathervanes.

COUNTRY CURTAINS, At the Red Lion Inn, Stockbridge, MA 01262-0955. 800-937-1237. Free, 72 pp. Many fabrics, colors, styles, and textures of curtains.

DOMESTICATIONS, Hanover, PA 17333-0040. 717-633-3313. Free, 95 pp. Contemporary styles and patterns in comforters, curtains, rugs, blankets, table linens, children's bed linens.

EDDIE BAUER HOME COLLECTION, P.O. Box 3700, Seattle, WA 98124-3700. Free, 56 pp. Comfortable country home decorating accents — wicker, bear cookie jar, goose down comforters, furniture.

FINISHING TOUCHES, 4555 Lyman Dr., Hilliard, OH 43026-1282. 800-468-2240. Free, 56 pp. Much imagination is evident in these light-hearted and folkart decorating accents, toys, and garden and kitchen touches.

GOODWIN WEAVERS, P.O. Box 408, W. Cornish Rd., Blowing Rock, NC 28605. $5, 20 pp. 100% cotton loom-woven throws, pillows, rugs, table linens, canopies, wall hangings.

GUMP'S, MAIL ORDER DIVISION, 1707 Falcon Dr., Ste. 102, DeSoto, TX 75115. 800-284-8677. Free, 47 pp. Rare, unique, imaginative home decorations and accessories, serving dishes.

POTTERY BARN, Mail Order Dept., P.O. Box 7044, San Francisco, CA 94120-7044. Free, 36 pp. Country comfortable furniture, dinnerware, rugs, home accessories.

RENOVATOR'S SUPPLY, Renovator's Old Mill, Millers Falls, MA 01349-1097. 800-659-3211. Free, 64 pp. Period fixtures and accessories for your home — cast iron bathtubs, china sink and toilets, vintage-look fixtures, tin ceilings and cornices, weathervanes, indoor and outdoor lighting.

RUE DE FRANCE, 78 Thames St., Newport, RI 02840. 800-777-0998. $3, 36 pp. Authentic lace curtains, panels, table linens, pillows (all machine washable) and French accessories. Elegant.

SUGAR HILL, P.O. Box 1300, Columbus, GA 31902-1300. 800-252-8248. Free, 47 pp. Traditions and heritage of the South expressed in unique home furnishings — country dough bowl, furniture, pendulum clock, reed boxes.

TAPESTRY, Hanover, PA 17333-0135. 800-833-9333. $2, 64 pp. Fresh looks for the home at exceptional values—seasonal decor, table linens, sweetheart chair, wicker and lattice accessories, Shaker furniture, storage towers, Oriental screens and accent tables.

TEAK CONNECTION, 2391 SE Dixie Hwy., Stuart, FL 34996. 407-287-0463. $2, 32 pp. Anything and everything teak — swimming platforms, shelves, accessories for boats such as dish and cup holders, tables.

TOUCH OF CLASS CATALOG, 1905 N. Van Buren St., Huntingburg, IA 47542-9595. 800-457-7456. Free, 72 pp. Victorian, southwestern, other bedroom linens and accessories.

WARM THINGS, 180 Paul Dr., San Rafael, CA 94903. 415-472-2154. Free, 16 pp. Goose down comforters, slippers, robes, pillows, cover ensembles.

YIELD HOUSE, P.O. Box 5000, N. Conway, NH 03860-5000. 800-258-0376. $3, 42 pp. Country accents at their best—furniture and decorating pieces. Also furniture kits.

Housewares
(see also *Cookware* and *Smorgasbord*)

BARRONS, P.O. Box 994, Novi, MI 48376-0994. $2, 48 pp. Hundreds of the world's finest china, flatware, and stemware patterns and fine gifts at substantial savings.

COLONIAL GARDEN KITCHENS, Hanover, PA 17333-0066. $2, 96 pp. Helpful household and kitchen equipment such as a rolling laundry sorter, long-handled dustpan, cushioned seat on wheels for gardening or low tasks; portable pine footpath; canister that stores, pours, and measures; lots of really clever items.

COMPLETE COLLEGIATE/TRAVELER, P.O. Box 11145, Fairfield, NJ 07004. 201-808-9249. $2, 12 pp. Necessities and luxuries for the college-bound and traveler—bath tote, storage bags, folding clothes dryer, travel organizer bags, folding drinking cup, others.

HOLD EVERYTHING, Mail Order Dept., P.O. Box 7807, San Francisco, CA 94120-7807. Free, 40 pp. Stylish containers, storage units for bath, closet, kitchen, laundry room, garage.

HOUSE OF 1776, P.O. Box 472927, Garland, TX 75047-2927. Free, 24 pp. Fine names in china, crystal, stainless, sterling silver, and giftware at discount prices.

INTERNATIONAL WINE ACCESSORIES, 11020 Audelia Rd. B113, Dallas, TX 75243. 800-527-4072. $3, 36 pp. Designer wine racks, stemware, natural grapevine tables, books and videos, decanters, wine cellar construction plans and kits.

REPLACEMENTS, LTD., 1089 Knox Rd., P.O. Box 26029, Greensboro, NC 27420. 919-697-3000. Free, brochure. Call for replacements in your china, crystal, flatware pattern.

Infant/Maternity Supplies
(see also *Clothing—Children thru Teens; For Children Only; Handcrafts,* and *Toys, Dolls, Games*)

BABY BUNZ & CO., P.O. Box 1717, Sebastopol, CA 95473. Free, brochure. Several styles of cotton, no-pin diapers and diaper covers; biodegradable disposable diapers; cotton undergarments from Sweden; accessories.

BABY WORKS, 11725 NW West Rd., Portland, OR 97229. Free, 20 pp. Cloth diapers (prefolded or no-fold) *without* pins, leaks, or hand-rinsing; diaper covers, training pants, accessories.

BABYBJORN, Regal & Lager Scandinavian Products for Children, P.O. Box 70035, Marietta, GA 30007. 404-565-5522. Free, 32 pp. Children's nursery products from Scandinavia. Colorful, latest in practicality.

ELIZABETH LEE DESIGNS, HC65, Box 12, Bluebell, UT 84007. 801-454-3738. Free, 8 pp. Patterns for the breastfeeding mother.

INGI, P.O. Box 45, Chagrin Falls, OH 44022-0045. 800-338-4644. Free, 23 pp. Very chic European nursery collection—coordinated layettes, nursery accessories.

KINDER CONNECTION, 1688 Montalto Dr., Mountain View, CA 94040. 415-968-2181. Free, 15 pp. Baby supplies, jogging strollers, indoor/outdoor play structures, cloth diapers.

MOTHERS WORK MATERNITY, 1309 Noble St., 6th Fl., Dept. NG, Philadelphia, PA 19123. 215-625-9259. Free, 32 pp. Fashions for work and play for the mother-to-be.

MOTHERWEAR, P.O. Box 114, Northampton, MA 01061. 413-586-3488. Free, 38 pp. Fashions and helpers for the nursing mother; baby clothing.

NATURAL BABY CATALOG, 114 W. Franklin Ave., Pennington, NJ 08534-1405. Free, 52 pp. No-pin cotton diapers and Velcro diaper covers, everything for nursing, toys of natural materials, lambskin items, organic cotton clothing, soft shoes, herbal and homeopathic remedies.

ONE STEP AHEAD, P.O. Box 517, Lake Bluff, IL 60044. 800-950-5120. Free, 48 pp. Nursing and nursery supplies, safety and "out and about" equipment, toys, even a birthday party kit!

PARENTING CONCEPTS, P.O. Box 1437, 526 Grizzly Rd., Lake Arrowhead, CA 92352. 800-727-3683. $1, 16 pp. Practical and attractive items for new babies and moms including lullabies on tape.

RIGHT START CATALOG, THE, Right Start Plaza, 5334 Sterling Center Dr., Westlake Village, CA 91361-4627. Free, 60 pp. Wonderfully different nursery items, toys, carriers, strollers; gifts for mom, dad, grandparents.

International/Regional Specialties
(see also *Food* categories, *Handcrafts; Smorgasbord;* and *Travel*)

AUSSIE CONNECTION, 825 NE Broadway, Portland, OR 97232. Free, 18 pp. Specialties from Down Under—oilskin raincoat, wool jumper (sweater), sheepskin-lined slippers and boots, handmade boomerangs, and others.

BLARNEY, Blarney Woollen Mills (NJ), INC., 373D Rt. 46W, Fairfield, NJ 07004-9880. $2, 40 pp. Classic gifts from Ireland—Irish coffee glasses, sweaters, Waterford crystal, Belleek, other giftware.

BOIS FORT GALLERY, 130 E. Sheridan, Ely, MN 55731. 800-777-7652. Free, 19 pp. Native American and outdoor photography, handcrafts, paintings, books, children's books, audio cassettes.

CARE PACKAGE CATALOG, P.O. Box 684, Holmes, PA 19043. 800-428-1257. Free, 32 pp. Exotic gifts and fashions from around the world—toys from Russia, baskets from the Philippines, hand-carved napkin rings from Kenya, embroidered clothing from Guatemala, wonderfully different.

CLADDAGH JEWELLERS, Eyre Square Centre, Galway, Ireland. 800-473-3259. Free, 10 pp. Lovely bracelets, rings, watches with the romantic Claddagh design (two hands holding a heart).

DIETZ MARKET, P.O. Box 2243, Durango, CO 81302. 800-321-6069. Free, 24 pp. Best of the West — jalapeño suckers, barbecue sauce, lariat wreath, monthly salsa selection, Women's Bean Project basket (to help homeless women in Denver), colored corn necklaces, tin luminarias.

EXIMIOUS OF LONDON, 1000 Green Bay Rd., Winnetka, IL 60093. 800-221-9464. Free, 32 pp. The best of the British tradition—leather jewel boxes (for him or her), Limoges porcelain, wooden games, handpainted soldier bookends, monogrammed watch, more.

GREAT ALASKA CATALOG, 5750 Glacier Hwy., Juneau, AL 99801. 314-754-4215. Free, 32 pp. Jewelry, posters, housewares, stuffed animals, videos depicting wolves, puffins, Eskimos, bear, moose, other Alaskan natives.

LA PIÑATA, No. 2 Patio Market, Old Town, Albuquerque, NM 87104. 505-242-2400. Free, 5 pp. Several sizes and many designs of piñatas and paper flowers.

LOUISE HEITE'S ICELANDIC CATALOGUE, P.O. Box 53, Camden, DE 19934-0053. 800-777-9665. Free, brochure. Icelandic products—yarn, sweater kits, weaving and spinning kits.

PEAVIAN LOGIC, P.O. Box 45, Hawaii National Park, HI 96718. 800-554-1407. Free, 26 pp. Collection of products about Hawaii's natural environment—videos, postcards, stamps, glow-in-the-dark T-shirts.

PO POLSKU, 12 Saranac Ave., Lake Placid, NY 12946. 518-523-1311. Free, brochure. Almost 100 folkcrafts made by local craftsmen in Poland—toys, inlaid boxes, traditional clothing, wildflower pictures and cards; also books and audio tapes.

PUEBLO TO PEOPLE, P.O. Box 2545, Houston, TX 77252-2545. 800-843-5257. Free, 36 pp. Direct from cooperatives in South and Central America are colorful clothing, jewelry, coffee beans, baskets, toys, Christmas decorations, and more. All handmade. Non-profit organization.

SCOTLAND BY THE YARD, Rt. 4, Quechee, VT 05059. 802-295-5351. Free, brochure. Fine Scottish imports— cardigans, Thistleware pottery, kilt pins, clan crest jewelry, tartan ties, CDs of pipes and drums.

SCOTTISH LION IMPORT SHOP, THE, P.O. Box 1700, N. Conway, NH 03860. 603-356-5517. Free, 64 pp. Lovely things from Scotland—skirts, tams, and scarves in over 400 tartans; Shetland wood sweaters, jewelry, patterned handbags, Edinburgh crystal, Thistle pottery, shortbread, Highland dirks, and that's just half of the catalog!

TASTE OF BRITAIN, P.O. Box 1425, Norcross, GA 30091-1425. Free, brochure. Union Jack gifts; cookbooks; Norfolk lavender bath products; cheese selection; sweets, chocolates, biscuits, jams, marmalades, sauces, pickles, desserts, teapots and cosies, beverages, kitchen staples.

WORLD AWARENESS, INC., Dept. 1, 890 Twin Towers, Ypsilanti, MI 48198-3882. 800-472-8860. Free, various. This non-profit organization presents aids to global awareness— games, cassettes, stories from around the world (5% goes to projects in poor areas of the world).

Jewelry
(see also *Art & Special Treasures; Handcrafts; International/Regional Specialties;* and *Outdoors*)

A.G.A. CORREA, P.O. Box 401, Wiscasset, MA 04578-9987. 800-341-0788. Free, 40 pp. Fine jewelry inspired by the sea—Turk's head tie bar, center of effort pendant chain, crescent moon charm, dangling bowline earrings.

GLORI NICKEL-FREE JEWELRY, H&A Enterprises, Inc., 143-19 25th Ave., P.O. Box 489, Whitestone, NY 11357. 718-767-7770. Free, 7 pp. Nickel-free earrings and jewelry "guaranteed friendly to sensitive skin."

JAMES AVERY CRAFTSMAN, P.O. Box 1367, Kerrville, TX 78029-1367. Free, 25 pp. Sterling silver and gold jewelry— with gemstones, classic designs, seasonal themes, Christian symbols, charms.

MARY LAURA'S, 701 Carlisle Blvd. NE, Box 12615, Albuquerque, NM 87195. Free, brochure. Handcrafted sterling silver and gemstone jewelry from the Zuni Indians.

MUSEUM OF JEWELRY, 3000 Larkin St., San Francisco, CA 94109. 800-258-0888. Free, 31 pp. Many styles of jewelry— Renaissance, Victorian, contemporary, Russian, art deco, Georgian.

NATURE'S JEWELRY, 27 Industrial Ave., Chelmsford, MA 01824-3692. Free, 100 pp. Wide variety of styles and kinds of jewelry with animal, floral, fauna, fish, scenic subjects—some dressy and some just for fun.

SIMPLY WHISPERS, Roman Research, Inc., 33 Riverside Dr., Pembroke, MA 02359-1910. 800-451-5700. Free, 58 pp. Fashion earrings for sensitive ears—made entirely from surgical grade stainless steel. Up-to-the-minute designs and old-fashioned prices.

TORY'S JEWELRY, 106 Washington St., Marblehead, MA 01945. 800-67-TO-RYS. Free, 15 pp. Lovely handmade gold and sterling jewelry.

Models & Miniatures

(see also *Collectibles; Craft Supplies; Handcrafts;* and *Toys, Dolls, Games*)

AUTHENTIC MODELS, 104 S. Mill St., P.O. Box 520, Creswell, OR 97426-0520. 503-895-4555. Free, 15 pp. Detailed model kits for such things as country wagon, royal fire engine, Gutenberg press, field cannon, street organ, miniature musical instruments, folkart, many kinds of ships.

BLUEJACKET SHIPCRAFTERS, P.O. Box 425, Stockton Springs, ME 04981. 800-448-5567. $2, 24 pp. Fine ship modeling kits, building materials, and plans.

DOLLHOUSE FACTORY, Box 456, 157 Main St., Lebanon, NJ 08833. 908-236-6404. $5.50, 118 pp. Very complete catalog of doll houses, supplies, miniatures, and instructional books.

DUNKEN CO., INC., 511 Main St., P.O. Box 95, Calvert, TX 77837. 409-364-2020. Free, 20 pp. Kits and molds to cast your own toy soldiers, war game soldiers, collectors' soldiers, fantasy figures.

EWA MINIATURE CARS USA, 369 Springfield Ave., P.O. Box 188, Berkeley Heights, NJ 07922-0188. 908-665-7811. $2, 88 pp. Model cars from over 300 manufacturers plus books, manuals, posters, videos, and magazines.

FLYING MODEL ROCKETS, Estes Industries, Hi-Flier Manufacturing Co., P.O. Box 227, Penrose, CO 81240. Free, 64 pp. Just what the title says — from starter kits to many styles of rockets to software for analyzing performance.

GREENBERG CATALOG, 21027 Crossroads Cir., P.O. Box 1612, Waukesha, WI 53187-1612. Free, 28 pp. Hobby books, magazines, videos on toy trains, doll houses, radio control models, miniatures, collectibles.

GREENLEAF PRODUCTS, INC., P.O. Box 388, 58 N. Main St., Honeoye Falls, NY 14472. 800-847-2545. Free, 14 pp. Artistically designed doll houses, also miniature lighting.

HOBBY BUILDERS SUPPLY, P.O. Box 921012, Norcross, GA 30092-7012. $5, 64 pp. Doll house kits, plans, and a myriad of accessories — lighting, windows, hardware, furniture kits.

LILLIPUT MOTOR CO., INC., P.O. Box 447, Yerington, NV 89447. 415-326-0993. Free, brochure. Schuco micro-racer series of die-cast, clockwork motor cars.

LUNAR MODELS, 106 Century Dr., Cleburne, TX 76031. 817-556-0296. Free, 38 pp. Models of varying skill levels for space ships, vehicles, figures, and alien beings.

MODEL EXPO, P.O. Box 1000, Mt. Pocono Industrial Park, Tobyhanna, PA 18466-1000. $3, 92 pp. Beautiful, detailed models of ships, ship model fittings, modeler's tools, reference books.

PACIFIC AIRCRAFT, 14255 N. 79th St., Scottsdale, AZ 85260. $3, 16 pp. Original designs of fine military, civilian, and commercial aircraft models.

PRECIOUS LITTLE THINGS, The Fieldwood Co., Inc., P.O. Box 6, Chester, VT 05143-0006. 802-875-4127. $3.50, 32 pp. Nice color photographs show the detail of these adorable accessories for doll houses — food, stoneware, elegant furniture, much more.

ROSE'S DOLL HOUSE, 5826 W. Bluemound Rd., Milwaukee, WI 53213. 800-926-9093. Free, 27 pp. Detailed doll house miniatures and accessories.

SHELDON'S HOBBIES, 2135 Old Oakland Rd, San Jose, CA 95131. 408-943-0872. Free, 22 pp. Hundreds of kits and supplies for radio-controlled trucks, planes, cars.

SHOWCASE MODEL CO., P.O. Box 470, State College, PA 16804-0470. 814-238-8571. Free, 36 pp. Display models of airships, aircraft, aviation weathervanes, rockets. Another catalog of ship display models.

TOWER HOBBIES, P.O. Box 9078, Champaign, IL 61826-9078. 800-523-0187. $3, 288 pp. Radio-control models (cars, boats, planes), accessories.

Music & Movies

(You'll find plenty of audio and video gifts here. See also *Books & More; For Children Only; International/Regional Specialties;* and other categories for videos about special subjects; see also *Handcrafts* for handmade musical instruments.)

ALPHA COLLECTION, Bradford Consultants, P.O. Box 4020, Alameda, CA 94501. 510-523-1968. Free, 18 pp. Organ and choral music recorded in the cathedrals, churches, and schools of the British Isles.

AMERICAN PIE OLDIES, P.O. Box 66455, Los Angeles, CA 90066. 310-821-4005. $2, 114 pp. 45 rpm singles, CDs, cassettes, movie videos, mostly "oldies and goodies."

BAINBRIDGE RECORDS, P.O. Box 8248, Van Nuys, CA 91499-4195. 800-621-8705. Free, 16 pp. LPs, CDs, and cassettes of classical, jazz, sound effects, easy listening music.

BOSE EXPRESS MUSIC, The Mountain, Framingham, MA 01701-9323. 800-451-BOSE. $6 refundable, 288 pp. 75,000 titles of rock, classical, jazz, blues, Nashville, opera, world music on CD, tape, video, laserdisc, mini disc, plus accessories. Cost of catalog refunded with first order. Collector's Club offers free CDs.

BOSTON MUSIC CO., 172 Tremont St., Boston, MA 02111. 617-426-5100. Free, various. Several catalogs covering musical gifts, instrumentals, choral, organ, piano. They can provide any music currently in print.

CRITIC'S CHOICE POSTINGS VIDEO, P.O. Box 549, Elk Grove Village, IL 60009-0549. $2, 116 pp. Thousands of movies for every taste—comedy, classics, musicals, drama, foreign, action.

ELDERLY INSTRUMENTS, 1100 N. Washington, P.O. Box 14210, Lansing, MI 48901. 517-372-7890. Free, various. Several very inclusive catalogs — records, cassettes, and CDs; books, instructional tapes, and video cassettes about music; electric and acoustic instruments and accessories; used instrument list.

FUSION VIDEO, 17311 Fusion Way, Country Club Hills, IL 60478-9906. Free, 48 pp. All kinds of videos—history, family, classics, inspirational, foreign, music, nostalgia, science fiction, collections, more!

GREAT CHEFS, P.O. Box 56757, New Orleans, LA 70156-6757. 800-321-

1499. Free, 8 pp. Great chefs come to your home via video to prepare their specialties.

GREEN FROG PRODUCTIONS LTD., 200 N. Cobb Pkwy., Ste. 138, Marietta, GA 30062-3538. 800-227-1336. Free, 8 pp. Audio and video cassettes for railroad enthusiasts.

GREEN LINNET RECORDS, 43 Beaver Brook Rd., Danbury, CT 06810. Free, 49 pp. CDs and tapes of music that spans the globe.

H&B RECORDINGS DIRECT, 2186 Jackson Keller, San Antonio, TX 78213. 800-222-6872. Free, 48 pp. CDs — classical, musical and film scores, choral, children's, piano and organ, instrumentals.

HEARTLAND MUSIC, 605 S. Douglas St., P.O. Box 1034, El Segundo, CA 90245-1034. Free, 16 pp. Cassettes, CDs, records of favorite artists from the 40s up to today — slow dancing, soft rock, Elvis, Floyd Cramer, George Strait, and more.

INTERNATIONAL HISTORIC FILMS, INC., P.O. Box 29035, Chicago, IL 60629. 312-927-2900. Free, 30 pp. British cinema, authors, royal family, antiques, gardens, and landmarks on video.

KEYBOARD WORKSHOP, Box 700, Medford, OR 97501. 503-664-7052. Free, 30 pp. Special keyboard skills taught via video or cassette with printed material — Southern gospel piano, ragtime, syncopation, echoes, transposing, chord substitutions, etc.

KICKING MULE RECORDS, P.O. Box 158, Alderpoint, CA 95511. 707-926-5312. Free, 46 pp. CDs, cassettes, music books, teaching tapes, videos for acoustic guitar, banjo, dulcimer, harmonica, harp.

LARK IN THE MORNING, P.O. Box 1176, Mendocino, CA 95460. 707-964-5569. Free, 72 pp. Over 100 kinds of musical instruments (percussion, winds, bagpipes, strings, harps, reeds), instrument kits, books, videos.

MULTITIME MEDIA, P.O. Box 1210, Dublin, OH 43017-6210. 800-860-DISC. Free, 16 pp. CDs of carefully mixed classical music and nature's songs, or nature sounds alone (falling rain, ocean surf, thunderstorm, birds in a meadow). Also CD sleeve binders, DJ Express for carrying 400 CDs.

MUSIC DISPATCH, P.O. Box 13920, Milwaukee, WI 53213. Free, various. Several catalogs: one with music, CDs, cassettes, books for guitar and electric bass; another with music for piano and voice, songbooks and more.

MUSIC STAND, THE, 1 Rockdale Plaza, Lebanon, NH 03766. 802-295-9222. Free, 63 pp. Gifts and ideas from the performing arts — clothing, jewelry, and accessories with musical instruments, ballerinas, and Broadway musicals; also music stands, tapes and CDs, and practical accessories for musicians.

NATIONAL EDUCATIONAL MUSIC CO., LTD., 1181 Rt. 22, Box 1130, Mountainside, NJ 07092. 800-526-4593. Free, 51 pp. Band and orchestra instruments from amati to zildjian (woodwinds, brasswinds, percussion, cymbals, drums, keyboards and synthesizers, recorders, string instruments, accessories).

ORGAN HISTORICAL SOCIETY, P.O. Box 26811, Richmond, VA 23261. Free, 46 pp. Recordings (CD, cassette), books, sheet music.

PATTI MUSIC CO., 414 State St., P.O. Box 1514, Madison, WI 53701-1514. 608-257-8829. $2, 82 pp. Piano and organ music, metronomes, tuners, manuscript paper and teaching aids, statuettes.

PLAYER PIANO CO., INC., 704 E. Douglas, Wichita, KS 67202. 316-263-3241. Free, 112 pp. Large selection of player piano parts, accessories, piano rolls.

POCKET SONGS, 50 S. Buckhout St., Irvington, NY 10533-2204. 914-591-5100. $2, 128 pp. Cassettes and CDs that allow you to remove the vocalist and become the star performer. Also a catalog, "Music Minus One," for singers of classical songs or players of musical instruments.

QUALITON IMPORTS, LTD., 24-02 40th Ave., Long Island City, NY 11101. 718-937-8515. Free, various. Several large catalogs of CDs—classical, jazz, and international music.

READER'S DIGEST VIDEO COLLECTION, Reader's Digest, Order Dept., Pleasantville, NY 10570. Free, 48 pp. Humor, workout, living history, other countries, wildlife, children's movies.

RECORD ROUNDUP, P.O. Box 154, Cambridge, MA 02140-0900. 617-661-6308. Free, 74 pp. CDs, cassettes, videos of every kind of music from around the world — including children's, folk, reggae, gospel, Cajun, rock 'n roll, classical, soul.

REGO IRISH RECORDS & TAPES, INC., 64 New Hyde Park Rd., Garden City, NY 11530-3909. Free, 50 pp. Just what the name says—music, song, storytelling, and entertainment from Ireland—traditional and contemporary.

RHYTHM BAND INSTRUMENTS, P.O. Box 126, Fort Worth, TX 76101. 817-332-5654. Free, 46 pp. Rhythm instruments, videos, sheet music, musical games, and teaching aids.

RICK'S MOVIE GRAPHICS, P.O. Box 23709, Gainesville, FL 32602-3709. Free, 62 pp. Reprints, star photos, and movie theme commercial posters plus original material for films from the early 1950s right up to today's hottest titles.

SAMPLER RECORDS, LTD., P.O. Box 19270, Rochester, NY 14619. 800-537-2755. Free, 26 pp. Cassettes, CDs, and LPs of folk music, music of Ireland and Scotland, Shaker music, instrumental hymns, music for harp and dulcimer, fiddle tunes, historic dance tunes, music for children.

SOUND DELIVERY, P.O. Box 2213, Davis, CA 95617-2213. Free, 548 pp. Gigantic listing (over 85,000 titles!) of mostly pop and classical cassettes and CDs.

SOUNDSATIONS!, 370 Mt. Vernon, Grosse Pointe Farms, MI 48236. 313-885-1539. Free, 23 pp. For musicians—MIDI software and hardware, RAM cartridges and expanders, computer software and interfaces, cassettes and CDs, drum and keyboard patches, rhythm pattern packages, discount musical equipment.

VIDEO ARTISTS INTERNATIONAL, 158 Linwood Plaza, Ste. 301, Fort Lee, NJ 07024-3704. 201-944-0099. Free, 12 pp. Performing arts video collection with such stars as Maria Callas, John Coltrane, Makarova, Jascha Heifetz, and others.

VIDEO LIBRARY, 7157 Germantown Ave., Philadelphia, PA 19119. 800-669-7157. Free, 8 pp. Videos to rent by mail. All kinds of movies—Australian, British, comedy, adventure, documentaries, family, fine arts, drama, foreign, health, horror, instruction, musicals, science fiction, vintage, Westerns; also audio books, video games, and laserdiscs.

VIEW VIDEO, INC., 34 E. 23rd St., New York, NY 10010. 800-843-9843. Free, 20 pp. Over 125 special interest videos from dance, art, classical, jazz, health and fitness, sports, parenting, children's interactive programming.

WIRELESS, P.O. Box 64422, St. Paul, MN 55164-0422. Free, 48 pp. "For fans and friends of public radio." Cassettes, videos, CDs, sweatshirts, books based mostly on radio programs and similar fun themes.

WORKSHOP RECORDS, P.O. Box 49507, Austin, TX 78765. 512-452-8348. Free, 80 pp. Music lessons in books and on cassettes, instruments, accessories mainly for guitar, banjo, fiddle, harmonica, dulcimer, mandolin.

WORLD DISC/NATURE RECORDINGS, 915 Spring St., P.O. Box 2749, Friday Harbor, WA 98250. 206-378-3979. Free, various. Cassette tapes and CDs offering soothing and beautiful nature sounds, innovative contemporary classic music, and intriguing mixes of nature's sounds and relaxing music.

Outdoors
(see also *Animals, Birds, Fish (and Lovers of Same!); Environmentally Friendly;* and *Sports & Recreation*)

A5 ADVENTURES, INC., 1701 N. West St., Flagstaff, AZ 86004. 602-779-5084. Free, 15 pp. Packs, portaledges, haulbags, slings for climbers.

AKERS SKI, INC., P.O. Box 280, Andover, ME 04216. Free, 40 pp. Cross-country skis, equipment.

ANDERSON ARCHERY CORP., Box 130, Grand Ledge, MI 48837. 517-627-3251. Free, 48 pp. Supplies for the hunting archer.

ANGLER'S SUPPLY HOUSE, P.O. Box 996, Williamsport, PA 17703. 717-323-7564. Free, 50 pp. Books, tools, kits, supplies for fishermen to make their own gear or buy it ready-made.

BACKCOUNTRY BOOKSTORE, P.O. Box 191, Snohomish, WA 98291-0191. $1, 62 pp. Over 2,200 titles on backpacking, climbing, skiing, watersports, bicycling, adventure trekking.

BASS PRO SHOPS, 1935 S. Campbell, Springfield, MO 65898-0400. 417-887-1915. Free, 156 pp. "Basic plus" for outdoorsmen — clothing, hunting and fishing gear, camping equipment.

BENNETT MARINE VIDEO, 730 Washington St., Marina del Rey, CA 90292. 800-733-8862. $2.50, 48 pp. Marine videos on fishing, sailing, power-boating, watersports.

BERRY SCUBA CO., 6674 N. Northwest Hwy., Chicago, IL 60631. Free, 40 pp. Gauges, fins, slates, pneumatic guns, wetsuits, accessories.

BIKE NASHBAR, 4111 Simon Rd., Youngstown, OH 44512-1343. 216-782-2244. Free, 84 pp. Clothing, accessories, safety gear for the cyclist.

BOOK CHANDLER, Harbour Bookshop, 12 Fairfax Pl., Dartmouth, Devon TQ6 9AE United Kingdom. Free, 11 pp. Nautical books—history, knots, cruising, boat building, seamanship.

BOUNDARY WATERS CATALOG, Piragis Northwoods Co., 105 N. Central Ave., Ely, MN 55731. Free, 40 pp. Equipment for canoeists, winter sports, camping; books on outdoors.

CABELA'S, Catalog Sub. Dept., 812 13th Ave., Sidney, NE 69160-0001. 800-237-8888. Free, 210 pp. Rugged outdoor clothing, hunting and fishing gear, outdoorsman gifts.

CAMPER'S CHOICE, 502 4th St. NW, P.O. Box 1546, Red Bay, AL 35582-1546. Free, 54 pp. RV parts and accessories—from awnings to filtration systems to mini-blinds.

CAMPMOR, Box 997-B, Paramus, NJ 07653-0997. 800-525-4784. Free, 134 pp. Great prices for every outdoor activity—tents, inflatables, camping gear, clothing, books, maps, videos, backpacks, cooking equipment.

CASCADE OUTFITTERS, P.O. Box 209, Springfield, OR 97477. Free, 66 pp. "Grand Canyon tested river equipment" — kayaks, clothing, rafts, dry boxes and bags, camping equipment, all you'll need.

COLDWATER CREEK, Sandpoint, ID 83864-0907. 800-262-0040. Free, 48 pp. Celebrating the out-of-doors in clothing, jewelry, prints, home accessories.

COLORADO KAYAK, P.O. Box 3059, Buena Vista, CO 81211. 800-535-3565. Free, 32 pp. Drysuits, canoes, whitewater guides, helmets, footwear, roof racks, flotation devices.

DUNN'S, INC., Hwy. 57E, P.O. Box 449, Grand Junction, TN 38039-0449. 800-223-8667. Free, 112 pp. Upscale clothing, books, accessories for the sportsman.

EARLY WINTERS, P.O. Box 4333, Portland, OR 97208-4333. 800-821-1286. $2, 64 pp. Clothing made for snow country plus handloomed wool sweaters from Peru, pocket planetarium that shows the night skies and constellations, brain teaser games, workout wear.

EDDIE BAUER, P.O. Box 3700, Seattle, WA 98124-3700. 800-426-8020. Free, 52 pp. Good value clothing, classic styles for men and women who spend time outdoors.

EXTRASPORT, 5305 NW 35th Ct., Miami, FL 33142-3203. 305-633-2945. Free, 23 pp. Specialty clothing for on and off the river.

FOUR CORNERS RIVER SPORTS, Box 379, Durango, CO 81302-0379. Free, 32 pp. Whitewater equipment — kayak, canoes, videos, clothing, paddling jackets.

FROSTLINE KITS, 2525 River Rd., Grand Junction, CO 81505-2525. 800-548-7872. Free, 32 pp. Sew your own quality parkas, stuff sacks, vests, jackets, down comforters and jackets, ski bags, bags and packs, luggage, sleeping bags, and tents from kits.

GANDER MOUNTAIN, P.O. Box 248, Wilmot, WI 53192-0248. Free, 208 pp. Supplies for many outdoor interests — boating, camping, hunting, archery, hiking.

INTEGRAL DESIGNS, P.O. Box 40023, Highfield P.O., Calgary, Alberta Canada. T2G 5G5. 403-640-1445. Free, various. Tents, shelters, and action wear for outdoor (mostly winter) activities.

L.L. BEAN, L.L. Bean, Inc., Freeport, ME 04033-0001. 800-341-4341. Free, 84 pp. Top quality men's and women's casual, outdoor clothing, comforters, hiking boots.

LEISURE OUTLET, 421 Soquel Ave., Santa Cruz, CA 95062. Free, 8 pp. Discounted equipment for camping, golf, backpacking, travel, photography.

MAD RIVER CANOE, Box 610, Waitsfield, VT 05673. 802-496-3127. Free, 32 pp. Canoes and accessories.

MARMOT MOUNTAIN INTERNATIONAL, 2321 Circadian Way, Santa Rosa, CA 95407. 707-544-4590. Free, 39 pp. Top-of-the-line apparel and sleeping bags for polar conditions.

MOUNTAIN PRESS PUBLISHING CO., 2016 Strand Ave., P.O. Box 2399, Missoula, MT 59806. 800-234-5308. Free, 20 pp. Books on the out-of-doors — earth science, guide books, frontier adventures, horse and vet, roadside geology, and history.

MOUNTAINEERS BOOKS, 1011 SW Klickitat Way, Ste. 107, Seattle, WA 98134. 800-553-4453. Free, 9 pp. Books on outdoors sports—bicycling, mountaineering, nature and conservation, outdoor instruction, paddling, travel, and winter sports.

NETCRAFT FISHING TACKLE, 2800 Tremainsville Rd., Toledo, OH 43613. Free, 83 pp. Everything for the fisherman — bags, boat accessories, net making supplies, fish scents, waders.

NORTHWEST OUTDOOR CENTER, 2100 Westlake Ave. N, Seattle, WA 98109. 206-281-9694. Free, 16 pp. Boats, books, and gear for kayaking.

OFFSHORE ANGLER, 1935 S. Campbell, Springfield, MO 65898-0140. $4, 140 pp. "Offshore, inshore, flats, flyfishing, backcountry, surf" equipment, clothing, boat gear, related gift items and toys.

OVERTON'S, 111 Red Banks Rd., P.O. Box 8228, Greenville, NC 27835. 800-334-6541. Free, 116 pp. Equipment for almost all water sports—boating equipment, swimsuits, water skiing gear, books, videos, safety equipment, children's gear.

PARKWAY SYSTEM, THE, 241 Raritan St., S. Amboy, NJ 08879. 908-721-5300. Free, 23 pp. Advanced yet practical equipment for sport and commercial divers—jumpsuits, hoods, grabber boots, gloves, drysuits, regulators, vests.

PATAGONIA MAIL ORDER, INC., 1609 W. Babcock St., P.O. Box 8900, Bozeman, MT 59715-2046. 800-336-9090. Free, 91 pp. Two catalogs, for adults and kids. Rugged outdoor clothing of exceptional quality.

PATIO, THE, P.O. Box 925, San Juan Capistrano, CA 92693. Free, brochure. Outdoor furniture, pool games, hammocks, bird feeders, weathervanes.

REI, Sumner, WA 98352-0001. Free, 180 pp. Quality outdoor gear and clothing—tents, sleeping bags, cookware, tall men's sizes, watches, water sports equipment, footwear, much more.

SAILBOARD WAREHOUSE, INC., 300 S. Owasso Blvd., St. Paul, MN 55117. 800-992-SAIL. $4.95, 84 pp. Sailboard buyer's guide and catalog— boards, sails, wetsuits, masts/booms, more.

SIERRA TRADING POST, 5025 Campstool Rd., Cheyenne, WY 82007. Free, 32 pp. Discounted famous brands of outdoor clothing, equipment.

SIERRA CLUB, Mail-Order Service Guide, 730 Polk St., San Francisco, CA 94109. Free, 43 pp. Explore and appreciate the earth's scenic and ecological resources through books, audio tapes, calendars, children's books, posters, and logo items.

SIMS STOVES, P.O. Box 21405, Billings, MT 59104. 406-259-5644. Free, 16 pp. Camping equipment—folding woodburning stoves, wall tents, cast iron cookware, pack saddles, cookware sets, prospecting equipment, books on outdoors cooking.

STAFFORD'S, 808 Smith Ave., P.O. Box 2055, Thomasville, GA 31799-2055. 800-826-0948. Free, 48 pp. Fashionable and functional casual wear "tested by South Georgia briars." Special styles such as quail embroidered field shirt, hunting jeans with canvas sewn on the front, waxed cotton jackets, plus gifts for hunters and outdoorsmen and women.

SWISS ARMORY, 2838 Juniper St., San Diego, CA 92104. 800-43-SLICE. Free, various. Many styles of Swiss Army knives—even left-handed and those carrying names of favorite sports teams.

TIDEWATER SPECIALTIES, U.S. Rt. 50, Box 158, Wye Mills, MD 21679-0158. Free, 80 pp. Gifts and gear for wildlife enthusiasts, dog owners and trainers, and outdoor sportspersons; books and housewares with wildlife motifs; your own "animal crossing" sign, sporting neckties and watches, floor mats, and sweatshirts.

U.S. CAVALRY, 2855 Centennial Ave., Radcliff, KY 40160-9000. 800-333-5102. $3, 126 pp. Military and adventure equipment.

VOYAGEUR, P.O. Box 207, Waitsfield, VT 05673. 800-843-8985. $2, 22 pp.

High performance canoe and kayak gear—bags, seats, paddles, safety equipment, etc.

WEST MARINE, Catalog Sales Div., P.O. Box 50050, Watsonville, CA 95077-5050. Free, 104 pp. Quality boating gear and apparel—including flag accessories, dinghies, harnesses, scrimshaw Christmas ornaments, compasses, basic items like pumps.

WILD ROSE GUIDEBOOKS, P.O. Box 240047, Anchorage, AK 99524. 907-274-0471. Free, 52 pp. Books, maps, videos for outdoor adventures—parks and refuges, RV/car touring, hikes, backpacking, safety, adventure stories, scenery, much more.

WOMYN'S WHEEL, P.O. Box 2820, Orleans, MA 02653. Free, 36 pp. Cycling clothing and products for women.

WYOMING RIVER RAIDERS, 601 SE Wyoming Blvd., Casper, WY 82609. 800-247-6068. $1, 40 pp. Canoes, rafts, and many very handy accessories.

Photography

B&H PHOTO-VIDEO, 119 W. 17th St., New York, NY 10011. 212-807-7474. Free, 30 pp. New and used equipment for the professional photographer.

CAMJACKET, 2610 Adams Ave., San Diego, CA 92116. 800-338-8759. Free, brochure. Modular camera "jacket" system for camera bodies and interchangeable lenses. Replaces the traditional camera bag.

OMEGA ARKAY, 191 Shaeffer Ave., P.O. Box 2078, Westminster, MD 21158. 410-857-6353. Free, 64 pp. Professional photographic and darkroom equipment.

PORTER'S CAMERA STORE, INC., P.O. Box 628, Cedar Falls, IA 50613-9986. 800-682-4862. $5, 120 pp. Huge selection of photography equipment, books, developing supplies, accessories.

W.B. HUNT CO., INC., 100 Main St., Melrose, MA 02176. 617-662-6685. Free, 72 pp. Cameras, darkroom equipment, film, paper, accessories.

Religious

(see also *Books & More* and *Music & Movies*)

ABBEY PRESS, 341 Hill Dr., St. Meinrad, IN 47577-1001. $1, 44 pp. Christian specialty gifts—for home, children, holidays. Precious Moments and other collectibles.

AMERICAN BIBLE SOCIETY, P.O. Box 5656, Grand Central Station, New York, NY 10164-0851. Free, 40 pp. Inexpensive Bibles and Scripture booklets in many languages, large print, Braille; booklets for youth; coloring books, activity books for children; audio and video cassettes.

BEST TO YOU, Hwy. 16 E, P.O. Box 1300, Siloam Springs, AR 72761-1300. Free, 48 pp. Christian cards, calendars, Nintendo games, books, housewares with Scripture verses.

CHRISTIAN BOOK BARGAINS, P.O. Box 1009, Dover, OH 44622. Free, 64 pp. Books, videos, Nintendo games, perpetual calendars, games, toys.

CHRISTIAN BOOK DISTRIBUTORS, P.O. Box 6000, Peabody, MA 01961-6000. 508-977-5050. Free, 44 pp. Over 5,000 titles from 90 top Christian publishers at great savings. Every subject—reference, children's, counseling, even entertainment and teaching videos and computer software.

COMMUNICATION RESOURCES, P.O. Box 2625, N. Canton, OH 44799-6115. Free, 24 pp. Church clip art on diskette and paper.

GREAT CHRISTIAN BOOKS, 229 S. Bridge St., P.O. Box 8000, Elkton, MD 21922-8000. $5, refundable, 36 pp. Over 7,000 Christian books at big discounts—children's, home school, Puritan and Reformed classics, music, games, family books; children's videos.

JUDAICA CLASSICA, 125 E. 85th St., New York, NY 10028. 212-722-4271. Hundreds of handcrafted Jewish ceremonial objects in glass, wood, and silver from Israel, America, and Europe. Call for specific items you are interested in.

LIVING EPISTLES SHIRTS, P.O. Box 77, Klamath Falls, OR 97601. 800-874-4790. Free, 17 pp. Christian messages, designs on T-shirts, sweatshirts, tank tops, scoop necks, roll-ups.

PRECEPT MINISTRIES, P.O. Box 182218, Chattanooga, TN 37422. 615-892-6814. Free, 104 pp. Christian books, tapes for adults, teachers, and teens.

PRINTERY HOUSE, THEE, Conception Abbey, Conception, MO 64433-0012. Free, 28 pp. Christian greeting cards, art, folk art from El Salvador, pendants, bronze door plaques.

WORD FAMILY, P.O. Box 10662, Des Moines, IA 50336-0662. Free, 48 pp. Christian music (contemporary and traditional) on cassettes or CDs, books, videos, children's products.

Science
(see also *For Children Only*)

ACCESS MAPS & GEAR, 321 S. Guadalupe, Santa Fe, NM 87501. 505-982-3330. Free, 16 pp. Relief maps, computer-generated contour imagery, compasses, travel guides, map puzzles, globes, roadside geology books, geologic highway maps, atlases.

AMAZING CONCEPTS, P.O. Box 7.16, Amherst, NH 03031. 603-673-4730. Free, brochure. "Far-out science" kits, plans, equipment — lasers, stun guns, coil guns, thermal telescope, other exotic tools.

AMERICAN WEATHER ENTERPRISES, P.O. Box 1383, Media, PA 10963. 215-565-1232. Free, 20 pp. Devices for the weather watcher — barometers, thermometers, tygrometers, rain gauges, home weather stations, sundials, books, software.

ANATOMICAL CHART CO., 8221 Kimball, Skokie, IL 60076. 800-621-7500. Free, 84 pp. Mostly hilarious, but also educational products dealing with skeletons; the charts seen in doctors' offices on puzzles, nightshirts, and the like. Also a great array of scientific kits for children—even a science-kit-a-month club. catalog of "barebones" books and videos on nutrition, child care and women's health, anatomy, nature, ecology, medical reference books.

ASTRONOMICS/CHRISTOPHERS, LTD., 2401 Tee Circle, Ste. 105/106, Norman, OK 73069. Free, various. Birding optics, spotting scopes, binoculars.

BIRDING, P.O. Box 4405, Halfmoon, NY 12065. 518-664-2011. Free, 31 pp. Scopes, tripods, binoculars, accessories from top manufacturers.

EDMUND SCIENTIFIC CO., 101 E. Gloucester Pike, Barrington, NJ 08007-1380. 609-573-6260. Free, 112 pp. Complete line of equipment for the technical and science educator (and hobbyist) plus classroom motivators and prizes, experiment kits, science discovery toys.

FINAL FRONTIER, 1516 W. Lake St., Ste. 102, Minneapolis, MN 55408. 800-24-LUNAR. Free, 32 pp. Space collectors' catalog—books, satellite images, models, patches, slides, videos, posters, murals, software, etc.

HUBBARD SCIENTIFIC, Dept. MPB, P.O. Box 760, Chippewa Falls, WI 54729. Free, 8 pp. Raised relief topographic maps.

MAP STORE, INC., 5821 Karric Sq. Dr., Dublin, OH 43017. 800-332-7885. Free, 16 pp. Business maps of various geographical areas and scales, wall-mounted maps, folded city maps, street guides; computer-generated maps of census area, zip codes, or market area.

OPTIC OUTFITTERS FOR BIRDERS, 716 S. Whitney Way, Madison, WI 53711. 608-271-4751. $2, 40 pp. Binoculars, spotting scopes, tripods, accessories.

RAVEN MAPS & IMAGES, 34 N. Central Ave., Medford, OR 97501. Free, 15 pp. Relief and flat maps for framing.

SKULLDUGGERY, 624 South B St., Tustin, CA 92680. 800-336-7745. Free, 35 pp. Unique natural history gifts, fossil replicas, skeleton puzzles, animal skulls, woodcarvings, jewelry.

SKY & TELESCOPE, Sky Publishing Corp., P.O. Box 9111, Belmont, MA 02178-9111. 800-253-0245. Free, 32 pp. Astronomy books, star atlases, videos, slides, audio tapes, posters, photographs, calendars, globes.

WORLDSAT INTERNATIONAL, INC., Box 224, Malton P.O., Mississauga, Ontario L4T 3B6 Canada. Free, various. Spectacular satellite images from space, puzzles, globes, digital atlases, and other space-age finds.

ZEPHYR SERVICES, 1900 Murray Ave., Pittsburgh, PA 15217. 412-422-6600. Free, 72 pp. Software programs dealing with stellar database, images of our universe, asteroids, satellite predictions as well as programs for diet planning, coin collecting, math tutorials, and other scientific subjects.

Smorgasbord
(a wonderful selection of gifts that overlap several categories)

ALSTO'S HANDY HELPERS, P.O. Box 1267, Galesburg, IL 61401. Free, 56 pp. "Wish I'd thought of these" kinds of tools and practical helps for garden, home chores, clean-up, pest control, deck, and patio. One-of-a-kind items.

ARMCHAIR SHOPPER, P.O. Box 306, Grandview, MO 64030-0306. 800-729-1111. Free, 96 pp. Mainly decorative items for the home and collectibles —centerpieces, dolls, seasonal decorations, country crafts, toys.

ATLANTA CUTLERY, Box 839, Conyers, GA 30207. 800-883-0300. $2, 68 pp. Knives and cutting tools from around the world.

BAG 'N BAGGAGE, Corporate Headquarters, 11067 Petal St., Dallas, TX 75238. 800-788-2808. Free, 21 pp. Nice selection of gifts for traveler, golfer, business person.

BEST CATALOGS IN THE WORLD, Publisher Inquiry Services, 951 Broken Sound Pkwy. NW, Bldg. 190, Boca Raton, FL 33431-0857. $6, 80 pp. A catalog of catalogs to order to expand your shopping alternatives.

BLUE CHIP GIFTS, P.O. Box 6748, Lubbock, TX 79493-6748. 800-747-3137. Free, brochure. Gifts and greeting cards with business or financial themes.

BROOKSTONE HARD-TO-FIND TOOLS, 5 Vose Farm Rd., P.O. Box 803, Peterborough, NH 03460-0803. 800-926-7000. Free, 64 pp. Not tools in the traditional sense, but tools that make life easier such as panoramic rear view mirror to eliminate blind spots, non-fog bath mirror, motion-activated night light, compact hair dryer/iron, so many more handy items.

BUTTERFLY VIDEO, Box 184-C13, Antrim, NH 03440. 603-588-2105. Free, 16 pp. Dance lessons on video—ballroom, country, children's dance, exercise, even theatrical make-up techniques.

CALLAWAY GARDENS COUNTRY STORE, Callaway Gardens Resort, Inc., P.O. Box 2000, Pine Mountain, GA 31822-2000. Free, 20 pp. Specials (like muscadine sauce, green or red pepper jelly, peach spread, apricot butter), wildflower prints, golf pro collection.

CELEBRATION FANTASTIC, 1620 Montgomery St., Ste. 250, San Francisco, CA 94111. Free, 40 pp. Romance, whimsy, and imagination spring from this catalog. Special treats such as Limoges Christmas decorations, singing Santa socks, decoupage Christmas plates, hand-embroidered pillows, hand-painted shirts, other delights.

CHARLES KEATH, LTD., P.O. Box 48800, Atlanta, GA 30362-1800. Free, 40 pp. Imaginative gifts of clothing, home decorations, holiday accessories.

CHRISTMASTIME TRADITIONS, 300 Ravine St., Pounding Mill, VA 24637. 703-963-NOEL. Free, 16 pp. Christmas decorations—door posters, outdoor scenes, music boxes, little accents.

COCKPIT, THE, P.O. Box 019005, Long Island City, NY 11101-9005. 800-272-WINGS. Free, 44 pp. Large selection of aviation and military-inspired outer wear, accessories, gifts.

COLORFUL IMAGES, 1401 S. Sunset St., Longmont, CO 80501-6755. Free, 48 pp. Wonderful assortment of housewares, clothing, decorative objects, labels, toys.

COMB CORP., 720 Anderson Ave., St. Cloud, MN 56395. Free, 56 pp. Authorized liquidator offers great savings on items for kitchen, office, exercise room, traveler, security, electronics, more.

COMPANY OF WOMEN, 102 Main St., P.O. Box 742, Nyack, NY 10960-0742. Free, 32 pp. Profits benefit the Rockland Family Shelter, which serves victims of domestic violence, rape survivors, and the homeless. Interesting array of products celebrating women—toasts from wise women etched on glasses, suffragette mug, women-who-dared calendar and postcards, music by women, books about women, art prints, personal safety devices.

COOK BROS., INC., 240 N. Ashland Ave., Chicago, IL 60607. 800-345-8442. $2.50, 80 pp. Wholesale distributors—dozens of gifts in each of many categories — luggage, watches, jewelry, cameras, calculators, games, sporting goods, tools, auto and home accessories, home decor, dolls.

COUNTRY MANOR, Rt. 211, P.O. Box 520, Sperryville, VA 22740. $3, 60 pp. Charming country decorating accents, dolls, decorated sweaters, handcrafts.

COUNTRY STORE, 5925 Country Ln., P.O. Box 990, Greendale, WI 53129. Free, 36 pp. Country gifts for country folks—afghans, country cookbooks, collectibles, home decorating, country comedy and critter shirts, books, kitchen items.

DAISY KINGDOM, 134 NW 8th Ave., Portland, OR 97209. Free, 48 pp. Holiday gifts and crafts to make or purchase—really cute cross-stitch, appliqué, pillow kits, iron-on transfers, rubber stamps, little gifts.

DAVID KAY, One Jenni Ln., Peoria, IL 61614-3198. Free, 48 pp. Lovely gifts to enhance home and garden—carved mahogany doorstops, needlepoint pillows, wicker wine rack, French antique garden furniture, so many choices.

DAY-TIMERS, INC., P.O. Box 27000, Lehigh Valley, PA 18003-9859. 215-206-9000. Free, 98 pp. Many styles of calendar organization systems, desk accessories, binders, and other items to get you organized.

ESPECIALLY FOR YOU, 2475-A E. Bay Dr., Largo, FL 34641. 813-531-6442. Free, 15 pp. Personalized gifts for educational administrators, teachers, and support staff—apple gifts, school desk bookends, lunch tote bag, imprinted pencils, other appealing items.

FAITH MOUNTAIN CO., P.O. Box 199, Sperryville, VA 22740. 800-822-7238. $3, 40 pp. Delightful home decorating accents, folkart, women's casual wear, dried floral arrangements and wreaths, decorated sweaters, the best of nostalgia.

GEARY'S, 351 N. Beverly Dr., Beverly Hills, CA 90210-4794. Free, 52 pp. Gifts from frivolous to fabulous—tableware, art, children's specials, fine crystal, comical decorating touches.

GLOBAL MARKETING (U.S.), INC., P.O. Box 24386, Fort Lauderdale, FL 33307. 305-771-0068. Free, brochure. Soaps, bath and shower products, decorative storage containers, party crackers (not the eating kind!).

HAMMACHER SCHLEMMER, Operations Center, 2515 E. 43rd St., P.O. Box 182256, Chattanooga, TN 37422-7256. Free, 60 pp. The latest in electronic, health, and men's wear; gifts you might not find anywhere else.

HANNDY HINTS, P.O. Box 83015, Milwaukee, WI 53223. 414-353-5520. $2.50, various. Country-style note pads, T-shirts, sweatshirts, bumper stickers, coffee mugs, rubber stamps.

HANOVER HOUSE, P.O. Box 2, Hanover, PA 17333-0176. $1, 56 pp. Clever gadgets, novelties, toys. Something for everyone.

HERRINGTON, 3 Symmes Dr., Londonderry, NH 03053. Free, 92 pp. Fine audio, video, motoring, golf, boating, photography, sports, and skiing equipment, accessories.

HOLCRAFT, P.O. Box 792, Davis, CA 95616. $1, 32 pp. Santa any way you like him—at the end of a bungee cord, cookie molds, papier-mâché from Germany, pine cone Father Christmas. Also angels, snowmen, fairy tale nesting dolls.

HORCHOW, P.O. Box 620048, Dallas, TX 75262-0048. Free, 32 pp. Refreshing collection of home decorating items, ladies' clothing, home furnishings.

INITIALS, 409 Williams St., P.O. Box 246, Elmira, NY 14902-0246. $3, 32 pp. Distinctive personalized gifts—toy boxes, sterling silver baby cups, brass door knockers, silk tuxedo scarf, Christmas stockings, more great ideas.

KIRSTEN PIPE CO., INC., P.O. Box 70526, Seattle, WA 98107-9987. 206-783-0700. Free, brochure. Their own pipes and cigars and replacement parts for pipes.

LEFTHANDERS INTERNATIONAL, P.O. Box 8249, 2713 N. Topeka Ave., Topeka, KS 66608. $2, 31 pp. Sporting equipment, cooking and serving aids, playing cards, craft instruction, scissors, notebooks, and accessories for the left-handed.

LIGHTER SIDE, THE, 4514 19th St. Court E, Box 25600, Bradenton, FL 34206-5600. $2, 80 pp. Lighthearted gifts such as chocolate tool kit, Trolls slippers, Betty Boop doll, Star Trek shirts, character sets, and rubber stamp sets.

LILLIAN VERNON, Virginia Beach, VA 23479-0002. 914-633-6300. Free, 96 pp. Great values in toys, home accents, toys, housewares—one-stop shopping!

LOUIS VUITTON LUGGAGE AND ACCESSORIES, 130 E. 59th St., New York, NY 10022. 212-223-3840. Free, 93 pp. Luggage, purses, wallets, and desk accessories of leather, silk, cowhide, cashmere, and canvas.

MARKLINE, 65 Mathewson Dr., P.O. Box 890190, E. Weymouth, MA 02189-0900. Free, 40 pp. Fascinating electronic wizardry, entertaining and practical tools and gifts such as a radio concealed in a baseball cap, potato chip maker, portable doorbell chime, waterproof outdoor clock, and lots more!

MARY MAC'S TEATIMES, P.O. Box 841 Langley, Whidbey Island, WA 98260. Free, 32 pp. For tea lovers, quality teas, tea foods, linens, stationery, accoutrements, publications, fabric tea bags.

MCMILLAN PUBLICATIONS, INC., 2921 Two Paths Dr., Woodridge, IL 60517-4512. Free, brochure. Dozens of railroad videos.

MILES KIMBALL, 41 W. 8th Ave., Oshkosh, WI 54906. Free, 66 pp. Inexpensive gadgets: personalized labels, bumper stickers, pet IDs; toys, bowler towel, banks, plant caddy, pet car seat, kitchenware.

MYSTIC SEAPORT MUSEUM STORES, 39 Greenmanville Ave., Mystic, CT 06355. Free, 48 pp. Gifts and decorative arts inspired by the sea—jewelry, notecards, nesting pirates, clothing, artwork. Also a book catalog with maritime subjects.

NATIONAL GEOGRAPHIC, P.O. Box 2118, Washington, DC 20013-2118. Free, 32 pp. Videos, books, gifts from nature, and history for all ages.

NATURE CO., P.O. Box 188, Florence, KY 41022. Free, 36 pp. All aspects of nature are celebrated in these unique gifts—malachite jewelry, sculptures, walking sticks, music from around the globe, puzzles, clothing with conservation themes, 3-D rainforest.

NEIMAN MARCUS, Mail Order Div., Marketing Management, P.O. Box 2968, Dallas, TX 75221-2968. $6.50, various. Clothing, housewares from a high-fashion department store.

NEW MORNING HERBS, Rt. 2, Box 262A, Grand Junction, TN 38039. 901-764-6171. $1, 51 pp. Herbs, perennials; herb notecards, book plates; handmade herb jars; books on herbs; country store handcrafts.

ORVIS, 1711 Blue Hills Dr., P.O. Box 12000, Roanoke, VA 24022-8001. 800-635-7635. Free, 110 pp. Women's and men's sporty clothing; gifts for traveling, kitchen, country decorating.

PARAGON, THE, P.O. Box 996, 89 Tom Harvey Rd., Westerly, RI 02891-0996. Free, 72 pp. Good values in tasteful gifts, toys, home accessories.

PENTREX, P.O. Box 94911, Pasadena, CA 91109. 818-793-3400. Free, 40 pp. Railroad videos and books.

PERIWINKLE GIFTS, 9553 W. 130th St., N. Royalton, OH 44133. Free, 48 pp. Wide selection of reasonably priced gifts from oak valets to coin counters to flashlights. Housewares, practical items.

PICCADILLY'S GALLERIA, 1301 E. 9th St., Cleveland, OH 44114. 216-579-4300. Free, 14 pp. Lovely English country accessories and gifts—Muffy Bear and clothing, Victorian moiré lamps, Kinkade paintings, Yankee candles, bunny booties, pewter picture frames.

PLOW & HEARTH, 301 Madison Rd., P.O. Box 830, Orange, VA 22960-0492. 800-866-6072. Free, 60 pp. Assortment of useful items for country living to add comfort, convenience, safety, or enjoyment to life—bird feeders, fireplace paraphernalia, games, gardening, and pet accessories.

POTPOURRI, Dept. 174-2, 120 N. Meadows Rd., Medfield, MA 02052. 508-359-5440. $2, 80 pp. Just plain fun gifts for everyone—home decorations, humorous nightshirts, lovely afghans, seasonal gifts.

PRACTICAL MARINE, 6288 W. Oakton, Morton Grove, IL 60053. 800-677-

5189. $1, 28 pp. Hundreds of marine and RV products, safety devices, tools, instruments, more.

PROMISES KEPT, P.O. Box 47368, Plymouth, MN 55447-0368. 800-989-3545. Free, 48 pp. Nice family gifts—toys, cedar chests, folding shopping cart, exercise equipment, gardening items, lots more.

S.T. PRESTON & SON, INC., Main St. Wharf, Greenport, NY 11944-0798. Free, 102 pp. Ship models, marine clocks and barometers, figureheads, scrimshaw, brassware, marine prints, and a lot of decorative nautical items for the home.

SAN FRANCISCO MUSIC BOX CO., P.O. Box 7817, San Francisco, CA 94120-7817. 800-227-2190. Free, 48 pp. Music boxes from romantic to nostalgic to made-for-children.

SCOPE, 50 Oser Ave., Hauppauge, NY 11788-5134. $2, 64 pp. Lots of electronic gifts; also kitchen, garden, and sports items.

SHARPER IMAGE, P.O. Box 7031, San Francisco, CA 94120-9703. Free, 36 pp. Up-to-the-minute technology such as towel warmer, electronic organizer, massaging sandals, portable gas candle lighter, unusual gifts.

SIGNALS, P.O. Box 64428, St. Paul, MN 55164-0428. 800-669-5225. Free, 40 pp. For fans of public television—books, videos, cassettes, sweatshirts, accessories, fun things featuring characters and programs from public TV.

SKY MALL, 1520 E. Pima St., Phoeniz, AZ 85034-9850. 800-424-6255. Free, 86 pp. A little of everything from leading catalogs— leisure equipment, clothing, housewares, electronic gadgets.

SMITH & HAWKEN, 25 Corte Madera, Mill Valley, CA 94941-1829. Free, 48 pp. Several catalogs: garden, clothing, tool, bulb, furniture, holiday/gift, home. Lots of natural materials.

SPECIAL DUTY, U.S. Cavalry, 2855 Centennial Ave., Radcliff, KY 40160-9000. $3, 126 pp. Law enforcement and security equipment. Everything from tactical gear to daggers to U.S. military insignia and surveillance equipment.

SPIEGEL, Ste. A, 1040 W. 35th St., Chicago, IL 60672-0040. 800-345-4500. $3 refundable, 88 pp. Women's and men's latest fashions, furniture, housewares, electronics, linens, decorating accents, etc.

SPORTY'S PILOT SHOP, Clermont County Airport, Batavia, OH 45103-9747. Free, 96 pp. Gifts, books, videos, clothing, equipment for the pilot.

STERLING CUSTOM LABELS, 9 Willow St., Winsted, CT 06098. 800-654-5210. Free, brochure. Woven-edge labels—choice of shapes, artwork, type style.

VERMONT COUNTRY STORE, Mail Order Office, P.O. Box 3000, Manchester Center, VT 05255-3000. 802-362-4647. Free, 128 pp. Basic, comfortable clothing, housewares, outdoor and cleaning aids, regional foods.

WALTER DRAKE & SONS, Drake Bldg., Colorado Springs, CO 80940-0002. Free, 104 pp. Many paper and other items for personalizing; household and helpful gadgets.

WHISTLE & ROLLSIGN STORE, 333 Valley Rd., Ste. 123, W. Orange, NJ 07052. Free, 34 pp. Videos, books, memorabilia for railroad enthusiasts.

WIND AND WEATHER, THE, Albion St. Water Tower, P.O. Box 2320, Mendocino, CA 95460. 800-922-9463. Free, 36 pp. Weathervanes, weather instruments, sundials, garden ornaments, and books on the same.

WOODENBOAT STORE, P.O. Box 78, Brooklin, ME 04616. Free, 32 pp. Books, tools, videos to buy or rent, kits for real or scale-model boats.

Special Needs

(special helps for those with various disabilities)

ACCESS WITH EASE, P.O. Box 1150, Chino Valley, AZ 86323. $1 refundable, 32 pp. Thoughtful helpers for those with arthritis, back problems, or other disabilities—hands-free hair dryer holder, big print address book and playing cards, shirt buttoner, suction dish brush for one-handed dishwashing, very practical and reasonably priced ideas.

ADAPTABILITY, P.O. Box 515, Colchester, CT 06415-0515. Free, 44 pp. Products for independent living for those with disabilities—crafter's stand to hold needlework and pattern for the one- or weak-handed, Dancin' Grannies exercise videos, therapy games.

AMERICAN BIBLE SOCIETY, P.O. Box 5656, Grand Central Station, New York, NY 10164-0851. Free, 40 pp. Includes Bibles in Braille, large print, special education series for those with learning difficulties.

AMERICAN SIGN LANGUAGE VIDEOTAPES, Sign Enhancers, 1320 Edgewater NW, Ste. B10, Rm. C1, Salem, OR 97304. 800-76-SIGN-1. Free, 10 pp. American Sign Language videos, deaf culture autobiographies, interpreting and translating, fairy tales, and kids' stuff!

ARTHRITIS SPECIALTY CATALOG, Sav-Mor Pharmacy, 110 E. State St., Nokomis, IL 62075. 800-336-8386. Free, 32 pp. Time and effort savers, books, dressing aids.

ASSOCIATED SERVICES FOR THE BLIND, 919 Walnut St., Philadelphia, PA 19107. 215-627-0600. Free, brochure. Recorded periodicals available free on tape to qualified blind persons.

ATTAINMENT CO., P.O. Box 930160, Verona, WI 53593-0160. 800-327-4269. Free, 35 pp. Contemporary products for people with special needs—picture prompt system, videos, talking software, slant boards.

BOOKS ON SPECIAL CHILDREN, P.O. Box 305, Congers, NY 10920-0305. 914-638-1236. Free, 12 pp. Books on health, play, independent living, teaching, counseling learning-disabled people, communications.

CLEO, INC., 3957 Mayfield Rd., Cleveland, OH 44121. Free, 192 pp. Items for the variously handicapped—furniture, homemaking aids, exercise and therapy equipment.

DANMAR PRODUCTS, INC., 221 Jackson Industrial Dr., Ann Arbor, MI 48103. Free, 105 pp. Products for special needs, attractive as well as adaptive. Catalog also in Spanish.

EQUIPMENT SHOP, P.O. Box 33, Bedford, MA 01730. 617-275-7681. Free, 30 pp. An engineer and an occupational therapist combined experience to bring the world of childhood play to those with disabilities—simple, durable equipment from around the world.

LARGE PRINT BOOKS-BY-MAIL, G.K. Hall & Co., Attn: Andy, 70 Lincoln St., Boston, MA 02111. Free, 16 pp. Hardcover and paperback mysteries, romances, non-fiction, adventure, Westerns, cookbooks, and reference books in large print.

LS&S GROUP, INC., P.O. Box 673, Northbrook, IL 60065. Free, 64 pp. Products for the visually impaired—games, security aids, magnifiers, telephone accessories, talking translators, Braille embossers, talking calculators, very practical helps.

NATIONAL ASSOCIATION OF THE DEAF, Bookstore, 814 Thayer Ave., Silver Spring, MD 20910-4500. 301-587-6282. Free, 11 pp. Books on sign language, research, biographies, signed songs and children's books; jewelry stationery, greeting cards, mugs, T-shirts featuring a signed word.

NATIONAL LIBRARY SERVICE FOR THE BLIND AND PHYSICALLY HANDI-CAPPED, Reference Section, Library of Congress, Washington, DC 20542. Free, 62 pp. Request the brochure, "Facts," that describes eligibility, types of services, bibliographies to order. Services include Braille, large print and Spanish large print books, books on tape and almost 70 popular magazines, music, sheet music, and instruction.

PRESTON, J.A. PRESTON CORP., P.O. Box 89, Jackson, MI 49204. 800-631-7277. Free, 166 pp. Products for physical therapy, rehabilitation, and special education—feeding aids, recreation, mobility aids.

PROPHECY DESIGNS, P.O. Box 84, Round Pond, ME 04564. 207-529-5318. Free, 16 pp. Charming Braille and printed greeting cards.

SCIENCE PRODUCTS, P.O. Box 888, Southeastern, PA 19399. 215-296-2111. Free, 16 pp. Vision boosters for hobbyists, the office, and outdoor activities; Braille clocks, bi-lingual talking clocks, magnifiers.

SPECIAL NEEDS PROJECT, 1482 E. Valley Rd. #A-121, Santa Barbara, CA 93108. 805-565-1914. Free, 16 pp. Books about physical and mental disabilities and health for children and their families.

TECHNICAL AIDS & SYSTEMS FOR THE HANDICAPPED, INC., Unit 1, 91 Station St., Ajax, Ontario L1S 3H2 Canada. 416-686-4129. Free, 72 pp. Products to help with personal care, dressing, homemaking, leisure for those with various handicaps.

WOODBINE HOUSE, 5615 Fishers Ln., Rockville, MD 20852. 301-468-8800. Free, 18 pp. Books for parents and teachers of children with disabilities. They have another catalog of general trade books on subjects from bicycling to historic preservation.

Sports & Recreation
(see also *Outdoors* and *Toys, Dolls, Games*)

CHAMPS SPORTS, 311 Manatee Ave. W, Bradenton, FL 34205. 800-766-8272. Free, 24 pp. "Not your average sports store." Clothing and equipment for martial arts and outdoor activities.

ESPN HOME VIDEO, ESPN Plaza, Bristol, CT 06010. 800-343-1834. Free, 16 pp. Videos on boxing, yachting, horseracing, motorsports, teaching kids sports, skiing, golf, outdoor sports, exercise and fitness, comedy.

MARK REUBEN GALLERY, 34 Princess St., Sausalito, CA 94965. 415-332-8815. Free, various. Hand-printed and sepia-toned pictures of sports legends.

M-F TRACK & FIELD CATALOG, P.O. Box 8090, Cranston, RI 02920-0090. 800-556-7464. Free, 64 pp. For serious track and field participants. Training equipment and everything for a competition except the athletes.

PERFORMANCE BICYCLE, Performance, One Performance Way, P.O. Box 2741, Chapel Hill, NC 27515-2741. 800-727-2433. Free, 71 pp. Latest advances in clothing, parts, accessories for bicycles, mountain bikes, in-line skates.

RAINBO SPORTS SHOP, 4836 N. Clark St., Chicago, IL 60640. 312-275-5500. $3, 32 pp. Ice skating competition dresses, videos, skates, carrying bags, gifts for skaters such as porcelain figures, jewelry, books, stickers.

ROAD RUNNER SPORTS, 6310 Nancy Ridge Dr., Ste. 107, San Diego, CA 92121-3266. 800-551-5558. Free, 110 pp. Apparel and equipment for running, cycling, swimming, fitness, aerobics, walking, volleyball, soccer.

SIMPLY THE BEST SPORTS, 5535 N. Long Ave., Chicago, IL 60630-1376. 800-237-8493. Free, 16 pp. Variety of items with the name of your favorite team—jackets, caps, sports bag, medallions, jerseys, more clothing.

SOCCER INTERNATIONAL, Dept. K4, P.O. Box 7222, Arlington, VA 22207. 703-524-4333. $2, 15 pp. A complete soccer gift and equipment catalog. Includes such novelties as soccer greeting cards, bumper stickers, party supplies, embroidered patches, and T-shirts in addition to standard uniforms and training aids.

SPORTS SECTION, THE, 140 Oregon St., El Segundo, CA 90245-4212. Free, 48 pp. You'll cheer over the selection of practice jerseys, caps, sweatshirts, T-shirts, jackets, Christmas stockings, trash cans, clocks, puzzles, and videos from your favorite pro and college teams.

SYSKO'S BASKETBALL BOOKS & VIDEOS, 266 Railroad Ave., P.O. Box 6, Benton, WI 53803. 608-759-2105. Free, 20 pp. Biographies, history, instructional, references for basketball.

Stationery & Paper Goods
(see also other categories for notecards, calendars, etc., with special themes)

ACCENTS, 215 Moody Rd., Enfield, CT 06083. Free, 36 pp. Greeting cards, stationery, wrapping paper, related paper goods at good savings.

AMY ALLISON CARD SHOP, THE, P.O. Box 303, Elmira, NY 14902-0303. Free, 32 pp. Quantity discounts on good quality greeting cards for every occasion, seasonal gifts, personalized items, gift wrapping supplies.

CURRENT, Express Processing Center, Colorado Springs, CO 80941-0001. 800-525-7170. Free, 100 pp. The more you order, the more you save on quality stationery, cards, calendars, ornaments, children's gifts, wrapping paper, gift items.

EARTH CARE PAPER, INC., P.O. Box 7070, Madison, WI 53707. 608-223-4000. $2, 36 pp. Recycled paper cards, gift wrap, and environmental gifts.

FOREIGN CARDS, LTD., P.O. Box 123, Guilford, CT 06437. 800-231-1684. Free, brochure. Postcards from around the world.

GOOD NATURE DESIGNS, 1630 E. 2nd St., Dayton, OH 45403. 800-733-0722. Free, 16 pp. Recycled paper notecards in several attractive styles.

HEIRLOOM EDITIONS, 520-B, Rt. 4, Carthage, MO 64836. 417-358-4410. Free, 70 pp. Victorian prints, cards, paper products, flue covers.

MERRIMADE, 27 S. Canal St., Lawrence, MA 01843. 508-686-5511. Free, 24 pp. Personalized stationery, placeware, playing cards, plastic drinkware, name sticks.

PAPER DIRECT, 205 Chubb Ave., Lyndhurst, NJ 07071-0618. 800-272-7377. Free, 87 pp. Wide assortment of design papers for copiers, laser printer, desktop publishing; recycled papers.

VICTORIAN PAPERS, P.O. Box 411341, Kansas City, MO 64141-1341. Free, 48 pp. For the romantic—lovely greeting cards, stationery, calling cards, and accessories from the Victorian era.

Toys, Dolls, Games
(see also *Collectibles; Craft Supplies; For Children Only; Handcrafts; Infant/Maternity Supplies;* and *International/Regional Specialties*)

BARON BARCLAY BRIDGE SUPPLIES, 3600 Chamberlain Ln., Ste. 230, Louisville, KY 40241. 800-274-2221. Free, 64 pp. Cards, playing accessories, hundreds of books on bridge, videos, even computer software for when you can't get a foursome!

BITS & PIECES, 1 Puzzle Pl., B8016, Stevens Point, WI 54481-7199. 800-JIGSAWS. Free, 44 pp. International puzzle collection satisfies the child in everyone. Jigsaws, 3-D, skill games, board games, illusions, conversation pieces.

CHILDCRAFT, P.O. Box 29149, Mission, KS 66201-9149. Free, 80 pp. Beyond toys! Discovery tools for kids—building sets, personalized puzzles or bags, pocket skis, holiday crafts, 3-D model of U.S. Capitol, more.

CONSTRUCTIVE PLAYTHINGS, 1227 E. 119th St., Grandview, MO 64030-1178. 800-448-7830. Free, 48 pp. Sturdy, colorful toys that kids will love. Ages infant through elementary school.

FAMILY GAMES, INC., P.O. Box 97, Snowden, Montreal, Quebec H3X 3T3 Canada. 514-485-1834. Free, brochure. Environmental and multi-cultural board games, card games, puzzles, and magnetic games.

FAO SCHWARZ FIFTH AVE., P.O. Box 182225, Chattanooga, TN 37422-7225. 800-635-2451. Free, 59 pp. Kids' paradise—infants through teens. Electric riding toys, matching outfits for girl and her doll, infant play area with activity gadgets on the rim, art sets, more imaginative playthings.

HEARTH SONG, Mail Processing Center, 6519 N. Galena Rd., P.O. Box 1773, Peoria, IL 61656-1773. Free, 52 pp. Hard-to-find, quality playthings for children—halfpenny dolls, Valentine baking set, Ukrainian egg decorating kit, lap loom, folk toys, more "to honor the innocence and joy of childhood."

INTO THE WIND, 1408 Pearl St., Boulder, CO 80302. Free, 79 pp. Wide variety of kites, boomerangs, windsocks, kite making supplies, gliders.

JOHNSON SMITH, 4514 19th St. Court E, P.O. Box 25500, Bradenton, FL 34206-5500. 813-747-2356. Free, 80 pp. "Things you never knew existed ... and other items you can't possibly live without." Practical jokes, optical illusions, TV show paraphernalia, funny stuff.

KLUTZ, 2121 Staunton Ct., Palo Alto, CA 94306. 415-424-0739. Free, 65 pp. Wacky, pure fun gifts—*The Official Icky Poo Book*, magic and juggler's tricks, string games, stilts, rubber stamp bug kit. Get the idea?

MAHER STUDIOS, P.O. Box 420, Littleton, CO 80160. 303-798-6830. Free, 20 pp. Handcarved wooden ventriloquists' puppets, videos, books, and comedy routines.

ORIENTAL TRADING CO., INC., P.O. Box 3407, Omaha, NE 68103-0407. Free, 66 pp. Cute array of seasonal stuffed animals, balloons, children's jewelry, and imaginative novelties for children or the young at heart.

WORLD WIDE GAMES, P.O. Box 517, Colchester, CT 06415-0517. Free, 60 pp. This catalog doesn't stop at games although there are lots of those (skittles, board games, games of skill, wooden games). Also brain-teasers, mazes, jigsaw puzzles, sliding puzzles, triazzles (hexagon with triangular puzzle pieces), kaleidoscopes, kites.

Travel
(see also *Books & More* and *Music & Movies*)

BARRON'S EDUCATIONAL SERIES, INC., P.O. Box 8040, 250 Wireless Blvd., Hauppauge, NY 11788. Free, 39 pp. Foreign language books, cassettes, CDs; study guides for beginners, business people, and advanced students.

COMPLETE TRAVELLER BOOKSTORE, 199 Madison Ave., New York, NY 10016. 212-685-9007. $2, 56 pp. Numerous travel guides, field guides, language phrasebooks and cassettes, maps, travel gear.

FAMILY TRAVEL GUIDES CATALOGUE, Carousel Press, P.O. Box 6061, Albany, CA 94706-0061. 510-527-5849. $1, 30 pp. Children's travel game books, family-oriented travel guides to specific areas.

NATIONAL PARK VIDEOS, Handbooks and Films, Harpers Ferry Historical Association, P.O. Box 197, Harpers Ferry, WV 25425. 304-535-6881. Free, 48 pp. Books, videos, films, and folders on such diverse topics as industry and invention, exploration and settlement, earth matters, great Americans, and more—all connected with the natural and historical treasures of our nation.

MAGELLAN'S, P.O. Box 5485, Santa Barbara, CA 93150. 800-962-4943. Free, 46 pp. Travel essentials—currency converters, travel games, security devices, dual-voltage appliances, luggage.

PERSONAL COURIER AUDIO TAPES, Educational Excursions, P.O. Box 180355, Dallas, TX 75218. 214-328-9377. Free, brochure. Master storyteller and British historian Dr. Ronald Hutton presents spellbinding commentary on the British Isles—historical fact and legend—for travelers and history fans alike.

PUBLICATIONS FROM THE NATIONAL PARK SERVICE, Div. of Publications, Sales Information Desk, National Park Service, Harpers Ferry, WV 25425. 304-535-6018. Free, 10 pp. Photocopied list of books relating to various national parks or events surrounding national historic sites.

RAND MCNALLY, P.O. Box 1697, Skokie, IL 60076. 800-234-0679. Free, 64 pp. Beyond the traditional road atlas and including videos on foreign languages and countries, globes, travel accessories.

STORY BEHIND THE SCENERY, KC Publications, P.O. Box 14447, Las Vegas, NV 89114-4447. Free, 30 pp. Gorgeous photography in books for most of the national parks. Some in Spanish, French, German, Japanese. Some on audio cassette.

TRAVEL MEDICINE, INC., 351 Pleasant St., Ste. 312, Northampton, MA 01060. 800-872-8633. Free, brochure. Books and equipment for healthy traveling—water disinfecting products, mosquito nets, medical kits.

TRAVELER'S CHECKLIST, 335 Cornwall Bridge Rd., Sharon, CT 06069. 203-364-0144. $1, brochure. Hard-to-find traveler's supplies — U.V. sensometer (tells what strength sunscreen to use), packable hat with brim that folds, backpack/seat combination, alarms.

TRAVELLING BOOKS, P.O. Box 77114, Seattle, WA 98177. $1, 30 pp. Travel books, maps, accessories for the independent and adventurous traveler.

WHOLE WORLD LANGUAGE CATALOG, Audio-Forum, Ste. LA80, 96 Broad St., Guilford, CT 06437-2635. 800-243-1234. $2, 51 pp. Self-instructional foreign language courses (dozens of languages) on audio cassettes; music, movies, videos about other countries.

Western & Equestrian

ANN CHAPMAN, 246 N. Main St., Galena, IL 61036-2253. 800-397-1982. Free, 48 pp. Western clothing, classic British sporting bags, housewares for horsemen, dishware with horse designs.

AUSTIN-HALL BOOT CO., 491 N. Resler, Ste. B, P.O. Box 220990, El Paso, TX 79913-0990. Free, 30 pp. Made-to-measure leather cowboy boots.

BOOK STABLE, THE, 5326 Tomahawk Trail, Ft. Wayne, IN 46897-0474. $1, 44 pp. Equestrian books, magazines, videos plus rubber stamps, stationery, bookmarks, memo pads for horsemen.

DREAM RIDERS, Dept. C, P.O. Box 1277, Orinda, CA 94563. 510-283-1433. Free, 20 pp. Books for young horse lovers and their families.

EQUESTRIAN ENTERPRISE, 380 Concord Woods Dr., Smyrna, GA 30082-5210. Free, 24 pp. So many gift items for horse lovers—porcelain, jewelry, clothing, books, paper goods, novelty items.

HALF HALT PRESS, INC., 6416 Burkittsville Rd., Middletown, MD 21769. 301-371-9110. Free, 18 pp. Equestrian books—on competition, for children and youth, on advanced and basic techniques.

KENTUCKY DERBY, PARTY KITS AND EQUESTRIAN GIFTS, 8007 Vinecrest, Ste. 9, Louisville, KY 40222. 502-425-2126. Free, 16 pp. Party kits (food baskets, horse-shaped cutting board and crackers), equestrian gifts (needlepoint pillows, bookmarks, belt buckles, umbrellas, clothing, key holder, art).

OLD WEST OUTFITTERS, 7213 E. 1st Ave., Scottsdale, AZ 85251. 602-949-1900. $3, 60 pp. "Frontier dry goods" — broomstick skirts, Western shirts for men and women, suspenders, belts, Old West lawmen's badges, vests, horse collar mirror, cast-iron cookware.

PEGASOS PRESS, 535 Cordova Rd. #163, Santa Fe, NM 87501-4143. 800-537-8558. Free, 23 pp. Books and videos for the equestrian—riding, horse health, biographies, children's and young adult racing, picture books, handicapping.

SHEPLERS WESTERN WEAR, P.O. Box 7702, Wichita, KS 67277-7702. 800-833-7007. Free, 48 pp. Western style clothing and boots for women and men.

SOUTHERN TACK SHOP, 2176 Hillsboro Rd., Franklin, TN 37064. 800-844-4546. Free, various. Gifts, supplies for horsemen—riding jackets, bridles; horse jewelry, calendars, decorative tins, button covers, note pads.

SUITABILITY, 1355 W. 89th St., Cleveland, OH 44102. 216-631-1136. Free, 14 pp. Horse-print fabrics; patterns for horses (saddle pads, shin/ankle boots) and horse lovers (saddle suit vests, jodhpurs, tuxedo shirts), horse button covers.

TRAFALGAR SQUARE EQUESTRIAN BOOKS, P.O. Box 257W, N. Pomfret, VT 05053. 802-457-1911. Free, 26 pp. Books on training, showing, instruction, jumping.

WAGON WHEEL WESTERN WEAR, 2765 W. Jefferson, Ste. D, Springfield, IL 62702. 800-641-5562. Free, 46 pp. Gear for the horse—pads, saddles, English riding accessories, boots, barn and stable supplies.

5.
Gifts to Make

There are many magazines and books available with directions for making gifts with any skill or hobby. See *Catalogs: Craft Supplies* and *Magazines: Crafts; Metalworking;* or *Woodworking* for creative kits, pattern books, and equipment for making just about anything. The ideas that follow are simple and will make easy, yet appreciated, gifts.

❧ NOT FOR EATING! ❧

Cooked Play Dough

1 cup flour	1 tablespoon vegetable oil
½ cup salt	2 teaspoons cream of tartar
1 cup water	Food coloring

Mix in a saucepan and cook, stirring constantly, over medium heat until a ball is formed. Pur on a floured board or waxed paper and knead until smooth. Keep tightly covered. Will keep several weeks.

Cookie Cutter Candles

Find a shape of cookie cutter you like. Cut a base of heavy cardboard slightly larger than the cutter and punch a hole in the center for a wick. Place the base over the open side of the cutter. Cut a small stick (or use a pencil) to lay across the closed side of the cutter. Tie a string to the stick and run it down through the hole in the base. Tie a knot in the end of the string to keep the base tight up against the cutter. Place the cutter, cardboard-side down, on a cutting board that has been covered  with newspaper. Melt crayons or wax in a double boiler; watch carefully! Pour just a little melted wax through an opening in the cutter. Let that harden before adding a little more. Remember that the base is only cardboard. Gradually fill the cutter. Once the candle is hardened, set the mold in hot water a few seconds to loosen the sides and then remove the candle.

Dough Ornaments

1 pound baking soda	1¼ cups water
1 cup cornstarch	Food coloring (optional)

Mix all ingredients in a saucepan. Cook over low heat, stirring constantly until dough forms a ball like pie crust. Cool; then roll with a rolling pin. Cut shapes with cookie cutters or form your own designs. Poke a hole near the top with a toothpick. Dry overnight on a cookie sheet (don't cook). Paint with felt-tip pens or oil paints. Slip colored ribbon or yarn through the hole for hanging on the Christmas tree. Use other seasonal shapes and decorate for package toppings. Spray with acrylic spray and they'll last a long time.

Fragrant Winter Trivet

From quilted material, make a 3½" square pouch. With right sides together, stitch along three sides. Turn right side out. Fill with a mixture of the following: Mix materials such as balsam fir needles, coriander seed, sandalwood chips, rosemary, cloves, cinnamon, or whole allspice. Mix ingredients in a paper bag or glass bowl, add a small amount of evergreen or bayberry oil gradually—about ¼ or ½ ounce per gallon of dry ingredients. Place in glass jars with airtight lid or in self-sealing plastic bag and store in cool, dark place for two to six weeks. Shake gently about once a week and add more fragrance after the first two weeks if needed.

After filling trivet, be sure it is still relatively flat. Stitch remaining side. Place a cup of hot drink on it and it will send out a lovely fragrance.

Potpourri

Place small pine cones, leaves, and dried flower petals in a self-sealing bag. Add a few drops of fragrance oil. Store in the freezer for several days. (To dry flowers, hang upside down in a dark, well-ventilated room for about three weeks. Especially suitable specimens are roses, okra and iris pods, silver dollar eucalyptus, yellow or purple statice, yarrow, and safflower.)

Simmering Potpourri

Use same directions for curing ingredients as Fragrant Winter Trivet, but use such ingredients as spina cristi, marigold flowers, whole anise, whole cloves or allspice, cinnamon chips, ginger root slices, whole coriander seed, whole sage, uva ursi leaves, sandalwood chips, whole juniper berries, orange or lemon peel, windmill pods, tilia flowers, globe amaranth, sunflower petals, and orange or orange and clove oil. To use, place 2-3 tablespoons of potpourri per cup of hot water and simmer in an open pan on the stove. This will release a wonderful fragrance into the air for hours (but be sure to check water levels and add hot water as needed).

Sweet-Scented Ornaments

1 package unflavored gelatin	3 tablespoons ground cloves
³/₄ cup applesauce	¼ cup cornstarch
1.9 ounce jar ground cinnamon	

In a small saucepan, soften gelatin in applesauce for a few minutes. Over medium heat, stir constantly until barely simmering. Remove from heat. Combine cinnamon, cloves, and cornstarch in medium bowl. Stir in applesauce mixture. Turn onto waxed paper and knead. Divide dough in half and wrap one half in plastic. Use all the dough within 30 minutes. Roll dough to ¼" thick. Cut with cookie cutters. Use a straw or toothpick to make holes for hanging with ribbon or string. Dry on wire rack overnight.

❧ EASY HANDWORK GIFTS ❧

Alphabet Book

Cut 26 rectangles of felt (any size larger than about 8" square). From a contrasting color felt or fabric, cut each letter of the alphabet and the outline of an item that begins with that letter. Glue one letter and item on each "page." Arrange in order. (You can glue two pages back to back.) Punch holes in left side of the stack and fasten pages together with ribbon or a metal ring.

Bag Full of Memories

Make some fabric gift bags from holiday prints, gingham, children's prints, or other designs. Use them year after year and watch them "fill" with memories. Cut two pieces of fabric the size you want the bag to be (make several bags of different sizes). With the pieces right sides together, sew down one side, across the bottom and up the other side ¼" from the edges. To make the casing for the ribbon, press the top of the side seams open. Turn the top edge down ¼" and press. Fold that edge down 1¼" and pin. Sew along the lower edge of the casing as close to the edge as you can. Press the casing. Turn the bag right side out. To make openings for the ribbons, carefully snip the threads on the outside of the bag along the side seams of the casing. Cut two ribbons (⅞" wide and twice the length of the bag). Pin a safety pin to one end of one ribbon and pull it through the opening, leaving equal lengths of ribbon on each side of the bag. Repeat with the second ribbon. Decorate bags with iron-on appliqués or stencil additional designs with fabric paint. Place gift inside and tie each side of the bag with the ribbons.

Candy Bar Sled or Car

Use a mini-size candy bar for the body. Using cake frosting in tubes as the glue, attach peppermint candies for wheels or candy canes for sled runners. Attach a round chocolate candy for the steering wheel. Refrigerate to set frosting.

Cherub Gift Bags

Place gift in a colored lunch bag (or a brown one that child has painted or colored) and fold the top edge closed. Fold a 6" round paper doily in half and staple it over the top of the folded bag. To make the cherub's face, trace around a soup can on pink construction paper. Cut out the circle. Punch two holes from black construction paper with a hole punch and glue them as eyes on the face. Draw a smile on the face and draw two hearts (or use heart stickers) at each end of the smile. For hair, curl 8" strips of curling ribbon with the blade of scissors and glue the curls around the face. Glue the face to the doily on the front of the bag.

Christmas Balls

Cut out eight circles from stiff wrapping paper. Fold each in half (decorated side in). Glue each outside half to the half of another piece until all pieces are glued together forming a ball. When dry, make a large knot in a piece of colored yarn or embroidery floss and thread through the center with a long needle to make the hanger.

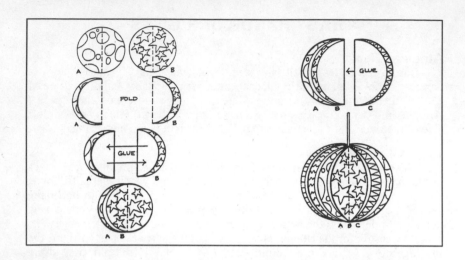

Christmas Candy Train

Keeping all ingredients wrapped, glue a roll of Life Savers to a 5-stick package of gum. Glue two square candies (e.g., Starbursts) together, then to one end of the Life Savers. To the other end of the Life Savers, glue a red or green foil-wrapped Hershey's Kiss chocolate candy (for the smokestack). Glue peppermint candies for wheels. (Use craft glue or a hot glue gun.)

Gingerbread Creation

Don't worry about the architecture. Just let your imagination run free with graham crackers cemented together with canned frosting. Decorate with sprinkles, candies, little marshmallows, and tube icing.

Hand-Decorated Wrapping Paper

1. Decorate butcher paper with rubber stamps, finger paints, or original crayon designs.
2. Cut a shape out of a potato or sponge. Dip in paint and print onto the paper.
3. Lay a paper doily on white paper. Rub a crayon over the doily for a lacy design.

Hand-Printed Pot Holder

Purchase a plain colored pot holder. Brush fabric paint on a child's hand and press hand firmly onto the pot holder. Follow the directions on the paint jar for setting the paint and washing the fabric.

Paper Crackers

For each cracker use the cardboard tube from a roll of bathroom tissue or cut the tube from a roll of paper towels in half lengthwise. Place the tube in the center of one long edge of a piece of colored 8" x 11" tissue paper. Roll the paper around the tube and tape the straight edge with transparent tape. Use curling ribbon to tie the paper close to the tube at one end. Fill tube with little candies or toys. Tie paper at remaining end of tube. Decorate paper with stickers or felt-tip pens. Give these as party favors or stocking stuffers.

Personal Tic-Tac-Toe

Draw the tic-tac-toe grid on a piece of wood. Be creative in the two playing piece shapes you choose (person's initials, horse and cow, cowboy hat and boot, star and crescent moon, dog and bone, etc.).

Photo Statues

With scissors carefully cut around a person from an 8" x 10" photograph, leaving a straight edge and border at the bottom of the shape. Spray the back of the photo with spray adhesive and glue it to a piece of foam core board (available in art supply or craft stores). When the adhesive is dry, cut out the shape with a sharp craft knife. Paint or stain two strips of wood molding as long as the picture's base. Glue the photo between the two strips to form a base so the picture will stand alone.

Punched-Tin Luminaria

(Luminaria are traditional Southwestern or Latin American holiday outdoor decorations.)

Clean an opened tin can and pinch all rough edges flat and smooth. Fill the can with water and freeze until the ice is solid. Remove from the freezer. Using a permanent-ink marker, draw a design (Christmas tree, star, bell, etc.) with dots around the sides of the can. Leave 1" from the bottom undecorated. Place the can on a towel so it won't slip (and to protect the countertop). Position a nail on each dot and hammer until it hits the ice (the ice prevents the can from being crushed during hammering). When you have completed the pattern, place the can in the sink until the ice melts. Pour out the remaining water. To use, place a votive candle in the can, being careful not to cut yourself on the sharp edges of the design. Line your sidewalks with the luminaria and light them each night for a lovely effect during the holidays.

Scented Stationery

Add 4 or 5 drops of your favorite essential oil to a cotton ball and lay between sheets of stationery. Close the box or seal all in a plastic bag for a week. The sweet fragrance will travel with your letter.

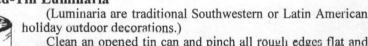

❧ EASY GIFTS FROM THE KITCHEN ❧

Bean Soup Mix

Mix 1¼ cups of legumes (navy, small navy, red kidney, large lima, or black beans; black-eyed or green peas; lentils) and place in a jar (with a cross-stitched lid?) or in a fabric bag. Tie the instructions on with ribbon or yarn.

Instructions: Wash and soak beans overnight. Drain and place in 4-quart pot with 2 quarts water or stock, 1 pound ham or ham hocks, 2 medium onions, 1 green pepper (chopped), 2 stalks celery (chopped), 2 cloves garlic (minced), 15 oz. tomatoes, and 2 tablespoons lemon juice. Cover and bring to a boil. Simmer 1 hour. Add 1 pound smoked sausage and cook another 45 minutes. Add salt, pepper, and cayenne to taste. (Can omit meat and add carrots).

Blueberry Syrup

1 cup fresh or frozen blueberries   1-2 tablespoons maple syrup

Combine in a saucepan with 1 tablespoon water. Heat until mixture bubbles. Stir and mash blueberries. Strain if necessary.

Cranberry Chutney

2 cups water	1 cup raisins
2 cups sugar	2 tablespoons brown sugar
1 lb. cranberries	1 teaspoon powdered ginger
½ cup vinegar	¼ to ½ teaspoon garlic powder (op.)
1 teaspoon curry powder	slivered almonds (optional)

Boil water and sugar five minutes. Add remaining ingredients except almonds and bring to a boil. Cook 10-15 minutes. Add almonds.

Hot Cocoa Mix

8-qt. box of instant powdered milk	2-lb. can Nestle's Quik
1 16-oz. box powdered sugar	11-oz. jar dry coffee creamer

Mix well and store in tightly covered container. Stir ⅓ cup mix into 1 cup boiling water.

Instant Spiced Tea Mix

1 cup lemon-flavored instant tea	1 teaspoon cinnamon
2 cups Tang	1 tablespoon ground cloves
3 cups sugar	

Mix well and store in airtight container. Stir 2 heaping teaspoonfuls into a cup of boiling water.

Russian Tea Mix

1 1-lb., 2-oz. jar Tang	1 teaspoon cinnamon
½ cup lemon flavored tea	½ teaspoon cloves
1¼ cup sugar	

Mix all ingredients and store in a tightly closed jar. Use 2 teaspoonfuls in a cup of boiling water.

Chinese New Year Cookies

6-oz. semi-sweet chocolate pieces	3-oz. can Chinese noodles
6-oz. butterscotch pieces	7½-oz. salted peanuts

Melt chips in top of double boiler. Stir in noodles and nuts by hand. Drop by teaspoonfuls onto waxed paper and chill.

Frosted Spiced Pecans

1 egg white	¼ teaspoon cinnamon
2 tablespoons cold water	¼ teaspoon cloves
½ cup sugar	¼ teaspoon allspice
½ teaspoon salt	2 cups pecan halves

Beat egg whites slightly with a fork. Add water and sugar and stir. Blend in spices, but do not beat. Add pecans and stir until each nut is well coated. Pour onto a greased cookie sheet. Bake at 250° for one hour until toasted golden. Test and stir often so that pecans don't stick together in globs. When the nuts are a pleasing color, place them on waxed paper until cold. Store in airtight container.

Hurry-Up Cookie Mix

(Give this with a new cookie sheet or mixing bowl set and the recipes. Courtesy of Jackie Hostage.)

8 cups all-purpose flour	1 tablespoon salt
3 cups sugar	1 tablespoon baking soda
2 cups brown sugar, firmly packed	3 cups vegetable shortening

In large mixing bowl, combine all ingredients except shortening. Cut in shortening with two knives, one cup at a time until evenly distributed and mixture resembles coarse meal. Store in tightly closed container for up to 3 months. To use: Follow directions below for desired cookie.

1. Preheat oven; grease cookie sheets. Combine ingredients below in mixing bowl. Beat well.
2. Stir in additional ingredients. Drop batter by teaspoonfuls onto prepared cookie sheets.
3. Bake as directed or until cookies are golden. Cool on wire racks.

Flavor	1: Combine	2: Stir in	3: Bake
Chocolate Chip (2 dozen)	3 c. Cookie Mix 2 T. Milk 1 egg	1 c. chocolate chips 1 c. chopped nuts 1 t. vanilla	10-12 min. at 375°.
Oatmeal Spice (3 dozen)	2 c. Cookie Mix 1 t. pumpkin pie spice 3 T. milk 1 egg	2 c. regular oatmeal 1 c. chopped raisins	12-15 min. at 375°.
Fresh Apple (3 dozen)	2 c. Cookie Mix 1¼ t. apple pie spice 2 T. milk 1 egg	½ cup finely chopped apple ½ c. chopped raisins ½ c. chopped nuts	10-12 min. at 375°. (Good with vanilla icing.)
Breakfast Cookies (3 dozen)	2½ c. Cookie Mix 2 T. frozen orange juice, undiluted, thawed 1 egg 1 T. grated orange rind	½ cup Grape-Nuts cereal ½ pound bacon, cooked, drained, crumbled	10-12 min. at 350°. (Cookies should be lightly browned but still soft.)

Hurry-Up Fudge

16 oz. powdered sugar
½ cup cocoa
¼ cup milk

1 stick butter or margarine
1 tablespoon vanilla
½ cup chopped nuts

Blend powdered sugar and cocoa in microwave-safe mixing bowl. Add milk and butter. Don't mix these in; just place them in the bowl. Heat in microwave oven for 2 minutes. Stir just to mix ingredients. Add vanilla and nuts; stir until blended. Pour into greased or buttered 8"- or 9"-square container and freeze for 20 minutes or refrigerate for 1 hour.

Kindergarten Fudge

2 cups powdered sugar
¼ cup cocoa

¼ cup crunchy peanut butter
2-3 tablespoons evaporated milk

Sift sugar and cocoa. Cut in peanut butter. Blend in enough milk for a workable consistency. Roll between 2 sheets of waxed paper to desired thickness. Cut into squares and let set.

O, Nuts!

½ cup brown sugar, packed # 6 cups round cereal
½ cup dark corn syrup # 1 cup pecans, walnuts, or peanuts
¼ cup margarine # 1/2 cup slivered almonds
½ teaspoon salt

Preheat oven to 325°. Grease jelly roll pan with margarine. In a 3-quart saucepan, heat sugar, corn syrup, margarine, and salt over medium heat, stirring constantly, until sugar is dissolved (about 5 minutes). Remove from heat and stir in remaining ingredients until well coated. Spread mixture in pan and bake 15 minutes. Cool 10 minutes. Loosen mixture with metal spatula. Let stand until firm (about 1 hour). Store in covered container. Makes about 8 cups.

Poppycock

²/₃ cup almonds # 1 cup margarine
1¹/₃ cups pecans # 1/2 cup white corn syrup
2 quarts popped corn # 1 teaspoon vanilla
1¹/₃ cups sugar

Combine almonds, pecans, and popped corn. Boil sugar, margarine, and syrup until it turns a tan color. Add vanilla. Stir quickly and pour mixture over the nut mixture. Turn out onto a buttered tray or board. When cool, break into small chunks. (You can omit nuts and substitute more popped corn.)

Pralines Even I Can Make

2 cups sugar # 2 cups chopped pecans
1 stick margarine # 20 large marshmallows
5 oz. can evaporated milk # 1³/₄ cups graham cracker crumbs

Combine sugar, margarine, and milk in heavy saucepan. Bring to a boil. Stir for 3 minutes. Remove from heat and add marshmallows. Stir until marshmallows have melted, then add pecans and graham cracker crumbs. Drop by teaspoonfuls onto waxed paper. Makes 40-60 pralines.

≈TREATS FROM WILMA'S KITCHEN ≈

(*From Wilma's Kitchen* gives down-home recipes developed by Wilma Warren for her own farm produce. These are easy to mix and great for giving. Put one recipe into an appropriate container. Be sure to include the cooking instructions. For dozens of "like Mama used to make" recipes, send $6.95 to Mrs. John Warren, Rt. 1, Box 512, Wolfe City, TX 75496.)

Corn Bread Mix
4 cups corn meal # 4 teaspoons salt
2 cups flour # 2 teaspoons baking soda
2 tablespoons sugar # $3/4$ cup shortening
4 teaspoons baking powder
   Blend ingredients and store in tightly covered bowl in refrigerator up to several weeks. To use, mix 1 cup of the mix, 1 egg, and enough buttermilk to make a soft dough. Bake in muffin or corn stick pan at 450° for 15 minutes. Makes about 8 muffins.

Biscuit Mix
8 cups flour # 1 teaspoon baking soda
1 tablespoon salt # 1 teaspoon cream of tartar
¼ cup baking powder # $3/4$ cup shortening
   Blend all ingredients and store in refrigerator. Keeps well. One cup makes 6 or 8 biscuits. Add enough buttermilk to make soft dough. Roll out on floured board and spread with melted shortening, margarine, or butter. Fold over and cut into biscuits. Bake about 12-15 minutes at 450°.

Pancake Mix
8 cups flour # 4 tablespoons baking powder
1 cup sugar # 2 teaspoons baking soda
2 cups corn meal # ½ cup shortening
2 teaspoons salt
   Mix ingredients and store in cool place until needed. Use 1 cup mix, 1 egg, and enough buttermilk to make medium thin batter. Start with ½ cup plus 1 tablespoon buttermilk for each cup of mix. Cook on griddle. Serve with warm syrup or honey.

Salsa Picante
   Wilma says, "This hot sauce can be added to any Mexican food if not hot enough to suit your taste. It's the sauce that adds the heat."
2 cups ripe tomatoes # 1 large onion
2 cloves garlic # 1 teaspoon salt
½ cup jalapeño peppers # 2-4 tablespoons vinegar
2 tablespoons salad oil
   Cut tomatoes into quarters and put through blender with peppers, onions, and garlic. Mix all in a saucepan and simmer about 15 minutes. Makes about 2 cups.

Appendix

❧ SMALL ELECTRIC APPLIANCES ❧

There is hardly a task that does not have an electrical appliance that does it for you. Have fun figuring out how to pamper someone!

Personal Care
Whirlpool bath
Massagers, vibrating cushion
Heating pad
Automatic skin refresher
Facial sauna
Sun lamp
Facial cleaner
Shaving cream warmer
Electric shaver
Manicure machine
Lighted make-up mirror
Portable hair dryer
Blow dryer
Curling iron, diffuser
Electric curlers
Iron, steam iron
Hot curling brush
Electric hair trimmer
Electric toothbrush

Food Preparation
Knife, knife sharpener
Can opener
Peeler
Food dehydrator
Food bag sealer
Food grinder
Peanut butter machine
Grater, salad grater/shredder that
    shoots slices into a bowl
Blender, mini-chopper, hand-held
    blender
Potato chip maker
Curly cutter
Mixer—hand or on stand
Bread kneader, bread baker
Juicer
Skillet

Indoor grill
Griddle
Waffle iron
Toaster, toaster broiler
Potato baker
Crisper (keeps dry foods such as
    crackers, chips, powdered
    sugar, etc. fresh)
Fry pot
Slow cooker
Steamer
Crêpe maker
Doughnut maker
Cupcake, muffin maker
Pizza baker
Cookie, canapé, candy maker
Mini-oven
Hot dog, burger cooker
Yogurt maker, ice cream freezer
Popcorn popper
Espresso, French press coffee or
    cappuccino machine
Coffee bean grinder/brewer

Serving Aids
Coffeemaker (from 1 to 30 cups)
Electric iced teapot or teakettle
Bun warmer
Portable one- or two-burner range
Warming tray
Plate warmer
Ice crusher

Other
Fabric steamer
Aluminum can crusher
Hand-held vacuum
Shoe polisher
Scissors

❧ GENERAL BIRTHDAY INFORMATION ☙

Symbolic Birthstones & Flowers

Month	Birthstone, *Meaning of Stone*	Flower, *Meaning of Flower*
January	Garnet, faithfulness	Carnation (white), purity
February	Amethyst, peacemaking	Violet, modesty
March	Bloodstone, courage	Daffodil, welcome (or jonquil)
April	Diamond, innocence	Daisy, innocence (or sweet pea)
May	Emerald, true love	Lily of the Valley, doubly dear
June	Pearl	Rose (red), love
July	Ruby, true friendship	Larkspur, lightness
August	Sardonyx, conjugal happiness	Poppy, forgetfulness (or gladiolus)
September	Sapphire, repentance	Aster, always cheerful
October	Opal, hope	Calendula
November	Topaz, friendship	Chrysanthemum, hope
December	Turquoise, happiness in love	Holly, rejoice together (or narcissus)

Signs of the Zodiac

Sign	Dates *	Symbols	
Aries	March 21-April 20	Ram	♈
Taurus	April 21-May 20	Bull	♉
Gemini	May 21-June 20	Twins	♊
Cancer	June 21-July 22	Crab	♋
Leo	July 23-August 22	Lion	♌
Virgo	August 23-September 22	Virgin	♍
Libra	September 23-October 22	Scales	♎
Scorpio	October 23-November 21	Scorpion	♏
Sagittarius	November 22-December 21	Archer	♐
Capricorn	December 22-January 19	Goat	♑
Aquarius	January 20-February 18	Water Bearer	♒
Pisces	February 19-March 20	Fish	♓

* Dates may vary by one day depending on year of birth.

❧ ANNIVERSARY SYMBOLS & GIFT IDEAS ❧

Along with etiquette, these symbols have changed in recent years, but that just gives you more flexibility in selecting a gift. The top listing is the more traditional symbol; the bottom listing, the more modern one. Many more ideas are listed under *Gift Ideas: Anniversaries* or in special interest gift categories.

Year Symbol: Gift Ideas

1 **Paper:** Magazine subscription, book, cookbook, stationery, photograph album, grocery bag of paper products (recycled paper perhaps), playing cards, tickets to special event, gift certificate, coupon for yard or housework, bridge tallies, matching party napkins and paper plates, sheet music.
Clock, plastic, furniture: Clock — travel, alarm, kitchen, digital, kitchen timer, chiming clock, sundial, outdoor; plastic storage containers for closet or cabinet, chairs for patio, kitchen utensils, Lucite photo frame or recipe book holder; furniture such as occasional table or chair, desk, bookshelves, folding table and chairs, TV trays.

2 **Cotton:** Matching T-shirts, shirts, or nightshirts; sheets or pillowcases, placemats and napkins; cotton hammock; a crocheted ornament or item; tote bag; handmade Christmas tree skirt or stocking; throw pillow; quilt or afghan; bath set; apron; beach towel; handkerchiefs (monogrammed); how about cotton candy?
China: Bud vase, candy dish; serving dish, cup and saucer, or other piece in their pattern; china flowers; china painting on a trivet or plate.

3 **Leather:** Real leather or leather-looking photograph album, briefcase, wallet, belt, purse, driving gloves, luggage or luggage tag, desk accessories, coat, boots, skirt.
Crystal, glass: Set of glasses (see Gift Ideas: Bar Gifts), pitcher, hand mirror, bud vase, glass Christmas tree ornament, bottle of wine, candy dish, salt and pepper shakers, coasters, glass baking dishes, stained glass window ornament or lamp, candleholders, parfait or sherbet glasses, dressing table set, crystal collectible figurine; how about a liquid crystal display (LCD) watch or calculator?

4 **Fruit, flowers, silk:** Basket of real fruit, fruit tree; dried, silk, or cloth flowers; bouquet of real or chocolate flowers; rose bush or other flowering plant or bulb for the garden; hanging basket or potted plant; art print or notecards with flowers or fruit on them; silk pillowcases, sheets, pajamas, gloves, underwear, or blouse.
Appliances, rayon, nylon, or other synthetic silks: Popcorn popper, ice cream or yogurt maker (see Appendix: Small Appliances); nylon outdoor gear or clothing; see above for silk items.

5 **Wood:** Wooden spice rack, candleholders, bookends, picture frame, trinket box, jewelry box, salad bowl set, cutting board, rocking chair, croquet set, duck decoy, golf tees; woodcarving, decorative item for the home, tree for yard, piece of furniture, cord of firewood.
Silverware: Silver or silver-plate flatware (serving piece or odd piece like iced tea spoon or grapefruit spoon in their silver pattern), tray or trivet, pendant, napkin rings, candleholders, thimble (see

Gift Ideas: Silver Gifts for more ideas).

6 **Candy, iron:** Boxed candy; shaped candies such as rose, basketball, sports car, etc.; travel or steam iron; cast iron cookware, fireplace andirons or tools, trivet, hibachi, lawn furniture, plant stand.

Wood, sugar: See 5th Anniversary; anything sweet (candy, cookies, jelly, cake), cookie bouquet, shaped cake or candies.

7 **Wool, copper, brass:** Wool blanket, sweater, pants, scarf, caps, socks, stadium blanket; a needlepoint or knit item or a kit for her to make; afghan; copper tea kettle or cookware; knit golf club covers, old copper penny for a coin collector; brass candleholders, bowl, planter, door knocker.

Desk sets: Pencil holder, electric pencil sharpener, paperweight, desk picture frame or picture of spouse or family for desk, calendar (perpetual, made with your photographs, daily planner), desk organizer, bookends for desk, pen and pencil set.

8 **Bronze, pottery:** Pottery or ceramic dishware, pitcher, bowl, wind chimes, flower pot, cookie jar or jam jar; bronze door knocker, candlesticks, or statue.

Linens, laces, electrical appliances: Linens for bed, bath, table, or kitchen; linen suit; lacy lingerie, blouse, handkerchief, sachet, dresser scarf; lace-trimmed pillow or dresser scarf; lace collar; espresso maker, popcorn popper, etc. (see Appendix—Small Electric Appliances).

9 **Pottery, willow:** See 8th Anniversary above for pottery suggestions; willow basket.

Leather, china, glass, or crystal: Leather (see 3rd Anniversary above); china, glass, or crystal serving ware, decorative items, candleholders, jewelry.

10 **Tin, aluminum:** Decorative tin box, tintype (an old kind of photograph made now in specialty shops), cookie cutters, cookie tin (full); aluminum baking pans, tennis racquet, fishing rod, step ladder, barbecue grill.

Diamond jewelry: Pin, watch, brooch, pendant, ring, earrings, necklace.

11 **Steel:** Stainless steel cutlery, steak knife set, cookware, pocket knife, shish kabob skewers; hobby tools.

Fashion jewelry: Initial, special religious or hobby symbol, neck chains, earrings.

12 **Silk, linen:** See 4th Anniversary for silk, 8th Anniversary for linen.

Pearls, nylon: Pearl earrings, choker; mother-of-pearl inlaid box or jewelry; nylon lingerie or outdoor gear or clothing.

13 **Lace:** See 8th Anniversary.

Textiles, furs: Coat, reupholster a chair or sofa, throw pillow or rug, anything handwoven, wall hanging, fur-lined gloves or slippers; "real fur" (a furry pet!).

14 **Ivory:** Ivory-handled steak knives, carving set, letter opener, cocktail picks, carving, or brooch.

Gold or agate jewelry: All lengths of gold chains, pins, bracelet, ring, earrings; gold coin; agate pendants, earrings, pins.

15 **Crystal, glass:** See 3rd and 9th Anniversary.

Watch: (two time zones; waterproof; stop watch; digital with alarm;

dressy; rugged outdoor)

20   China: It may be time to start a new set. See 2nd Anniversary.
Platinum, occasional furniture: Some "silver-like" jewelry is platinum; furniture such as tables, chairs, patio furniture, night stand, etc.

25   Silver: Two silver goblets (see also *Gift Ideas: Silver Gifts* or 5th Anniversary).

30   Pearl, personalized gifts: See 12th Anniversary; personalized stationery, T-shirt, license plate, mailbox, tote bag, golf club or tennis racquet cover, front door knocker.
Diamond: Jewelry or diamond needle on a stereo.

35   Coral: Jewelry, coral-colored lingerie, linens, or clothing.
Jade: The real thing or jade-colored jewelry or clothing, chess set, figurine.

40   Ruby, garnet: Ring or earrings, ruby-red glassware, or box of ruby-red grapefruit.

45   Sapphire, tourmaline: Jewelry.

50   Gold: Jewelry or watch or gold coin made into a medallion.
Emerald: Jewelry or maybe something from the Emerald Isle (Ireland).

55   Emerald, turquoise: See 50th Anniversary; turquoise jewelry or colored dress or blouse or bed linens

60/75   Diamond: Jewelry; tie tack or cuff links.
Gold: See 50th Anniversary.

❧ PERPETUAL GIFT OCCASION CALENDAR ❧

MONTH: _____

1		**17**	
2		**18**	
3		**19**	
4		**20**	
5		**21**	
6		**22**	
7		**23**	
8		**24**	
9		**25**	
10		**26**	
11		**27**	
12		**28**	
13		**29**	
14		**30**	
15		**31**	
16			

Index

Adult—basic, gift ideas, 33-5

Animals, birds, fish and wildlife, magazines, 115-6

Animals, birds, fish (and lovers of same!), catalogs, 146-8

Anniversaries, gift ideas, 35-6

Anniversary symbols and gift ideas, 217-9

Antique collector, gift ideas, 36-7

Antiques, arts and, magazines, 116-7

Archaeologist, amateur, gift ideas, 37

Art and special treasures, catalogs, 148-9

Artist, gift ideas, 37-8

Arts and antiques, magazines, 116-7

Automobiles, magazines, 117

Aviation, magazines, 118

Baby, gift ideas, 19-21

Bachelor, gift ideas, 38-9

Backpacker, gift ideas, 39-40

Bar gifts, gift ideas, 40-1

Bar mitzvah, gift ideas, 41

Bat mitzvah, gift ideas, 41

Beauty, health and, catalogs, 178-9

Billiards player, gift ideas, 41

Birthday information, general, 216

Birthstones, 216

Boater, gift ideas, 41-3

Boating and sailing, magazines, 118-9

Books and more, catalogs, 149-52

Bowler, gift ideas, 43

Bridesmaid, gift ideas, 43

Business, magazines, 127-8

Buying guides, magazines, 119

Calendar, perpetual gift occasion, 220

Camper, gift ideas, 43-5

Canoeist, kayaker and, gift ideas, 45

Car enthusiast, gift ideas, 45-6

Catalogs, 145-203

Children, catalogs, 171-4

Children thru teens, magazines, 119-20

Christmas specials, gift ideas, 46-7

Clergy, gift ideas, 47-8

Clothing, catalogs, 152-4
  children thru teens, 152
  general, 152-3
  men, 153
  women, 153-4

Collectibles, catalogs, 154-6

Collectors, 48-9, 121
  gift ideas, 48-9
  magazines, 121

College graduation, gift ideas, 49-50

College student, gift ideas, 50-1

Computer enthusiast, gift ideas, 51-2

Computing, 121-2, 156-7
  catalogs, 156-7
  magazines, 121-2

Cook, gift ideas, 52-5

Cookware, catalogs, 157

Country living, magazines, 123

Craft supplies, catalogs, 157-64
  assorted, 157-9
  basketry, 159-60
  caning, 159-60

Craft supplies, catalogs, cont.
  decorative arts, 163
  jewelry making, 160
  needlework, 160-2
  painting, 163
  rubber stamping, 163
  woodworking, 163-4
Crafts, magazines, 123-5
Crafts enthusiast, gift ideas, 55-6
Cyclist, gift ideas, 57-8
Dancer, gift ideas, 58
Decorating, homes and, magazines, 133
Desk dweller, gift ideas, 58-9

Elderly at home, gift ideas, 60-1
Electric appliances, small, 215
Electronic marvels, gift ideas, 61-2
Electronics, audio, video, magazines, 125
Electronics, catalogs, 164
Eleven to fourteen-year-old, gift ideas, 28-30
Entertaining, food and, magazines, 129
Entertainment world, magazines, 126
Environmentalist, gift ideas, 62-3
Environmentally friendly, catalogs, 164-6
Equestrian, western and, 111-2, 202-3
  catalogs, 202-3
  gift ideas, 111-2
Ethnic interests, magazines, 126-7

Family, gift ideas, 64-6
Family historian, gift ideas, 70-1
Family life, magazines, 127
Farewell gifts, gift ideas, 66-7
Federal Express, shipping tips, 13-4
Fifteen to eighteen-year-old, gift ideas, 30-3
Financial and business, magazines, 127-8
Fireplace gifts, gift ideas, 67
Fisherman, gift ideas, 67-8

Fishing, magazines, 128-9
Fitness, health and, magazines, 131-2
Fitness buff, gift ideas, 68-9
Floral gifts, catalogs, 166
Flowers, symbolic, 216
Food, catalogs, 166-71
  assorted, 166-8
  international, 168-9
  meats, 169
  regional, 169-70
  sweets, 170-1
Food and entertaining, magazines, 129

Games, sports and, gift ideas, 102-3
Gardener, gift ideas, 69-70
Gardening, 129-30, 174-5
  catalogs, 174-5
  magazines, 129-30
Genealogist, gift ideas, 70-1
Gift ideas, 19-114
Gift profile, 15-8
  blank form, 17-8
  creating, 15-6
Gifts, helpful hints for giving, 9-18
Gifts from the kitchen, easy, gifts to make, 210-3
Gifts to make, 205-14
  easy gifts from the kitchen, 210-3
  easy handwork gifts, 207-9
  not for eating, 205-6
  treats from Wilma's kitchen, 213
Gifts, shipping tips, 13-4
Golfer, gift ideas, 71-2
Grandparents, gift ideas, 72
Groomsman, gift ideas, 73
Guns, hunting and, magazines, 133-4

Handcrafts, catalogs, 176-8
Handwork gifts, easy, gifts to make, 207-9
Handyman, 73, 131, 178
  catalogs, 178
  gift ideas, 73

Handyman and hobbyist, magazines, 131

Hanukkah gifts, stocking stuffers and, gift ideas, 103-4

Health and beauty, catalogs, 178-9

Health and fitness, magazines, 131-2

Health needs, special, gift ideas, 97-101

High school graduation, gift ideas, 73-5

Historian, family, gift ideas, 70-1

History and military, magazines, 132-3

History buff, gift ideas, 75-6

Hobbyist, handyman and, magazines, 131

Home furnishings, catalogs, 179-81

Homes and decorating, magazines, 133

Host/hostess, gift ideas, 76-7

Housewares, catalogs, 181

Housewarming, gift ideas, 77-8

Hunter, gift ideas, 78-9

Hunting and guns, magazines, 133-4

Infant supplies, maternity and, catalogs, 181-2

International specialties, regional and, catalogs, 182-3

Jewelry, catalogs, 183-4

Jogger, gift ideas, 92

Kayaker, canoeist and, gift ideas, 45

Lefties, gift ideas, 79

Magazines, 115-45
general interest, 130-1

Man—basic, gift ideas, 80-1

Maternity supplies, infant and, catalogs, 181-2

Metalworking, magazines, 134

Military, history and, magazines, 132-3

Miniatures, models and, catalogs, 184-5

Model building, magazines, 134-5

Models and miniatures, catalogs, 184-5

Motorcycles, magazines, 135

Motorcyclist, gift ideas, 81

Movies, music and, catalogs, 185-8

Music, magazines, 135-6

Music and movies, catalogs, 185-8

Musician, gift ideas, 81-2

Needleworker, gift ideas, 82-3

New parents, gift ideas, 83-4

Nursing home resident, gift ideas, 84-5

One-year-old, gift ideas, 21

Organizer, gift ideas, 85-6

Outdoors, 136-7, 188-91
catalogs, 188-91
magazines, 136-7

Outdoors lover, gift ideas, 86-7

Paper goods, stationery and, catalogs, 200

Perpetual gift occasion calendar, 220

Person living abroad, gift ideas, 88

Pets and pet lovers, gift ideas, 88-9

Photographer, gift ideas, 89-90

Photography, 137, 191
catalogs, 191
magazines, 137

Politics and opinions, magazines, 137-9

Reading, good, magazines, 131-2

Recreation, sports and, catalogs, 199-200

Regional specialties, international and, catalogs, 182-3

Religious, 139, 191-2
catalogs, 191-2
magazines, 139

Retirement home resident, gift ideas, 90-1

Romantic, the, gift ideas, 91

Runner, gift ideas, 92

Sailing, boating and, magazines, 118-9
Science, 139-40, 192-3
  catalogs, 192-3
  magazines, 139-40
Scuba diver, gift ideas, 92-3
Seamstress, gift ideas, 93-4
Security and safety conscious, gift ideas, 94-5
Senior citizens, magazines, 140
Shipping, 12-4
  addressing packages, 14
  containers for, 13
  cushioning packages, 13-4
  insurance, 13
  sealing packages, 14
  USPS abbreviations, 12
  wrapping packages, 14
Silver gifts, gift ideas, 95
Single woman, gift ideas, 95-6
Six to ten-year-old, gift ideas, 25-8
Skier, gift ideas, 96-7, 109
  snow, 96-7
  water, 109
Smorgasbord, catalogs, 193-7
Snow skier, gift ideas, 96-7
Special needs, 140, 198-9
  catalogs, 198-9
  magazines, 140
Sports and games, gift ideas, 102-3
Sports, magazines, 140-2
Sports and recreation, catalogs, 199-200
Sports fan, gift ideas, 101-2
Stationery and paper goods, catalogs, 200
Stocking stuffers and Hanukkah gifts, gift ideas, 103-4
Swimmer, gift ideas, 104-5
Swimming pool owner, gift ideas, 105

Teacher, gift ideas, 105-6
Teaching, magazines, 142
Tennis player, gift ideas, 106
Three to five-year-old, gift ideas, 23-5
Toys, dolls, games, catalogs, 200-1
Trains, magazines, 142
Travel, 142-3, 201-2
  catalogs, 201-2
  magazines, 142-3
Traveler, gift ideas, 106-8
Two-year-old, gift ideas, 21-2

United Parcel Service, shipping tips, 13-4
United States Postal Service, 12-4
  abbreviations, 12
  shipping tips, 13-4

Vegetarian, gift ideas, 108-9

Walker, gift ideas, 92
Water skier, gift ideas, 109
Water sports, magazines, 143-4
Wedding, gift ideas, 109-10
Wedding showers, gift ideas, 111
Western and equestrian, 111-2, 202-3
  catalogs, 202-3
  gift ideas, 111-2
Winter sports, magazines, 144
Woman—basic, gift ideas, 112-3
Women, magazines, 144
Wood hobbyist, gift ideas, 113-4
Woodworking, magazines, 144-5
Writers, 114, 145
  gift ideas, 114
  magazines, 145

Zodiac signs, 216